◆ THE HERITAGE GUIDE ◆

THE
ITALIAN RIVIERA

A complete guide to Liguria, including Portofino,

Cinque Terre, Portovenere, Genoa and Sanremo

D0048485

Touring Club of Italy

OB 2 FERS

in Liguria
AGENZIA REGIONALE

I am particularly happy to have been called upon to present this Guide to Liguria to readers in and outside Italy. The main purpose of the book, produced by Touring Club of Italy in collaboration with the Ligurian Regional Authorities, is to focus attention on a part of the country that occupies a far from secondary place on the international tourism circuit, but whose resources, attractions, and many-sided qualities remain unknown to many of those who visit the area, including the Ligurians themselves.

Liguria has a century-long tradition as a tourist destination. From the earliest days it realized the huge potential the region offered, and over the years successfully created the well-oiled organizational machine that was needed to satisfy the demands of the tourists who came. Today, at the dawn of the third millennium, at a time when so many of the old certainties are being swept away by the continuous process of change, Liguria has resolutely taken up the challenge posed by the increasingly complex requirements of catering for a public that knows more, and thus expects more.

This guide is very much in tune with this delicate transitional stage, in which tour operators are to be found drawing up new, more flexible criteria for the vacations they organize, and offering more diversified packages as a result.

Its various sections not only outline the merits of the region's rich cultural, historical and artistic heritage, but also describe in great detail the wide range of interesting and exciting leisure-time pursuits that can be enjoyed in the region.

The pages that follow provide an easy-to-consult, attractively-presented introduction to Liguria, which, while devoting due attention to its illustrious past and to its many areas of environmental interest, is also keen for tourists to discover the many other attractions that make this such an ideal place to spend a vacation. The overall image that comes across is one of a dynamic region that is fully aware of its ability to provide hospitality of the highest order, a region where tourism – its main natural resource – is managed carefully, seriously, and inventively.

Recent market research into what brings foreign tourists to Italy – quite apart from the fact that to many people the very name Italy is synonymous with vacationing – found a whole series of motivations ranging from art, the landscape and the natural environment to good food and wine, the climate, the warmth and friendliness of the people, and the high quality and variety of products. Without wishing to seem biased, I cannot help wondering whether any of these qualities can be said not to apply to Liguria alone.

The region does indeed seem to offer something of everything. A visit to Genoa is a journey back into Italian history, to the city's great days as a maritime republic and the age of princely rule; Genoa is also a vibrant modern city with a host of attractions, the spectacular Aquarium being one of the first to spring to mind. Visitors to the Riviera (as the region's shores are known to most foreign tourists, especially to those from English-speaking countries) will find one of Europe's finest stretches of coast: the sea here is wonderful, as are the many historical seaside towns, which now provide tourists with amenities of the very highest standard. Those who venture inland into the valleys, meanwhile, will find a quite different, more secluded world, its old mountain towns a living reminder of life in olden times, before modern society rediscovered the sea.

The coasts, the valleys and the mountains all have their own special appeal – be it of a cultural or environmental nature. The thematic tours that conclude the main itineraries section of the book give detailed information on hiking in the hills, on the towns that fly the 'orange flag of excellence', on the gastronomic delights and wines, and on a whole range of opportunities for sports enthusiasts, to say nothing of the tours through the special cultural and literary parks which the region has been so proud to create as a way of enhancing the quality of tourism on offer.

The message we in Liguria are perhaps keenest to convey, though, is surely the simplest one of all. We want everyone to be aware of something we have always known: that every guest of the region – from wherever in Italy or the world they have come – will be welcomed here as a friend.

Franco Amoretti
Head of the Agriculture and Tourism department, Regione Liguria

I am delighted to have been called upon by the Touring Club of Italy to say a few words of introduction about my own region of Liguria, through this prestigious volume.

I would first of all like to applaud the decision to publish this English-language edition of the Heritage Guide to the region. Touring Club of Italy deserves credit for the many high-quality publications it has produced over the years and for the efforts it has made to foster an awareness – in Italy and abroad – of just how much this country has to offer in terms of natural beauty, art, archaeology and history, and of the facilities and services it offers to its visitors.

Liguria is a region with a long and important history. Its geographical location at the crossroads of some of Europe's main trading and migratory routes, and as a commercial and industrial hub, has made it a place of transit but also of sojourn, thanks to its favorable climate and sunny position overlooking the Mediterranean Sea. It has been a vacation destination since the very earliest days of tourism, and to this day the region attracts large numbers of visitors from around the world, who among other things come to enjoy such gastronomic delights as the local olive oil, vegetables, red and white wines, and various kinds of pasta: in short, the very essence of the 'Mediterranean diet'. Liguria also grows flowers that are renowned throughout the world for their quality, their beautiful colors often serving to decorate major international events.

The administration I run is committed to safeguarding the region's natural environment, giving its support to all initiatives based on the principles of sustainable development, to the preservation of cultural traditions, and to tourist activities, striving constantly to improve the quality of life in the towns on the coast and up in the hills and to provide the very best services for local residents and visitors alike.

Meanwhile the regional capital Genoa – the city of Christopher Columbus – is now the focus for a series of major initiatives that look set to enhance the international status of the city as it prepares to take on the role of European cultural capital in 2004.

We look forward to welcoming you in Liguria. Arrivederci!

Sandro Biasotti
President of Regione Liguria

Touring Club of Italy
President and Chairman: *Roberto Ruozi*

Touring Editore
Chief Executive Officer: *Armando Peres*
Managing director: *Marco Ausenda*
Deputy director: *Renato Salvetti*
Editorial director: *Michele D'Innella*

Series editor: *Anna Ferrari-Bravo*
Editorial co-ordinator: *Gino Cervi*
Senior editor: *Cinzia Rando*, with the collaboration of *Guglielmo Martinello* for the section
"Other places: hotels, restaurants, curiosities. Addresses, opening times"
Editorial secretary: *Laura Guerini*
Technical consultant: *Enrico Foti*
Maps: *Servizio cartografico del Touring Club Italiano*

Contributors:
Nanni Basso, for "The silent towns"; *Ferdinando Bonora*, for "Art in Liguria", "Genoa: the history and culture of a city-port"; *Luca Clerici*, for "Literary and culture parks in a border region"; *Stefano Fera*, for "Liguria's many faces" and the box on pp. 18-19; *Il decumano*, for "Chronology", and chapters 5, 6 and 12; *Albano Marcarini*, for "Walking and cycling in Liguria"; *Lorenzo Marsano*, for "From seafood to mountain fare: traditional local specialties that never fail to surprise", "Liguria: one big open-air gym", "The marinas: modern structures and charming surroundings where the world of the sea meets that of the land"; for chapters 1, 2, 3, 4, 7, 8, 9, 10, 11, and for the section "Other places: hotels, restaurants, curiosities. Addresses, opening times" (excluding hotels and restaurants); *Lisandro Monaco*, for "Liguria: a visitor's guide".

Other contributors:
David Lowry (English translation)
Francesca Brusa (copyediting, indexes and captions)
Cristina Gatelli (illustration research)
Studio Gatelli (layout)
Graffito/Cusano Milanino (MI), for the maps in the main section of the guide, revised by *Sergio Seveso*
Enrico Bergonzi, for the drawing on p. 47 and the plates on pp. 50-51 and 164-165
(text by *Federica Rando*)

Cover photo: *view of Portofino* (Liguria Region Tourism Archive/Roberto Merlo)

This guide was produced thanks to the efforts of the in Liguria Regional Agency.

This edition was promoted by Settore Iniziative Speciali di Touring Editore.
Director, Angela Moioli, Corso Italia 10, 20122 Milano, tel. 028526538-473; fax 028526510

Great care has been taken in the creation of this guide to ensure the accuracy of the information supplied. Nevertheless, the publishers cannot accept responsibility for variations in opening times, telephone numbers, addresses, access conditions or other variations, nor for any damages or inconvenience caused as a result of information contained in the guide.

Filmsetting: Emmegi Multimedia, Milano
Printing and binding: Bolis Poligrafiche S.p.a. Bergamo
Cover printing: Publinova Italiana, Rozzano (MI)

Touring Club Italiano, Corso Italia 10, 20122 Milano
www.touringclub.it
© 2001 Touring Editore, Milano
Code: L2V
ISBN: 88 365 2114-2
Printed in February 2001

Contents

Introduction
History, culture and tourism in the region

Itineraries
Detailed descriptions of the tourist sites

Painted facades in Camogli

1 Historic Genoa

2 Modern Genoa

3 The port, the New Walls, the fortresses

The 'Lanterna', symbol of Genoa

4 Greater Genoa and the metropolitan district

5 Savona and environs

*A filigree vase,
Campo Ligure*

6 The Albenga valleys

7 Imperia and environs

Olive groves near Imperia

8 Sanremo and Valle Argentina

9 Ventimiglia and the Ligurian Alps

G. Canavesio, fresco. Church of S. Bernardo, Pigna

10 Portofino and Tigullio

11 The Chiavari area

12 La Spezia, the Cinque Terre and easternmost Liguria

The 'Lovers' Walk' between Riomaggiore and Manarola

Itineraries

Information for travelers and Indexes
Where to eat, where to stay, other tourist attractions

Recco's famous 'fugassa al formaggio'

Itineraries in the Genoa area.
Index of maps and plans

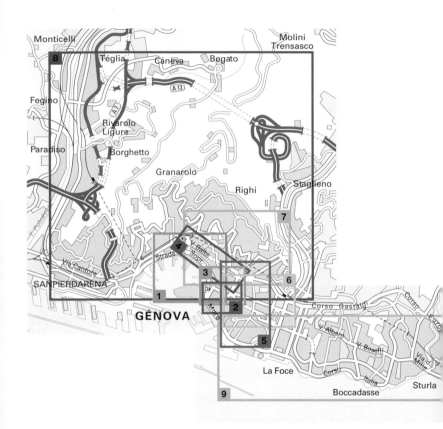

Genoa: a view of the port, with the 'Matitone' (literally 'big pencil') skyscraper

The provincial map brings together all the Genoa area tour maps used in this guide. The numbered list below gives the title and page reference of each tour.

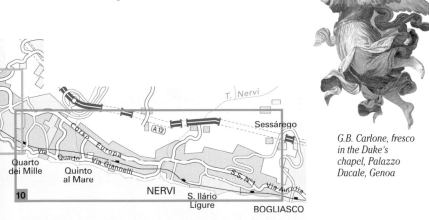

G.B. Carlone, fresco in the Duke's chapel, Palazzo Ducale, Genoa

Town plans
Genoa I (1:7.000), p. 45
Genoa II (1:14.000), pp. 70-71
Genoa III (1:45.000), pp. 88-89
Genoa IV (1:100.000), pp. 90-91
Nervi (1:18.000), p. 97

Plans of buildings and monumental sites
Cathedral of San Lorenzo, p. 53

Piazza Banchi, p. 59
Santa Maria Assunta in Carignano church, p. 77
Santa Maria di Castello church, p. 56

Gallery plans
Palazzo Reale National Art Gallery, p. 68
Palazzo Rosso National Art Gallery, p. 65

Excursions through Liguria and index of maps and plans

The regional map on these pages brings together all the area tour maps used in the guide (except for Genoa and its surroundings). The numbered list (opposite page, bottom) gives the title and page reference of each tour.

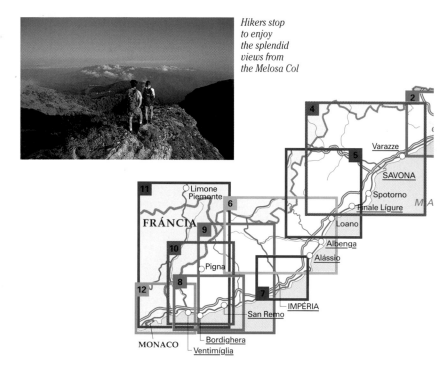

Hikers stop to enjoy the splendid views from the Melosa Col

The beautiful 'Bay of Silence' set against the colorful houses of Sestri Levante

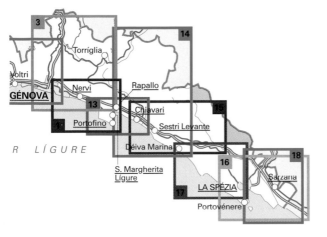

How to use this guidebook

The guide opens with a series of introductory chapters outlining some of the main features of the region, followed by the guide proper, organized into itineraries. At the back of the book is an exhaustive list of addresses and useful information.

The color blue is used to indicate the most interesting monuments, museums, streets and squares in the city itineraries, and for the places worth stopping off at on the out-of-town excursions.

A **single asterisk** (*) denotes something of special interest; double asterisks (**) mean that the place described is of outstanding interest.

The abbreviation "elev." and figures in meters indicate the **altitude** above sea level of the towns and villages described; the most up-to-date population figures available at the time of going to press (pop.) are also given for municipal areas.

Other towns, monuments and artworks deserving attention are shown in *italics*.

Towns and monuments not shown in blue but nevertheless worth visiting are given in **bold type**.

Cervo**

This highly attractive seaside resort (elev. 66 m, pop. 1,261), which appears at its most picturesque at night, sits on a hill sloping gently down to the sea. From the stronghold, *Via Salineri* leads down to the splendid **church of San Giovanni Battista*** (1686-1734), rightfully considered as one of the best expressions of the Ligurian Baroque. Designed and begun by Giovanni Battista Marvaldi, it has a large stuccoed concave facade overlooking the sea; the belltower, added in 1771-74, was designed by Francesco Carrega.

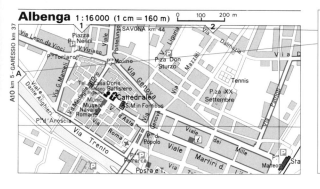

Albenga 1 : 16 000 (1 cm = 160 m)

The street maps are divided up into **grids** with letters and numbers so that monuments, museums etc. can be located using the map references given in brackets in the descriptions.
E.g. *Cattedrale di S. Michele* (A1)

In the case of particularly complex walking tours, the suggested route is shown in blue on the **street maps**.

If the monument is off the map the closest map reference is given.

For extra visual clarity, monuments are **classified according to importance** as follows:

 monuments of outstanding artistic interest (3D drawing on the map)

 monuments of great interest (in black)

 monuments of interest (in dark brown)

other buildings (in light brown)

For a complete list of symbols used on the street maps see p. 14.

7.2 The coast to the north-east
7.3 The Porto Maurizio valleys

The **maps** accompanying each excursion trace the suggested route in color, and show places worth stopping at along the way. The starting and finishing points are marked with a flag. For a complete list of symbols used on these maps see p. 14.

The **floor plans** of some of the more complex monuments are designed to facilitate the visit. Any reference numbers or letters are explained in the legend accompanying the plan or given in brackets in the description.

Cathedral of San Lorenzo

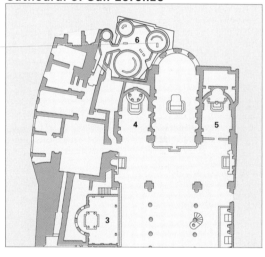

The descriptions are accompanied by **photographs**, taken by leading photographers, which illustrate some of the most beautiful sites, the most important monuments and other particularly interesting aspects of the region.

The **boxes** that appear here and there in the book shed more light on various things of interest by telling anecdotes or giving extra, more detailed information about the places and artworks described.

13

How to use this guidebook

Information for travelers

Hotels are listed with their official star ratings. Restaurants are rated according to quality using the traditional silverware symbols (on a scale of one to five).

Visiting arrangements and opening times given for **museums** and **cultural institutions** are correct at the time of going to press. However, some subsequent changes may have been made to hours or schedules.

There are brief descriptions of **other places of interest**, including tourist amenities, places of entertainment and recreation, local festivals, and craft shops selling the typical products found throughout the region, with details of how to find them.

Varese Ligure

Page 189   ⊠ 19028
i   *IAT* (seas.), Via Portici 73, tel. 0187842094.

Hotels, restaurants, campsites and holiday camps

❡   *Amici.* Via Garibaldi 80, tel. 0187842139. Closed Wednesday in winter, Christmas-New Year. Parking facilities, garden.

Museums and cultural institutions

at Cassego, 10 km
   Museo della Tradizione Contadina di Cassego (farming museum). Via Provinciale 150. Closed Sunday. Visits by prior arrangement, tel. 0187843005.

Arts and crafts

   Cooperativa Agricola Casearia Val di Vara. Locality Perassa, tel. 0187842108. Cheeses and other dairy produce.

☐   Visitors should be aware that museums, monuments and archaeological sites are usually closed all day on 1 Jan, at Easter, on 25 Apr, 1 May, the first Sunday in June, 15 Aug and 25 Dec. Note also that visiting hours for churches are not given unless they differ from the normal opening times (traditionally 8am - noon and 4pm - 7 pm).

Key to symbols used in the maps and street plans

	Main thoroughfare		Monument of outstanding interest
	Main road		Monument of particular interest
	Other roads		Other monuments to visit
	Street with steps		Church
	Rail line and station	*i*	Tourist information office
	Cableway, funicular, chair lift	P	Principal parking area
	Contour map showing elevation and grade	+	Garden, hospital

Key to symbols used in sightseeing tours

→	Sightseeing tour	=	Highway
▷	Start of itinerary		Main road
◁	End of itinerary		Other roads
Lavagna ●	Main locality of the itinerary	⌂	Church
Carasco ●	Nearby locality	∴	Ruin, prehistoric remains
	Urban area	🏛	Villa
	Park and nature reserve	✳	Natural curiosity

Introduction

History, culture and tourism in the region

A stretch of the coast near Camogli

Liguria's many faces

Most Europeans think of Liguria as the sunny Italian Riviera: a string of seaside resorts on a stretch of coast famous for its historic towns, verdant countryside, rocky shores and villas; a region whose social and urban history is inevitably bound up with its role as a destination for vacationers. Anyone passing through the region today by car or by train sees precisely what they would expect to see from the map: a long thin curving strip of coastline squeezed in between the sea and the mountains glimpsed in the dazzling gaps between one tunnel and the next, or more panoramically from the viaducts. And that would seem to be it: just a string of famous seaside resorts as announced on the loudspeakers of the train stations, or written on the exit signs punctuating the highway that runs through the region from Tuscany to France.

The impression today's travelers have is probably not unlike that of 16th-century seafarers who, in their effort to escape danger as the coast disappeared from view, would resort to the *Holy Name* litany, a practice in which the main sanctuaries, churches and the saints to whom they were dedicated were recited in geographical order from east to west. Liguria seems to be stuck with this widespread geographical notion of being a narrow strip of land by the sea, such as might be defined by a nautical log concerned only with the immediate coastal area, almost denying the existence of what may lie behind. Industrial development and mass tourism must surely take some of the blame for reinforcing this impression, quite the reverse of the way things were up to about a century ago, before the majority of the population abandoned the inland areas and moved to the coast.

Liguria's contrasting worlds: busy seaside resorts (top left, Portofino) and old

But as the best publications on the region are always at great pains to point out, Liguria is not really just one region, but a collection of several very different ones. And this plurality does not end with the traditional breakdown into *Levante* (a reference in Italian to the rising sun, i.e. eastern Liguria), *Ponente* (western Liguria, beyond which the sun sets), and the Genoa area in between, a tripartite division established in the early Middle Ages by Berengar II as the Obertenga, Aleramica, and Arduinica marches. The region can also be divided along its length, and indeed there has always been a profound dichotomy between the coast and the mountainous areas inland. This plurality, together with the fact that Liguria is percentage-wise Italy's most mountainous region and the one with the shortest distance between the mountains and the sea, is what has always made the region unique.

Until relatively recently, even in areas like the Cinque Terre – the famous 'five lands' that seem to hang, as if suspended, over the sea – there was a deep rift in the population that was all about the opposite pull exerted by the land and by the sea. Not only were the peasant folk who tended the vines on the terraces high up over the waves unable to swim, but they also treated sailors and fishermen with the same scorn many people have for gypsies. The seafaring folk repai' them with the same coin, considering them as lowly serfs. In the inland area behind Albenga, the antagonism was even more complex: the flat valley bottom area formed a third area between the maritime and mountain communities. In the words of an old local proverb: "If you touch the hand of a sailor man, take to your heels as fast as you can!".

Liguria is full of such stratifications, a hybrid world full of unresolved conflicts. Its history is proof of this: a complex tangle of obscure goings-on that can only be interpreted in micro-historical terms, that is to say concerning just one valley, or one town. Indeed, this highly fragmentary situation is probably one reason why no in-depth historical study has ever been carried out into the region as a whole.

'Unknown' ancient Liguria

One symptom of all this is the vexed question of how the region was organized in Roman times. The line taken by historians during the Fascist regime programmatically insisted on the continuity between past, present and future splendor, while 'social-democratic'

historians probably went too far in the opposite direction, de-Romanizing much of what had been celebrated during the twenty years of Fascist rule. Between the 1950s and 1960s, archaeologist Nino Lamboglia carried out some extensive and quite remarkable work throughout Liguria, introducing new scientifically significant techniques, and becoming the pioneer of underwater archaeology. Thanks to his efforts it was possible to progress from mere conjecture to more accurate field work.

The substantial finds made in western Liguria were not matched by anything as extensive in the Genoa area, so it seemed reasonable to suppose that today's regional capital was little more than a fishing village in Roman times. In fact after a period in the 5th century BC as a major trading port, frequented by Greek and Etruscan merchants, it was destroyed in the

farming ways (bottom right, near Monterosso); Alpine and Mediterranean flora

205 BC during the Second Punic War by Magone, brother of Hannibal, because of its alliance with Rome. According to the 'social-democratic' interpretation, Genoa did not rise again until the Middle Ages, one explanation for this being that the Roman road built in region in 109 BC, the *Aemilia Scauri*, by-passed Genoa altogether, cutting diagonally across instead from Vado (Vada Sabatia) up to Tortona (Derthona).

The findings of more recent excavations in parts of the ancient heart of Genoa torn apart by World War II bombing are refuting this interpretation, demonstrating that in Roman times the city was probably just as big and important as it is today. This being the case, we are once again asked the question of whether the city that grew up and flourished around the port was adversely affected by the lack of a major link with the inland road network, and if so to what extent.

The conflict between coastal and inland areas, barely perceivable nowadays, has always been central to Liguria's historical development. In the late ancient and early medieval period, population movements away from or back to the coast usually depended on the degree of the threat from Saracen pirates. As a result, relations between the *castellari*

Colorful, closely-set houses inland and on the coast. Above: the stone houses of Castel Vittorio; below: painted facades in Camogli

(the fortified towns in the hills) and the coastal settlements were both complementary and antagonistic. The complex system of towns that grew up as a result formed the backbone of the region and were the region's most interesting feature.

The urban settlements on the coast grew in size in the Middle Ages, after Genoa successfully rallied around it Liguria's other towns and led them to victory against the Saracens. This achievement ushered in a period of relative peace and at the same time confirmed Genoa's hegemony of the Riviera.

One of the most striking features of the 4th-century 'Peutingerian Chart' is the fact that the succession of towns along the coast corresponds almost exactly to that on a modern map. The density of coastal settlements is usually explained by the lack of space inland, which, though true, is only part of the explanation. What helped urban life to flourish in such an extraordinary way by the sea was the very nature of the coast itself. With the exception of the Magra estuary and the Albenga flood plain, which until relatively recent times were too boggy to be settled, Liguria did not really have marshland, unlike the Tuscan and Lazio coasts further down the Tyrrhenian, which were urbanized much more recently as a result. Low, sandy shores were impossible to settle in ancient times because they were difficult to defend and subject to malaria. By contrast, the Ligurian coast was healthy, not least of all because of the abundance of fresh water flowing down from the mountains. It was also easy to defend because of the high cliffs and the fact that the many inlets and rocky places offered a safe haven only to those who knew them thoroughly and were thus able to negotiate the often treacherous waters.

The succession of coastal towns thus became the most visible and hence familiar face to travelers in the past, who nearly all came to Liguria from the sea. Charles de Brosses left an interesting record of this in the early 18th century, when he wrote: "In general we can say that there is no finer stretch of coast than that known as the Riviera of Genoa; it is an uninterrupted sequence of well-constructed, and populous towns and villages".

An inland area rich in history

And yet, however populous the Liguria coast may have appeared, until the days of great emigration to the Americas, the majority of the population lived in the inland parts of the region, in scattered towns and villages or

Andrea Doria, the negotiating admiral

Although we know for sure that Andrea Doria was not born in Genoa, his name is inextricably bound up with the city. Doria sought fame away from his homeland, as a *condottiere* in central and southern Italy. From Rome, where he was a palace guard at the court of Pope Innocent VIII (the Genoese Giovanbattista Cybo), he went into the service of Guidobaldo da Montefeltro, of the d'Aragona, and of Giovanni Della Rovere. It was not until he reached the ripe old age of fifty that he began to learn seafaring skills. After early assignments at the beginning of the century for the Banco di San Giorgio, he took command in 1525 of the papal fleet and of that of Francis I. In 1528 he signed the famous pact with Charles V, which was viewed by his contemporaries and by many later historians as high treason.

farmsteads, nearly all of medieval origin. These areas were the theater of much in-fighting for territorial control, but also of battles against interference from neighboring states, especially from Savoy. The fragmentation of the territory was extreme: there was a great variety of forms of local government run by an array of commissaries, captains, *podestà*, and feudal lords.

The territory around the Neva valley behind Albenga, for example, was controlled by the Clavesana then by the Del Carretto family before being ceded to the Republic in the early 17th century, whereafter it was bitterly fought over by Genoa and Savoy. Zuccarello, the center of the marquisate of the Del Carretto, was the home town of the young Ilaria, the wife of Paolo Guinigi of Lucca who died in childbirth and was immortalized in the famous monument by Jacopo della Quercia in Lucca cathedral and even more so by the Romantic cult that grew up around her in the late 19th and early 20th centuries.

Astronomer Gian Domenico Cassini

Control of Ligurian territory did not require any great military might: in most cases it came about spontaneously, as a result of the urbanization in Genoa of the feudal families, who came there in the hope of increasing their wealth and reputation by taking part in the financial enterprises of the day. One such period was that of the bankers of Charles V, 'noble usurers' who were meritorious inasmuch as they grew rich at the expense of the most powerful people on earth, and left behind them a whole series of palaces and villas of truly incomparable beauty. Traveling along what were once the ancient salt routes connecting the Po Valley with the sea, on which these wonderful but now almost abandoned little towns stand, one is struck by just how well developed these urban centers of a great ancient civilization were. In the village of Pigna in the upper Nervia Valley inland from Ventimiglia, for example, the birthplace of Carlo Fea still stands intact in a little square behind the parish church, which incidentally has a fine rose window by Giovanni Gagini. Born in this little out-of-the-way village in 1753, Fea went on to become one of Italy's first and greatest archaeologists. Earlier, in 1625, Gian Domenico Cassini, one of the foremost mathematicians and astronomers of his day, who lived in Bologna and Paris (where he became Louis XIV's first astronomer), was born in Perinaldo, a little town in the neighboring valley.

Doria did begin negotiations with the Hapsburg while he was still serving under the king of France, and yet, reprehensible though his behavior may seem, it did conform to the ethic of the Genoese patricians, whose special financial skills and cosmopolitan vocation persuaded them to regulate relations with the various foreign powers under strict contractual terms. Viewed in this way the party at fault was not the Genoese admiral but Francis I, who was continually behind with payments: on expiry of the contract, Doria simply found a better position. The choice was decisive for the city, which in this way entered the Hispano-Hapsburg sphere of influence, and enabled the Genoese nobility to raise their status from that of mere merchants to *hombres de negocio*, financiers who were experts in bills of exchange. Andrea Doria was also a capable settler of disputes typical of an open class like the Genoese patrician order, which could be entered with money. Not only did he pacify the old and the new nobility, through the compulsory aggregation into the 28 *alberghi* led by the main families, he also put down the revolt led by Gian Luigi Fieschi, thereby increasing his own power and that of the republic.

This world, which seems so far removed from the present day, has left us other great examples of urban civilization, in the form of highly dignified decoration, art, and architecture. It is perhaps no coincidence that among the popes remembered as great patrons of the arts were several of Ligurian origin. Tommaso Parentucelli, of Sarzana (who became Pope Nicholas V in 1447), formed the original core of the Vatican Library with his own personal book collection, and commissioned works by some great artists. Then there were the two great city-planning popes: Francesco Della Rovere, of Celle Ligure, elected Pope Sixtus IV in 1471, and his grandson Giuliano Della Rovere of Albisola, who became Pope Julius II in 1503. The work they did as patrons of art and culture is so well known as to require no further comment.

All of this helps to demonstrate that a true knowledge of Liguria cannot be limited to the coast, but requires patient exploration of its mountains and valleys, along the ancient routes that lead into what are at times quite inaccessible, isolated places. There used to be a time when such advice would have fallen on deaf ears, or at least would have been followed only by a very limited group of travelers. This has now changed: contemporary tourism is developing in a way that is seeing greater interest in hiking and in the environment and history of the places visited. We might say that tourism today is now two-speed: one kind goes at the speed of the motor car, the other at walking pace.

In Liguria this division is seen in the distinction between weekend and summer vacation tourism on the coast, centering around the traditional infrastructures designed for beach life and sailing, and a new kind of 'mountain' tourism, that goes at a much more leisurely pace, on foot, on horseback or by mountain bike, and which is giving rise to a whole network of amenities ranging from mountain huts to farm holidays, throughout the whole of inland Liguria.

The High Ligurian Mountain Trail

One of the most interesting initiatives taken by the regional authorities in response to this new tourist demand is the creation of the so-called 'High Ligurian Mountain Trail', a system of routes established about a decade ago by the Ligurian Chamber of Commerce Union that winds its way through the entire Ligurian stretch of the Apennines, enabling those who walk it to discover a secret, more beautiful Liguria. These ancient pathways open up a completely unexpected world in which the chief element of surprise is the seemingly paradoxical vicinity of mountain (and in some cases Alpine) scenery and the sea. The peak of Mt. Saccarello, which at 2,200 meters is the highest point of the trail, commands an astoundingly panoramic view across the mountains to the sea stretching away to the horizon. Similar views are to be had from other peaks – Mt. Galero, Mt. Carmo, Mt. Beigua to name just three – and from the many passes and look-out points along the way.

The High Trail is also an opportunity to discover traces of the ancient Ligurian cults, such as symbols and masks carved into the rock to ward off evil spirits. Then there are the many examples of rural architecture: shepherds' huts built in stone and covered over with turf, or wooden huts with thatched roofs, *neviere* (cold stores filled with snow), hump-backed bridges and medieval towns depopulated as a result of emigration. There are many other towns where small communities still live and carry on their farming and sheep-rearing activities, keeping their ethno-cultural and linguistic traditions alive.

But perhaps the most surprising discovery to be made on the High Trail is the fact that Liguria is very evidently changing, quite independently of the will of its inhabitants, into a kind of large nature reserve. The spontaneous formation of what amounts to one enormous regional park has come about less because of the existence of protected areas, than as a consequence of the fact that human life there has all but disappeared. On the one hand this has meant that huge areas of abandoned farmland have now fallen into a state of neglect, with some serious hydro-geological results, but on the other it has allowed ecosystems which elsewhere have been partly or completely wiped out to re-establish themselves. So while we might feel sad at the overgrown state of the olive groves and chestnut woods planted in the 18th century, the collapse of terraced farmland and the crumbling of their characteristic dry stone-walling, we must at the same time take heart in the idea that the natural environment has in this way had the opportunity to be reinstated. The fact that farm buildings and country homes have not proliferated here as they have in so many other Italian regions, which until recently was bemoaned as a misfortune for Liguria, is in today's global de-industrialized western world now being seen as one of the happier accidents of history. The quality of the natural environment could in the medium to long term become a major economic resource, especially in terms of a new more careful and controlled development of the territory for the purposes of tourism.

One interesting example of this has been the restoration of the ancient town of Colletta di Castelbianco. This small medieval settlement, a short distance inland from Albenga, which was uninhabited for decades, has now been brought back to life by a shrewd property development scheme that successfully combined quality restoration of the architecture with the installation of advanced technological facilities. Colletta was reconstructed stone by stone and at the same time completely wired up to the modern information technology network, and is an extremely interesting pilot experiment at a European level of what might be described as a 'telematic village'.

Another significant example of how the natural environment can become a tourist attraction is the Aquarium in Genoa, which has proved such a hit with the public as to have become one of Italy's most visited museum structures. The great interest for visitors here is not only the huge variety of underwater species on show, but also the way in which the presentation of marine life is part of a more wide-ranging program to protect and improve the quality of the marine environment at large.

From this point of view Liguria can offer some truly memorable experiences. Whale-watching trips can now be made in the summer months to the so-called 'Cetacean Sanctuary', in the triangle of sea between Marseilles, Genoa and Corsica, where sightings of various species of dolphins – including the bottlenose dolphin – and of larger cetaceans, such as fin whales, sperm whales and grampus are not uncommon.

Genoa: a regional capital waiting to be discovered

Of course no one can hope to understand and love Liguria, or really appreciate its historical and environmental treasures, without getting to know its ancient capital Genoa. This is perhaps Italy's most unjustly unknown city, shunned not only by the tourists that flock to the beaches along the Riviera, but even by many of its own residents. As historians point out, Genoa's importance lies both in the fact that it was the region's *mater et domina*, and because it is also the most northern of the continent's southern cities. That is to say it still encapsulates so much of urban culture in the Mediterranean. This city is Arab, Spanish, Greek, Sicilian and Turkish: it is, in a word, Ligurian.

Genoa is in many ways a larger version of the typical Ligurian seaside town, vertically organized with steep, narrow streets, slate roofs and painted facades. Painted facades are to Ligurian architecture what olive oil is to the Mediterranean diet: they are what binds the various parts together, representing the state of transition from solid to liquid, from the two-dimensional to the three-dimensional. They are quintessentially Mediterranean, in that they are a transfiguration of form, among other things as a result of the climate and the passing of time, to the point where the tablature of the facade begins to suggest associations with impressed surfaces and palimpsests.

There are two theories as to why painted facades are so widespread in Liguria. The first is connected with the proverbial stinginess of the Ligurian people but is not particularly convincing, one reason being that in the past stone and marble were not particularly costly. The second, more credible explanation has to do with the narrowness of the city streets: adding architectural attributes to walls, even if they took up no more than a few dozen centimeters, would have reduced the usable space in between – something that

The austere but impressive front of Genoa's Ducal Palace, by Andrea Vannone

Trompe l'oeil effects are to be found both on noble palaces and ordinary houses in Genoa

could not be allowed on streets usually no more than two meters wide.

Genoa's Mediterranean quality has also come about through the new influx of immigrants who today, as in the past, find it easier to fit in here than elsewhere. Ethnic integration is indeed one of the city's greatest success stories. Take, for example, the Durazzo family from Albania (the surname is the Italian name for the port of Durrës), which began as a successful family of silk weavers but went on to become one of the most outstanding and powerful dynasties in Genoa, Italy and abroad. They built some of the city's most sumptuous palaces, such as the one in Via Balbi (today's *Palazzo Reale*) because it was the Genoese residence of the Savoy royal household, and villas in Santa Margherita and Albisola, the latter known as Villa Faraggiana after its last owners.

Genoa's palaces and villas are perhaps the most pleasant surprise for visitors to the city, although time and patience are needed to appreciate their architecture to the full. The fact is that Genoa does not make a great show of itself, unlike so many other Italian cities which have that most typical of Italian urban features: the *piazza*. Genoa has very few, and the ones it does have are either 19th- or 20th-century creations (and thus outside the ancient city) or not really *piazze* at all. And without squares to face onto, the *palazzi* can only really be appreciated from within. This also explains why sculpted doorways are so important, as embodiments of the architecture to which they belong. Perhaps Genoa's most outstanding monuments are in fact that extraordinary run of portals that line Strada Nuova, the 'Via Aurea', or Via Garibaldi as it is now more democratically known. Possibly designed by Galeazzo Alessi in the years in which he was concerned with Genoese projects, the street was laid out in the second half of the 16th century. It originally came to a dead end, with a nymphaeum and monumental fountain at the western end, serving only as an access corridor to the palaces. It was not until the 18th century, when the Strada Nuovissima (present-day Via Cairoli) was opened up, that it was connected to the other monumental street, the 17th-century Via Balbi, which was already its Baroque continuation.

Walking down these streets today is always an emotional experience, given the way in which it demonstrates the sublime relationship between interior and exterior that is so typical of Mediterranean architecture. Here, every single element is indicative of the desire, at the highest architectural level, to capture the light from the sea, hence the profusion of balconies, loggias, hanging gardens, terraces, nymphaea, peristyles, and stairs, all of which exert an inescapable centripetal force. Here one can see how perfectly the Dutch artist Maurits Escher understood the Mediterranean world in general, and in particular that of Genoa and Liguria, which he so loved to visit: it is easy to imagine oneself caught up in the architecture of one of his inventions.

Chronology

6th-5th cent. BC. The original nucleus of Genoa grows up on the Castello hill. The town soon becomes a major trading center frequented by Greek and Etruscan merchants.

1st cent. The amphitheater in Luni is built. The Augustan Trophy (Trophée des Alpes) is built (13-15) at La Turbie, above Monaco. In the Augustan division of Italy (15-17) the Regio IX, Liguria, is delimited by the Varo river (west of Nice), by the Magra and by the Po.

2nd cent. The Via Postumia, from Genoa to Aquileia via Tortona and Piacenza is opened (148), followed by the Via Æmilia Scauri: from Pisa to Luni and to Tortona; from here the road continues as the Via Fulvia to Turin and as the Via Iulia Augusta to Vado (Vada Sabatia), Albenga and Ventimiglia. The Roman colony of Luni is founded (177).

197-180 AD. The region comes under Roman occupation after repeated military campaigns on Ligurian soil. Stability is not reached until the following century.

4th cent. AD Genoa's first cathedral, part of the Ambrosian church, is dedicated to St. Siro.

5th cent. (first half) The Baptistery of Albenga is built.

6th-8th cent. Change of sovereignty in Liguria: from Byzantine rule (from 553) to Longobard rule (from 644), a period that is brought to an end in 774 by Charlemagne, King of the Franks. In 811 Carolingian Genoa is the northern coastal stronghold of the March of Tuscia.

9th cent. Genoa: with the construction of the defense walls, San Siro (outside the walls) loses its cathedral status, and is replaced by San Lorenzo.

10th cent. (second half) The Arduinic March (in the west, centering on Albenga and the county of Ventimiglia), the Aleramic March (Vado-Savona) and the Obertenghi March (in Genoa and the east) are established.

1016 Luni is destroyed during a Saracen attack; in 1058, malaria and the silting up of the port force the inhabitants to abandon the town and settle in Sarzana, to which Pope Innocent III transfers the diocese in 1204.

1091 The marquises of Clavesana take possession of Albenga, formerly held by the Arduini.

11th-12th cent. Genoa paves the way to become a great commercial power: from 1097 it provided ships for the First Crusade; in 1099 the separate local 'compagne' were brought together as the 'Compagna Communis', the body that went on to establishe communal independence; and in the war against Pisa (1118-31) for control of Corsica.

12th cent. Communal institutions and independent bodies are established at Porto Maurizio (in the early part of the century), in Savona (1122-27), Albenga (1159), Sarzana (1169), and Noli (1187).

1118 The now Romanesque-style church of San Lorenzo is consecrated in Genoa.

1155-63 Genoa: new, bigger walls are built to replace the previous 9th-century *enceinte*.

1162 Emperor Frederick I Barbarossa, enfeoffs the Riviera from Monaco to Capo Corvo and the Apennines to the Commune of Genoa le Riviere. This process – preceded by the purchase of Portovenere (1133) and the foundation of Chiavari (1147, with planning extended until 1178) – legitimizes Genoa's expansionist policy in the region, one which became more marked in the 13th century.

1191 Acre (the modern Israeli port of Akko), seized from the Muslims during the Third Crusade, becomes the hub of Genoa's colonial system in the eastern Mediterranean.

1217 The church of Santo Stefano in Genoa is consecrated.

1245-52 The Basilica dei Fieschi is built near Chiavari.

1250 The death of Frederick II, who had guaranteed the independence of Albenga and Savona, enables Genoa to impose its hegemony over the two cities.

1257-62 Genoa: Guglielmo Boccanegra – representing the merchant classes – is Captain of the People; communal government gives way to seigniorial rule.

1261 Genoa's territorial expansion continues, with the subjugation of Ventimiglia; in 1276 Porto Maurizio is brought under Genoese control, but obtains in return the title of chief town of the vicariate of western Liguria.

1278 The church of San Matteo is rebuilt in Genoa.

1284 The Genoese fleet puts the Pisan fleet to rout at Meloria; as a result Genoa's main rival in the Tyrrhenian loses its historic role as a naval and commercial power.

1298 The old conflict with Venice for mercantile supremacy in the Levant, begun in 1204, continues

Knights on a Genoese boat in 1187

23

with Genoa's victory at the naval battle of Curzola. Peace is eventually established, without winners or losers, after the war of Chioggia (1378-81).

1313-14 Giovanni Pisano is in Genoa to work on the tomb of Margaret of Brabant.

1320-46 Genoa: the third ring of defense walls, the Mura Vecchie, are built, and fortified with ramparts two centuries later (1536).

1339 Simone Boccanegra is the first doge of Genoa, imposed by the anti-noble movement after twenty years of fighting between Guelphs (the Fieschi and Grimaldi) and Ghibellines (the Spinola and Doria).

1343 La Spezia is elevated by Genoa to *podestà* jurisdiction status.

1359 The Doria sell to Genoa the feudal rights over the town of San Romolo: Sanrömu, in local dialect, hence Sanremu and later Sanremo.

14th-15th cent. The most tumultuous period in the history of the Republic, which is torn apart by internal wars and caught between the ambitions of Milan and France (Visconti, Sforza and French seigneuries by turns rule over Genoa between 1353 and 1499; subjugation to the rule of Louis XII continues until 1506), while continued losses in Sardinia, Corsica and the eastern Mediterranean mark the city's decline as an important naval power.

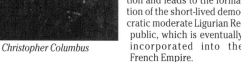

Christopher Columbus

1447 Tommaso Parentucelli, native of Sarzana, becomes Pope Nicholas V; in 1471 Francesco Della Rovere, from Celle Ligure, becomes Pope Sixtus IV, and in 1503 Giuliano Della Rovere, from Albisola, is named Pope Julius II.

1451 Christopher Columbus is born in Genoa.

1489-90 Vincenzo Foppa is active in Savona.

1496 Emperor Maximilian I re-establishes the autonomy - removed by Genoa in 1451 - of the marquisate (Del Carretto) of Finale. A century later (1598) it passes under the direct control of Spain; in 1713 Austria sells it to Genoa.

1528 Acting during the Franco-Spanish war for control of Italy, Andrea Doria obtains from Charles V - in exchange for the inclusion of Genoa into Spain's political and economic system - recognition of the autonomy and territorial integrity of the Republic; the agreement includes the definitive subjugation of Savona.

1547 The Fieschi conspiracy against the Andrea Doria seigneury is brutally repressed.

1548-56 Galeazzo Alessi is active in Genoa. Major works include Villa Cambiaso Giustiniani, Santa Maria Assunta in Carignano, and the gateway to the Molo.

1551 Genoa: 'Strada Nuova dei Palazzi', now Via Garibaldi, is laid out.

1576 Oneglia, a feudal dependency of the Doria since 1298, is sold to Emanuele Filiberto of Savoy.

1591 After the renovation of Palazzo San Giorgio (1570), work begins on Palazzo Ducale in Genoa.

1600-1627 Rubens and Van Dyck stay in Genoa on several occasions.

1605-1746 The Guidobono majolica workshop is active in Savona.

1626-33 Genoa: the fourth and final defense walls, the Mura Nuove, are built.

1656-96 The Albergo dei Poveri hospice is built in Genoa.

1684 French puts renewed pressure on Genoa, which refuses to disarm its fleet and suffers naval bombing between 18 and 28 May.

1746 The imperial troops (in the War of Austrian Succession) occupy Genoa on 6 September; they are forced out of the city in the revolt that began on 5 December, possibly with the Balilla episode.

1751 Genoa: the Accademia Ligustica di Belle Arti is founded.

1768 The Treaty of Versailles decrees the transfer of Corsica - which long before had risen up in rebellion under Pasquale Paoli - from the Genoese Republic to France.

1796-1805 The offensive launched by Napoleon's troops, beginning with the defeat of the Piedmontese at Montenotte (11-12 April 1796), sweeps away the old political and institutional organization and leads to the formation of the short-lived democratic moderate Ligurian Republic, which is eventually incorporated into the French Empire.

1805 Giuseppe Mazzini is born in Genoa.

1814-15 The Congress of Vienna establishes that Ligurian territory - now known as the Duchy of Genoa - to the House of Savoy under Vittorio Emanuele I.

1826-31 Genoa: Carlo Barabino builds the Carlo Felice Theater.

1835-51 Genoa: the monumental cemetery of Staglieno is created.

1840-46 The Durazzo Pallavicini park at Pegli is laid out.

1849 The Republican uprising in Genoa fails.

1852 Genoa: founding of Ansaldo the firm which, after taking over the Taylor and Prandi mechanical plant at Sampierdarena, begins locomotive building activities.

1853 The opening of the Turin-Genoa railroad line marks the beginning of the regional rail network; it is followed by the opening of the Milan-Genoa line (in 1867), the Genoa-Ventimiglia line (1872), Genoa-La Spezia (1874), and Turin-Savona (1884).

1855 "Doctor Antonio", a novel written in English by Giovanni Ruffini, set mainly in Bordighera, is published in Edinburgh, attracting a sizable crowd of British vacationers to the small seaside town.

1860 The Piemonte and Lombardo steamships with Garibaldi's legendary army 'The Thousand' on board, sets sail from Quarto al Mare (later Quarto dei Mille), in the night between 5 and 6 May.

1861 The first census of the united Italy establishes that Liguria has a population of

778,000. One hundred years later, in 1961, the number has risen to 1,735,349.

1867 The well-to-do English tradesman Sir Thomas Hanbury and his brother Daniel begin to lay out their botanical garden on the sloping sight at Cape Mortola.

1874 Genoa spreads eastward, with the incorporation into the municipal area of six coastal communities and the Val Bisagno, increasing the city's population by 130,000.

1875-82 Extensive work is done to expand and redevelop the port of Genoa.

1892 Genoa: the Italian Workers' Party is founded, later to become (1895) the Italian Socialist Party.

1898 La Spezia: inauguration of the new mercantile port.

1903 Genoa: the Independent Port Consortium is established.

1906 The municipal casino opens in Sanremo.

1923 Porto Maurizio and Oneglia are merged together to form the city of Imperia. The Genoa-Casella narrow gauge railway opens.

1926 With the incorporation into the city of 19 surrounding municipalities (from Voltri to Sant'Ilario Ligure and Pontedecimo), 'Greater Genoa' comes into being.

1941 9 February. British warships bomb Genoa.

1943-44 La Spezia suffers enormous damage in air raid attacks.

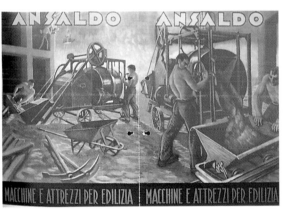

Foundry workers in an advertising poster of the Genoese firm Ansaldo

1945 On 24 April Genoa rises up and forces the German garrison to surrender before the arrival of Allied troops in the city on 27th.

1951 The Italian Song Festival in Sanremo is held for the first time.

1956 Genoa: The San Lorenzo Treasury museum, designed by Franco Albini, is opened.

1959 A major Iron Age necropolis dating back to the 8th-7th centuries BC is discovered near Chiavari.

1962 Genoa: The Cristoforo Colombo International Airport, built on a strip of reclaimed land near Sestri Ponente, is opened.

1965 With the completion of the A7 (Milan-Genoa) Liguria's highway network begins to take shape: in 1970 the A6 (Turin-Savona) is opened, followed in 1971 by the A10 (Genoa-Ventimiglia) and the A12 (Genoa-Livorno); in 1975 the A15 (Parma-La Spezia) is opened to traffic; work on the A26 (Voltri-Gravellona Toce), begun in 1976, is finished in 1995.

1972 Genoa: construction of the outer breakwater at Pra begins, stage one in the creation of the new port at Voltri.

1975 Genoese poet Eugenio Montale is awarded the Nobel Prize for Literature.

1984-92 Genoa: redevelopment work is carried out on the ancient port, a project that continues also after the celebrations for the 500th anniversary of the discovery of America.

1985-89 The Regional Authorities push for greater environmental protection, creating eight regional nature parks: Beigua, Cinque Terre, Bric Tana, Piana Crixia, Montemarcello-Magra, Portofino (to which the protected marine area is added in 1998), Antola and Aveto.

1986 The *Carte e Cartografi in Liguria* mapmaking exhibition is held in Albenga, La Spezia, Imperia and Savona. In Genoa, the new Cristoforo Colombo airport is opened and work begins on the subway network.

1987 Genoa is the venue for two major art exhibitions *Giovanni Pisano in Genoa* and *The Age of Rubens*.

1990 Genoa: the modernized Carlo Felice Theater and the Righi and Sant'Anna funicular railways are opened.

1991 The census records 1,676,282 residents in Liguria, down on 1971 (1,853,578) and again on 1981 (1, 807, 893); Genoa's population is also in decline: from 762,895 inhabitants (1981) to 675,639.

1992 The exhibition *Genoa and the Baroque Age* is held at Palazzo Spinola di Pellicceria.

1995-97 The mid-Nineties see a series of major art exhibitions at Palazzo Ducale: *Pierre Puget*; *Bernardo Strozzi*; *The Uncovered City*, *Urban Archaeology in Genoa 1984-94* (at the Commenda di S. Giovanni di Pré); *The Art of Freedom: Antifascism, War and Liberation in Europe*; *Van Dyck: Great Paintings and Collectors' Items in Genoa*; *Futurism, the Major Themes: 1909-44*; *Christiana Signa* (at Sant'Agostino).

1998 The EU Council of Ministers for Culture, meeting in Brussels on 28 May, name Genoa 'European Cultural Capital' for the year 2004.

1999 The Cinque Terre National Park comes into being, alongside the existing regional Promontory and Eastern Isles Nature Park. On 5 December a major historical retrospective *El Siglo de los Genoveses* opens at Palazzo Ducale. In the same month it is announced that Genoa will host the G8 summit of the heads of the seven most industrialized nations, in June 2001.

Art in Liguria

Liguria: art by the sea

It is impossible to approach the question of Liguria's artistic heritage without going beyond the region's present border, not only into neighboring territories but also further afield to far-off places that have left their mark on the region in various ways down the ages. The old cliché that describes Liguria as an isolated region hemmed in by the mountains and the sea and inhabited by a rather churlish people is simplistic. The region has in fact always been a major crossroads: for geographical and historical reasons it was the frontier between the land and sea routes, between mainland Europe, the Mediterranean, and indeed the rest of the planet. In the field of cultural output, artists and their clients in Liguria have for centuries been exposed to foreign cultures through the arrival here of works created elsewhere, and of foreigners themselves. Visitors are greeted by an extraordinary heritage – much of it still in its original location, the rest now housed in the many museums – that takes them on a voyage of discovery encompassing everything from the modern world back to earliest times.

From rock carvings to Roman ruins

The most remote traces are to be in westernmost Liguria, in the Balzi Rossi cave dwellings, one of Italy's most important prehistoric sites (along with those at Finale and Toirano), which were settled for over a hundred millennia from the Lower Paleolithic to around 10,000 years ago. Here we find the earliest forms of pictorial expression: the outline

Christian symbols and floral decorations on the colorful Byzantine mosaic in the Baptistery, Albenga

of a horse carved into a rocky wall, and some fifteen female statues, symbolic 'Venuses' of fertility and plenty.

In the Maritime Alps, around Mt. Bego (now in French territory), a remarkable open-air sanctuary dating back to the Bronze Age has some 100,000 rock carvings. The Iron Age necropolis at Chiavari is documented at the local archaeology museum, with burial gifts indicative of a society already organized into social classes in the 8th-7th centuries BC. Even richer is the necropolis of pre-Roman Genoa (5th-3rd cent. BC), where archaeologists found sophisticated ceramics and other imported items, now on show at the museum in Pegli.

The long process of Romanization – obstructed by the stalwart resistance of the indigenous populations, the eventual subordination of whom was celebrated by the imposing Augustan Trophy at La Turbie (13th-5th cent. BC) – led to the foundation of provincial towns: Luni (177 BC), a center for the export of Apuan marble; Albintimilium (Ventimiglia) in 180 BC; and Albingaunum (Albenga) a century later.

This latter town's magnificent baptistery contains the most important Byzantine mosaic in northern Italy outside Ravenna. Here, and elsewhere, marble creations and other works testify to the subsequent period of Longobard rule.

The influence of the overseas world of the Macedonian revival, between the 10th and 11th centuries, is seen in the church architecture and 'crutch-style' cloister capitals at the abbey of San Fruttuoso di Capodimonte, set in a beautiful bay on the Portofino promontory. Similar features were found in Genoa when the church of *San Tomaso* was demolished in the 19th century. These finds are now exhibited in the museum of *Sant'Agostino*, a treasure house of sculptural fragments that have come to light as a result of the destructive activities of the last two centuries.

Maestro Guglielmo, Crucifix. Sarzana Cathedral

The age of the Communes and the Seignories

The Genoese Commune, established in 1099, was by the 12th century already pursuing a vigorous expansionist foreign policy along the coast and inland, pitting itself against feudal powers and other local communities, in some cases reaching agreement with them, in others establishing power by force, or founding towns. One of these was Chiavari (1147-78), a stronghold against the Fieschi, lords of Lavagna, whose most lasting legacy is the palace and Gothic basilica of San Salvatore across the Entella river, built in 1245 by Sinibaldo Fieschi (later Pope Innocent IV).

Many territories held out against Genoa, establishing their own independent artistic cultures to rival that of the capital. The Commune of Savona capitulated in 1528, bringing to an end a renascence whose leading figures included two Della Rovere popes (Sixtus IV and Julius II), Giuliano da Sangallo working as the architect of the family palace, and such painters as Donato de' Bardi and Vincenzo Foppa. The Del Carretto marquises held onto Finale until 1598, when it passed into the hands of Spain and later to Austria, which did not sell it to Genoa until 1713.

Over on the eastern border with Tuscany, the town of Sarzana, which had long been fought over by Pisa, Lucca, Milan, Genoa and Florence, became part of the Republic of Genoa in 1562. The successor of the ancient Luni, on the old Via Francigena pilgrim route from the north to Rome, has in its cathedral the *Cross of Maestro Guglielmo*, the earliest example (1138) of the painted crucifix genre that abounded in Tuscany and Umbria.

In the late Middle Ages and early Renaissance, towns were built and decorated by artists from outside, thus bringing to the area artists and architects from other parts of Europe and the Mediterranean: the Islamic and Byzantine East, the Iberian Peninsula, France and also Flanders, commercial interests in which resulted in the extensive presence of Flemish masterpieces. Artists from other Italian regions also contributed works down the ages: Manfredino da Pistoia, Giovanni Pisano, Barnaba da Modena, Giovanni Mazone, Carlo Braccesco, Matteo Civitali, Andrea Sansovino, to name but a few.

Exquisite reliquaries and other sacred items brought to or crafted in Genoa over the

Giovanni Pisano, funerary monument of Margaret of Brabant. Museo di Sant'Agostino, Genoa

El siglo de los Genoveses

The term 'century of the Genoese' – coined by non-Italian historians Spooner, Ruiz Martín and Braudel – refers to the period between approximately 1528 and 1563, when Genoa was at the forefront of international finance, investing vast amounts of revenue in prestigious buildings, paintings, sculpture and other works that can be enjoyed to this day.

The radical changes in foreign and domestic policy as well as in art that came about in 1528 were largely the work of one man: Andrea Doria.

This *condottiere* was admiral of a fleet of warships that first served the French king Francis I. When this contract expired, Doria transferred his allegiance to emperor Charles V. On the one hand this finally expelled the French, who in turn with the Duchy of Milan had controlled the city for over 130 years, and on the other resulted in the now free city of Genoa entering an alliance with Spain and the Empire that lasted over a century. This also enabled Genoese entrepreneurs operating on the main European markets to extend their

*P. P. Rubens, Venus and Mars.
Galleria di Palazzo Bianco, Genoa*

sphere of influence by advancing considerable amounts of capital to powers loyal to the Hapsburgs to pay for their wars among other things, and deriving profits that were proportionate to the complexity and risks of the operations. Which is why it was said that the Spanish galleons returning from the legendary El Dorado were laden with gold that "was born in the Americas, died in Spain and was buried in Genoa".

In the same year constitutional forms were introduced whereby the running of the Republic was placed in the hands of the aristocracy alone (originally organized into 28 family groupings known as *alberghi*), with doges holding office for two years. After making the noble gesture of refusing seigneury over the fatherland he had liberated, Andrea Doria created for himself a lifetime role in the College of Supreme Inspectors, extremely powerful regulators who supervised the work of the entire government, including that of the doge. 1528 was also the year in which Andrea Doria (named Prince of Melfi in 1531)

centuries are beautifully displayed in the San Lorenzo Treasury Museum, a world-famous example of post-war museum design (by Franco Albini, 1956).

Much of the architectural work from Romanesque times to the great architectural works of the 16th and 17th centuries and through to the 19th century was the work of Lombard or Ticino masters, who were highly specialized stonemasons and sculptors. Among the main families in which artistic creativity was passed on from father to son were the Gagini, the Carlone, and the Orsolino.

In western Liguria, between Albenga and Briga, the Piedmontese Giovanni Canavesio and the Biazaci created polyptychs and frescoes in a popular realist style in the late 15th century, while the Niçois Lodovico Brea produced even more refined works in the Ligurian-Provençal style in Taggia, Savona and Genoa.

The 'century of the Genoese' (see box) began in 1528. Roman artists were invited to work in Genoa while Genoese artists were sent to Rome to learn about

Shadows and light in Villa Durazzo, Santa Margherita Ligure

decided to create his own suburban palace, for the decoration of which he enlisted the services of Perin del Vaga, Giovanni Angelo Montorsoli and other artists from the circles of Raphael and Michelangelo. It marked the triumphant arrival of the Roman late Renaissance in a city which until then was still dominated by Po valley and other nordic styles, with the occasional Tuscan influence. For decades thereafter Palazzo del Principe was the main stylistic reference point, its figurative content widely emulated by other members of the nobility in their city residences and villas.

artistic developments there. In 1548 Perugia-born Galeazzo Alessi designed a revolutionary 'Roman-style' palace for Luca Giustiniani in Albaro (now the School of Engineering), which served as a prototype for other similar buildings in the city for centuries to come. The same architect built for the Sauli family the huge basilica of *Santa Maria Assunta*, a scaled-down version of one of the proposed ideas for St. Peter's in the Vatican. In the *Cinquecento* much decorative use was made of fresco and stuccowork for both the interiors and exteriors of buildings, producing a riot of figures, colors, allegorical and architectural inventions that created in the city a fantasy world most of which is now either lost or poorly restored. During this fruitful period Luca Cambiaso, Giambattista Castello (il Bergamasco), the Semino, the Calvi, and later Lazzaro Tavarone and Bernardo Castello did much decorative work on palaces and churches, as well as producing a wealth of paintings.

A. Van Dyck, Anton Giulio Brignole Sale. Galleria di Palazzo Rosso, Genoa

17th century: the flourishing season of the Genoese Baroque

As relations with Flanders continued and intensified, Liguria was home to a flourishing colony of Flemish painters and silversmiths, which in the early 17th century included first Peter Paul Rubens, then Antonie Van Dyck, who produced altarpieces and splendid portraits and other paintings. Rubens' *Circumcision* in the church of the Gesù in Genoa (1605) is considered by some critics to be the first Baroque painting in the history of art. So impressed was Rubens by the quality of Genoese residential architecture, he drew up a detailed repertoire of plans for the buildings which was published in Antwerp in 1622. Many aristocrats bought artworks on the international market, and commissioned local and foreign artists to paint others. In the space of a few generations, this resulted in the creation of several splendid picture galleries, whose collections are now private and not usually open to the public, or which have been sold by their owners and dispersed. However, some works now hang in the public art galleries: notably the ones in Genoa's Palazzo Rosso, Palazzo Bianco and the National Galleries in Palazzo Spinola and Palazzo Reale. Well represented here are Titian, Tintoretto, Veronese, Guido Reni, the Carracci, Guercino, Procaccini, Caravaggio, Mattia Preti, Aurelio Lomi, Orazio and Artemisia Gentileschi, Luca Giordano, Rubens, Van Dyck and others besides. The presence of these artists in Liguria in the 17th century produced a pictorial culture which, with its original and varied idioms, developed its own independent style incorporating a wide variety of inspirations. The main names here were Giovanni Andrea Ansaldo, Gioacchino

A. V. Ščusev, Russian church of Cristo Salvatore, Sanremo

Assereto, Giovanni Bernardo Carbone, the Carlone, Valerio Castello, Giovanni Andrea and Orazio De Ferrari, Domenico Fiasella, il Grechetto, Giambattista Paggi, and Bernardo Strozzi. Later in the 17th century, Baroque civilization brought masterpieces in the form of sculptural works by Marseilles artist Pierre Puget, Genoese artist Filippo Parodi, clearly inspired by Bernini, and grand paintings – frescoes and canvases that transfigured palaces and churches – painted by Domenico Piola and his son-in-law Gregorio De Ferrari, from Porto Maurizio.

The Ricca architects of Lavina di Rezzo (Imperia) built some interesting churches in the 17th and 18th centuries in western Liguria and the Genoa area.

The votive shrines to be found all over Genoa and in other towns in Liguria – mostly dedicated to the Virgin Mary and dating back to the 17th and 18th centuries – testify to the intensity of popular piety, when unknown stone-cutters worked alongside such famous sculptors as Francesco Maria Schiaffino. This period also saw a wealth of artistic *presepi*, or nativity crèches, complete with dressed wooden figurines; many of these remain on show also outside the Christmas period in permanent exhibitions and museums. Wooden sculptures in the 17th and 18th centuries – the Bissoni and Anton Maria Maragliano were masters of the art, which continued to the 19th century – produced theatrically realistic sacred groups, along with crucifixes and processional chests, which are still brought out for the devotional processions that take place throughout the region, most notably on Good Friday in Savona and on 24 June in Genoa, the feast day of the patron saint John the Baptist. Domenico Parodi and Lorenzo De Ferrari continued the late Baroque style into the early 18th century, creating sumptuous 'mirror galleries' that were miniature versions of the one in Versailles. Pictorial art in this period was dominated by the powerful, visionary work of Alessandro Magnasco. Cultural dependence on France, largely a consequence of the naval bombing of 1684, was seen in many fields. In architecture it reached its peak just after the middle of the century with Palazzo Durazzo Bombrini, built in Genova Cornigliano by Pierre Paul de Cotte, a grandiose Paris residence at the mouth of the Polcevera, which brought to the region some major innovations in living styles.

The age of Neoclassicism

With Rococo now out of fashion, Neoclassicism firmly established itself in the 1770s and 1780s: in and out of town, new buildings appeared and palaces and gardens were modernized, thanks to the work of Charles de Wailly, and later of Andrea Tagliafichi, Gregorio Petondi, Giambattista Pellegrini and others. Lombard architect Simone Cantoni rebuilt the central section of Palazzo Ducale, which had been devastated by fire in 1777. In 1781 his brother Gaetano designed the cathedral of Porto Maurizio.

The Genoese scene in the period following the *ancien régime* until 1835 was dominated by Carlo Barabino, the architect and urban-planner who masterminded the creation of the modern city, drawing up development plans and designing new buildings, including the Carlo Felice Theater and the adjoining Fine Arts Academy. This institution was founded in 1751 by the enlightened aristocracy who, with donations from their own picture galleries, created and gradually enlarged the museum there for the benefit of its students.

Architecture and the city: the modern urban form

19th- and early 20th-century developments in the capital and other towns in the region first borrowed from the forms of the ancient patrician villas, reduced to mere surface decorations on middle-class homes, then began to adopt a varied range of architectural and decorative features also seen in other parts of Italy and abroad, blending historical styles, Eclecticism and Art Nouveau, with interesting though rarely original results. Exceptions here are the phantasmagoric creations of Florentine architect Gino Coppedè, who designed the Mackenzie castle and other fanciful buildings.

Two major squares laid out in Genoa in the 1930s are emblematic of the opposite directions in which Italian architecture was moving on the eve of World War II: Piazza della Vittoria, designed by Marcello Piacentini, demonstrated rhetorically, but elegantly, the regime's aspirations to the grandeur of Imperial Rome; Piazza Rossetti, by Luigi Carlo Daneri, offered a refined version of the simple modernity of European rationalism.

The major works of contemporary architecture that have appeared in the last few decades have been hotly debated. They include the museums of Albini and Helg; the viaduct over the Polcevera river by Morandi and Cherubini; the reconstruction of the Ferraris football stadium (Gregotti), of the Carlo Felice Theater (Rossi, Gardella, Reinhart) and of the San Silvestro complex for the new Architecture school (Gardella, Grossi Bianchi); the design of the San Benigno Center by the American practice S.O.M.; and Renzo Piano's redevelopment of the Old Port for the 1992 Expo.

In the 19th century Liguria was discovered by a foreign élite, attracted by the landscape and by the climate, many records of which survive. The Villa Pallavicini park in Genoa Pegli, opened in 1846, was conceived no longer just for private use, but as an attractively landscaped tourist attraction. Close to the border with France, Englishman Thomas Hanbury created an important acclimatization park for exotic plants. Bordighera was adorned with the work of Charles Garnier, the architect who designed the Opéra in Paris. One reminder of the stay of czarina Maria Alexandrovna in Sanremo in 1874 is the Russian church of Cristo Salvatore, by A. V. Ščusev, the designer of the Lenin Mausoleum.

One of Italy's most extensive collections of oriental art came from Edoardo Chiossone, who bequeathed to the City of Genoa the treasures he collected during his long stay in Japan (1875-98), later added to with other acquisitions and now displayed in a modern museum.

Other museums document art and sculpture from the last two centuries by Ligurian and other artists. The region boasts an extensive collection of modern and contemporary art, exhibited also in various private galleries.

One of the latest museums is the Amedeo Lia art gallery in La Spezia, made possible through the patronage of a collector of ancient art.

Alongside the various new developments, an interest in the past began to develop in the late 19th century, with the beginning of research and restoration work which – thanks initially to the efforts of Alfredo D'Andrade and a level of freedom of action that would be unthinkable today – brought back to life aspects of the Middle Ages that had been lost but which were now given a new appeal: examples are Palazzo San Giorgio, Porta Soprana and *San Donato* in Genoa; San Paragorio in Noli and the Baptistery in Albenga. The retrieval of vestiges of the ancient world continues today, though with quite different criteria: the region's towns and cities are preserving the best of their past as they look ahead to the future.

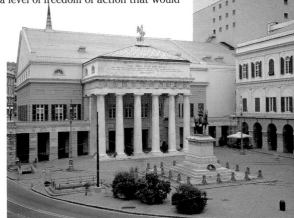

19th- and 20th-century architecture in the Carlo Felice Theater, Genoa

Liguria: a visitor's guide

Thanks to its mild climate – temperate in winter and cool in summer – Liguria attracts tourists all year round. The best period to visit the region, however, is from early springtime on, when the flowers are already in full bloom, the days are warm, the most beautiful places are seldom crowded and it is sometimes even possible to go for a swim in the sea. Spring is also the time when certain climatic conditions cause a meteorological phenomenon known in dialect as the *caligo*: a mist created by a process known as advection that results in the formation of fog banks during the hottest hours of the day, when the sea is still cold and the air is heated by the sun. These usually quite dense banks of mist, which appear in the open sea, are a danger to shipping but a spectacular sight to anyone observing them from high ground.

The region's website – *www.regione.liguria.it* – is a useful source of information about Liguria.

The regional capital

The city at the heart of Liguria is a beautiful though in many ways strange place. Anyone arriving in Genoa from the north by car or train misses its most attractive side: as singer-songwriter Ivano Fossati put it, Genoa should be approached from the sea, from where it appears in all its imposing beauty. For like all coastal towns, Genoa is two-dimensional, like the backdrop of some huge theater. From the Old Port area, the bay describes a semi-circle, around which is ranged a city center that appears almost to tumble down to the sea from the hills behind. Central Genoa is full of treasures and contradictions: splendid palaces are squeezed in between dark, narrow alleyways; imposing doorways face onto run-down street corners. The *Lanterna* lighthouse (the symbol of the city) is now dwarfed by the new pointy skyscrapers and coal plant that surround it; to the east, but still in the city, lies the ancient picturesque fishing village of Boccadasse. The city is a tangle of streets leading every which way, with elevated highways, bridges, underpasses, and trains emerging from tunnels a few meters from the third-story windows of apartment blocks. In the center are *trattoria* and other places to eat and drink at all hours of the day, and all manner of shops. Then, when you emerge from the labyrinth you suddenly find yourself in a completely different place: the more sober, elegant city of Palazzo Ducale, Piazza De Ferrari, Via XX Settembre, Via S. Vincenzo, Piazza Colombo.

From Ponte Spinola, opposite the Aquarium, boats take visitors on guided tours of the city from the sea, following a route that takes in the whole of Genoa's historic center and the port, to Ponte Somalia and back: the round trip takes approximately 45 minutes. These tours are run by *Alimar* (*Servizi Turistici Marittimi, Calata degli Zingari 16126 Genoa, tel. 010256775, fax 010252966*), and *Cooperativa Battellieri del Porto di Genova* (*Calata degli Zingari 16126 Genoa, tel. 010265712*). Boat tours cost 10,000 lire.

A bird's-eye view of the port of Genoa, with the city's hills behind

Another way of seeing Genoa from the south (at an even lower price) is by taking the elevator in the Bigo (*tel. 0102485710*), the pronged, derrick-like structure located at the center of the Expo area. Other intriguing observation points are the far end of the Aquarium Pier, or better still the amazingly panoramic belvederes on the Castelletto and Righi esplanade. Detailed information about the city can be found at *www.comune.genova.it/città.htm* and at *www.apt.genova.it*.

Parks and nature reserves

Liguria has no fewer than six large regional parks, two smaller park areas and four nature reserves, spreading over a total of 60,000 ha, or nearly 12% of Ligurian territory. In addition to this, the region boasts the High Mountain Trail, a major hiking route that winds its way for 440 km through the mountains, and two other large parks: the Alpi Liguri and Finalese Parks.

The **Bric Tana Regional Nature Park**, a hilly, 170-ha area, cloaked in chestnut and other woods in the Savona area (headquarters at Millesimo: *Municipal Department, tel. 019564007*), is important in particular for the presence of surface and underground karst formations, and the Bormida river with its limestone pinnacles. Also in the province of Savona is the 794-ha **Piana Crixia Regional Nature Park** (*Piana Crixia Municipal Department, tel. 019570021*), with characteristic gullies and eroded sand and clay crevices; the main attraction here is the *fungo di pietra*, a giant mushroom-shaped rock. The **Beigua Regional Nature Park** (*Beigua Park Authority, Corso Italia 3, Savona, tel. 01984187300*), covers an area of 18,160 ha straddling Genoa and Savona provinces. The landscape ranges from mountains rising to an altitude of 1,200 m down to the first gentle slopes that rise up from the coast, and has two quite

Liguria's nature parks attract many bird-watchers

distinct climates that create two totally different worlds. The park contains traces of the very earliest human civilization (prehistoric rock carvings) and of man's more recent activities: pre-industrial iron foundries, glassworks and paper mills. Here too is Tiglieto Abbey, the home of Italy's first Cistercian community, and the so-called *Convento del Deserto*, near Varazze, a monastery of the Discalced Friars order. The next park to the east is the **Antola Regional Nature Park**, a 7,680-ha area administered from Busalla (*Via XXV Aprile 17, tel. 0109761014*). Dominated by Mt. Antola and crossed by the old salt routes, this park is noted for its wealth of exceptional flora and fauna – in particular its rare butterflies – but also for its ancient architecture, such as the Castello della Pietra and other fascinating manor houses dating back to the days of the imperial feuds, and its old mills. Also in Genoa province is the 4,660-ha **Portofino Regional Nature Park**, which spreads over the municipalities of Camogli, Chiavari, Portofino, Rapallo, Recco, Santa Margherita Ligure, and Zoagli (*Park Authority at Santa Margherita Ligure, Viale Rainusso 1, tel. 0185289479*). The heart of the reserve, a protected area since 1935, is the famous promontory, or *Monte di Portofino*, which rises to a height of 600 m and measures over 3 km across. In the park, which since June 1998 has also included a marine reserve, is the splendid ancient abbey of **San Fruttuoso di Capodimonte**. More typically mountain scenery is to be found in the **Aveto Regional Nature Park** (*Park Authority at Borzonasca, Via Marré 75/A, tel. 0185340311*), which comprises the extensive Lame forest and Liguria's highest Apennine mountain peaks (1,600 and 1,800 m), with extensive pastureland for the rearing of cattle that yields a typical cheese. Borzone Abbey offers cultural interest. The 13,152-ha **Promontories and Eastern Isles Regional Nature Park** (*Park Authority in Levanto, Palazzo Comunale, tel. 0187920893*) lies between the provinces of Genoa and La Spezia, and protects the areas that have not yet become part of the **Cinque Terre National Park**, based in Riomaggiore (*for information contact the Town Hall, tel. 0187920633*). This newly-created park, which slopes steeply down to the coast, has been reinforced over the centuries with dry stone wall terraced farmland. Clinging to the cliffs amongst the vineyards lie the *Cinque Terre*:

Nature parks and protected areas

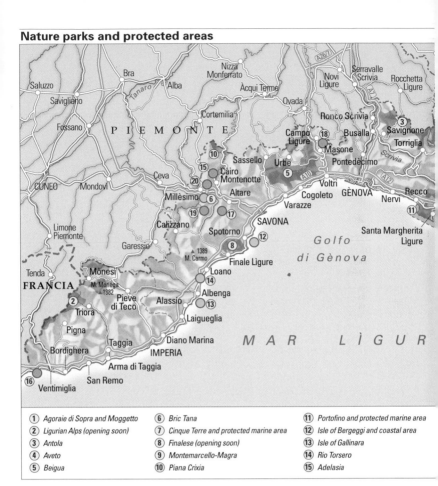

1. Agoraie di Sopra and Moggetto
2. Ligurian Alps (opening soon)
3. Antola
4. Aveto
5. Beigua
6. Bric Tana
7. Cinque Terre and protected marine area
8. Finalese (opening soon)
9. Montemarcello-Magra
10. Piana Crixia
11. Portofino and protected marine area
12. Isle of Bergeggi and coastal area
13. Isle of Gallinara
14. Rio Torsero
15. Adelasia

here, the natural and man-made worlds blend to form a landscape of rare beauty. The flora varies from ilex and cork-oak to olive and vines. Completely within La Spezia's provincial borders, the **Montemarcello-Magra Regional Nature Park** (*Park Authority at Sarzana, Via Paci 2, tel. 0187691071*), protects an area of great archaeological interest: the Vara river, in particular, is dotted with charming historic villages, castles and old water-mills.
Three of the region's four nature reserves are in Savona province: the **Gallinara Isle Regional Nature Park** (*administered from Albenga, Piazza S. Michele 17, tel. 0182541351*) is home to one of the largest colonies of herring gulls in the northern Tyrrhenian, to early Mediterranean species of flowers, and to some rare reptiles (the island's marine environment survives virtually intact, and protection is soon to be extended further out to sea); the **Rio Torsero Regional Nature Reserve** (*administered from Ceriale, tel. 0182990024*) comprises an area of great importance to paleontologists because of the abundance, variety and excellent state of preservation of fossils from the Pliocene (interesting examples can be observed in the reserve's own museum in Peagna); the **Bergeggi Regional Nature Reserve** (*tel. 019859017*) occupies a stretch of coast taking the form of cliffs rich in caves and inlets, and the island opposite, on which stand various ruined buildings (a protected marine area is to be created here because of the wealth of undersea life off the island's cliffs, and for its geological and biological importance).
The **Agoraie di Sopra and Moggetto Nature Reserve** in Genoa province (*run by the regional division of the State Forestry Department, Viale Brigate Partigiane 2, Genoa; tel. 010586831*) lies on the western slopes of Mt. Aiona. Here are four perpetual lakes of rare beauty as well as some seasonal ones, and the so-called Moggetto, or Lastro Tarn; the Agoraie di Sopra group of lakes includes the Lago degli Abeti (Lake of the Silver Firs),

	National park
	Regional nature park
●	State-run nature reserve
○	Regional nature reserve
○	Other protected areas
	Protected marine areas

④ ①

⑦

⑨

0 ___ 12 km

⑯ *Hanbury Botanical Gardens*
⑰ *Osiglia Lake*
⑱ *Prato Rondanino Botanical Gardens*
⑲ *Mt. Camulera*
⑳ *Rio Parasacco*

so named after the petrified fir forest on the lake bottom, which can still be seen. Other natural reserves to be created are the *Ligurian Alps Regional Nature Park*, along the Nervia, Argentina and Arroscia valleys and rising up to 2,000-m peaks, at the foot of which grow lilies and orchids; the *Finale Area Regional Nature Park*, between Finale Ligure and Noli; and the *Hanbury Botanical Gardens*, at Capo Mortola, near Ventimiglia. More information on Liguria's parks can be found at *www.comunic.it/parks/regione.liguria/index.htm*.

Getting around in Liguria

The main highways serving the region are the A12 for those coming from the east as far as Genoa, continuing as the A10 from Genoa west to Ventimiglia. From the north the region is accessed via the A15 Parma-La Spezia, the A7 Milan-Genoa, the A26 Santhià-Voltri, and the A6 Turin-Savona.

The A10 and A12 cover the entire sweep of the coast, and are extremely panoramic, though frequently subject to strong winds as well as being choked with vacation traffic, so long queues are inevitable at certain times of the year and most weekends. On Sundays, of course, the traffic is most intense on the northbound carriageways as the Lombards and Piedmontese head home. Those who can travel at less busier times are well advised to do so: one of the most pleasant ways of avoiding the Sunday rush home is to set off after midnight having enjoyed a leisurely dinner in one of the many excellent and inexpensive trattorias to be found in the inland areas.

The same applies for those taking the A6 north from Savona to Turin: long stretches of this highway have one overtaking lane only shared by the opposite carriageways, whereas the stretch of the southbound carriageway of the A7 (Milan-Genoa) climbing over the Giovi Pass seems more like an awkward provincial road than a modern highway (both are now being widened). The A26 is much faster-moving.

The state road that runs the length of the region is the Via Aurelia, a panoramic road with some exceptionally beautiful stretches. It is best appreciated out of season, taking time to enjoy the places along the way. Between La Spezia and Sestri Levante the Via Aurelia pushes inland as far as the Bracco Pass. An alternative route is the coast road from La Spezia toward Riomaggiore, although motorists should be sure to fill up their cars before setting off: there is not a single gas station to be found on the road to Levanto. Those who do take this route will, though, be rewarded by the spectacular landscape of the *Cinque Terre* and beyond to Levanto itself, Bonassola, Deiva Marina, and then the long, narrow tunnels before Moneglia. These former railroad tunnels allow for the passage of one direction of cars only, so be prepared for long waits here: the lights regulating the alternate flow of traffic stay red for anything up to a quarter of an hour at a time.

In summer in particular, attempts to reach the *Cinque Terre*, Camogli, and Portofino by car would be foolhardy to say the least. The train is by far the best way of getting around on land, and boats leave daily from the main towns to take day trippers to the most picturesque seaside spots. A car is something you definitely do not want to have to worry about when visiting San Fruttuoso, out on the Portofino promontory between Portofino and Camogli, which can in fact only be reached by boat or, for the more athletic, on foot along the signposted paths.

From Savona to Genoa Nervi a light metropolitan railway runs a regular service for which a single ticket covers the train and the buses in the entire urban area. The train stations of La Spezia and each of the five stations in the Cinque Terre sell a special return tourist ticket from La Spezia to Monterosso al Mare, that can be used for a whole day to hop on and off any of the many regional trains that stop at the stations.

Air travelers land at Genoa's *Cristoforo Colombo* airport (*tel. 0106015410*), to the west of the city at Sestri Ponente (reached from Genoa by the highway for Ventimiglia, exiting at *Genova Aeroporto*). The *Volabus* bus service connects the airport with Genoa's main train stations *Principe* and *Brignole*.

Luni (La Spezia) has a *Military Airport* (*tel. 0187673180*) open to civil traffic for tourist activities. The region's other airport is in the plain of Villanova d'Albenga (Savona), which also provides a tourist service covering the whole of western Liguria.

The other approach is of course from the sea: the port of Genoa in particular, but also those of La Spezia, Savona and Imperia, provide a regular service on national and Mediterranean routes with passenger and car ferries. The region's numerous marinas provide mooring facilities for pleasure craft of all sizes, and offer excellent amenities (see itinerary pp. 217-18).

Foreigners in Liguria

Toward the end of the 1800s foreign travelers, especially those coming from northern Europe, began to appreciate Liguria's beauty. To the west the English discovered Bordighera, Sanremo, and Alassio. They were followed by the Russians and then by the Germans, who rediscovered the charms of the inland towns and villages, where large numbers of visitors from Germany still come to spend their summer vacation. The remarkable Villa Hanbury at Capo Mortola (Ventimiglia), the casino and palm trees of Sanremo, and the hotels of Bordighera are lasting testimonies of the love for Liguria visitors from abroad have shown. Many famous writers and artists came here, including Monet and Hemingway, who marked their stay on the famous *artists' walk* at Alassio (the futurists invented something similar in Albisola). The medieval town of Bussana Vecchia, destroyed a century ago by an earthquake, was salvaged by a colony of Dutch and Germans and is now an artists' town.

Among those who frequented Liguria's eastern shores were Dickens, Goethe, Maupassant, Nietzsche, Wagner, Shelley and his wife Mary Wollstonecraft, and Byron, after whom the Arpaia Cave in Portovenere is named.

Portofino in particular has always been, and still is, a meeting place for movie kings and queens, leading financial figures, and politicians.

Special places

A lot of places in Liguria, while usually categorized as being merely of 'curiosity value', are interesting places to visit nonetheless. In the Argentina Valley, some 800 meters above

Alberto Sordi in "Racconti d'Estate", a film set in Liguria by G. Franciolini

sea level, is the village of **Triora**, once thought to be the haunt of witches: during a period of famine in the late 16th century, a delegation of inquisitors arrived here to rid the place of what was considered to be the evil that was manifesting itself through these women. The dramatic happenings of those far-off times are remembered today in a Witches' Monument, in some strange-sounding street names, in the Museum of Ethnography and Witchcraft, and of course in the many shops selling souvenir gnomes, witches, elves and love potions. Above Bordighera lies **Seborga**, which has for years claimed its independence as a principality under its reigning monarch George I, and above Sanremo lies the town of **Bussana Vecchia**, the artistic colony (described by some as a commercial art business) that settled here in the 1960s and after a difficult beginning – various unsuccessful attempts were made to evict the newcomers – is now a flourishing community. The beautifully-situated **Verezzi**, which commands beautiful views in every direction, is the venue each summer for a major Theater Festival.

Eastern Liguria will delight anyone keen to get away from motor traffic: the splendid blend of art and architecture that is the **abbey of San Fruttuoso** can only be reached from the sea or on foot; **Palmaria Isle**, also off limits to automobiles, conceals its natural beauty in difficult-to-reach caves; and the other smaller island off Portovenere, the **Isle of Tino**, is a military area that is only opened to the public on 13 September, in celebration of Venerio, the patron saint of the Gulf of La Spezia. The inland area above the Aveto valley is a hiker's paradise: the **Agoraie Forest** offers high mountain scenery that is truly unusual for a region on the sea.

Names

The names that have been attributed to the various stretches of the coast say it all: Riviera of the Flowers (the westernmost shores), Riviera of the Palms (between Marina di Andora and Varazze), Paradise Gulf (from Bogliasco to the Portofino promontory), Gulf of the Poets (at La Spezia), Bay of Fables and Bay of Silence (Sestri Levante), and Blue Bay (Lerici).

Handicrafts

Of the many craft activities offered in the region, here are some of the best known. Altare, which is known for its glassmaking, has a master glassmakers' school and glassblowing center (with an interesting museum). Albisola is a center for ceramic pottery, and Campo Ligure is famous for the traditional craft of filigree work. The Tigullio and Val Fontanabuona are famed for their fabric manufacture: velvet in Zoagli, damask, brocade and lampas in Lorsica, lace in Rapallo and Portofino, and macramé in Chiavari. This town is also famous for the traditional making of chairs, while nearby Val Fontanabuona is a center for slate, which is quarried

Artwork in Bussana Vecchia (above) and slate handicrafts in Valle Fontanabuona

in these parts; Gattorna is a center for the manufacture of wooden toys, Uscio (Terrile) is renowned for its tower clock manufacture, and Avegno for its bell foundry. Chiavari has been producing 'campanine' chairs, with their elegant, simple design, since the early 19th century.

Not surprisingly, fishing-net making and other marine crafts are widespread. And given the attention to detail and originality that goes into the construction of naval vessels in Liguria, shipbuilding, which is central to the region's economy, could also arguably be included among the region's traditional craft activities.

Sport

A whole range of sporting activities – on land and at sea – can be pursued in Liguria. As well as water polo (a discipline in which the region excels), swimming, and windsurfing (sea conditions here are ideal), there are sailing schools in nearly all the coastal towns (*F.I.V. Liguria, tel. 010589431*), and windsurfing schools in many: in Alassio (*tel. 0182642516*), Bordighera (*tel. 0184266567*), in Genoa at Bagni Italia (*tel. 0103620685*), at the Centro Surf Club (*tel. 0103629668*), at Genoa Vernazzola (*tel. 0103770365*), and at Genoa Voltri. There are also plenty of scuba-diving centers, the addresses of which can be found in magazines specializing in the sport. Water-skiing centers can be found in Alassio and La Spezia (*tel. 0187504013*).

Given the prevalently mountainous nature of the terrain, there are also plenty of

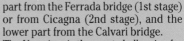

For extreme sports enthusiasts

Liguria offers plenty of opportunities for kayak enthusiasts. Here are some of the best known and best equipped.

A key location in the province of Imperia is the *Argentina* river, the upper part of which is reached from Molini di Triora, the central part 4 km up from Mt. Badalucco, and the lower part from Badalucco itself.

Most canoeists in the Savona area head for the *Orba* river, the upper part of which is reached from San Pietro d'Olba, the central part from the Tiglieto bridge and the lower part downstream from the dam of Ortiglieto lake.

The most popular river for the sport in Genoa province is the *Lavagna*, the highest part of which is reached from the Molino bridge for Boasi, the upper part from the Ferriere bridge (1st landing stage) or after the confluence with the Urri river (2nd landing stage), the central part from the Ferrada bridge (1st stage) or from Cicagna (2nd stage), and the lower part from the Calvari bridge.

The *Vara* river is the most challenging for canoeists in the La Spezia area. The highest part is reached 2 km up from Varese Ligure (uppermost stage), at the bridge at km 3 of the SS566 (2nd highest stage), below the Ponte S. Margherita dam (middle stage), or from the Vizza power station (lower stage); the lower part of the river is reached below the weir under the Brugnato highway viaduct.

For further information, visit the website (*http://www.federcanoa.org*) or contact *Federazione Italiana Canoa Kayak, Viale Tiziano 70, Roma, tel. +390636858188-36858247; fax +390636858171;* or in Genoa, *Via Malta 2, tel. 010587338.*

Anyone in western Liguria looking for something even more challenging than these 'whitewater' descents should head for Loreto, near Triora, where bungee jumps are organized from March to October by the Outdoor Bungee Center 1. Here the drop is 119 m.

More information can be found at *www.bungee.it* and at *http://-www.bungee.it/ntbc1/indexntbc1i.html.*

opportunities for cyclists and mountain bikers (*F.C.I. Liguria, tel. 0105704116*), and for hikers, who can find out about what the region offers by contacting *Associazione Alta Via dei Monti Liguri* (*tel. 010204448*). Even joggers are catered for, with numerous specially laid-out tracks (*F.I.D.A.L. Liguria, tel. 010884349*). Of special interest to hikers are the 'Cinque Terre and Riviera Trails' run by *CAI's La Spezia section* (*tel. 018722873*). Mountaineers can choose from a seemingly endless range of high-altitude itineraries: Mt. Galero, the High Mountain Trail, Reopasso, Mt. Antola, Mt. Aiona, Mt. Cantomoro, Mt. Nero, Mt. Roncalla, Groppo delle Ali, Mt. Penna, Mt. Maggiorasca, Mt. Tobbio *(contact the Italian Alpine Club CAI in Genoa, tel. 010310584)*. Downhill and cross-country skiers will find slopes and trails at Alberola and Calizzano (Savona), Colla Melosa and Monesi di Triora (Imperia), Mt. Alfeo (reached from Gorreto, Genoa), Mt. Aiona (reached from Rezzoaglio, Genoa), Mt. Montarlone (reached from Rovegno, Genoa), Mt. Maggiorasca, Mt. Penna, Santo Stefano d'Aveto (Genoa), Mt. Antola (reached from Torriglia, near Genoa), and Mt. Gottero (reached from Varese Ligure, near Genoa).

Rock climbers can choose from a number of facilities: near Albenga, in Val Pennavaira; and at Finale Ligure there is an outdoor area of European standards, with some 2,000 routes in limestone; at Triora there is a mid to large limestone area; and at Muzzerone (road to Portovenere as far as Le Grazie) is another mid to large limestone area (though not of the most advanced type) in an attractive setting (a guide is needed to find the cliffs that form sheer drops over the sea); there are artificial areas at Genoa-Borzoli and Deiva.

Liguria is also well equipped for horse-riding (*F.I.S.E. Liguria, tel. 010 541585; F.I.T.E.E.C.–A.N.T.E. Liguria, tel. 0185337585*), canoeing and kayaking (*F.I.C.K. Liguria, tel. 010587338*). There are golf links at Garlenda (tel. 0182580012), Sanremo (*tel. 0184557093*) and Lerici (*tel. 0187970193*). Finally, daredevils who prefer the thrill of parachuting can contact the *Flying Club at Sarzana* (*tel. 0187673180*) and at *Genoa* (*tel. 010564335*).

Itineraries

Detailed descriptions
of the tourist sites

The picturesque hilltop village of Apricale

Genoa: the history and culture of a city-port

"You will see a right royal city, set against a mountainous hill, proud in its people and its walls, and whose very appearance proclaims it as lady of the sea...".
(Petrarch, *Description of Genoa*, 1358)

"This extraordinary city devouring the world is the greatest human adventure of the 16th century. Genoa seems to be the city of miracles".
(Fernand Braudel)

"If ever a diabolically capitalist city can be said to have existed before the capitalist age in Europe and the world, then it is Genoa, opulent and sordid at the same time".
(Fernand Braudel)

The port and the city have been closely bound up with one another since earliest times. **Genoa** (elev. 19 m, pop. 641,437) grew up on the sea, around 500 BC, with the role it would continue to play ever after (though with mixed fortunes) as the point of intersection between two major transport systems: the sea lanes of the great watery plain of the Mediterranean, and the land routes that cut across the Apennines to northern Italy and the rest of Europe. These were mainly trading routes, but over the centuries also served to bring different peoples and cultures into contact with each other.

The original settlement that grew up here took advantage of a number of favorable conditions: this was the northernmost point of the Tyrrhenian Sea, lying within easy reach of the Po Valley, and had a natural harbor consisting of an inlet defended by a small peninsula that was enlarged after the 12th century to become today's Old Pier.

The mostly Etruscan merchants heading for the Greek colony of Massalia (Marseilles) and other destinations, came into contact and soon established links with the

Excavation work between the Spinola and Calvi bridges, Genoa, in a 1755 print. Sea and Seafaring Pavilion, Genoa

local populations who had been living on the Ligurian shores for several centuries.
The first fortified citadel grew up on the Castello hill, the high ground which was cho-
sen in the Middle Ages as the site for the bishop's palace-castle and later a large
monastery, until its dissolution by Napoleon and in the mid-19th century.
An ally of Rome during the Second Punic War and destroyed by the Carthaginians in 205
BC., Genoa was rebuilt soon afterwards by the Romans, reaching the size it would more
or less maintain until the 11th century, bordered to the south by the Castello hill and to
the north by the thoroughfare leading roughly from Palazzo San Giorgio, on the sea, to
the Porta Soprana gateway, boundaries within which the cathedral of *San Lorenzo* also
lay. The regular urban grid pattern of the area introduced by the Romans was continued
in the Middle Ages, with various alterations and additions. Very little can be seen of the
original city, which was protected in the 9th century by the original defense walls that
are now no more than a memory. Much does survive meanwhile from the city that grew
up at the time when seafaring began again in earnest in the early decades of the second millennium. For centuries transformation of the city was based not on demolish-
ing the old, but on putting existing structures to new uses wherever possible. Thanks
to this, the visit to the old town is a fascinating journey through history.
Finding your way through Genoa's *carrugi*, the narrow old alleyways lined with tall buildings is not as difficult as it might at first seem. Making sense of the maze is fairly easy,
once you have a clear idea of the main thoroughfares which were opened up to allow the
passage of people, animals and goods, along the shore and inland, where they eventually turn into *creuze*, the walled suburban pathways that eventually become mule-tracks.
The waterfront buildings known as the *Ripa*, beneath which runs what is left of the arcaded street built by the owners of the buildings, are a splendid example of urban planning begun in 1133 by the young commune. From Piazza Cavour, created after the covering over of the original port, a seemingly insignificant alleyway – Vico delle Camelie
– turns left and runs almost parallel to the arcaded waterfront, becoming busier and
busier to the west. This series of streets and squares – Via delle Grazie, Piazza S. Giorgio (the old Roman forum and a marketplace since medieval times), Via Canneto il Curto, Via S. Pietro della Porta, Piazza Banchi (another major trading place and the business
hub until the creation in the 19th century of Piazza De Ferrari), Via S. Luca, Via Fossatello,

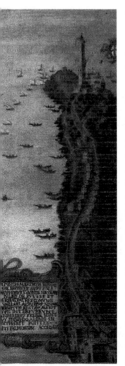

Via del Campo, Via Pré and beyond – is still one of the city's main
thoroughfares. Other streets run inland from the coast in a fan-
like arrangement in the direction of the eastern Riviera and the
Po Valley, cutting across the long thoroughfare mentioned
above: in the older part of town Via S. Bernardo, Via Giustiniani
and Via Canneto il Lungo head toward Porta Soprana (the mid-
12th century 'Barbarossa Walls'), continuing from there as a single street into the district that was totally transformed in the last
two centuries, and where little of the earlier city remains, as far
as the Bisagno river, the eastern edge of the city before 1874. In
the area urbanized after the year 1000, mention must also be
made of the street that until the 19th century was the main point
of entrance into the city, not from the land but from the sea, and
still an excellent introduction to the old city for anyone coming
from the Aquarium and the Expo site: Via al Ponte Reale, Piazza and Via Banchi, Via Orefici, Via and Piazza Soziglia, branch-
ing off into Via Luccoli and Salita S. Caterina in one direction and
Via dei Macelli di Soziglia in the other.
One thing that makes medieval Genoa different from other ancient cities in Italy is the lack of a large central public square, the
need for which was not perceived by a society fragmented into
factions, each with their own little square (the best surviving example is the Doria family's Piazza S. Matteo) that was the hub of
their sphere of influence; Genoa was a collection of *contrade*.
Buildings in stone, marble and brick erected in that period
abound: tall houses, with impressive arcades (now walled-up)
and traces of mullioned windows, the occasional surviving
tower, Romanesque and Gothic churches, and stretches of defense walls of a city which between the 13th and 14th century,

having vanquished the Pisans and Venetians, was one of the richest and most powerful mercantile cities in the Mediterranean and the entire continent. The buildings themselves were radically altered down the ages to suit changes in lifestyles and taste.

From the mid-15th century, sculpted portals and other elegant Renaissance decorations in marble, black stone and slate began to decorate the old merchants' homes which to keep up with changes on the international business scene were gradually turning into bankers, a process that built up to a crescendo with the splendor of the 'century of the Genoese', between the 16th and 17th centuries. The city, now one of Europe's financial capitals, linked to Spain and the Empire, enjoyed its second Golden Age, a period testified to by sumptuous palaces, elaborate Baroque churches, the countless paintings now in the places of worship, museums or private homes. Public and private schemes opened up new roads and squares, and redeveloped existing ones. It was in this period that Piazza Banchi took on its current appearance. In the mid-16th century the extraordinary phenomenon that was Strada Nuova (today's Via Garibaldi) began to happen, a milestone in the history of European urban planning. The seats of civil and religious power, of medieval origin, themselves underwent major transformations: the dome and the presbytery of the cathedral were redesigned and Palazzo Ducale was reorganized. The ancient tradition of the so-called 'Rolli' palaces – examples of refined, representative hospitality in Genoa in the 16th and 17th centuries – depended on the sumptuous private residences that were opened up to important personages on official visits. Some 150 palaces were divided up into five 'rolli', or official lists. Rubens himself was struck by this practice and collected several drawings of these buildings, which are now exhibited at the Royal Institute of British Architecture. The system of public hospitality organized through the 'Rolli' palaces, all in Genoa's historic center, was quite unique. Meanwhile luxurious villas were appearing all around the city, and the defense system was being improved: first (from 1536) by strengthening the 14th-century *enceinte* with earthworks and ramparts designed to withstand firearms (the 'Old Walls'); and later (between 1626 and 1633) with the erecting of more extensive walls on the mountain ridges and along the shores, from the lighthouse to the Bisagno river (the 'New Walls').

The downside to this opulence, in a period when money was concentrated in the hands of the few, was the appearance of an underclass of beggars. The huge *Albergo dei Poveri*, the 17th-century hospice built to help the disadvantaged, is a reminder of this. In 1684 the fleet of the 'Roi Soleil' heavily bombed Genoa to induce the reluctant republic to enter the economic and social sphere of influence of France, a country that would exert a strong cultural pull on the city for the whole of the 18th century: influencing fashion, art, architecture, design, literature and science.

In 1797, as revolutionary fever spread, the rule of the biennial doges, backed up by the aristocracy in accordance with the 1528 constitution, finally came to an end. After a number of years as the Democratic Ligurian Republic, Genoa was annexed to the Napoleonic Empire in 1805. The Emperor's defeat in 1815 led to union with the kingdom of Savoy, which thus gained the major seaport it had been longing to control for centuries in vain. With the 19th century the modern city began to take form: large sections of the ancient city were totally transformed and new quarters appeared on the fringes. The Gothic church of *San Domenico* was pulled down to make way for a new neoclassical opera house (named after the sovereign Carlo Felice) in the *piazza* that gradually developed into the hub of the modern city. In the mid-1800s, the new middle classes and old nobility began to move out to the hills. The values they held dear were being lost: the city they had known was decaying. Today's Greater Genoa was created in two stages (in 1874 and in 1926) with the incorporation of 25 municipalities into the old city, which had hitherto been contained within the New Walls. The metropolis now extends 33 kilometers along the coast and well up the inland Polcevera and Bisagno Valleys.

The creation of highways and railroads, the expansion of the port, industrial growth and extensive building work in the 20th century did much to alter the city's appearance. Some of these changes have undoubtedly been for the worse, but in many cases the results have been interesting and indeed laudable.

Modern Genoa finds itself in the enviable position of a city that enjoys a superb location and has a rich artistic heritage to offer those who seek it out. This surprising and often contradictory city is booming once again, and now looks forward to a splendid future, as it makes the most – after decades of neglect – of the splendors of its past.

1 Historic Genoa

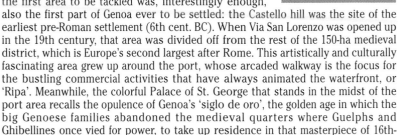

City profile

When large-scale restoration work on the ancient heart of the Ligurian capital began back in the early 1990s, the first area to be tackled was, interestingly enough, also the first part of Genoa ever to be settled: the Castello hill was the site of the earliest pre-Roman settlement (6th cent. BC). When Via San Lorenzo was opened up in the 19th century, that area was divided off from the rest of the 150-ha medieval district, which is Europe's second largest after Rome. This artistically and culturally fascinating area grew up around the port, whose arcaded walkway is the focus for the bustling commercial activities that have always animated the waterfront, or 'Ripa'. Meanwhile, the colorful Palace of St. George that stands in the midst of the port area recalls the opulence of Genoa's 'siglo de oro', the golden age in which the big Genoese families abandoned the medieval quarters where Guelphs and Ghibellines once vied for power, to take up residence in that masterpiece of 16th-century town-planning, the 'Strada Nuova' (now Via Garibaldi).

Decades later, the westward extension of the street, Via Balbi, was laid out, largely through private initiative. But the palaces of political and religious power remained within 'Barbarossa's walls' (1155), which even today form the symbolic boundary of the ancient city, though only the Vacca and Sant'Andrea gateways remain. Today, after the devastation of the last war and decades of neglect, energies have at last been channeled into upgrading the city. Attractive noble residences have thus been restored to their former glory (gaining enormously on the property markets in the process) and eye-catching pastel-colored facades have appeared on many other buildings. The same subtle shades are also to be found in the old port area, which was extensively redeveloped for the 1992 Expo, an event that helped focus the city's attention once again on its age-old, and vitally important contact with the sea.

Genoa: the old port, which underwent an extensive redevelopment by architect Renzo Piano for the 1992 Columbus Celebration Expo

1.1 The waterfront: from Piazza del Principe to the Molo Vecchio

Walking tour around the Ancient Port of Genoa *(see plans pp. 45, 49 and pp. 70-71)*

The starting-point of this walking tour is Piazza del Principe, the inevitable point of entry into the city for anyone arriving by road, rail or sea. After a brief initial detour down Via Fanti d'Italia to the Maritime Station, it continues along Via Gramsci to Piazza Caricamento. The tour also takes in the almost parallel streets just behind the waterfront buildings (Via Pré and Via del Campo) and the whole exhibition area of the old port. Finally, Via del Molo heads back inland to the ancient quarters.

Palazzo Doria Pamphily or Palazzo del Principe* (II, B1). The visual appeal of this palace, built by order of Andrea Doria, has been all but destroyed by the busy road and rail arteries that now surround it. The traffic impinges in particular on the facade, which has an elegant portal created by Silvio Cosini from a design by Perin del Vaga, who was commissioned by Andrea to decorate the entire residence (1528-33). And the Florentine artist certainly did the admiral proud, as the **Andrea Doria apartments** clearly show (*open: Sat 3-6pm, Sun 10am-1pm; by prior arrangement, tel. 010255509*). The visit begins in the vestibule (*Lives and Triumphs of the Roman Kings*), and continues with the **Heroes Loggia** (*The Doria Family's Ancestors**) and the **Salone della Caduta dei Giganti**, whose frescoes depict the *Giants being Struck Dead by Zeus**. Also in this room is Sebastiano del Piombo's celebrated 1526 **Portrait of Andrea Doria, Admiral of the Papal Fleet****. The Gallery has a magnificent series of *tapestries** of the battle of Lepanto (Brussels, 1582-91).
The **south side** arcades and terraced avant-corps form the attractive backdrop to the garden (undergoing restoration in 2000), which is divided into a series of terraces laid out in the late 16th century. At the center of the park stands

Taddeo Carlone's *Fountain of Neptune* (1599); the *Triton Fountain* (1543) is by Giovanni Angelo Montorsoli.

Stazione Marittima (II, B1-2). Restoration work in the early 1990s has retrieved the former splendor – and functional efficiency – of this eclectic three-floor building (1930), a major terminal for the great ocean-going liners in the 1930s and '50s. Worth noting is the *Customs Hall*, decorated with travel frescoes painted at the time of construction. The *Ponte dei Mille*, behind, was used by travelers of a quite different kind: this was the quay from which steamships packed with emigrants bound for the Americas departed. The ponderous reinforced concrete *Grain Silo* to the east of the station (1901) is a major piece of industrial archaeology now awaiting redevelopment for new uses.

Via Gramsci (II, B-C2-3). The former Via Carlo Alberto – the name of the street that used to include today's Via Adua (II, B1-2) – has been a construction site for a good ten years: first for the 1992 Expo and then for the building of the subway, all of which has caused major traffic disruption. Excellent shops are to be found in the buildings on the town side, which are nearly all 19th century.

S. Giovanni di Pré (II, B2). Two places of worship are contained in this complex, which dates back to 1180, a date

Genoa: the gardens of Palazzo Doria Pamphily, against a marine background in a period photo

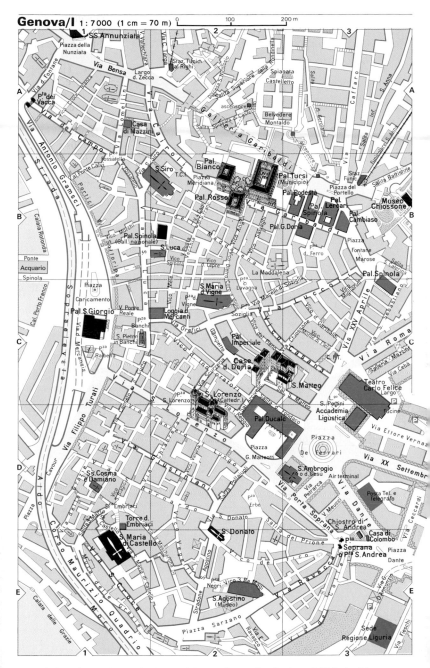

recorded in the tablet at the base of the fine cusped belltower, which has three rows of mullioned windows. It was built over an earlier church dedicated to the Holy Sepulcher, to which the presumed ashes of St. John the Baptist were brought from the Holy Land in 1098. The church was rebuilt by the Knights Hospitallers of St. John of Jerusalem (now the Order of Malta). Of greatest interest is the upper church, whose nave is separated from the aisles by heavy columns and bare stone arches. The blind span is the result of the reorganization of the church as a public place of worship in 1731, when the facade was also altered.

The restructuring of the adjoining

In the footsteps of Fabrizio De André

Singer-songwriter Fabrizio De André had always looked forward to spending his retirement in his native city but, alas, fate decreed otherwise. In the early 1960s Genoa saw a wealth of new musical talent (including well-known singer-songwriters Gino Paoli, Bruno Lauzi and Luigi Tenco), the young Fabrizio being among them. He was a great admirer of the French *chansonniers*, especially Georges Brassens. In 1968, Mina sang his highly successful *La Canzone di Marinella*, a hit that marked his real breakthrough onto the music scene. In his poetical songs he always sided with the losers, the misfits and the have-nots, themes which, together with the sheer musical quality of his songs, assured him favor with the youth movements of the day. In the second half of the 1970s, in keeping with his political beliefs, he moved to a farmstead at Tempio Pausania in northern Sardinia, where he and his companion Dori Ghezzi were kidnapped and held hostage for four months in 1980. The following year, not surprisingly, he wrote a song about the experience entitled *Hotel Supramonte*. When *Creuza de Mã*, an LP entirely in Genoese dialect, was released three years later it was greeted with rave reviews. It is considered to be his finest album and was voted best album of the 1980s by music critics. His last works brought further confirmation of the lively creative talents of a man who, even in his later years, was a rallying point for the entire Italian music world.

Genoa: the porticoed Via Pré, full of Mediterranean charm

Commenda, the old hospice convent now used to house temporary exhibitions, dates back to 1508. The elegant colonnade is surmounted by two tiers of loggias.

Via Pré (II, B2-3), lined with shops and stalls that give it something of the appearance of an Arab *souk*, offers an alternative route to Via Gramsci, continuing the itinerary inside the old quarter immediately behind the waterfront. The origins of this narrow street (the 'meadows' of the name suggest an unsubstantiated rural past) date back to the 11th-12th centuries; the few surviving medieval houses only add to its unmistakably Mediterranean charm.

Porta dei Vacca or Porta S. Fede (I, A1). It was the western opening in the 1155 walls. This gateway, incorporated into 17th-century buildings, has two bulky, semicircular towers that are connected by a main arch with a crenelated walkway and decorated on the inside by a colonnaded porch.
The street beginning behind Porta dei Vacca, **Via del Campo** (I, A1), was immortalized in song by the late Fabrizio De André (see box). The upper portions of some of its noble buildings have elegant fronts: note the 17th-century *Palazzo Cellario* (no. 10) and *Palazzo di Antonio Doria Invrea* built in 1540 (no. 9). Though the frescoes which once adorned the upper part have, regrettably, all but faded away, the memorial inscription on the column to Giulio Cesare Vacchero, who was put to death in 1628 for high treason, is still clearly visible. Further along, on the right, is the 13th-century Piccamiglio tower.

Piazza Fossatello (I, B1). This square was laid out in 1540, at the same time as the extension of *Palazzo di Cipriano Pallavicino* (no. 2), when it was given a fine mannerist facade. Note also the 1612 *Palazzo Centurione* (no. 1), in particular the beautiful *doorway* with Doric pilaster strips and a frieze of weapons.

The names of the quarters – used for the storage of foodstuffs – of the **Darsena** (II, B2) recall the old colonial days of Genoa the 'Superba'. The complex, opened in 1895, is currently being converted to new uses: the Faculty of Economics and Trade has already moved into the Scio quarter.

Via di Sottoripa (I, B-C1). This porticoed public street was laid out as early as 1133, when workshops and market stalls were made available upon payment of excise duty. And trade and commerce are still very much in evidence here, both in the first part, restored in the late 19th century, and in the latter section, which still has the original low arches. The skyscraper built here in the postwar years is, alas, quite out of keeping with the style of the area.
Piazza Caricamento (I, B-C1), which has long abandoned its former function as the city's rail terminal is now a pedestrianized area: the new underpass (1992) conveys road traffic from Via Gramsci to Piazza Cavour.

Palazzo San Giorgio* (I, C1). Tradition has it that while imprisoned in this building (then a Customs House) in 1298, Marco Polo dictated to his fellow-prisoner Rustichello da Pisa the account of his travels that later became the book "Il Milione". The building (*open: Sat 10am-6pm; on request, tel. 0102412754*), now the Port Authority headquarters, was built in 1260 by People's Captain Guglielmo Boccanegra (to a design by the monk Fra' Oliverio), to give the city

authorities a place to govern from, a purpose it served for just two years. In 1407, the palace became the property of the newly-established bank, Banco di San Giorgio, hence the current name. In 1570 the new wing facing the sea was added, and decorated on the outside (1606-08) by Lazzaro Tavarone with an impressive set of frescoes. The building was restructured in 1912 by Lodovico Pogliaghi, and painstaking restoration work in 1990 recreated the original splendor of the 16th-century building. Inside, the majestic **Salone delle Compere** (Buying Room) houses the *Statues of the Protectors of the Bank* and a number of fine paintings (*Madonna Queen of Genoa with St. George*, by Domenico Piola, 17th cent., the *Genoese Coat of Arms* and the *Symbols of Justice and Fortitude*, painted in 1490-91 by Francesco De Ferrari, and *St. George of the Genoese and the Bank's Emblem*, by Luchino da Milano, 1444). The *Sala dei Protettori* is dominated by Giovanni Giacomo della Porta's monumental fireplace (1554). The medieval building owes its present-day appearance to the late 19th-century restoration work done by Alfredo D'Andrade, who also renovated much of the interior.

The Expo District (II, C-D1-2-3). Redeveloping the ancient port of Genoa was always going to be a major challenge, even for an architect of the caliber of Renzo Piano, especially after the 1992 Columbus Celebration Expo,

Genoa: Palazzo San Giorgio, where Marco Polo dictated the account of his travels, "Il Milione"

the disappointing success of which cast considerable doubt on the future of the area.

The fears have proven unfounded, thanks in no small measure to the **Aquarium**** (II, C3; *open: 9.30am-7pm, Sat, Sun and holidays 9.30am-8pm; October-February closed Mon*), Europe's largest aquarium and Italy's third most visited monument. It was conceived on a huge scale, with 5,000 specimens of 500 marine species, 62 tanks and almost 10,000 m² of display space. In the **Big Blue Ship**, fish and crustaceans are found alongside rare reptiles and plants from Madagascar.

Offices and trading buildings are housed in the four buildings of the *Free Port*, part of the original 1595 complex, which since renovation once again boasts brightly-colored facades, and the *Millo Quarter* (1876), which also houses the *Museo Nazionale dell'Antartide Felice*

Ippolito (I, C1; *open: 9.45am-6.15pm, Sun and holidays 10am-7pm; June-September 2-10pm; closed Mon*). The main theme of the exhibition, backed up by modern multi-media aids, is the research work in the *Baia Terra Nova* base, the only Italian station in Antarctica.

The old *Cotton Warehouses* (II, C-D1-2) contain a modern multiplex cinema, the *Città dei Bambini* (kids' city, see box), and the Old Port's third exhibition center, the *Sea and Seafaring Pavilion* (*open: 10.30am-6pm, Sat, Sun and holidays 10.30am-7pm; October-February 10.30am-5.30pm, Sat, Sun and holidays 10.30am-6pm, closed Mon*), with historical items and beautifully reconstructed tableaux showing life as it was on board ship and in the old ports. Another area is dedicated to the great navigators. Note in particular the *vessel containing the ashes of Christopher Columbus*, found in Santo Domingo in 1877.

Making science and technology fun

La Città dei Bambini, Italy's largest learning and play center, invites children to "discover and learn while they enjoy themselves". This 'Kids' City', on the third floor of the old Cotton Warehouse building, was made possible by the joint efforts of the Genoese consortium *Imparagiocando* (literally 'learning through play') and the *Cité des Sciences et de l'Industrie* in Paris. The two guided exploratory routes through the 2,700-m² site, aimed at children of different ages (3- to 5-year-olds and those aged 6-14), present various static and dynamic exhibits that allow children – and the grown-ups accompanying them – to have fun and at the same time expand their cognitive horizons. The space was designed with the needs of its young visitors very much in mind. Particular attention has been placed on safety, but also on other aspects such as lighting, the shape and color of the furnishings, designed to help children feel completely at ease and give them that all important sense of security. The inlay-work carpet guides visitors along the two routes, with specialist helpers on hand to give assistance where needed, answering children's questions and showing them how to get the most out of the various activities. *Città dei Bambini* is open every day except Mondays, 10am-6pm (*for further information: tel. 0102475702, fax 010 2475712, e-mail cdibimbi@split.it, Internet: www.cittadeibimbi.net*).

Porta del Molo* (II, D2). Also known as Porta Siberia (possibly from *cibarie*, or foodstuffs) this grandiose opening in the 16th-century sea walls was designed by Galeazzo Alessi (1553) both as a stronghold for the port area and as a collection point for customs duties. On the seaward side, an ashlar exhedra is wedged in between the two bastions; the other side takes the form of a Doric portico with three fornices. On top of the gateway is an artillery platform.

1.1 From piazza del Principe to the Molo Vecchio

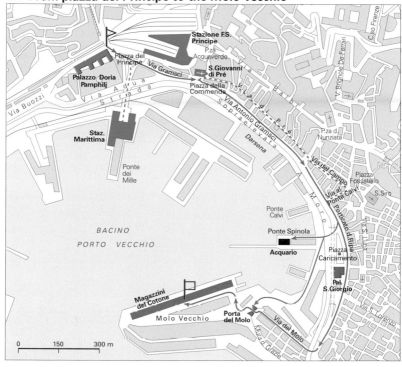

Via del Molo (II, D2-3). The street that runs inland behind Porta Siberia through the Molo quarter tells a host of intriguing stories. It is odd that Genoa should have a church dedicated to the patron saint of the city's great rival Venice: the *church of San Marco* (II, D3), built in 1173 but rebuilt in the 17th century, has on its left side a stone with a bas-relief *Lion of St. Mark,* part of the spoils of the Sack of Pula (1380). On the opposite side of the street, at no. 23, is the 16th-century *Palazzo del Magazzino del Grano*, a corn store, with a fine rusticated portal; further on is the *Aedicule (or Shrine) of St. John the Baptist* (1634), the former arrival point of the procession of 24 June, which now ends at

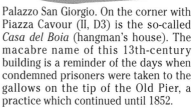

Palazzo San Giorgio. On the corner with Piazza Cavour (II, D3) is the so-called *Casa del Boia* (hangman's house). The macabre name of this 13th-century building is a reminder of the days when condemned prisoners were taken to the gallows on the tip of the Old Pier, a practice which continued until 1852.

Genoa: the Aquarium, with 5,000 specimens of 500 marine species and almost 10,000 m² of display space

The Ancient Port of Genoa

Genoa's old port is both the most modern and the historically richest part of the city. This explains the complexity of architect Renzo Piano's project for the 1992 celebrations of the discovery of America, which set out to recover Genoa's port area in a way that would highlight its historical importance as the area that links the city with the sea, a role which urban transformations (most notably the great divide created by the highway overpass) had all but destroyed. The redevelopment scheme aimed to stitch the two parts of the city together again, putting Genoa back in touch with the sea and giving the port a new lease of life by locating new, major public attractions there. These have indeed now turned it into one of the city's most important cultural districts. At the same time the port proper has been redeveloped, and links have

Palazzo San Giorgio

Piazza delle Feste

Aquarium

Via del Mare

Italy Pavilion

been established between the once isolated architectural elements from different periods of history: the 17th-century Free Depot, the Cotton Warehouses (a 19th-century industrial building) and the Millo quarter, dating back to the last quarter of the 19th century. Far from altering the character of the area, the new features enhance the sense of history: the Bigo, the Italy Pavilion, and the Aquarium all conjure up strong naval images of great symbolic significance.

Millo Building

Bigo

Porta del Molo

Former Cotton Warehouses

1.2 The political and religious center: from the Cathedral to Santa Maria di Castello

Walking tour through the heart of ancient Genoa *(see map p. 54)*

This tour covers the area enclosed by the first circle of walls. Piazza Cavour and Via Turati lead to Via S. Lorenzo and the cathedral, continuing along the north side into Piazza S. Matteo, round into Piazza Matteotti, then south-east to Porta di Sant'Andrea. From here the road leads down to the church of *San Donato*, then up to *Sant'Agostino* and, after the convent buildings of *Santa Maria di Castello*, down again to visit three parallel streets: Via S. Bernardo, Via dei Giustiniani and Canneto il Lungo, the main thoroughfares of the medieval city.

Cathedral** (I, C-D2; *open: 8am-noon and 3-7pm, Sun and holidays 8am-12.15pm and 4-7.15pm*). The cathedral of *San Lorenzo* is over a thousand years old: founded in the 9th century, it took precedence over *San Siro* because of its position within the first city walls. At the beginning of the 12th century reconstruction work in the Romanesque style began. Surviving ele-

The facade of San Lorenzo Cathedral, Genoa

ments from this never-to-be-completed operation include the two **side doors** of *San Giovanni* (1 on the plan on p. 53) – next to the baptistery – and of *San Gottardo* (2), on Via S. Lorenzo. The cathedral began to take on its present mainly Gothic appearance in the early 1300s, with the creation by Norman stonemasons of the first tier of the facade, with the alternating black and white bands typical of the Tyrrhenian area. Also from this period are the two *column-bearing lions* and (on the corner with the street) the saint with sundial whose pose has earned him the nickname 'The Knifegrinder'. The second tier of the facade, pierced with paired windows, was completed toward the end of the century; the tier above, also with paired windows but dominated by the great rose window, was added in the 1400s, as was the loggia that takes the place of what would have been the left-hand tower. The 16th-century saw the completion of the belltower and the addition of the dome, by Galeazzo Alessi. The steps, flanked by two lions (by Carlo Rubatto), were built in 1840 following the opening up of Via S. Lorenzo and the lowering of the level of the piazza.

Inside, the wall behind the facade is decorated with an interesting 14th-century fresco (*Last Judgment and Glorification of the Virgin*). In the north aisle on the left, just after the entrance to the baptistery, is the **Chapel of St. John the Baptist*** (3), with an exquisite front created in 1451 by Domenico and Elia Gagini. Inside the chapel, which has statues by Matteo Civitali and Andrea Sansovino, is the early 13th-century urn which supposedly contains the saint's ashes. The Lercari chapel (4) at the far end of the north aisle is decorated with **frescoes*** by Giovanni Battista Castello (*Assunta, Coronation of Mary, Saints and Prophets*) and by Luca Cambiaso (*Marriage of the Virgin, Presentation of Jesus in the Temple*), dated 1565-69. In the south aisle is an unexploded artillery shell that fell on the cathedral during a 1941 air raid, and an altarpiece (*Crucifixion with Mary, John and St. Sebastian**) by Federico Barocci (1597), in the Senarega chapel (5). Note also the wooden *choir*, by Anselmo de' Fornari, Gian Michele Pantaloni and Francesco

Cathedral of San Lorenzo

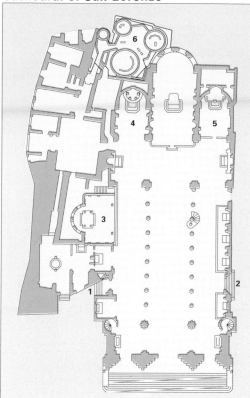

1 Portal of St. John the Baptist
2 Portal of San Gottardo
3 Chapel of St. John the Baptist
4 Frescoes by G.B. Castello and Luca Cambiaso
5 Altarpiece by Federico Barocci
6 Treasury

the Last Supper, it is now believed to be a 9th-century work of Islamic art. Note also the Roman chalcedony *dish with the Head of John the Baptist* (1st cent.): the glazed severed head of the saint and the gilt silver-work are 15th-century additions. In the same room is the **casket with the ashes of St. John the Baptist***, by Teramo Danieli and Simone Caldera (1438-45), still carried in procession through the streets of the city on 24 June, and the *casket of Barbarossa**, possibly given by Frederick I in 1178. The *Zaccaria Cross** is a Byzantine reliquary (10th cent., refashioned in the 13th cent.) in gold leaf with oriental gemstones and pearls: the fragments of wood inside are traditionally thought to have come from Christ's cross.

Along **Via Tommaso Reggio** (I, C-D2), which skirts the north side of the cathedral, are numerous political and religious buildings, some of them connected by overhead walkways. Among the most interesting are *Palazzetto Criminale* (1581), now the home of the State Archive, with a raised courtyard onto which three arcaded floors open; and the 13th-century *Alberto Fieschi and Abati palaces*, which – together with the *Grimaldina prison tower* from the same period – were incorporated into the Ducal Palace (see below).

Zambelli (1514-46), and the frescoes on the apse semi-dome and vault (*St. Lawrence Points to the Poor as the Treasures of the Church* and *Martyrdom of the Saint*), painted by Lazzaro Tavarone (1622-24).

The sacristy (entrance – 6 – to the left of the presbytery on the north side of the church) leads to the **Museo del Tesoro di San Lorenzo*** (*open: 9am-noon, 3-6pm; closed Sun*). This treasury is exhibited in four underground spaces – a central hexagonal chamber and three *tholoi* leading off from the alternate sides – designed in 1956 by Franco Albini. The beautifully atmospheric setting, with its black stone walls, enhances the beauty of the exhibits. One of the most interesting is the *sacro catino**, a green glass basin that was an important element in the Holy Grail tradition: originally thought to have been used by Jesus at

Detail of the casket with the ashes of St. John the Baptist

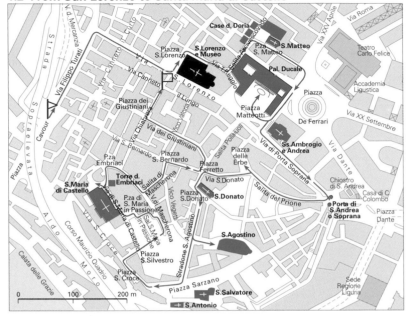

Piazza S. Matteo** (I, C2-3). This is where, in 1528, Andrea Doria announced to the people of the city the constitutional changes that introduced the oligarchy and marked the beginning of the 'Golden Century' of Genoa *La Superba* (*el siglo de los Genoveses*). This was the Doria family's private square and the buildings erected around it symbols of their power. *Palazzo di Andrea Doria* (no. 17), was given to the *condottiere* by the city senate in 1528. Much earlier, in 1298, the adjoining *Palazzo di Lamba Doria* (no. 15) had been presented by the city to Lamba Doria, who had defeated the Venetian fleet in the Battle of Korcula. On the left-hand side of the square are *Palazzo di Domenicaccio Doria* (no. 16) and *Palazzo di Branca Doria* (entrance at no. 1 Vico Falamonica), whose characteristic dark and light bands date the building to the second half of the 13th century. Though older in origin (1125) the **church of San Matteo*** also has black and white stripes, the result of

remodeling in 1278. This was the Doria family's place of worship, and the inscriptions on the lower part of the facade celebrate their military exploits. The interior, richly-decorated with frescoes, marble and stuccowork, was transformed in the 16th century by Giovanni Angelo Montorsoli, Giovanni Battista Castello ('il Bergamasco') and Luca Cambiaso, by order of Andrea Doria, whose remains lie in the *sarcophagus* in the crypt.

The little **cloister**, tucked away on the left of the church, has pointed arches on paired columns (1308-10).

The Doria houses in Piazza San Matteo, Genoa

Palazzo Ducale** (I, C-D2-3). This monumental building, by Andrea Vannone (1591-c. 1620), was returned to its original splendor for the Columbus celebrations in 1992. This operation restored the sumptuous fresco decorations on the side overlooking Piazza De Ferrari and Simone Cantoni's magnificent neoclassical facade (1783) in Piazza Matteotti: two tiers with paired columns topped by an attic decorated with statues and trophies. The interior, now used for temporary exhibitions and cultural events, has a double colonnaded courtyard; a double staircase leads to the upper loggia, where the official reception rooms are concentrated, around the western court. The most interesting rooms are the **chapel**, with frescoes (scenes from Genoa's glorious past) painted around 1655 by Giovanni Battista Carlone, and the **Sale del Maggiore e del Minor Consiglio**, two richly-decorated halls rebuilt in 1780-83 after a fire.

G. B. Carlone, fresco in the Duke's chapel. Palazzo Ducale, Genoa

Ss. Ambrogio e Andrea (I, D2-3). This church of ancient origin (6th-7th cent.), known by the Genoese as the **church of Gesù**, was rebuilt by the Jesuits in 1589. Giuseppe Valeriani, member of the Society of Jesus, created a single central space and large central dome, a layout designed to heighten the effect of the sumptuous Baroque decorations, which include frescoes by Giovanni and Giovanni Battista Carlone (ca. 1625-28), stuccowork and inlaid marble. The church also has some important paintings, most notably the **Circumcision****, painted by P. P. Rubens for the high altar, and **St. Ignatius Healing a Woman Possessed****, also by Rubens, in the north transept chapel. The 3rd chapel on the right has an *Assumption* by Guido Reni (1616-17).

Porta di Sant'Andrea (or Soprana)** (I, E3). This gateway separates the historic center from modern Genoa, in a beautiful position that has become one of the most celebrated views of the city. This tall twin-towered fortification (*open: Sat and Sun 9am-noon and 3-6pm; by prior arrangement, tel. 0102465346*), which formed part of the 9th-century walls, was rebuilt in 1155 in a style similar to the western gateway (Porta dei Vacca, see p. 46): the pointed arch opening between the two semicircular towers has an arcaded stringcourse, and crenelated walkway.

San Donato* (I, D-E2). The walk to this church passes through an area where the colorful facades of restored buildings alternate with the sad reminders of World War II air raids. This beautiful church, one of the best examples of the Romanesque-Gothic (early 12th cent.), has a splendid octagonal **belltower**** with two rows of paired windows (the third is a 19th-century addition), which was used as a model for the 'matitone' of San Benigno. The late 19th-century additions (the rose window and the colonnaded pseudo-porch) did nothing to enhance the original architectural features, which include a splayed portal with split arch. Note on the right-hand side the 17th-century shrine with the *Dove of the Holy Spirit*, enclosing a statue of the *Madonna and Child*. Inside, six of the columns separating the aisles from the nave are Roman. Above the row of columns is a false matroneum punctuated by paired windows. On the altar at the end of the south aisle is a *Madonna and Child* by Niccolò da Voltri (1401). The chapel of *San Giuseppe*, situated halfway down the north aisle, has a remarkable **triptych***, with hinged panels, depicting the *Adoration of the Magi* (by Joos van Cleve, ca. 1515).

Sant'Agostino (I, E2; *open on request, tel. 0102511263*). Although this church was deconsecrated more than two centuries ago, it did not suffer the same fate as other Gothic churches in Genoa, many of which were demolished to make way for the broad avenues of the modern city. The building, adjoining an Augustinian monastery, was in use as a place of worship before 1260. The three-section facade

A new lease of life for the carrugi

In the 1990s Genoa's youth rediscovered the historic center. Life began to change here with the opening in 1991 of the new Architecture School, around which (especially in and around Piazza San Donato and Piazza Sarzano) bars and coffee shops began to appear catering for students at lunchtimes. Gradually, these *ragazzi* (budding architects or otherwise) soon began frequenting the area after dark, even though it  was still something of a district of ill-repute. Gradually the Piano di S. Andrea, Piazza S. Donato and Piazza delle Erbe districts came back to life, this latter square in particular taking on the role of central gathering place at weekends. More cafés and restaurants aimed at an older clientele began to appear, while the districts' shopkeepers, who had once been in the habit of shutting up shop as soon as it began to get

is decorated with the familiar black and white bands; the 15th-century **campanile*** has a pointed polychrome majolica spire surrounded by four smaller pinnacles. Before being turned into an auditorium (1995), the church was used as a store for works of art and architecture salvaged from the destruction of 19th-century clearance schemes and World War II air raids. These and other exhibits are now on display in the **Museo di Sant'Agostino** (I, E2; *open: 9am-7pm, Sun 9am-12.30pm; closed Mon and holidays*), a former monastery complex with charming *triangular cloister* (14th-15th cent.). The other rectangular complex was completely refurbished when the building was transformed into a museum (Franco Albini and Franca Helg, 1977-80). Items on show include the *seal from the gravestone of Simonetta and Percivale Lercari** (1259), formerly in the cemetery of San Giovanni di Pré, and the remains of the **Funerary Monument of Margaret of Brabant****, wife of the emperor Henry VII of Luxembourg, by Giovanni Pisano 1313-14, formerly in the church of San Pietro di Castelletto. Also worth noting are a 13th-century fresco (*Banquet at Bethany*) by Manfredino da Pistoia and, in the 18th-century section, the *Repentant Magdalene** by Antonio Canova (1796).

Piazza Sarzano (I, E2). This elongated square at the bottom of Stradone S. Agostino was left derelict for decades after the last war. It has now come back to life, thanks mainly to the opening of the **Faculty of Architecture**, built in 1987-92 over the ruins of the 17th-century *monastery of San Silvestro*, which in turn incorporated various sections of the 11th-century bishop's palace. The creation of

this new university department, masterminded by architect Ignazio Gardella, also involved the former *church of San Salvatore* (1653), now a university lecture theater. To the right, on a slightly lower level than the piazza, is the *oratory of St.*

Santa Maria di Castello

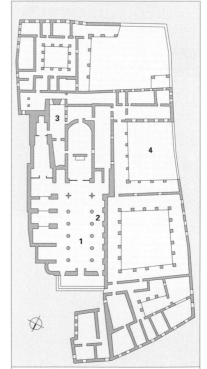

1 Church
2 Canvas by Bernardo Castello
3 Works by Barnaba da Modena and Lodovico Brea
4 Cloister with fresco by Joos von Ravensburg

dark, would now stay open until midnight. Not that this transformation of the area has been completely free of problems: the construction site for the redevelopment of Piazza delle Erbe, which still shows clear signs of the devastation here during World War II, has been held up by Italy's proverbial bureaucratic sluggishness, and not all the local residents show a liking for the groups of youngsters that gather below their windows until all hours. But the changes are here to stay: and new establishments are now springing up also around Via della Maddalena.

Anthony Abbot, built in the early 17th century as the headquarters of the so-called 'Casaccia'. Inside is a splendid chest (*St. James Slaughters the Moors**) attributed to Pasquale Navone; a *White Christ*, by Anton Maria Maragliano (1710), and a *Black Christ*, the processional crucifix fashioned in 1639 by Domenico Bissoni. Also from the 17th century is the small *kiosk* with fountain at the north-east end of the square, by Bartolomeo Bianco.

Santa Maria di Castello* (I, E1; *open: 9am-noon and 3.30-6.30pm*). The 'castle' of the church's name is a reminder of the fortifications that defended the hill in pre-Roman times and were reorganized in the Byzantine and Longobard periods, hence the early Christian origins of the church which now stands on the site, built in the 10th-11th centuries as a kind of 'co-cathedral'. The present Romanesque building dates back to the 12th century: a basilica-style layout with broad nave and side aisles, and a false matroneum above the arches. The columns and capitals use materials retrieved from elsewhere and are mainly Roman (2nd-3rd cent.). In 1441 Pope Eugene IV assigned Santa Maria di Castello to the Dominicans, who added the chapels of the city's large families; the octagonal dome was built in the following century.

One of the many interesting works inside the church (see plan, 1) is the *Martyrdom of St. Peter of Verona** in the 4th chapel on the right (2), by Bernardo Castello (1597). However, the works of greatest artistic merit are to be found in the **Sale dei Ragusei** (3; *open on request, tel. 0102549511*). These rooms – so named because they were used in the 16th and 17th centuries by merchants from the Dalmatian port of Ragusa (as Dubrovnik used to be known in Italian) – are entered from the south transept through the sacristy and contain a *Madonna and Child** by Barnaba da Modena and a *Coronation of the Virgin** painted by Lodovico Brea (1513). No less interesting is the convent: the **Loggia of the Annunciation** in the second of the three cloisters (4) has a superb *fresco** by German artist Joos von Ravensburg (1451), who covered the vaulting with tondi surrounded by elaborate floral motifs. The *Grimaldi Chapel*, adjoining the upper loggia, has the grand *Polyptych of the Annunciation*, by Giovanni Mazone (1469).

To the left of the church is the 41-m high **Embriaci Tower** (I, D1), built in the 12th century. This is the only tower allowed to be more than 80 hands high when a law was introduced in 1296 limiting the height of all city buildings. *Salita Mascherona*, lined with medieval buildings, leads down to *Piazza S. Bernardo*, onto which the somewhat dilapidated facade of the 16th-century *Palazzo Salvaghi* looks: the two statues of savages guarding the entranceway allude to the family name. There are plenty more vestiges of the past (archways, walled capitals, sculpted portals) along **Via S. Bernardo** (I, D1-2), a street created to form a thoroughfare from Porta Soprana down to the port. It was thus much traversed by merchants heading to or coming from the east. From *Piazza Ferretto*, **Via dei Giustiniani** leads to Piazza dei Giustiniani, where *Palazzo Giustiniani* (rebuilt in the 1700s) has a facade with a bas-relief depicting the *Lion of St. Mark* taken from the city of Trieste after the battle of Chioggia in 1380. Running parallel to Via dei Giustiniani is *Via Canneto il Lungo*, with several noble buildings: note the medieval *Palazzo Baruffo* (no. 23), with its rusticated tower.

Genoa: the 41-m-high Embriaci Tower, built in the 12th century

1.3 The market squares and the redevelopment of medieval Genoa: from Piazza S. Giorgio to Luccoli

Walking tour through the area to the north of the city center *(see map p. 60)*

This walking tour, dominated by late-Renaissance architecture, runs from Piazza S. Giorgio, along Via Canneto il Curto to Piazza Banchi. It then continues along Via S. Luca, turns into Via della Maddalena and down through Vico alla Posta Vecchia, Via delle Vigne and Vico delle Vigne, back toward Piazza Banchi. Via degli Orefici leads to Piazza Campetto and Piazza Soziglia, from which Via Luccoli heads up toward the 'Strade Nuove'.

Piazza S. Giorgio (I, D1). It is difficult to imagine this peaceful little square, quite near the busy Via S. Lorenzo, as a center of city commerce. And yet that is precisely the role the piazza played until the 11th century, when it was a market square (especially for the trading of salt). The *church of San Giorgio*, documented as early as 964, housed the Genoese standard, and celebrated civil rites. The church, rebuilt for the Teatini family (1695-1700), has a curving neoclassical facade (1859). The central-plan interior, dominated by an impressive dome, contains three paintings (*Martyrdom of St. George*) by Luca Cambiaso.

The history of the adjacent *church of San Torpete* is quite similar. Probably founded by Pisan merchants in the 12th century, it later became the church of the Cattaneo family, which in 1730 had the church rebuilt by Giovanni Antonio Ricca the Younger; the facade dates back to the same period as that of San Giorgio. The building, which still belongs to the Cattaneo family, has an oval, richly-stuccoed interior and is topped by a slate-covered dome.

The walk along **Via Canneto il Curto** (I, C-D1) takes in a number of charming little squares. After crossing Via Canneto il Lungo (at the *Croce di Canneto*) and Via S. Lorenzo, the street meets *Vico del Filo*, an old quaint alleyway leading to the cathedral square.

Piazza Banchi (I, C1). The name refers not to today's disorderly *bancarelle* (market stalls) but to the counters (*banchi*) used by the moneychangers of 'La Superba', who in the 13th and 14th centuries were obliged to conduct their business outside in the square, with all the risks that entailed. Only when the Madonna interceded to stop the plague did the Senate agree to provide a more dignified banking place. The architect Vannone was commissioned to design the **Loggia dei Mercanti*** (1589-95), an elegant rectangular space with barrel-vaulted ceiling supported by arches on paired columns (blind on the side facing onto Via S. Luca and Piazza Senarega). Decoration is limited to the band of *sculpted trophies* facing onto the square, the two open sides by Taddeo Carlone, and the fresco (*Enthroned Madonna and Child with St. John the Baptist and St. George*) on the rear wall, painted in the late 1500s by Pietro Sorri. The building, which in 1855 became Italy's first Commercial Exchange, is now used to house temporary exhibitions.

Genoa: Piazza Banchi, whose name refers to the counters ('banchi')

Piazza Banchi

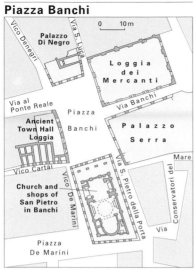

Vannone redeveloped the whole square in collaboration with Giovanni Ponzello at the same time as the building of the new loggia. This included the self-financed project for the **church of San Pietro in Banchi** (1572-85), built on a terrace over the shops as a compromise to keep the merchants happy without breaking the vow to build a place of worship. This central-plan church, topped by

Genoa: Gallery of Mirrors, Palazzo Spinola

a dome with three pinnacles (the fourth never materialized), was restored in the 1990s, and the *frescoes* on the facade, painted by Giovanni Battista Baiardo (ca. 1650), are once again clearly visible.

Via S. Luca (I, B-C1), a busy shopping street catering for all modern needs from clothes and footwear to electrical appliances, is the central stretch of the *carrugio dritto* (literally 'straight alley') that ran from Piazza S. Giorgio all the way to Porta dei Vacca. In amongst the shop windows are mannerist doorways (no. 12 is particularly noteworthy) and frescoed facades (*Palazzo Faruggia*, at no. 14).

Mid-way is *Piazzetta S. Luca*, a little square that was long fought over by the Grimaldi (Guelph) and Spinola (Ghibelline) households. The latter family built the lopped-off Torre Spinola and, in 1188, the **church of San Luca** (I, B1-2), whose present form dates back to 1626-50. The central-plan **interior**** was beautifully decorated in 1695 by Domenico Piola (*Coronation of the Virgin, Scenes from the Life of St. Luke, The Virtues*). The splendid altarpiece (*Nativity Crèche**) on the left-hand altar is by Giovanni Benedetto Castiglione, 'il Grechetto'. Note also two works by Filippo Parodi, the marble group (*Immacolata*) on the high altar and the wooden *Deposition of Christ* – also by Domenico Piola (1680-81) – in a niche to the right of the entrance.

Galleria Nazionale di Palazzo Spinola* (I, B2; *open: 9am-7pm, Sun and holidays 2-7pm; closed Mon*). The palace that now houses this art gallery was, ironically, built in 1593 by the Spinola's rivals, the Grimaldi. It was designed to separate *Piazza Inferiore* and *Piazza Superiore di Pellicceria*, onto which the two opposing entrances open. Bequeathed to the state in 1958, the palace has Baroque furnishings of exceptional quality and a fine **Gallery of Mirrors** (second floor) frescoed by Lorenzo De Ferrari (*Venus and Bacchus with Cupid, Pan Beaten by Cupid, Triumph of Galatea*). The collection of paintings, including

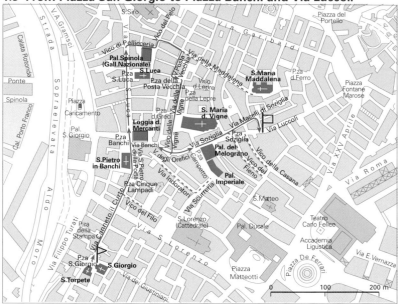

works by illustrious artists, begins with a *Resurrection* attributed to Tintoretto; in the following room is a *Portrait of a Nun** by Bernardo Strozzi and the *Journey of Abraham** by il Grechetto. In the second room upstairs note in particular the four *Evangelists** by Antonie Van Dyck, *Sacred and Profane Love** by Guido Reni and the *Marriage of the Virgin*, by Valerio Castello. The third room has a sketch (*Last Supper**) by Giulio Cesare Procaccini and a *Virgin at Prayer** by Joos van Cleve. The third floor is reserved for works that do not form part of the Spinola bequest, most notably an **Ecce Homo**** by Antonello da Messina and an **Equestrian Portrait of Giovanni Carlo Doria*** by Peter Paul Rubens. Other works include two paintings (*Sts. Erasmus and Jerome**, *Holy Bishop and St. Pantaleon*) by Carlo Braccesco, and an elaborate mirror frame (*Myth of Paris*) by Filippo Parodi and *Justice** sculpted by Giovanni Pisano for the Tomb of Margaret of Brabant.

At the far end of **Via della Maddalena** (I, B1-2), the main thoroughfare of the district of the same name, stands the *church of Santa Maria Maddalena* (I, B2-3), documented as early as 1150. The present building is the result of a late 16th-century remodeling by Vannone. In the second half of the 17th century the dome was added and the interior

divided into a central nave and side aisles by paired columns, a design based on the *church of San Siro* (see p. 66). These alterations were rather too grandiose for a church of this size, but the awkward architectural aspect is largely offset by the *frescoes* (1729-37), painted by Sebastiano Galeotti and his pupil Sigismondo Betti.
Returning down Via della Maddalena, the junction with Vico della Posta Vecchia (the medieval '*Quattro Canti di S. Francesco*', (I, B2), leads to Piazza della Posta Vecchia, formerly owned by the De Franchi family. *Palazzo di Stefano De Franchi* (no. 2) has a *piano nobile* with fine frescoes by Bernardo Castello depicting *Episodes from Jerusalem Delivered*. *Palazzo di Agostino De Franchi* (no. 1, in a poor state of repair) is famous in particular for a tender of 1565 between the client and builders Bernardino Cantone and Giovanni Battista Castello, which was of fundamental importance for the design of residential buildings in the historic part of the city.

Santa Maria delle Vigne (II, C2). The colorfully-named streets (Apple Alley, Hare Lane, Goose Square) around this church hark back to the rural days of the area, which was eventually engulfed by the growing city in the 10th and 11th centuries. The church, whose own name means 'of the vines', dates back to 981, although all that remains of this early period is the **belltower** with two- and five-light windows and an octagonal spire, set over an arch between the clois-

ter and the left-hand side of the church. The building was completely redesigned by Daniele Casella in around 1640.
The neoclassical facade was finished in 1842.
With the exception of the *Incisa-Vivaldi Tomb* (1304), beneath the belltower arch, there is no trace of the graveyard that once adjoined the medieval church. The modern church does, however, retain the original basilica-style layout. The most important decorative element inside is the fresco (*Mary in Glory*) on the presbytery vault by Lazzaro Tavarone (1612); the late 14th-century *Madonna* above the chapel at the end of the south aisle is attributed to Taddeo di Bartolo.

Via degli Orefici (I, C2). This crowded shopping street was once a popular meeting place for merchants, bankers and noblemen from the 'Strade Nuove'. Its name ('Street of the Goldsmiths') is as appropriate today as it was when it was originally named, since jewelry shops still abound. Note the important historical and artistic details in between the shop windows, such as the magnificent slate decoration over the door of no. 47 (**Adoration of the Magi***), property of the Gagini family (15th cent.) and – on the corner with Piazza Campetto - the votive shrine with *Madonna and Saints* (a copy, the original is in the Museo dell'Accademia Ligustica), commissioned by the corporation of goldsmiths.
The story goes that the young designer who won the coveted commission was murdered by an envious rival the day the work was unveiled (1640).

Precious metals were evidently also worked in the nearby *Vico degli Scudai* and *Vico degli Indoratori* if the street names are anything to go by ('of the Coinmakers' and 'of the Gilders' respectively). At no. 2 Vico degli Indoratori stands *Palazzo Valdettaro-Fieschi*, with a good *portal** (ca. 1460) by Giovanni Gagini. Note also, at no. 8 Vico degli Scudai, the almost perfectly-preserved *Casa Camilla*, an early 13th-century dwelling.

Piazza Campetto (I, C2). The 16th-century **Palazzo del Melograno** is named after the pomegranate tree that grew around the portal. The ground-floor is now rather incongruously occupied by a department store, an unlikely setting for the nymphaeum (*Hercules Slaying the Hydra*) in the courtyard by Filippo Parodi; the *piano nobile*, frescoed by Domenico Piola, Domenico Guidobono and Giacomo Boni, is now used as offices. The adjacent **Palazzo di Giovanni Vincenzo Imperiale** (I, C2), was designed round about the same time as its neighbor (it was finished before 1560) by Giovanni Battista Castello, who created the elaborate stucco decorations on the facade (stylized hermae and mascarons on the second piano nobile, putti and telamons at mezzanine level) and the *entranceway*, now an antiques shop; Castello also designed the *fireplace* on the second piano nobile, which, like the other upper levels, has lost its decorations. Opposite this building is the beginning of *Via di Scurreria* (derived from the medieval name 'scutaria'), opened up in the second half of the 16th century by Gian Giacomo Imperiale, who thus assured himself a convenient access to the cathedral.

Genoa: the historic Klainguti pastry shop in Piazza di Soziglia

Piazza di Soziglia (I, C2) is perhaps best known for its historic pastry shops: the interior of Romanengo dates back to the 19th century, while Klainguti rose to fame in the early 20th century. Leading off to the left in the north-east corner of the square is *Via dei Macelli di Soziglia* (I, B-C2-3). All that remains of the *Macello Nuovo*, the public slaughterhouse (1291-1319) which gave the street its name, is a bricked-in arcaded portico, facing onto the fashionable *Via Luccoli* (I, B-C2-3). Note (at no. 23), the Rococo facade of *Palazzo Franzone*.

1.4 The 'Strade Nuove': from Piazza delle Fontane Marose to Piazza Acquaverde

Walking tour through the quarters added in the 16th and 17th centuries *(see map pp. 66-67)*

This itinerary is dominated by the noble 16th/18th-century mansions that line the so-called 'Strade Nuove' (new streets). From Piazza delle Fontane Marose the route leads along the monumental Via Garibaldi and its continuation, Via Cairoli. After a brief detour to the church of San Siro, the tour continues with Largo della Zecca and Piazza della Nunziata, and the long, straight Via Balbi.

Piazza delle Fontane Marose (I, B3). This square takes its name from a fountain that was the subject of a curious play on words: in the 13th century it was

owned *Palazzo Interiano Pallavicini* (no. 2), by Francesco Casella (1565) is frescoed with allegorical figures.

The opening up of the adjacent Via Interiano in 1864-70 created an important road link between Piazza delle Fontane Marose and Piazza del Portello (I, B3).

Via Garibaldi★★ (I, B2-3; see illustration below). When the 'Strada Nuova dei Palazzi' was originally created it was to be for residential purposes only. Indeed the original street, designed by 'chamber' architect Bernardino Cantone (1551), was completely

Palazzo Bianco

Palazzo Rosso

Palazzo Doria Tursi
Palazzo delle Torrette

Palazzo Campanella

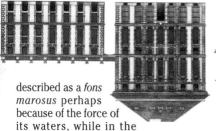

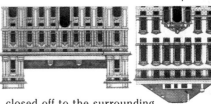

described as a *fons marosus* perhaps because of the force of its waters, while in the 15th-18th centuries the name changed to *morosus*, perhaps because of the nearby public brothel. The enlargement of the square as a result of the work done to level the streets (1832) further enhanced the views of the buildings that stand here, for example **Palazzo Spinola 'dei Marmi'** (no. 6; I, B-C3), built in 1445-59 on two sites that already belonged to the Spinola family two centuries earlier. The traditional black and white striped facade of the building (now a bank) has an interesting row of five niches, each containing a statue of a family member, probably by the Bissoni group (17th cent.). The four-light windows were added during restoration work in 1903; the trophies in the plinth date back to the previous century. The privately-

closed off to the surrounding streets. It was a costly privilege for those who succeeded in having palaces built there between 1558 and 1583, the revenue from their sale being used to finance various public works. The oasis of peace was finally opened up to traffic at the end of the 18th century; in the two centuries that followed the big families gradually gave way to civic institutions, banks, antique dealers and fashionable private clubs. This guaranteed the upkeep of these artistic and architectural treasures, which now form a pedestrian area.
The similarity with Milan's Palazzo Marino suggests the involvement of Galeazzo Alessi in the design of **Palazzo Cambiaso** (no. 1, Banca Popolare di Brescia), generally attributed to Bernardino Cantone (1558-60). The rooms on the piano nobile are decorated with mannerist frescoes (*Banquet of the Gods*,

Apollo and the Muses, Rape of the Sabine Women), by Andrea and Ottavio Semino. Opposite, **Palazzo Gambaro** (no. 2, built 1558-64, Banco di Chiavari della Riviera Ligure) has a marble portal with two reclining figures (*Prudence and Vigilance*) by Pietro Orsolino. One of the artists responsible for the interior decorations was Domenico Piola, who painted the *Allegory of Peace* in the main hall and the *Cherubs and Virtues* in the antechamber.

Next door is **Palazzo Carrega Cataldi** (no. 4, now the Chamber of Commerce), completed in 1561 to a design by Bernardino Cantone and Giovanni Battista Castello (the latter artist also painted the frescoes of *Apollo and Musicians* in the vestibule), while the splendid gilded Rococo *gallery* on the piano nobile was designed by Lorenzo De

club) by Bernardo Castello, Andrea Semino and Lazzaro Tavarone, who took their inspiration (*Peace between Pompey and Anthony, Scenes from the Life of Alexander the Great, Triumph of Caesar, Triumph of Augustus*) from the poet Gabriello Chiabrera. Civil wedding ceremonies are held in the hall on the piano nobile of **Palazzo Doria** (no. 6), noted for its impressive 18th-century *fireplace*. The building's facade was another joint effort by Bernardino Cantone and Giovanni Battista Castello (1563-67). The two architects also designed the still privately-owned **Palazzo Podestà** (no. 7, 1563-66), whose fine Mannerist *facade* has three figured rows and a beautiful *atrium* decorated with stuccowork, with a nymphaeum at the back of the courtyard. *Palazzo Cattaneo Adorno* (nos. 8

Palazzo Podestà — Palazzo Spinola — Palazzo Lercari Parodi — Palazzo Cambiaso
Palazzo Cattaneo Adorno — Palazzo Doria — Palazzo Carrega Cataldi — Palazzo Gambaro

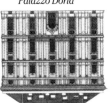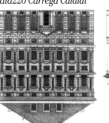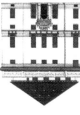

Ferrari (1743-44). The telamons decorating the portal of **Palazzo Lercari Parodi** (no. 3) were sculpted with mutilated noses as a reminder of the torturing of prisoners taken after a battle in Cyprus by a member of the Lercari family. Another interesting architectural feature of this building (1571-78) is the courtyard preceding the building proper: an innovative idea by Galeazzo Alessi and the first of its kind in Genoa. The fresco depicting the *Exploits of Megollo Lercari at Trebizond* in the hall on the second floor is by Luca Cambiaso, who indulged his vanity in this work by including a portrait of himself.

Until the frescoed facade of **Palazzo Spinola** (no. 5, Deutsche Bank) is restored, the most interesting feature of this building is the interior decoration of the piano nobile (now used by an exclusive private

and 10, 1584-88) is two houses in one, reviving a feature common in medieval Genoese architecture. *Palazzo Campanella* (no. 12), which was renovated in the second half of the 18th century, was badly damaged during 1942 air raids.

Palazzo del Municipio** (I, B2). Since 1848 the seat of Genoa City Hall, this grand building (1565-79), also known as **Palazzo Doria Tursi**, is conspicuous by its sheer size: the front is three times the length of the other buildings, an indication of the power wielded by Nicolò Grimaldi (the principal creditor of Philip II of Spain), who commissioned its construction. This imposing edifice, designed by Domenico and Giovanni Ponzello, has a magnificent colonnaded courtyard with double staircase leading to the upper loggia. Taddeo Carlone, who designed the impressive *portal*, was also involved in the decoration of the facade, which is enhanced by the color contrasts of white marble, pink stone and gray slate. In 1596 the palace passed into the hands of the Doria, who the following year began the construction of the side loggias and the garden. The clocktower was added in 1820, and *Public Offices* were incorporated on the side facing the Castelletto hill between 1960 and 1965 (design: Franco Albini and Franca Helg). In contrast to all this splendid architecture, the decorations appear quite spartan. There is nevertheless one item of particular interest inside: the famous *violin* (1742), which once belonged to Niccolò Paganini, is kept in the Council Room, the 'Sala della Giunta' (*visits: on request, tel. 0105572223*).

Galleria di Palazzo Rosso* (I, B2). When they reached the height of their power in the mid-17th century, the Brignole-Sale family did not want to miss out on the prestige of the 'Strada Nuova'. Their building, which took six years to complete (1671-77), has two *piani nobili*, to be divided between the two heirs. The building takes its name from the red stone facing on the facade. The beautifully-decorated interior has the city's largest art collection (*open: 9am-1pm, Wed and Sat 9am-7pm, Sun 10am-6pm; closed Mon and holidays*). The visit begins with a **Portrait of a Man*** (or **Muscovite Prince**) formerly attributed to Pisanello, and now thought to be by Giambono; and a *Young Man** by Albrecht Dürer (1506). The next room has a splendid **Judith with the Head of Holofernes**** by Veronese, followed by an *Annunciation** by Ludovico Carracci and *St. Sebastian** by Guido Reni; note also the superb **Death of Cleopatra**** by Guercino. Other important works on the first floor include those by Orazio Gentileschi (*Madonna and Sleeping Child**), Mattia Preti (*Clorinda Frees Olindo and Sofronia**), Bernardo Strozzi (**The Cook**, *Madonna and Bambino and St. Giovannino**) and il Grechetto (*Journey of the Family of Abraham*). Works upstairs include a sketch (*Phaeton before his Father Apollo*) by Gregorio De Ferrari for the fresco on the ceiling of the hall, destroyed during the air raids of 1942. The **Allegories of the Seasons*** by De Ferrari (*Spring, Summer*) and Domenico Piola (*Autumn, Winter*) survived the

bombing. The work forms a beautiful backdrop to the splendid portraits of **Geronima Brignole-Sale with her daughter Aurelia****, of *Anton Giulio Brignole-Sale* and of **Paolina Adorno Brignole-Sale****, masterpieces by Antonie Van Dyck.

Galleria di Palazzo Bianco* (I, B2). The 'white palace' was the other residence built by order of the Brignole-Sale. Giacomo Viano (1712-16) based the

P. Veronese, Judith with the Head of Holofernes. Galleria di Palazzo Rosso, Genoa

design on Palazzo Doria Tursi, but the architect had clearly exhausted his creative talents and the results were rather less than brilliant. The main interest of this palace is undoubtedly the art gallery contained within (*open: 9am-1pm, Wed and Sat 9am-7pm, Sun 10am-6pm; closed Mon and holidays*). The first room has an embroidered altarcloth (*Scenes from the Lives of Sts. Lawrence, Sixtus and Hippolytus**) donated in 1261 by Byzantine emperor Michael VIII Palaeologus. After the next two rooms, which have 16th-century Genoese and Italian paintings respectively, come four rooms dedicated to Flemish painting, beginning with Hans Memling (**Christ Blessing****) and Gerard David, who painted three panels of a polyptych (*Madonna and Child, St. Jerome, St. Mauro Abbot** and *Crucifixion**); and continuing with Jan Provost (*Annunciation**), Jan Metsys (*Charity*), Peter Paul Rubens (*Venus and Mars**) and the ever-present Van Dyck, with his *Christ of the Coin** and *Vertumnus and Pomona**. The visit continues with a section on Caravaggio

National Gallery, Palazzo Rosso

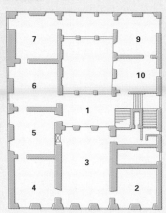
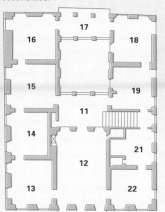

first floor

7   9

6   10

1

5

3

4   2

second floor

17

16   18

15   19

11

14

21

12

13   22

first floor

1 Loggia
2 Giambono, Albrecht Dürer, Palma il Vecchio
3 Paolo Veronese, Paris Bordon, Moretto, Jacopo Bassano
4 Ludovico Carracci, Guido Reni, G.C. Procaccini
5 Guercino
6 Orazio Gentileschi, Mattia Preti
7 Luca Cambiaso, Bernardo Strozzi

9 Sinibaldo Scorza, Grechetto
10 Domenico Piola, Bartolomeo Guidobono

second floor

11 Vestibule with loggia (Bernardo Schiaffino)
12 Salone (Gregorio De Ferrari)
13 Room of the Spring (Van Dyck, Gregorio De Ferrari)
14 Room of the summer

(Van Dyck, Gregorio De Ferrari)
15 Room of the fall (Domenico Piola, Antoine-Jean Gros)
16 Room of the winter (Domenico Piola)
17 Loggia
18 Giovanni Andrea Carlone
19 Giovanni Andrea Carlone, Carlo Antonio Tavella
21 Alcova
22 Domenico Parodi, Bartolomeo Guidobono

(**Ecce Homo***) and his followers, after which is a collection of Spanish paintings, most notably *St. Ursula** and *St. Euphemia** by Francisco Zurbarán. From this point on the gallery concentrates on 17th/18th-century Genoese artists: alongside the better-known artists such as Bernardo Strozzi (note his *St. Cecilia** and *St. Theresa in Glory**), il Grechetto (*Crucifixion**) and Valerio Castello (*Madonna of the Veil**), are interesting works by Gioacchino Assereto (*The Ecstasy of St. Francis**), Giovanni Andrea Ansaldo (*Salome Offering the Head of John the Baptist to Herod*) and Alessandro Magnasco, painter of the celebrated **Entertainment in a Garden at Albaro**** (see also p. 94).

A. Magnasco, Entertainment in a Garden at Albaro. Galleria di Palazzo Bianco, Genoa

Piazza della Meridiana (I, B2) This square is named after the 18th-century sun-dial (or *meridiana*) on the front of the Palazzo della Meridiana, built in 1541-45. Inside the *palace* (entrance at no. 4 Salita S. Francesco), are two fresco cycles (*Duel between Aeneas and Turnus*, in the courtyard, and *Ulysses Slays the Suitors*, in the room on the piano nobile) by Luca Cambiaso.

Today's **Via Cairoli** (I, A-B1-2) was once known as the 'Strada Nuovissima', literally a 'brand-new thoroughfare', opened in 1778-86 as an extension of the 'Strada Nuova'. This road, now permanently clogged with parked cars, has an interesting Renaissance building – *Palazzo di Gian Tommaso Balbi* (no. 18) – redesigned in the 1700s with an elaborate staircase.

San Siro (I, B1-2). This church, records of which date as far back as the 4th century, was the first cathedral of Genoa. When it lost this status to *San Lorenzo* (9th cent.), it was rebuilt by the Benedictines in Romanesque style. In 1580 the basilica was destroyed by fire, and subsequently rebuilt in its present form (1585-1619), possibly by Vannone. It was during this phase that the majestic *portal* on the right-hand side was added, while the facade was redesigned in 1821 by Carlo Barabino. The belltower, the only surviving part of the Romanesque church, was found to be unsafe and demolished in 1904.

The interior, whose nave is divided off from the aisles by paired columns, is richly decorated with colored marble and *frescoes* painted in two stages (1646 and 1664-76) by Giovanni Battista

1.4 From Piazza delle Fontane

Carlone; the stuccowork was added by his brother Tommaso. The splendid black marble and bronze **high altar** is a masterpiece by Pierre Puget (1670). Other works of art include an *Annunciation* by Orazio Gentileschi (1622) in the 1st chapel on the right and a fresco (*Saint in Glory*) by Gregorio De Ferrari on the vault of the 3rd; the 5th chapel on the left has a *Nativity Crèche** by Pomarancio, dated around 1606.

The mint building that gave its name to **Largo della Zecca** (I, A1-2) was demolished in 1927 to make way for the Garibaldi Road Tunnel (I, A-B2-3). The most interesting buildings in this noisy street are *Palazzo Rostan Raggio* (no. 4, now a school), a further example of the successful artistic partnership between Giovanni Battista Castello and Bernardino Cantone (1565-70); and *Palazzo Patrone* (no. 2, now a military headquarters) built in 1619-27 and with a remarkable fresco cycle (*Esther and Asahuerus*) in the vestibule, by Giovanni Carlone and Domenico Fiasella (1625-30).

To the right of Palazzo Rostan Raggio is the lower station of the **Righi Funicular Railway** (I, A2), a popular panoramic ride, with stops along the way at the various levels of the

The typical late 16th-century layout of the church of San Siro, Genoa

Circonvallazione a Monte. Via Valle-chiara (I, A1), meanwhile, leads to the *church of Nostra Signora del Carmine* (II, B3), built in the 12th century and still with a Gothic interior despite the numerous changes made down the centuries. The quaint neighborhood in which it stands has picturesquely named streets (Sugar Lane, Wisdom Way, Jujube Alley...).

With its grand, 175-meter-long *facade* that towers up behind Via Brignole De Ferrari (II, B3) the **Albergo dei Poveri** (II, A3), looks more like a royal palace than a hospice for the poor. The build-ing, which is now used by the universi-ty, took forty years to complete (1656-1696). It is a reminder of an age in which charity provided an opportunity for self-glorification, since the munifi-cence of the benefactors was rewarded with statues. Around the four court-yards runs a network of galleries, with a Greek-cross *church* in the center for the use of residents.

In *Via Lomellini* (I, A1), which leads down from Largo della Zecca to Piazza Fossatello (see p. 46), stands the *church of San Filippo Neri*, formerly adjoining a convent (now a school). Founded in 1674, it has a concave facade, a style not typically found in Genoa. The adjoining oratory (no. 10), built in 1749, has an exquisite statue of the *Imma-colata*, sculpted by Pierre Puget. A little fur-ther down, across the street, is the *Birth-place of Giuseppe Mazzini* (I, A1), which now houses the *Museo del Risorgimento* (*open: 9am-1pm; closed Mon, Wed and Sun*), presenting memorabilia, documents and works of art from the 1700s to the first decade of the Kingdom of Italy.

Piazza della Nunziata (I, A1). The only cycle of *frescoes* dedicated to Christopher Columbus in the city where the man who discovered America was born is to be found in the hall of *Palazzo Belimbau-Negrotto Cambiaso* (no. 1). It was painted by Lazzaro Tavarone in 1624. However, the most conspicuous building in this square – another area constantly filled with traffic – is the majestic **church of the Santissima Annunziata del Vastato*** (II, B3; *open: 7-11.30am and 4-6.30pm; Sun and holidays 7.30am-noon and 4.30-6.45pm*). It was rebuilt in 1591-1625 over an earlier late-Gothic church under the patronage of the Lomellini, a family whose properties at the time included the island of Tabarqa, off the north coast of Tunisia. The facade has two belltowers and a classical-style pronaos, added, amid much controversy, in 1867. The spectacular interior, in the shape of a Latin cross, displays a wealth of red and white inlaid marble, gilt stuccowork and frescoes, by some of the best Ge-noese painters: Giovanni and Giovanni Battista Carlone (the nave), Andrea Ansaldo and Gregorio De Ferrari (the dome), and Giulio Benso, whose *Annunciation* and *Assumption* in the choir are considered the most beautiful part of the interior decoration. The large canvas behind the facade (**Last Supper***) is by Giulio Cesare Procaccini.

Via Balbi (II, B2-3). This street was laid out by the Balbi family as a private street (1602-20), much in the same way as the 'Strada Nuova' had been created a few decades before. However, unlike its predecessor (today's Via Garibaldi), it is still awaiting pedestrianization. All the residences lining the street, designed by Bartolomeo Bianco, were owned by the Balbi family. The first **Palazzo Durazzo Pallavicini** (no. 1), the only one still privately owned, has four wings with loggias and a spectacular neoclassical staircase designed, like the *vestibule*, by Andrea Tagliafichi (1780). The *picture gallery**, with fine paintings by Italian and foreign painters, is closed to the public. **Palazzo Balbi Senarega** (no. 4), now the seat of the University's Literature and Philosophy Faculty, has a courtyard with loggias beautifully restored in the 1990s; the second piano nobile has *frescoes* by Valerio Castello and Gregorio De Ferrari.

The University Library is unusually located in the former *church of Ss. Gerolamo e Francesco Saverio* (1650-58), on the north side of the street. The apse wall in the reading room is decorated with *frescoes* by Domenico Piola.

Palazzo dell'Università* (II, B2). The former College of the Jesuits (1634-36) in the Baroque style bears more than a passing resemblance to Palazzo Doria Tursi. In addition to the architectural similarities, the two buildings occupy similar positions on sloping terrain. The declivity of the site obliged architect Bartolomeo Bianco to copy the idea of the atrium with raised courtyard and double staircase. To this he added a touch of 17th-century refinement, evident in such details as the paired columns of the portico. Following restoration work in the 1980s and '90s the palace has returned to its former glory.

National Gallery, Palazzo Reale

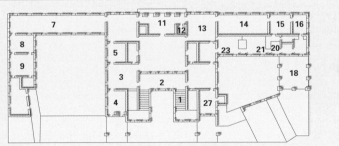

1 Stairs, left
2 Loggia
3 Room of the Battles (G.B. Pittoni, C.F. Beaumont, Francesco de Mura)
4 Room of Time (Domenico Piola, Grechetto, Francesco Bassano, Borgognone)
5 Room of Peace (Giovanni Francesco Romanelli)
7 Gallery of Mirrors (Filippo Parodi, Francesco Schiaffino)
8,9 Ante-chamber and Bedchamber of the Duke of Genoa (Valerio Castello, Guercino, Gian Gioseffo Dal Sole)
11,12 Chapel Gallery and Chapel (G.B. Carlone, Filippo Parodi)
13 Throne Room (Luca Giordano)
14 Audience Room (Van Dyck, Valerio Castello)
15 King's Bedchamber (Bartolomeo Guidobono, Van Dyck)
16 King's Bathroom (Maestro dell'Adorazione dei Magi di Torino)
18 Queen's Terrace
20 White Room (Giacomo Antonio Boni)
21 Queen's Bedchamber (Francesco de Mura, Bernardo Strozzi)
23 Queen's Drawing Room (Domenico Fiasella, Luca Giordano)
27 Room of the Dawn (Giacomo Antonio Boni, Bernardo Strozzi)

The *church of Ss. Vittore e Carlo* (II, B2), which is reached by a double staircase running parallel to the street, has a porticoed front that is the only one of its kind in Genoa. Used until 1974 by the Discalced Carmelites, it took nearly half a century to build (1629-73); the interior decorations were added in 1890-98.

*V. Castello,
The Chariot
of Time,
detail of the fresco.
Palazzo Balbi Senarega, Genoa*

Palazzo Reale** (II, B2-3). When the Savoy family took possession of this sumptuous building (1643-55) in 1824, it was indeed worthy of becoming the official 'royal residence'. The grand portal was added by Carlo Fontana in 1705; the courtyard of honor is flanked by brightly-painted walls. Beyond the triple arch, the terraced *garden* overlooking the sea has a black-and-white pebbled *walk* salvaged from the demolished monastery of the Turchine. The stairs to the left lead up to the piano nobile and the **Galleria Nazionale di Palazzo Reale*** (*open: 9am-7pm, Sun-Tue 9am-1.45pm*). The art collection, set against a backdrop of 17th-century frescoes and exquisite furnishings (18th-19th cent.), is seen at its most magnificent in the *Gallery of Mirrors*, noted also for its four statues (*Hyacinthus**, *Clizia*, *Amor* – or *Narcissus* – and *Venus*) by Filippo Parodi, and a marble group (*Rape of Proserpina*) by Francesco Schiaffino. The *Audience Chamber* has two important paintings: the *Rape of Proserpina** by Valerio Castello and the *Portrait of Caterina Durazzo**, by Antonie Van Dyck, who also painted the *Crucifixion* which hangs in the king's bedchamber. In the following room are two paintings from the Flemish school (*St. Catherine and the Heretics*, *St. Agnes is Led to the House of Pleasure*), by the so-called Maestro of the Adoration of the Magi of Turin. Note also the *silks**, painted as imitation tapestries by Giovanni Francesco Romanelli, in the *Sala della Pace*.

Palazzo Reale: the terraced garden with the courtyard of honor in the background

Genova/II 1:14 000 (1 cm = 140 m)

0 — 150 — 300 m

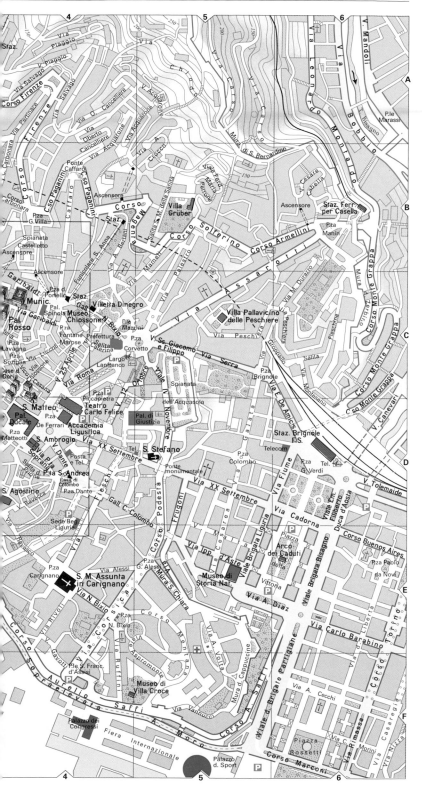

71

2 Modern Genoa

Profile

The expansion of the city in the early 1800s was largely the work of municipal architect Carlo Barabino, who, in creating today's Via XXV Aprile and the Carlo Felice Theater, established a new hub of city life around what later that century became Piazza De Ferrari. This period also saw the laying out of Via XX Settembre by mayor Andrea Podestà, along the course of the 17th-century Via Giulia. The new thoroughfare attracted the big names in the Genoese economy away from the port for the first time in the city's history.

The middle classes, who were now a force to be reckoned with, staked out their territory in the new residential districts established by Barabino. The longed-for urbanization of the high ground immediately behind the ancient city at last began to take place, along the Circonvallazione a Monte, as well as on the Carignano hill and down in the San Vincenzo plain. And as the city sprawled inexorably outward, so the rural outskirts disappeared, surviving only in a number of 16th-century villas – and their gardens – and the convent buildings dotted along the ridgeways above, and reached by quaint cobbled lanes, locally called *creuze*.

A similar fate was suffered by the old craftworkers' quarters, which late 19th-century urban planning had isolated from the medieval center. This area was far too tempting for a rapidly

Some of the new urban features from the last two centuries (left to right):

expanding city, which up to the 1970s also grew in population, desperate for space in which to create a business district; Piazza della Vittoria was created during the years of Fascism by covering over the Bisagno river estuary. This period also saw the opening up of Piazza Dante, followed after the war by major redevelopment of the Piccapietra and Madre di Dio areas, whose urban planning and architectural excellence is highly debatable. Not surprisingly, the new impetus for change in the 1990s saw the expanding business sector turning its attentions once again to the port area, leaving the modern city to take on the role of hub for cultural events and fashionable society for which it was originally designed.

Not that this will necessarily be so easy to achieve: when it comes to culture the ancient heart of the city is putting up some fierce competition.

2.1 The new quarters and the garden-city: from Via XXV Aprile to Piazza Corvetto and Carignano

Walking tour round the fringes of the ancient city *(see map p. 76)*

This tour, which takes us into 19th-century Genoa, begins at Via XXV Aprile and Piazza De Ferrari, already the hub of cultural life in the Ligurian capital in the late 19th century. From here, Via Roma leads to Piazza Corvet-

to, the elegant meeting point of the main roads of the modern city. The tour then follows the course of the 16th-century walls, heading south toward the fashionable district of Carignano on the hill overlooking the sea.

Via XXV Aprile (I, C3). This elegant shopping street (1825-28) was formerly called Strada Carlo Felice, a name that reminds us of the intention in creating this straight thoroughfare (in the manner favored by 19th-century town-planners) to connect the Savoy residence and all the 'Strade Nuove' with the new opera house of the same name (see below), which was under construction at the time.

Teatro Carlo Felice (I, C-D3; *open on request, tel. 0105381224*). Little did anyone expect, when Genoa's opera house was bombed during World War II, that it would remain closed for forty years thereafter, and yet it was not until 1987 that work began on rebuilding the theater. The damage was not even particularly devastating, and per-

Piazza De Ferrari, Galleria Mazzini, the Carlo Felice Theater

formances did indeed resume for a short period after the war. But the political diatribes began, and the sluggishness of the bureaucratic machine did the rest: the ruins of the theater came to symbolize the city's postwar decline. Then along came Ignazio Gardella, Aldo Rossi and Fabio Reinhart with their new design, which incorporated the pronaos and west porch of the original theater (designed by Carlo Barabino, 1826-31), from behind which the new building emerges: a towering volume topped by a glass pyramid that lights up when the theater is open, and now a familiar feature of the Genoese skyline. The design of the stage and the perspective of the auditorium are inspired by the architectural features of the city's old streets: the overall effect this creates, though undoubtedly visually appealing, is not entirely satisfying from a stylistic point of view. The dazzlingly sophisticated stage machinery, on the other hand, with its

four high-tech moving platforms, is among the most modern in Europe. All of which forms a stark contrast to the delightful 19th-century *Rissone Puppet Theater*, kept in the Niccolò Paganini room entered from the first foyer.

Piazza De Ferrari (I, D3). The heart of 20th-century Genoa, laid out between 1899 and 1923, is dominated by the spectacular circular bronze *fountain* (1936). An *Equestrian Statue of Giuseppe Garibaldi* (1892) stands on the corner between the Carlo Felice Theater and the *Palazzo dell'Accademia Ligustica di Belle Arti* (no. 5), also designed by Carlo Barabino (1826-31). Inside, a double staircase leads to the **Museo dell'Accademia Ligustica di Belle Arti*** (*open: 9am-1pm; Sun and holidays closed*). This is the picture gallery of Genoa's Fine Arts Academy, containing Ligurian art from the 14th to the 19th centuries. Works include: Giovanni Andrea De Ferrari (*A Saint Raises a Fallen Mason from the Dead**, *Adoration of the Shepherds**), Gioacchino Assereto (*Martyrdom of St. Bartholomew**), il Grechetto (*The Animals Entering the Ark**) and Francesco d'Oberto (*Madonna and Child with St. Dominic and St. John the Evangelist*). Arguably the most important works, however, are Perin del Vaga's superb **Polyptych of St. Erasmus***, and those by Bernardo Strozzi: *Lamenting the Dead Christ**, a fragment (*Head of John the Baptist*) and a sketch (*Paradise*) for the frescoes in the apse of the church of San Domenico, demolished in 1820 to make way for the new opera house.

With the exception of Palazzo Ducale (see p. 55) and the adjoining *Palazzo Forcheri* (no. 2), built in the late Middle Ages but subsequently much altered, and *Palazzo De Ferrari* (no. 3), built in the late 1500s, all the buildings facing onto the square are Eclectic in style. One notable example, on the corner between Via Dante and Via XX Settembre, is *Palazzo della Borsa* (the Stock Exchange, 1907-12), designed by Dario Carbone, with the help of A. Coppedè, who added the architectural decorations in the ground-floor rooms.

Via Roma (II, C4). This street has never attracted the sidewalk cafés that might have been expected to develop along a fashionable shopping thoroughfare, one possible explanation being the cold north winter wind. Some shopkeepers have indeed moved their businesses elsewhere, their places taken by offices and banks, which of course do little to bring the street to life, though the high-class jewelry shops and international designer boutiques help it to retain its elegance. With its perfectly straight layout and Neoclassical facades, Via Roma has all the typical features of the 19th-century street. It was opened in 1872 to connect the Circonvallazione a Monte with the business and cultural districts of the city center. The *Galleria Mazzini* (II, C4), which runs parallel to Via Roma, is a much livelier place during the day and when the book fair is held during holidays. The gallery has a glass and metal roof with elegant iron chandeliers, creating an elegant environment for theater-goers who used to stroll here after performances.

At the top end of Via Roma begins the *Salita S. Caterina* (II, C4), an ancient street that went up to the now demolished Murtedo Gateway. One interesting building along the lower part is **Palazzo Spinola Pessagno** (no. 3), built by Giovanni Battista Castello: the facade has some fine stuccowork and an impressive *portal* with herms and spiral tympanum.

Palazzo Doria Spinola (II, C4), also known as Palazzo della Prefettura, now houses the Prefecture and some provincial adminis-

tration offices. Attributed to Bernardino Cantone and Giovanni Battista Castello (1541-43), it lost its right-hand corner with the opening of Piazza Corvetto (see below); the 16th- and 18th-century frescoes on the facade suffer greatly in an area of such heavy traffic. However, beyond the *portal*, added around 1580 by Taddeo Carlone, is a magnificent Mannerist **courtyard*** with loggia: the upper level has interesting *city scenes* attributed to Felice Calvi (1584). Luca Cambiaso, with his father Giovanni, painted the frescoes (1545-50) on the ceiling of the main hall on the *piano nobile* (*Hercules Shoots Arrows at the Greeks Before the Gates of Troy*) and an adjoining room (*Hercules and the Amazons*).

It is quite a surprise in this modern part of the city to find, hidden away down a vaulted passage off *Largo Lanfranco* (II, C4) to the left of a modern bank, the **church of Santa Marta**. The modest facade of this ancient place of worship (remodeled in 1535) conceals an airy interior with nave and side aisles, and a large upper choir with two tribunes along the walls of the central tribune; the sumptuous decorations are Baroque. The apse is dominated by Filippo Parodi's splendid marble sculpture *St. Martha in Glory**; the *frescoes* are by Domenico and Paolo Gerolamo Piola, Valerio Castello, Lorenzo De Ferrari and Giovanni Battista Carlone. The cycle of paintings (*Ascension of Christ*) in the *Chapter House* (*open on request, apply at the church*) is all that survives of the 16th-century Benedictine convent.

Piazza Corvetto (II, C4-5). It was only to be expected that this circus, laid out in 1877 would become clogged with traffic, con-

Piazza Corvetto in Genoa, with the equestrian statue of Vittorio Emanuele II in the center

sidering that the Circonvallazione a Monte, the tunnels to the 'Strade Nuove' and other major city roads converge on it. And yet the piazza, with its trees, flowerbeds and grassy verges is one of Genoa's most beautiful. In the center stands the *Equestrian Statue of Vittorio Emanuele II* (1886), and the greenery continues into the Acquasola Park (see below) immediately to the south-east, and the *Villetta Di Negro Park* to the north-west. These latter gardens, entered from Piazzale Mazzini (adjoining Piazza Corvetto), with a *monument to Giuseppe Mazzini* (1882), have a varied collection of exotic plants planted in the 1700s by Ippolito Durazzo; the villa, built in 1802, was destroyed by allied bombing in 1942.

Museo d'Arte Orientale Edoardo Chiossone* (II, C4). Villetta Di Negro was the original home of this oriental art museum (*open: 9am-1pm; closed Mon and Wed*), relocated in 1971 in a modern building designed by Mario Labò. In 1875, the Japanese Imperial Government invited Edoardo Chiossone to run the Ministry of Finance Printing Institute (see box). During his stay (he never returned to Italy),

Chiossone collected some 15,000 items, some of which are the only ones of their kind in a western museum.

The visit begins with a series of 17th/19th-century bronze sculptures that survived the iconoclastic campaign of the late 19th century: note in particular the *Eleven-Headed Kwan-On**, from the Genroku period (1698-1703).

The display cabinets in the gallery on the side facing the sea have a bronze *ritual bell* and a collection of *spearheads and halberds** from the mid Yayoi period (1st cent. BC-1st cent. AD); the gilt bronze **Avalokitesvara***, possibly from Korea, dates back to the 7th or 8th century. Sculptures take pride of place in the gallery facing the hill, with two

wooden *Nio** from the early Kamakura period (12th/13th cent.). Also worthy of note are the 18th-century *Mask of Ran-Ryoo**, used by the 'Dragon King' in the

Armor from the late Edo period (19th cent.)

Bugaku Theater performances, and, in the extensive applied art collection, a pair of *cylindrical glazed porcelain vases* decorated with summer and autumn flowers, butterflies and dragonflies (ca. 1876). Note also the twelve *suits of armor* (16th/19th cent.) on display in the first hillside gallery, the burial gifts

2.1 From Via XXV Aprile to Carignano

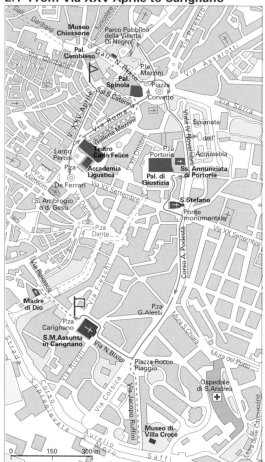

Giustizia all but masks the facade, which has a fine twin *portal* (1521). The interior is in the Mannerist style, the best examples of which are seen in the cycle of paintings by Giovanni Battista Castello (**Christ the Judge***, *Evangelists*) on the vault and in the pendentives of the presbytery, where three canvases also hang (*Annunciation, The Souls of the Just, The Souls of the Wicked*) by Luca Cambiaso. The 3rd chapel on the right has four allegorical statues surrounding the *Mausoleum of St. Catherine**, built in 1738-49 by Francesco Schiaffino: the sacellum containing the remains of the saint is held up on a marble base.

Santo Stefano* (II, D5). The facade is interesting, but the best part of the church is undoubtedly the rear. The steps that lead down to the church from Viale IV Novembre offer a perfect vantage point from which to admire the beautiful **apse***, a masterpiece of Romanesque architecture. Built over a plinth pierced with the small windows of the crypt, it has a series of blind arches, topped by a tier of smaller arches. The church, which was not consecrated until 1217, was built in the late 1100s over a Benedictine abbey founded around 960 by bishop Theodolph II. The front, which seems to hang suspended over Via XX Settembre (see p. 78), has the typical Genoese black and white striped facade, with a large rose window beneath a double two-light window. Rising up behind the pitched roof (a frequent feature of Genoese architecture) is the *campanile*, whose belfry, added in the 14th century, is in two sections with four- and five-light windows respectively. A false aisle was added on the north side of the church during postwar reconstruction work (1946-55), which also involved the rebuilding of the badly-damaged south wall. On the south wall inside is a splendid **Martyrdom of St. Stephen*** by Giulio Romano (1524). Note also behind the facade the *choir gallery** by Donato Benti and Benedetto da Rovezzano (1499), and the *Martyrdom of St. Bartholomew** by Giulio

from the Kofun period (6th/8th cent.), and the collection of paintings and prints.

The *Acquasola Esplanade* (II, C-D5) was created by Carlo Barabino in 1821. The gardens, once an elegant place filled with entertainment pavilions and Sunday afternoon strollers, mark the start of the Passeggiata delle Mura (literally 'wall walk'), along the route of the 16th-century *enceinte*, as the street names along the way remind us (*Mura di S. Chiara, Mura del Prato, Mura delle Cappuccine*). Opposite the Acquasola gardens begins Viale IV Novembre (II, C-D5). The Eclectic *Villetta Serra* (no. 3) houses the *Museo Biblioteca dell'Attore (open: 9am-1pm, Mon 2pm-7pm; closed Sat and Sun)*, a museum of 19th and 20th century stagecraft.

SS. Annunziata di Portoria (II, D5). This church, known locally as *Santa Caterina da Genova*, was built in 1488, but barely fifty years later, in 1536, the apse was demolished to make way for the new walls, only to be rebuilt twenty years after that. Palazzo di

Cesare Procaccini in the presbytery, where the blind arch motif outside is repeated. The much-remodeled *crypt* is dedicated to St. Michael, suggesting that this was an earlier Longobard church.

Ponte Monumentale (II, D5). This bridge affords a stunning view over Via XX Settembre and early 20th-century Genoa. The monumental construction (1893-99), designed by Cesare Gamba and Riccardo Haupt, has a large central arch over the road and two pedestrian arches at the sides. When it was built,

L. Cambiaso, Pietà. Church of S. M. Assunta, Genoa

Sauli* and **St. Sebastian***) sculpted in 1668 by Pierre Puget; the *St. John the Baptist* is by Filippo Parodi (1667), while Claude David sculpted the *St. Bartholomew* (1695). The most interesting paintings are the *Martyrdom of St. Blaise** in the 2nd altar on the right, by Carlo Maratta (1680), and the *Pietà** in the 3rd altar on the left, by Luca Cambiaso (ca. 1571). Note also the *St. Francis Receiving the Stigmata*, by Guercino, and the *organ* (1656), with doors painted by Paolo Brozzi and Domenico Piola.

the 16th-century *Porta dell'Arco* was moved to Via Banderali, below the Prato walls.

The leafy *Carignano* district, an elegant 19th-century residential neighborhood, is the location of the *Museo d'Arte Contemporanea di Villa Croce* (II, F4-5), a contemporary art gallery with over 200 artworks, housed in a 19th-century villa in its own park (*open: 9am-7pm, Sun 9am-12.30pm; closed Mon*), well known for its busy calendar of temporary exhibitions.

The daring **Ponte di Carignano** (1718-24), the bridge carrying today's Via Ravasco (II, D-E4), was designed again for the Sauli family by French architect Gerard de Langlade, who used an idea put forward by Alessi for this road link with Piazza Sarzano.

The steps on the right at the end of the four-span bridge lead up to the panoramic *walk** created over the 12th-century walls, leading to Porta di S. Andrea (see p. 55).

Santa Maria Assunta in Carignano* (II, E4). This church, built high up on top of the Carignano hill, was commissioned by the Sauli family. The design and construction – which took half a century to complete (1552-1602) – was by Galeazzo Alessi, who departed from the typical 'hillside' site of other churches in the city to create what for Genoa was a totally new kind of layout: a Greek cross set inside a square, and a central dome supported on piers with four smaller domes in the corners. The original design also envisaged four belltowers, but only the two over the facade (remodeled in 1722) were actually built. This interferes to some extent with the symmetry of the building, as is evident from the interior. In the niches of the dome-piers are two magnificent statues (**St. Alessandro**

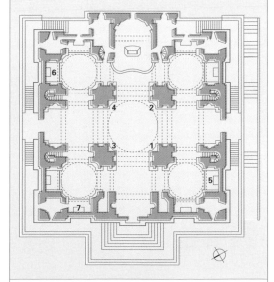

Santa Maria Assunta in Carignano

1 Statue of Sant'Alessandro Sauli (P. Puget)
2 Statue of St. Sebastian (P. Puget)
3 Statue of St. Bartholomew (C. David)
4 Statue of St. John the Baptist (F. Parodi)
5 Martyrdom of St. Blaise (C. Maratta)
6 Pietà (L. Cambiaso)
7 San Francesco (Guercino)

2.2 20th-century Genoa: from Piazza Dante to Via XX Settembre and Piazza della Vittoria

Walking tour through the area south-east of the historic center

This tour of the commercial and business heart of the city begins in Piazza Dante, then continues along the whole length of Via XX Settembre, to the monumental Piazza della Vittoria, beyond which emerge the ultra-modern Corte Lambruschini tower blocks.

Piazza Dante (II, D4). This square took the place of the former Borgo Lanaioli, which, as the name suggests, was once a center for woolmaking (*lana* = wool). One of the woolmakers who once worked here was Domenico Colombo, the father of the man who later discovered America. There is, however, no real proof that the so-called *Casa di Colombo* (I, E3; *open: Sat and Sun 9am-noon and 3pm-6pm; on request, tel. 0102465346*), was where the Columbus family actually lived. The building, an 18th-century reconstruction of an earlier house destroyed by French bombs in 1684, was restored (1987-88) in preparation for the 1992 Columbus celebrations, together with the adjoining **Cloister of Sant'Andrea** (I, E3), the only surviving part of the 12th-century Benedictine monastery, demolished in 1904. The paired columns have capitals carved with human figures and plant and animal motifs. The square that stretches out beneath was opened up in the 1930s. One of the architects involved

in the scheme was Marcello Piacentini, who also designed the thirty-floor *South Skyscraper* (1937-41), a 120-m building whose *Columbus Terrace* offers a spectacular view over the medieval quarters.

Via XX Settembre (II, D4-5). Until the 1980s this was Genoa's cinema and theater land. Now that leisure time activities have been decentralized, 'Via Venti', as it is known locally, is primarily a shopping street: department stores alternate with some of the town's 'historic' shops, some of which display that faded elegance the Genoese are so fond of. The street, designed by Cesare Gamba and opened up 1892-1900, is in any case beginning to show its age: as if the constant flow of motor traffic were not enough, the eclectic-style facades of its buildings are regularly daubed with slogans by extremist supporters of the city's soccer teams. This sense of neglect is perhaps most evident in the arcaded western section of the street up to the Ponte Monumentale (see p. 77).

Attempts to turn the once working-class area of **Portoria** into a business district failed. *Via XII Ottobre* (II, C-D4-5), now choked with traffic, has plenty of examples of post-war architecture at its ugliest. These buildings now dwarf the *church of Santa Croce e San Camillo de Lellis* (II, D4), thought to have been designed by Carlo Mutone

Genoa: aerial view of Via Dante and Via XX Settembre, the hub of the 20th-century city

2.2 From Piazza Dante to Piazza della Vittoria

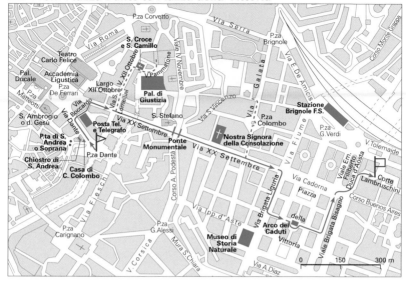

(1667). This little place of worship, topped by an octagonal dome, is entered from behind in Via Pammatone. The decorations inside create some trompe l'oeil architectural effects (*Triumph of the Cross*), added in the early 18th century by Gregorio and Lorenzo De Ferrari.

To the left of the church is the now somewhat dilapidated *Monument to Gian Battista Perasso* (1862), better known as the 'Balilla', the young recruit who according to tradition began the revolt against the Austrians in December 1746, here in Portoria. The *Staircase* and *Courtyard with Loggia* (1750-83) are all that remains of the former hospital of Pammatone, which was too badly bombed during the last war to be saved. The remains were incorporated into the ponderous *Palazzo di Giustizia*, the new law courts built between 1965 and 1970.

The *church of Nostra Signora della Consolazione e San Vincenzo* (II, D5), on the eastern, unporticoed stretch of Via XX Settembre, was built by the Augustinians in 1684-1706: the dome was added later (1769) and the facade was completed in 1864. The rich interior decoration of the nave and aisles is also nineteenth century. The most conspicuous work is the splendid **Crucifix*** painted on wood by the Maestro di Santa Maria di Castello (14th cent.), which hangs over the high altar. Note also the *picture gallery* in the refectory of the adjoining convent (*open on request, tel. 010561922*), which has a *Descent from the Cross* by Antonio Semino (1547) and a *Last Supper* at-

tributed to Luca Cambiaso. The *cloister* (1699-1708) has since 1899 been the site of the *Mercato Orientale*, a bustling market.

Named after the 'Genoese quarter' in Istanbul, *Via Galata* (II, D5) leads off from Via XX Settembre up to **Piazza Colombo**, an elegant porticoed quadrangle designed by Carlo Barabino and Giovanni Battista Resasco (1825-40): at the center of the square stands the *Fountain of the Winged Genie*, by Giovanni Battista Garré (1646), moved here from the Old Port. Beyond Piazza Colombo, Via Galata crosses **Via S. Vincenzo** (II, D5), a street with ancient origins (corresponding in part to the 'strata' around the Roman settlement), in which a number of late-medieval and Renaissance buildings still stand, including *Palazzo di Domenico Centurione* (no. 59), dated 1548, with a loggia to the rear of the building.

Museo Civico di Storia Naturale Giacomo Doria (II, E5). Genoa's much-visited natural history museum (*open: 9am-12.30pm and 3-5.30pm, Fri 9am-12.30pm; closed Mon and holidays*) was founded in 1867 and moved to its present home in 1912. It boasts a wealth of important zoological collections, including many non-European species; the *Entomology Collection* is the largest in Italy. The only disappointment is the presentation, no more than a sequence of display

Butterflies in the G. Doria Natural History Museum, Genoa

79

Frieze on the War Memorial Arch in Piazza della Vittoria, Genoa

cabinets, a method that has long been re-placed in scientific exhibitions by multimedia systems, but which in this museum are limited to the audio-visual presentation of documentaries screened in the small amphitheater and some fairly straightforward sound effects.

Piazza della Vittoria (II, D-E5-6). In 1999 the multinational beverages corporation Coca-Cola chose this square as the setting for a TV commercial that was seen throughout the world, one of the few claims to fame for a square that has never been loved by the Genoese, and which is usually dismissed as being a typical example of the 'Italian piazza' style created by the Fascist regime in the 1930s. The description is indeed quite an apt one: this huge monumental space (1923-38), was created by covering over the mouth of the Bisagno river, under the direction of Marcello Piacentini. The architect, together with Arturo Dazzi, also designed the *Arco dei Caduti* (1931), the memorial to the war dead at the center of the square, whose southern gardens feature a floral arrangement based on Columbus' three caravels.

To the north-east of the square is *Viale Emanuele Filiberto Duca d'Aosta* (II, D-E6), the location of the **Corte Lambruschini** business center erected in the 1980s on the corner with Corso Buenos Aires. As well as the two high-rise glass towers, which have become a new landmark for Genoa, the complex includes a hotel, and the *Teatro della Corte*, where the city's main theater company performs.

2.3 The Circonvallazione a Monte

Tour of the hills above Genoa, by public transport *(see map p. 82)*

Often considered as little more than a panoramic road that zig-zags its way along the hillside, this upper ring road is in actual fact one of the most successful examples of urban-planning carried out in 19th-century Italy. The tour, which is too long to walk and too nerve-racking to drive along, is best appreciated by public transport (bus no. 33 runs from Piazza Corvetto or the Porta Principe train station). The east-west route presented here heads out of town along tree-lined avenues whose names recall the personalities and events of the *Risorgimento*, a reminder that this route was laid out shortly after the unification of Italy.

Via Assarotti (II, B-C5-6). This long, straight and steep avenue which runs north-east up the hill from Piazza Corvetto was planned by Giovanni Battista Resasco (1852). It was the axis along which the hillward expansion of Genoa began, in a housing scheme for the well-to-do that was in a way the 19th-century equivalent of the opening up of the 'Strade Nuove' three centuries earlier, hence the similarity between the street fronts and the Mannerist facades of the 16th century. Also in neo-Renaissance style is the *church of Santa Maria Immacolata* (II, C5), built in 1864-73 by Maurizio Dufour. The central-plan interior is elaborately decorated; note in particular the exquisite metal and ivory inlay work on the early 20th-century domed *confessionals*.

Via S. Bartolomeo degli Armeni, which runs almost parallel to Via Assarotti, is a typical *creuza* winding up the hill that was part of the urban growth of the late 19th and early 20th centuries. Here, in its own park stands the beautiful late-Renaissance **Villa Pallavicino delle Peschiere*** (II, C5), now used by a brokerage firm. The main front of the villa, whose design is attributed to Galeazzo Alessi (though scholars disagree), has a three-arch entrance loggia, balustraded cornice and avant-corps; the interior was beautifully decorated (*Scenes from the Lives of Perseus and Ulysses, the Myths of Apollo and Diana*) by Andrea Semino, Luca

Cambiaso and Giovanni Battista Castello. Castello was also involved in the design of the monumental terraced *garden* (now cut across by Via Peschiera), which has a *nymphaeum*, with a mosaic grotto.

Piazza Manin (II, B6). This green, but congested square at the easternmost point of the Circonvallazione a Monte, and of the Mura Nuove (see p. 86), is the starting-point of the roads that head up into the Bisagno Valley, and the terminus of the *Genova-Casella railway* (II, B6; see pp. 105-106). The privately-owned *Villa Gropallo* (II, C6; *closed to the public*), is a 16th-century residence frescoed inside by Gregorio De Ferrari and Domenico Piola (the artist who painted the so-called '*Room of the Ruins*' *). The villa stands in grounds rich in Mediterranean and exotic flora, brought here in the 1700s by its then owner Ippolito Durazzo.

The **church of San Bartolomeo degli Armeni** (II, B5) is best known for the **Santo Volto*** kept in a chapel on the left (see box). Founded by the Basilians (1308), who in 1650 ceded the church to the Barnabites, the church is now rather unusually housed in a 19th-century building overlooking *Corso Armellini* (II, B5-6). The precious relic kept in the church, a gift from Constantinople to the Doge Leonardo Montaldo (in the second half of the 14th cent.), is reflected in some of the interior decorations, added when the church was redesigned in 1595 and 1775; the triptych on the high altar by Turino Vanni (*Madonna with Saints**) dates back to 1415.

Villa Grüber (II, B5) was built in the 16th century for Stefano De Mari, but subsequently transformed in the Neoclassical style; the square lookout tower is all that survives of the original building. Between 1979 and 1997 this residence (*now closed to the public*) housed the *Museo Americanistico Federico Lunardi*, a museum of pre-Columbian art, now to be relocated. The *park* with its English garden is open to visitors.

"Boys will be boys", they said in 1989 when young

The mystery of the Santo Volto

It's the age-old clash between science and faith. Although we are unlikely ever to know for sure if the reliquary kept in the *church of San Bartolomeo degli Armeni*, also known as the 'Holy Shroud' or 'Mandillo', really does bear an image of the face of Christ, studies carried out in the late 20th-century have dated the egg-based tempera portrait on linen to the Imperial Age. There are two versions to the story behind the shroud, based on a passage from St. John's Gospel: according to the first the effigy was impressed directly on the cloth by the face of Jesus; the other suggests it was the work of a painter sent by Abgar V, monarch of Edessa (the present-day Turkish town of Urfa). The relic, documented from the 4th century and venerated for the entire first millennium of the Christian era as a genuine portrait of the Redeemer, stayed here until 944, when it was transferred to Constantinople, an event still celebrated in the Byzantine Liturgy. It was in the capital of the Eastern Empire that the 'Holy Face' was set in the exquisite silver and gold filigree frame in which it is still kept; the ten embossed panels illustrate the first version of the portrait's origin and other episodes from its history until it was moved to Constantinople, the city it eventually left in 1362, when it was presented as a gift to future doge Montaldo in gratitude for his military services to the Emperor John V Palaeologus. Twenty-two years later the Santo Volto was housed in the *church of San Bartolomeo degli Armeni*. The relic was stolen by French troops in 1507, but retrieved by powerful Genoese bankers.

2.3 The Circonvallazione a Monte

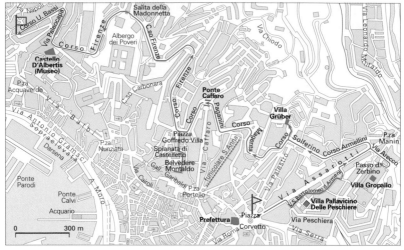

vandals (from good families) set fire to the charming wooden station of the *Funicular of Sant'Anna*, that takes passengers from *Corso Magenta* (II, B4-5) to Piazza Portello. Unfortunately, the youthful exuberance that destroyed the old building was not matched by the designers of its replacement, opposite which a flight of steps leads to the charming **Piazza Sant'Anna**, whose likenamed *church* (1584) has a fine marble *portal* with bas-relief (*Holy Family*). Inside, note the **Jesus and St. Theresa*** in the 2nd chapel on the left, attributed to Gerrit van Honthorst. The Carmelite convent (also 16th cent.) adjoining the church was restored in the 1990s: the *library and apothecary* still have their original furnishings.

Spianata di Castelletto (II, B4). The poet Giorgio Caproni wanted his stairway to paradise to be the *lift* from Piazza Portello to the **Montaldo Belvedere**** (I, A2-3). The top station stops some way short of heaven, but, as a photograph of 1910 al-

ready showed, it is a splendid vantage point from which to admire the view over the city: the entire historic center and the Old Port, in a panorama that ranges from the Carignano and Castello heights to the modern business center of Corte Lambruschini and San Benigno. Charming, too, is the glazed Art Nouveau-style station at the terminus at the Castelletto Esplanade, a name that reminds us of the major strategic importance of this point high above the city: the 'Castelletto', mentioned as early as 952, was crucial to the defense of Genoa until the stronghold's demolition in 1528. The fortress built by the Savoy in 1819 had an even shorter life: it was demolished thirty years later to make way for the new residential district (begun in 1858), which retains its original upper middle-class character.

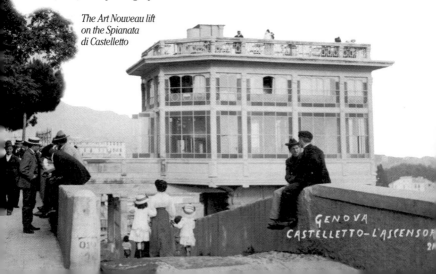

The Art Nouveau lift on the Spianata di Castelletto

Corso Firenze (II, A-B2-3-4) was laid out in 1910-20, as the Eclectic facades on the hillward side suggest. Among them stands the neo-Gothic *Bruzzo Castle* (II, A4), designed by Gino Coppedè in the early 20th century. Further on, opposite the midway station of the Zecca-Righi Funicular, stands the *church of San Nicola da Tolentino* (II, A3), jointly designed by Andrea Vannone and Cipriano Bianco (1597): much renovated down the centuries (the last work was done in 1970), it has exquisite marble decorations in the chapels.

A cobbled brick *creuza* leads up to the **Sanctuary of the Madonnetta** (II, A3, off map), or Sanctuary of Santa Maria Assunta, a place of worship built by the Augustinians, the religious order that the architect of the church Antonio Maria Ricca joined after work was completed (1696). The shrine is octagonal, as is the black and white pebbled parvis, whose boundary wall contains a marble *Pietà* by Domenico Parodi. The beautiful interior consists of a central luminous space from which two flights of stairs lead up to the presbytery. A third flight leads down to the *scurolo*, the small chapel containing the 15th-century statue of the *Madonnetta**, the 'little Madonna' after which the sanctuary is named. This in turn leads to the *crypt*, which has the celebrated artistic **Presepe***, or Christmas Crèche (*open: 9.30-11.30am and 3-6pm; on request, tel. 0102725308*), decorated with figures from the Genoese school of the 17th and 18th centuries. The sacristy has an *Annunciation** formerly attributed to the Niçois painter Lodovico Brea.

Castello D'Albertis (II, A2). Built during the neo-Gothic revival effectuated by four architects led by Alfredo D'Andrade (1886-92), this castle was commissioned by a colorful personality of the day, naval captain Enrico Alberto D'Albertis, who bequeathed to the city not only the castle itself but also the material displayed at the **Museo Etnografico** (*currently being restored; for information tel. 010282641*). These collections, gathered during his sea voyages to the Americas, South-East Asia, Oceania and New Guinea, include 11 meridians (built by D'Albertis himself), period weapons, nautical instruments and geographical publications, as well as exhibits displayed by the Catholic missions in America at the 1892 exhibition and a collection of pre-Columbian artifacts from Peru.

The western section of the Circonvallazione a Monte is largely characterized by the unscrupulous and uncontrolled building work done between the 1950s and 1970s, which virtually destroyed the rural character the area had retained until then. And yet at least one reminder of this lost world survives in the leafy square opposite the **Sanctuary of Oregina*** (III, A3), or *Sanctuary of Nostra Signora di Loreto*. This shrine, built in 1650-55 (the dome and facade – the upper part of which is decorated by windows and stuccowork – were added in 1707), housed until 1928 a chapel the reproduced the Santa Casa of Loreto. The sanctuary also has *Risorgimento* associations: tradition has its that the Madonna interceded in favor of the revolt against the Austrians in 1746, a miracle commemorated on 10 December each year with a visit by the mayor of Genoa.

Another place where time seems to have stood still is the churchyard of the **Basilica of San Francesco da Paola** (II, A1), an oasis of greenery in amongst the concrete of the surrounding residential area, and well known for the *belvedere** that looks out over the old port, down to which leads a brick road with the Stations of the Cross. The church (built in the 15th and 16th centuries

Nativity scene in the Sanctuary of the Madonnetta, Genoa

and remodeled in the 17th) was the natural choice as the sanctuary of sailors, whose *ex voto* depicting seafaring stories cover the walls of the hall in front of the entrance to the church, which has no facade. Inside the basilica note the beautiful *colored marble* decorations of the saint's chapel, and the altarpiece decorations, in particular the *Viaticum of St. Jerome* in the 2nd chapel on the right, by Giovanni Battista Paggi (1620), and the *Nativity Scene* in the 3rd chapel, painted in 1563-65 by Luca Cambiaso; the chapel at the end of the left-hand aisle has a *Washing of the Feet* by Orazio De Ferrari; the wooden statue of the *Assunta* in the apse is by Anton Maria Maragliano (17th cent.).

3 The port, the New Walls, the fortresses

Profile

Few cities are so tightly bound by the sea and the mountains as Genoa, which since ancient times has always set its sights firmly on the former, turning its back on the Apennine hills inland. This seaward focus was reinforced in the 1600s, with the erection of an impregnable defense system that in its day was the talk of Europe. Today, the imposing remains of these walls add an intriguing historical touch to the vast suburban park surrounding Genoa: a precious green space (and backdrop for cultural and sporting events) for a city that can hardly be said to have shown great concern for the environment as it has sprawled outward, something one glance at the Ligurian capital from the sea demonstrates only too well. The view from the sea also shows just how inextricably the city is bound up – for good or ill – with its port, and how, after the dark decades of immobility, it has now so resolutely taken up the challenge set by Europe's other major ports, making every possible effort to make up for lost time with the creation of the new Voltri terminal, a major infrastructure that is served by a network of road and rail links connecting the port to the very heart of the continent.

3.1 The port

Tour of the port area, on foot and by boat *(see plans pp. 88-89, 90-91)*

While Genoa's western coastal areas complain that the port's activities have swallowed up the green spaces, that the beaches have been destroyed by the wharves and that the highways come unbearably close to the built-up areas, the port planners complain that it is the city which suffocates the port. It is a problem faced by many ports, but made all the worse in Genoa by the lack of a hinterland. It is only to be expected, then, that Liguria's

capital should set its sights to the sea, and it is indeed here that the economy, investments, and employment are concentrated.

The earliest construction of a port on this site, which was already used as a natural harbor in Roman times, dates back to the 10th-12th centuries, the period in which the arcades of Via di Sottoripa (see p. 47) and Palazzo San Giorgio (see p. 47) were built. The second half of

Genoa: a view of the port, with the 'Matitone' (literally 'big pencil') skyscraper

the 14th century saw the creation of a dockyard with adjoining arsenal, but the first major development was the construction of the *Molo Nuovo* (II, D-E-F1), or New Pier, and the establishment of the 'free port'. The Savoy authorities ordered further work in the mid-19th century. But it was the Genoese Duke of Galliera, Raffaele De Ferrari, who put up the money needed to reorganize the complex, to a design by Adolfo Parodi (1875-82): various wharves were built between the old and new piers and protected by the *Molo Duca di Galliera* (III, C3), a 1,500-m outer pier. The subsequent stages in the port's development are best appreciated from one of the boat tours (*information: tel. 010265712*) that leave from Ponte Spinola (II, C3) and Calata degli Zingari (II, B1). Near to the International Trade Fair (see p. 93) is the mouth of the port, defended by an *outer breakwater* (III, B-C1-2) built between the 1920s and 1950s: this barrier, which incorporates part of the Duca di Galliera pier, is nearly 5,000 meters long. Beyond the *Aldo Moro Overpass* (III, B-C2-3-4), the panoramic *Corso Saffi* (II, E-F4-5-6) and *Corso Quadrio* (II, D-E3) flank the first stretch of the port, followed by areas reserved for pleasure craft and the large *ship repair yards* overlooking the **Bacino delle Grazie** (II, D-E1-2): among which are the *control tower*, similar in shape and height (50 m) to those found in airports. Beyond the Old Port and the Dockyard, begins the area used for passenger transport: cruise liners berth at the *Mille* (II, B-C1) and *Andrea Doria* bridges (II, B-C1); passenger ferries are accessed from the *Colombo* and *Assereto* bridges. Behind these bridges the skyline is dominated by the modern skyscrapers of the *San Benigno District*, built in the last two decades of the 20th century: the unmistakable *Matitone* (literally 'big pencil'), designed by a New York architecture firm, took its inspiration from the design of the bell-tower for the church of San Donato (see p. 55). More characteristic of the port scenario, meanwhile, are the large pale blue cranes of the container terminal at *Calata Sanità*, the quay built in 1988 onto the northern end of the New Pier, near the lighthouse (see p. 100).

Etiopia, Eritrea, Somalia, Libia; Massaua, Mogadiscio, Tripoli, Bengasi: names of the bridges and quays harking back to Italy's colonial past in Africa were used for the **Bacino di Sampierdarena** (III, B-C1-2), which

since its construction in 1926 has been dedicated to commercial shipping, as the imposing warehouses and goods handling equipment suggest.

The Cristoforo Colombo International Airport stands on reclaimed land (IV, E1-2) to the west of the port, and the view of Genoa from the plane is quite spectacular. Opposite the airport, protected by an outer breakwater built after the last war, are the large infrastructures of the **Petrol Port** of Multedo (IV, E1-2): a high-tech complex that has, regrettably, devastated the urban and natural environment. Technology is also very much in evidence at the **Voltri Container Terminal** (IV, E1, off map), the most modern and best equipped in the whole Mediterranean. This huge installation, defended by another 2,320-m breakwater, spreads over more than 1,000,000 m^2.

The Bacino delle Grazie with the control tower (above) and a shipyard

3.2 The New Walls and the outlying fortresses
Drive around Genoa's fortifications, approx. 17 km *(see plan pp. 90-91)*

The City Wall Park, the largest green space in the Genoese municipality (see box p. 88), comprises 876 hectares of beautiful woods and meadows punctuated by the imposing remains of the walls built along the ridge around the city and now open to visitors (*information, tel. 010565966*). The proposed tour really needs to be undertaken by car, since only certain stretches are served by public transport.

Mura Nuove. When these walls, the last in Genoa's history, were built, during the 'Siglo de oro', they were something of a status symbol, much admired by foreign courts, and a regular feature of pictorial representations of the city. They stretched for nearly 13 km (12,630 m to be precise) and described an almost equilateral triangle, coming to a point at Forte Sperone (see below). The building work, which took seven years (1626-33), was overseen by Ansaldo de Mari, father Vincenzo Maculano da Fiorenzuola and Giovanni Baliani, who were joined in 1630 by Bartolomeo Bianco.

The *enceinte* had to be modified after the Austrian sieges of 1746-47 and 1800, when they were found to provide inadequate protection against modern artillery fire. Clearly, fortified outposts were needed as reinforcements, and between 1818 and 1840 the Royal Sardinian Engineer Corps built the forts along the walls and in the surrounding hills using the Piedmontese construction technique. From the second half of the 19th century most of the stretches of the walls nearest to the sea were demolished as the city pushed its boundaries further and further outward along the coast.

Piazza Manin (see p. 81) is the starting point for the **Wall Road***, a scenic drive along the surviving inland stretch of the fortifications, some parts of which still have their original names. The *Mura di San Bartolomeo* (II, A-B6) are watched over by *Castle Mackenzie*, a brilliantly daring combination of medieval towers and turrets, Renaissance architectural features and Art Nouveau elements, by

The Genoese Walls in a 1684 print. Sea and Seafaring Pavilion, Genoa

Gino Coppedè (1896-1906). At the next turning a one-way street obliges motorists to leave the walls temporarily and continue along *Via Carso* (II, A-B5-6), climbing to the *Belvedere del Righi* (elev. 302 m; III, A4), which commands a spectacular view over the *City Wall Park**, the Bisagno valley and the eastern fortresses (see below); the panoramic terraces at the funicular station that connects with Largo della Zecca in the city below afford views of the port.

Construction of the *eastern forts*, designed by a group of architects under Jacques de Sicre, began in 1747. The first forts were *Quezzi, Richelieu* (named after the French officer who led the defense of the city during the 1746-47 siege), *Santa Tecla, San Martino* and *San Giuliano* forts (the last two not visible from the Righi belvedere); in the 19th century the *Quezzi Tower* (III, A5) and *Fort Ratti* (IV, D5) were added between Fort Quezzi and Fort Richelieu.

3.2 The New Walls and the Outer Forts

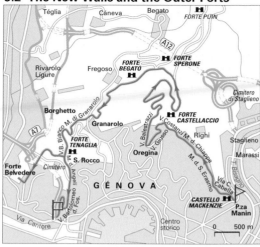

of summer theatrical performances and other cultural events.

It is still possible to walk along the communication trench that connected Fort Sperone with the **inner forts**, reached by getting off at Trensasco or Campi station on the Genova-Casella

Forte Castellaccio (elev. 507 m; IV, D4). This fort, a Guelph bastion mentioned as early as the 13th century and now a popular night spot, was rebuilt by Andrea Doria (1530) as a barracks and gunpowder store. Three hundred years later ramparts were built (1830-36) around the *Specola Tower* (1817-20), in which convicted criminals used to be hanged; this three-story building now houses a meteorological observatory.

The Forte Diamante, the furthest inland and highest of Genoa's outlying fortresses

Forte Sperone (elev. 512 m). This fortress, which pre-dates the New Walls was also the keep of the 17th-century *enceinte*, reached from *Via del Peralto* (III, A3, off map). The earliest records of the fortress, situated high up at the top of Mt. Peralto and altered in the late 1700s, date back to the 16th century. Its present appearance is the result of remodeling work (1826-27) by the Royal Engineers of the Savoy Household, which transformed the complex into a powerful citadel, now the setting for a season

railway (see pp. 105-106). Napoleon's engineers began the enlargement of the Pani redoubt, originally a supply post, which when completed in 1828 became **Fort Puin** (elev. 507 m; IV, D4). This well-preserved fortress, dominated by a quadrangular tower, is one of the main landmarks of the City Wall Park. A military road leads to *Fort Fratello Minore* (elev. 620 m; IV, C-D4), literally the 'younger brother' and the only survivor of the so-called 'Two Brothers', the dual front-line position during the siege of 1800. Italian poet Ugo Foscolo took part and was wounded in the defense of the stronghold,

Green spaces within easy reach of the office are quite a rarity these days, but for the Genoese, the City Wall Park is just a ten-minute drive out of the center of town. Many go there to find relief from the oppressive summer heat, or to make the most of the crisp sunny days that are so frequent in the Genoa winter. This extremely important natural environment boasts over 900 species of registered plants, and provides a habitat for foxes, squirrels, dormice, badgers, hoopoes and kestrels, as well as being of great historical value, because of the remains of the fortifications built here between the 17th and 19th centuries. The better-preserved parts are often used as the venue for cultural and recreational events: Forte Castellaccio, for example, contains two night spots, and a theater festival is staged in summer at Forte Sperone, as a part of a busy calendar of cultural events and exhibitions. The park also performs an educational function: until the new headquarters in Forte Begato are ready the Casetta Rossa in Via del Peralto is temporarily being used to house Genoa's Municipal Environment Department (*tel. 010561401*). Here, information is available on hiking

restructured in 1816-32 and now in a poor state of repair since being abandoned. *Fort Diamante* (IV, C4) is the furthest inland and the highest of all (elev. 672 m). This major stronghold, built in 1758, has survived virtually intact: its polygonal layout reinforced with curtain walls between salient corners is an excellent example of a typical 18th-century redoubt.

Forte Begato (elev. 472 m). This ponderous rectangular fortress with buttressed corners built by the Savoy army (1815-36) offers spectacular views over the center of Genoa and the Polcevera Valley. It is now being converted into offices for the City Wall Park and the new Visitors' Center

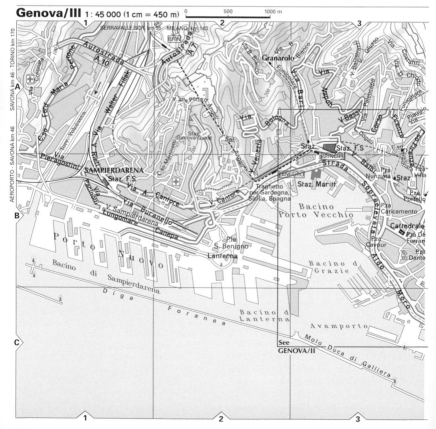

Genova/III 1 : 45 000 (1 cm = 450 m)

and walking tours inside the park area, which in the first weekend in April is the venue for the *MTB Genoa Cup*, the mountain bike challenge that attracts the best Italian practitioners of the sport. Sport of a non-competitive kind is also on offer here in the form of two keep-fit paths.

The MTB Genoa Cup Challenge

(currently housed in the Casetta Rossa in Via del Peralto) providing visitors with information on the area and its wildlife.

Beyond the fortress, the road descends steeply (excellent views) to *Portello di Granarolo*, beyond which it changes its name to *Mura di Granarolo* and, further on to *Via Bartolomeo Bianco* (III, A2-3), which moves away from the walls themselves.

Forte Tenaglia (elev. 216 m). This now abandoned fortress still shows clear signs of the damage the 'promontory entrenchment', a large horn-shaped construction facing the Polcevera valley, suffered during World War II. The stronghold, mentioned as early as the 16th century, was rebuilt between 1833 and 1836, when it acquired the shape that gave it its name (*tenaglia* = pincer).

From *Corso Martinetti* (III, A-B1-2), a *creuza* leads up to the last two fortresses outside the walls, both of which were built in the 19th century: *Fort Belvedere* (elev. 114 m), now a sports center, and *Fort Crocetta* (elev. 157 m).

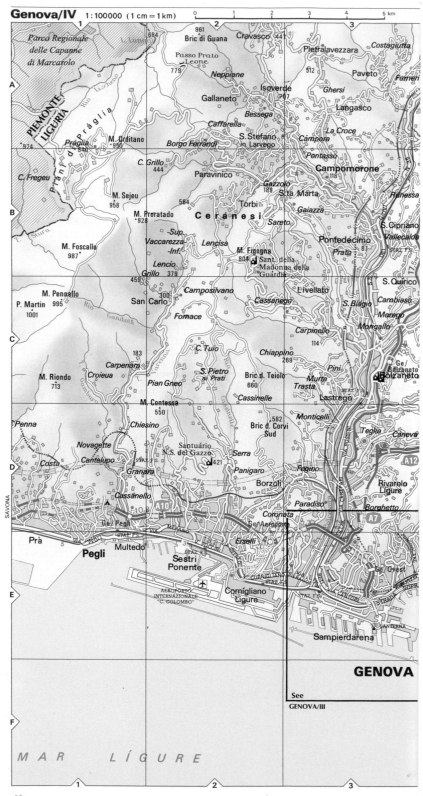

0   1   2   3   4   5 km

Parco Regionale
delle Capanne
di Marcarolo

L'Anna
684
961
Bric di Guana
Cravasco 441
Costagiutta

Passo Prato
Leone
779
Pietralavezzara
Paveto
Furnen

PIEMONTE

LIGURIA

Neppiane
512

Isoverde
207
Ghersi

Gallaneto
Langasco

Rio Razzalo

Bessega

Caffarella
La Croce

•974

Práglia
M. Orditano
•950

Práglia
840

Borgo Ferrandi
S. Stefano
in Larvego
Cámpora
Pontasso
Campomorone

C. Fregeu

Pian di Práglia

C. Grillo
444
Paravinico
Gazzolo
189
S.ta Marta
118
Rithessa

M. Sejeu
958
564
Torbi
Cerénesi
Gaiazza

M. Proratado
•928
Sareto
S. Cipriano
Vallecalde

Stura

-Sup.
Vaccarezza
-Inf.
Lencisa
Pontedécimo
Prata
87
STAZ.F.S.

M. Foscallo
987
Lencio
Grillo 379
M. Figogna
804
Sant. della
Madonna della
Guárdia

459
S. Quirico

M. Pennello
Rio Gandolfi
San Carlo
300
Camposilvano
Livellato
S. Biagio
Cambiaso

P. Martin
1001
995
Fornace
Cassanego
Carpinello
114
Morego
Mongallo

Rio Gambaro

183
C. Tuio
Chiappino
269
Pini
Ge/
Palazzeto
Bolzaneto

Carpenara
Croieua
S. Pietro
ai Prati
Bric d. Teiolo
660
Murta
Trasta
STAZ.F.S.

M. Riondo
713
Pian Gneo
Cassinelle
Lastrego

M. Contessa
550
•582
Monticelli
Teglia
Caneva

Penna
Chiesino
Bric d. Corvi
Sud

Novagette
Santuário
N.S. del Gazzo
421
Serra
Fegino
A12

Costa
Cantalupo
STAZ.F.S.
Granara
Panigaro
Borzoli
Paradiso
Rivarolo
Ligure
Borghetto

Cassánello
A10
Coronata
A7

SAVONA
Ge/ Pegli
STAZ. F.S.
VIA MERANO
Ge/ Aeroporto
Ge/ Ovest
STRADA SOPR.

Prà
Pegli
Multedo
Erselli
Cornigliano
STAZ.F.S.

Sestri
Ponente
Cornigliano
Ligure
Sampierdarena

AEROPORTO
INTERNAZIONALE
"C. COLOMBO"

GENOVA

See

GENOVA/III

MAR LÍGURE

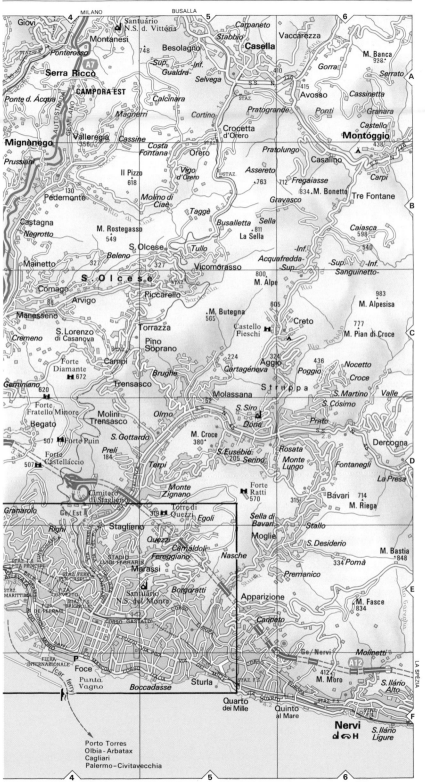

4 Greater Genoa and the metropolitan district

Profile

It is virtually impossible, along the coast at least, to detect a physical or historical dividing line that distinguishes between the districts annexed in 1926 to the city – thereafter known as 'Greater Genoa' – and those that remained outside the official city limits in the *Genovesato*, or province of Genoa. The transition is made all the more seamless by the fact that some of the more outlying areas seem to have closer ties with the city than others that actually fall within the metropolitan area. Arguably the most dynamic part of the province today is the western part, where industrial recession has necessitated a gradual transformation of the local economy. Hence the arrival, alongside the modern port structures described in the previous chapter, of large out-of-town shopping malls, unheard of in the Genoa area

Genoa: the picturesque fishing village of Boccadasse, with its colorfully-painted houses

before the 1990s. Also, the western extremities, though marred and in some cases totally disfigured by industrial activities and uncontrolled speculative property development, do conceal some quite unexpectedly beautiful (and recently upgraded) areas with great tourist appeal, some unknown even to the locals. To the east, meanwhile, Nervi is now not just a winter and summer seaside resort but also a focal point for artistic and cultural activities, in summer but also at other times of the year.

Val Polcevera, the valley which since ancient times has been the main route from the coast to the Po Valley, has suffered a rather similar fate to the western coast. In recent times it has seen some quite inexplicable building work for a city with such a dwindling population. Val Bisagno, on the other hand, displays closer links with the city center, not least of all because of the concentration there of some major public infrastructures (the cemetery, the central market, the football stadium and the prisons). This valley, too, saw major redevelopment work in the 1990s that put disused areas to new uses, and tried to solve Genoa's chronic traffic problem.

Small new industrial estates have sprung up in the Genoa hills, but their discreet presence has not (thanks partly to the now well-established awareness of the need for environmental protection) jeopardized the natural beauty of an area that has attracted vacationers for nearly a century.

Nowadays the area is particularly popular with hiking enthusiasts and lovers of other outdoor pursuits (trekking, mountain biking, canyoning etc.).

4.1 La Foce, Albaro and the coast to Nervi
Tour of the eastern city districts, by car and public transport, approx. 11 km
(see maps pp. 94-95 and 96-97)

The most convenient way of visiting the area east of the city is by bus, since parking is relatively easy at Piazza della Vittoria (see p. 80), where this tour begins, but much more difficult in the places on the way. The quickest way of getting to La Foce is by bus no. 20, which leaves from the terminus in Via Casaregis (II, F6). From here continue on foot along Corso Italia – with a detour to the Albaro district – or take bus no. 31 to Quarto dei Mille; bus no. 15 goes all the way to Nervi.

Foce (III, C4). In the 19th century this was an area of little houses and gardens, populated by fishermen and washerwomen, a long-gone world that survives only in prints and paintings. Today La Foce (literally 'the estuary', the mouth of the Bisagno river) has a quite different face. Development began toward the end of the 19th century, with the construction of the first residential area immediately to the south of the new railroad, and culminated in the Fascist period with the ambitious scheme that covered the river over. Piazza Rossetti (III, C4) is a large rectangular space facing the sea planned by Luigi Carlo Daneri and built between 1936 and 1955 (with an interruption to the work during World War II). The early post-war years saw the construction of the *church of San Pietro della Foce*, high up over the first part of Corso Italia (see below).

Fiera Internazionale (III, C4). The most important event in the Genoa trade fair calendar is the *Salone Nautico* (International Boat Show), held in October, hence the choice of this area by the sea when this exhibition site was created between 1959 and 1962, and the inclusion in the complex of a mooring basin for the display of pleasure boats. The four pavilions, built on land reclaimed from the sea, include the circular *Palazzo dello Sport,*

The Salone Nautico and Euroflora: two major international events at the Genoa trade fair

the venue for numerous musical and sports events. This building also houses the other major Genoese show, *Euroflora*, held every five years (next edition: 2001), during which it is transformed into a huge, highly functional display center.

Corso Italia* (III, C4-5). The Genoese have a strange relationship with their seafront. But this much-criticized promenade, so often likened to the Promenade des Anglais in Nice (a comparison that sits rather uneasily), is nevertheless always crowded with people on hot summer evenings and crisp winter's days. Corso Italia totally transformed the coastline when it was built between the two world wars. It differs from its French counterpart in its more pronounced residential character: the landward side of the avenue is lined with elegant private residences surrounded by gardens. One noteworthy example is the neo-Gothic Villa Canali, another unashamedly Eclectic creation by Gino Coppedè (1924-25). The seaward side is largely given over to bathing establishments, most of which boast a long, almost historical tradition, and other modern structures equipped for today's popular sports (squash, five-a-side football etc.).

Among the few features of the ancient waterfront that survive is the *abbey of San Giuliano* (III, C5), a medieval complex, largely rebuilt in the 15th century, badly damaged in the last war and now in a pretty sad state of repair after over half a century of neglect, although some repair work was done for the 1992 Columbus celebrations: note in particular the restored facade facing Corso Italia, with a late 16th-century *portal* in black stone.

The idea that a quiet little fishing village can still survive in the heart of a modern city is part of the attraction of **Boccadasse** (III, C5-6): it is always a treat to come here and eat an ice cream or a Genoese

4.1 From Foce to Albaro and Quarto dei Mille

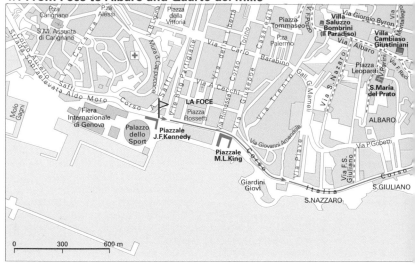

focaccia, or simply while away the time in the picturesque harbor with its colorfully-painted houses.

From Boccadasse, *Via Scalinata* leads to **Capo di Santa Chiara**, a spectacular panoramic point dominated by *Castelletto Türcke*, yet another creation by Gino Coppedè (1903). Another way of getting here is from *Via Caprera* (III, C6) and down Via di Capo di Santa Chiara. The *Augustinian monastery*, at no. 16 (*open on request, tel. 0103993315*) has a remarkable altarpiece (*Martyrdom of St. Sebastian**) by il Bergamasco.

A. Magnasco, Supper at Emmaus. San Francesco d'Albaro, Genoa

Villa Saluzzo Bombrini 'il Paradiso'* (III, B-C5; at no. 28 Via Francesco Pozzo). This is generally regarded as the villa that appears in the background of Alessandro Magnasco's *Entertainment in a Garden at Albaro*, which hangs in the Palazzo Bianco art gallery (see p. 65). It is quite plausible that the artist did indeed choose as the model for his famous painting the grounds of this splendid late 16th-century villa (*closed to the public*), setting up his easel in the western loggia, which affords a panoramic view over the Bisagno Valley. The porticoed wings are the most interesting architectural feature of this villa, built by Andrea Vannone. The cycles of

paintings inside are by Andrea Ansaldo, Bernardo Castello and Lazzaro Tavarone.

Via Albaro (III, C5). As early as the 14th century, Genoese high society came to spend their vacation on the hillier ground here that slopes gently down to the sea. That air of historical elegance still survives in this main street of today's modern district, which became part of the metropolitan district of Genoa in 1876. The leafy suburb, known also for its private clinics and modern sports complexes, has numerous Mannerist and Baroque villas, many of them set in their own grounds, and entered from the narrow back streets created out of the *creuze*. Via S. Nazaro, for example, has two noteworthy aristocratic residences: *Villa Raggi* (at no. 19), a 17th-century reconstruction of a building erected two centuries earlier, and *Villa Brignole Sale* (no. 20), also 17th century. *Villa Carrega Cataldi*, at no. 11 Via Albaro also dates back to the 17th century, while *Villa Saluzzo Mongiardino* (no. 1), where George Gordon Byron stayed in 1823, is 18th century. Also in Via Albaro stands the *church of San Francesco d'Albaro* (III, C5),

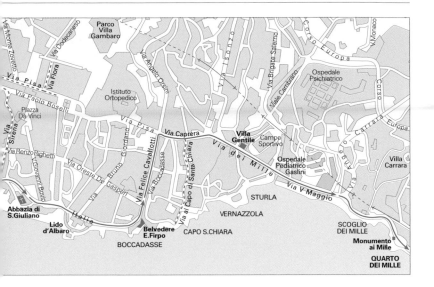

originally built in the 14th century but redesigned between the 17th and 19th centuries; the adjoining convent (*visits on request, tel. 0103628624*) houses a splendid **Supper at Emmaus*** by Alessandro Magnasco.

The tree-filled square behind the convent, *Piazza Leopardi* (III, C5), was until the 19th century a *prato pubblico*, or public green, hence the name of the *church of Santa Maria del Prato*ᐱ (III, C5), which dates back to 1172. After a long period of neglect, the church was redesigned in the Baroque style in 1730, with the addition of features that were removed during restoration work in 1951, which restored the original Romanesque appearance.

Villa Cambiaso Giustiniani** (III, C5). This villa on the corner between Via Albaro and Via Montallegro, which now houses the University's Engineering Faculty, was the first work in Genoa by Galeazzo Alessi: a grand residence, commissioned by Luca Giustiniani (work began in 1548) that became a paradigm of architectural culture in the city. This solid, square building stands in a dominant position inside a large park (partly open to the public). It has an airy ground-floor loggia beneath the facade; there is another loggia on the piano nobile at the rear of the building. The lunettes of the barrel-vaulting are the only part of the building with pictorial decoration: two frescoes by Giovanni Battista Castello (*Day*) and Luca Cambiaso (*Night*). The architectural ornamentation is richer: the sober classicism of the ground floor gives way on the level above to a style more obviously inspired by Roman Mannerism.

The names **Quarto dei Mille** and **Quinto al Mare** indicate the distance in Roman miles (four and five respectively) from Piazza S. Giorgio (see p. 58). But the word 'Mille' in the first refers not to miles but to the 'Thousand' soldiers that set sail from here with Giuseppe Garibaldi on his historic expedition to Sicily in 1860, an exploit celebrated by a *Monument* (III, C6) by Eugenio Baroni (1915). Today the rocky shore is a succession of bathing establishments, which continue almost without interruption all the way to Nervi.

Nervi*

Although the Art Nouveau hotels have now been converted into serviced apartments, the elegant old-world seaside resort atmosphere remains: it is easy to forget how near we are here to the city center – even the

The monument to the Thousand at Quarto

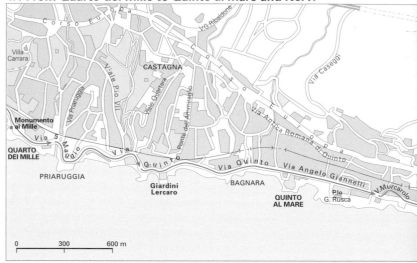

micro-climate is much milder than in Genoa proper. Links with the city are provided by the panoramic but tortuous Via Aurelia, or the chaotic *Corso Europa* (III, B-C5-6), opened up after the war below the hills further inland.

Restoration work in 1959 partly recovered the original appearance of the **church of San Siro** (A1), built in the first half of the 12th century and rebuilt in the 1600s. The medieval church contained a painting (*Saint Siro Enthroned between St. Andrew and St. Bartholomew*) attributed to Pier Francesco Sacchi, now kept in the rectory (*open on request, tel. 010321502*).

Anita Garibaldi Promenade** (A1-2-3). With its pink and yellow houses, beached boats, and medieval bridge over the mouth of the river, Nervi harbor is a quaint old corner of Liguria protected by an outer breakwater and the starting-point for the celebrated 'seafront promenade', which winds its way along the spectacular jagged rocks and up and down the natural steps. It is atmospheric both in winter, when the waves pound against the rocks, and in summer when the sea is unexpectedly crystal clear and the walk is brought to life by the popular bathing establishments, ice-cream parlors, bars and cafés. At one point along the walk, which offers views down to the hills of Portofino, the historic *Gropallo Tower* (A2), built in the 16th century as a watchtower to defend against attacks from Saracen pirates.

The Nervi Parks* (A2-3; *open: 8am-7.30pm, January, October 8am-5.30pm, February 8am-6pm, March, September 8am-6.30pm,*

The Anita Garibaldi Promenade at Nervi, one of the most scenic in Italy

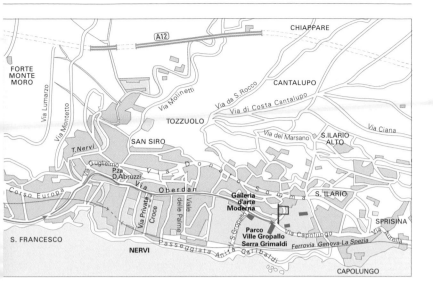

April 8am-7pm, November-December 8am-5pm). The grounds of the Gropallo, Serra and Grimaldi villas have been united to form a single 9-ha park, laid out in the English garden style with typical Mediterranean and exotic plants (palms, monkey puzzles and camphor), a delightful place made all the more charming by the presence of squirrels. It is no less rich culturally: *Villa Gropallo*, at no. 1 *Via Capolungo* (A2-3), houses the municipal library, the 17th-century Villa Serra houses the *Modern Art Gallery* (*nearing completion; for information, tel. 010282641*), with a valuable collection of 19th- and 20th-century Ligurian paintings and works by artists such as Arturo Martini and Felice Casorati. Art from the same period can also be seen in the *Frugone Collection*, exhibited in Villa Grimaldi Fassio (*open: 9am-7pm, Sun 9am-1pm; closed Mon*);

the grounds of this 18th-century residence, restored in 1960, have a magnificent *rose garden*, with 800 types of rose in flower from May to November; concerts, ballet perfomances and film seasons are held here in summer.

The **Museo Giannettino Luxoro** (A3), housed in an early 20th-century aristocratic residence in grounds, has a large applied art collection with holy-water stoups, majolica tiles and Christmas crèche statuettes. The museum (*nearing completion; for information, tel. 010322673*) also has an interesting art collection, including three paintings (*The Miserly Painter, The Ecstasy of St. Bruno*, and *St. Bruno in Meditation*) by Alessandro Magnasco.

There are excellent views from *Sant'Ilario Alto* (A3), a small town whose exceptionally mild climate has turned it into one of the most exclusive parts of eastern Genoa.

Nervi 1:18000 (1 cm = 180 m)

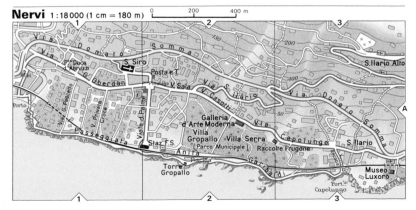

4.2 The Via Aurelia from Nervi to Recco and Mt. Fasce
Drive through the area to the east of Genoa, approx. 42 km

This stretch of the riviera from Nervi to the Portofino promontory is a riot of maritime pinasters, olive groves and bougainvillea. The particularly mild climate has made it a popular tourist area, despite the rather unfavorable nature of the coastline, with a prevalence of rocks and hardly any sandy beaches, although the difficult terrain has also saved the area from the kind of speculative building work that has defaced other parts of the coast. The atmosphere – and the weather – is quite different along the road away from the Via Aurelia inland from Recco toward Uscio. Here, a modern panoramic road heads back to Genoa through the suburbs (and former villages) of Apparizione and Borgoratti, and back to Corso Europa.

Bogliasco
In administrative terms this little Riviera town (elev. 25 m, pop. 4,579), belongs to the Genoa conurbation (Nervi-Sant'Ilario). It has the appearance of an elegant residential suburb, with an ancient center near the beach (the so-called Roman bridge is in fact medieval) and a typical fishing village character. It is watched over to the west by the *castello*, not really a castle but a defense tower built by the ancient Republic of Genoa. A little further on, a black-and-

Sori and the belltower of its church

white cobbled terrace built over a rock forms the scenic parvis of the *church of the Nativity*. Built by Giovanni Antonio Ricca the Younger (1731-37), it is an elliptical building enclosing a central octagonal space punctuated with pilaster strips.

Pieve Ligure
No one seems to mind the total lack of a beach here, although sunseekers are hard put to find a comfortable spot for sunbathing on the rocks. The town (elev. 70 m, pop. 2,618) is divided into two quite distinct parts. The modern town by the sea is now part of Bogliasco; the ancient settlement of Pieve Alta below Mt. Santa Croce is surrounded by terraced olive groves and dry stone walls. The 17th century *parish church of San Michele* dominates the main square, from which Via S. Bernardo leads to the *oratory of St. Anthony Abbot*, which has a remarkable collection of processional *crucifixes*, including one dating back to 1713 by Anton Maria Maragliano.

Sori
Another fishing community (elev. 14 m, pop. 4,450) with typical pastel-colored houses overlooking the beach. Behind them, in front of the Aurelia viaduct, stands the belltower of the elliptical *church of Santa Margherita*, with an interesting curvilinear facade. The church was designed by Giovanni Antonio Ricca the Elder (1711-14).

The Romanesque *church of Sant'Apollinare* (14th cent.), situated on a hill (elev. 260 m) just east of the town, is a favorite beauty spot for Sunday trippers, who come to enjoy the wonderful views here.

Recco
This little town (elev. 5 m, pop. 10,419) was razed to the ground in World War II during the 1943-44 air-raid attacks, intended to destroy the railway bridge but which hit Recco itself. The town was rebuilt after the war with a modern layout, the only points of artistic interest being the many 17th-century paintings now kept in the post-war *church of Ss. Giovanni Battista e Giovanni Bono*. Recco's principal attraction today, arguably, are its gastronomic delights: beginning with its '*fugassa*', a cheese focaccia specialty that has even made a name for itself abroad (see box).

4.2 From Nervi to Recco and to Genoa

A winding road (SS 333) heads inland from Recco to Avegno (elev. 92 m, pop. 2,107), best known for its well-established bell-making tradition. Further on, toward Uscio, lies Terrile (elev. 270 m), whose economy is based on the manufacture and worldwide export of tower clocks.

Uscio

This town (elev. 361 m, pop. 2,276) is perhaps best known for the *Arnaldi Health Colony*, established here during the health culture in vogue in the early 20th century. Less famous is Longobard past of the town, which later became a benefice of the Ambrosian church. This explains why the Romanesque *church of Sant'Ambrogio* (11th-12th cent.) is dedicated to the patron saint of Milan. There are plenty of reminders of Lombard building techniques both on the facade and inside, where the side aisles are separated from the nave by slate columns. The belfry and spire are 18th-century additions.

Colle Caprile (elev. 470 m), the hill connecting Uscio with the upper Fontanabuona Valley, lies on what was once a much-used transhumance route, as the name (*capra* = goat) suggests.

From Uscio to Genoa

The provincial road that heads back to the Ligurian capital through verdant countryside is bordered on one side by a series of small valleys that slope steeply down to the sea and on the other by the Apennine mountains, cut through, beyond Mt. Becco (elev. 894 m) by the *Valle del Lentro*, whose river is a tributary of the Bisagno. The road skirts Mt. Bastia (elev. 848 m), with the *Prati di Fascia* lookout offering an excellent view that takes in the entire eastern fortifications (see pp. 87-89). **Mt. Fasce** (elev. 834 m) is today marked by a forest of television relay antennae near the peak, a frequent sight in the Genoa area. The city itself can be admired in its entirety against the backdrop of the Maritime Alps from the various observation points along the descent toward the little village of Apparizione, now part of the conurbation.

The origin of the *'fugassa al formaggio'*

Flour, olive oil, salt, water and fresh, soft *prescinsêua* cheese are the ingredients that go to make Recco's famous cheese focaccia, the *pièce de résistance* of a town that boasts one of Liguria's richest culinary traditions. Tradition has it that this recipe dates back to the 16th or 17th century, when the town was constantly plagued by marauding Saracen pirates. Alerted to the danger by warning shots from the local garrison, the women, children and elderly fled to the hills, taking with them what flour, salt and oil they could find. The ingredients were kneaded together using water from the river, and the salt and oil could be traded with shepherds for cheese, slices of which were placed over a thin layer of dough, covered with another layer and given a sprinkling of salt and oil. Before baking, a few holes were made in the surface to allow the steam produced by the dough and the cheese to escape. The *fugassa* was then placed on a slate slab that had been heated on hot coals: in a few minutes the tasty savory pie was ready. Little could the poor folk have imagined as they mixed together their few simple ingredients that this emergency recipe would go onto become a regional specialty, one that is now famous way beyond Italy's borders.

4.3 Western Genoa, the Leira and Stura Valleys and the coast to Arenzano

A drive through the area to the west and north-west of Genoa, 27 km to Cogoleto and a further 37 km from Voltri to Tiglieto *(see map p. 103)*

The coastal strip to the west of Genoa is often unfairly described as little more than one big industrial estate. This is an oversimplification that ignores much of the history and culture of the area, as this tour, which begins at the Maritime Station (see p. 44), sets out to demonstrate. Many of the places along the way can be comfortably reached from the A10 expressway, exiting at Sestri Ponente (the airport), Pegli and at Voltri, which marks the end of the metropolitan area. The SS 456 road leads up into the Leira and Stura Valleys, while Via Aurelia (SS 1) continues along the coast to Arenzano and Cogoleto, and the border with the province of Savona.

Villa Rosazza. The Aldo Moro highway overpass offers the best view over the 'Scoglietto' residence, now a school. Built around 1565 for Ambrogio Di Negro, it passed in the 1700s into the hands of the Durazzo family, who in 1787 commissioned Andrea Tagliafichi to redesign the building. His alterations are particularly evident on the rusticated exterior, with frames and white friezes, a tympanum over the central section and statues in the cornice. At the same time the grounds were extended, with the creation – also by Tagliafichi – of an English garden around the original terraced complex with nymphaea: the part nearest the sea was destroyed by the arrival of the railroad (1854) and other urban expansion.

The 'Lanterna', symbol of Genoa

Lanterna* (III, B2). As the emblem of Genoa's independence, the old lighthouse is now the symbol of the city. The tower *(visits by request, tel. 0102465346)* was built in 1543 over the ruins of the Briglia fortress, the headquarters of the French garrison. The 117-m tower, which now shares its place on the skyline with the skyscrapers of the San Benigno district, is divided into two sections each one topped by arched corbelling; the flashing *light* at the top (*closed to the public*), has a range of 33 miles.

Sampierdarena

Not even Albaro (see p. 94) could boast such a concentration of suburban villas, most of which have now been swallowed up by the urban sprawl (III, B1-2). The three most noteworthy, all in *Via Daste*, are **Villa Grimaldi** 'Fortezza' (entrance at no. 14 Via Palazzo della Fortezza), **Villa Imperiale Scassi** 'Bellezza' (no. 3) and **Villa Sauli** 'Semplicità' (no. 8). The first two, built in the 1560s and now occupied by a school, are in the Alessi style. Villa Imperiale Scassi has frescoes by Giovanni Carlone (*Samson Fights the Lion*) and Bernardo Castello (*Scenes from the Life of David*, *Jerusalem Delivered*). Villa Sauli, by Bernardino Cantone (1558-63), is more original in style, but has suffered as a result of being divided up into apartments. Little remains of the once splendid park, which fell victim to urban and industrial growth. One exception is the now public garden of Villa Imperiale Scassi, above the traffic-clogged *Via Cantore* (III, B1-2), and, also in Via Daste, that of the 16th-century *Villa Doria* (no. 7), annexed to the complex of the Madri Franzoniane.

From Via Daste turn left into *Via Giovanetti*, in which stands the medieval *church of Santa Maria della Cella* (1206-13). Bombing in 1944 brought to light remains of the little *chapel* (probably 8th century) that is the 'cell' of the name: the ashes of St. Augustine were reputedly brought here in 725. The church underwent various alterations over the centuries, including the addition of a neoclassical facade in 1850, but the basilica layout (nave and side aisles) remains; the *Doria family tombs* on the walls of the presbytery, by Taddeo Carlone and his workshop (16th-17th cent.), are a reminder of its noble role as the private chapel of the Doria family until 1797. Interesting artworks include a *St. Bernard* by il Grechetto (4th altar on the right) and the *Madonna* and Child with St. Giovannino (1st altar on the left) by Luca Cambiaso (1562-65).

Via Ghiglione leads to *Piazza Gustavo Modena*, dominated by the Neoclassical *theater* of the same name (1833), restored and reopened in 1997. Continuing toward the sea, we come to *Villa Centurione 'del Monastero'* (late 16th cent.), so called because it was built over the ruins of a 13th-century Benedictine abbey. The decorations inside the building (also used as a school) are by Bernardo Castello.

Corniglianο Ligure (IV, E2). The rather disconcerting appearance of this suburban area today makes it difficult to imagine that this was once a favorite summer retreat for the aristocracy. Reminders of these quieter days remain in *Via Muratori* (first turn-off to the left in Via Ansaldo after the Polcevera bridge), in which stands **Villa Durazzo Bombrini**, built in 1752-73 by Pierre Paul de Cotte, also the designer of the *staircase** on the right of the vestibule, which was copied by Andrea Tagliafichi for Palazzo Durazzo Pallavicini in Via Balbi (see pp. 67-68). The villa is now used as offices.

From Piazza Massena, *Via Coronata* (III, A1) leads up to the hill of the same name toward the *oratory of the Assunta* (1729), which is richly decorated inside with gilt stuccowork and paintings, and the 15th-century *sanctuary of the Coronata*, rebuilt after World War II.

Sestri Ponente (IV, E2). 20th-century industrial development – shipbuilding, and iron and steel – culminated in 1960 with the launch of the 'Leonardo da Vinci', at the time the pride of the Italian navy. Now the suburb is perhaps one of the most attractive of Genoa's westernmost quarters, with a large pedestrian area and an offering range of social, cultural and commercial amenities. In *Piazza Micone*

stands the *parish church of Santa Maria Assunta* (1620), which has (in the 3rd altar on the left) a *St. Charles Borromeo in Adoration of the Virgin** painted in 1617 by Morazzone.

There is a splendid **view** from the *sanctuary of the Madonna del Gazzo* (IV, D2), on top of Monte Gazzo (elev. 421 m). The chalk and rock quarries to the north and eastern sides of the hill have done irreparable environmental damage, but to preserve what natural beauty remains, the *Parco Urbano di Monte Gazzo* was created, spreading over approximately 231 ha.

Multedo (IV, E1). The installation here first of foundries and then of the Petrol Port without due respect for the urban and natural surroundings have not completely succeeded in destroying all vestiges of the past: arguably the most interesting historical site in Multedo is *Villa Lomellini Rostan* (*closed to the public*), near the highway tollbooth at Pegli. Built around the mid-16th century, it is one of the most successful examples of a residence designed before Alessi, with large side loggias and an interesting interior layout. The ceiling of the main salon is decorated with paintings (*Coriolanus and his Mother**) by Bernardo Castello (1583). Nothing remains, however, of the splendid garden created in 1784 by Andrea Tagliafichi, destroyed in the 1950s to make way for a sports center.

Returning eastward, the *Ancient Roman Road of Pegli* leads to the *oratory of Sts. Nazaire and Celsus* (1613), frescoed inside (*Scenes from the Life of Christ and the Titular Saints*) by Lazzaro Tavarone. The road flanking the oratory leads up to the 16th-century *parish church of Santa Maria di Monteoliveto*, which has largely retained its original form, the only exception being the facade, redesigned in 1840.

Pegli
Another once flourishing seaside resort, Pegli (IV, D-E1) was in the second half of the 19th century the meeting-place for Europe's high society, to whom the local pharmacy would offer restorative effervescent drinks made with sea water. But though we might imagine what it must have been like in those days to stroll along the fine panoramic seafront promenade, the scene is spoilt today

The launch of the 'Michelangelo' at the Ansaldo shipyard, Sestri Ponente

by the all too familiar backdrop of ugly postwar apartment blocks, part of the speculative building wave that mercifully spared the leafy grounds of the aristocratic villas.

Villa Durazzo Pallavicini Park* (*open: 9am-7pm, October-March 10am-5pm; closed Mon*). Best reached by train (Pegli rail station is

The Villa Durazzo Pallavicini Park, Pegli

right next to the entrance to the park), the 18th-century *Villa Pallavicini* is visited principally for its magnificent gardens, laid out in 1840-46 by Eclectic architect Michele Canzio. The 97,000-m² park is a theatrical experience, in which the visitor is taken into an esoteric world of make-believe punctuated by typical architectural features (ornamental temples and bridges, grottoes, triumphal arches, pagodas and Turkish kiosks) that were fundamental to the Romantic tradition. The villa houses the **Museo Civico di Archeologia Ligure** (*open: 9am-7pm, Fri, Sat and Sun 9am–1pm; closed Mon*). Exhibits range from the Paleolithic period to Roman times. Particularly noteworthy are two prehistoric *burial places*: the Tomb of the Young Prince of the White Arenas* (dating back some 20,000 years), with a rich collection of funeral offerings, and *the Tomb of the Child with Squirrel-Tail Cape*, possibly from the early Neolithic period (10,000 BC). The inscription on the *Statue-Stele of Lunigiana* (4th-5th millennium BC) found at Zignago, near La Spezia, is in Etruscan characters; and the *Tablet of Polcevera** (117 BC), found in the Bocchetta Pass, carries a ruling by the Roman Senate on the dispute over territorial boundaries between Genoa and the 'Vituri Langenses' tribe. Two rooms are dedicated to the collection of Prince Otto of Savoy, with numerous objects found in the necropolises of Cuma and Capua.

Villa Doria Centurione. This mansion, built in the first half of the 16th century for banker Adamo Centurione and extended in

1592 by Andrea Vannone, still houses the **Museo Navale** (*open: 9am-1pm, Fri and Sat 9am-7pm, closed Sun and Mon*), but the display space is much less than it once was and would certainly benefit from the proposed but for now vetoed idea of relocating the museum to the Sea and Seafaring Pavilion (see p. 48). Italian maritime history is illustrated by nautical instruments, maps, models of historical vessels, cannon, armory and paintings, most notably the *Portrait of Christopher Columbus** attributed to Ridolfo del Ghirlandaio and the *View of Genoa in 1481* by Cristoforo de' Grassi. However, as long as the museum remains in its current premises, it is still possible to admire the exquisitely decorated interior of the villa (also used as a school), with frescoes by Lazzaro Tavarone and Nicolosio Granello: the latter artist painted the *Jason before Pelias** on the ceiling of the salon, where there is also a model of a 15th-century sailing-ship. Behind the villa, watched over by a 16th-century *tower*, is a now somewhat neglected public *park* laid out in 1548 by Galeazzo Alessi.

Voltri

Genoa's westernmost suburb (IV, D1, off map) has had its sights firmly set on the future since the building of a container terminal placed the little town firmly on the European sea transport map. Voltri has indeed displayed a commercial vocation since the late Middle Ages, when it exploited its position at the junction with the road up to the Turchino Pass; it was also a busy manufacturing center in pre-industrial times.

Andrea Ansaldo and Orazio De Ferrari, who were themselves from Voltri, were among those who created the altarpieces kept in the *churches of Sant'Ambrogio* (1620, with dome and belltower from the following century) and *Ss. Nicolò ed Erasmo*: the nave of the latter church, built in 1652, is divided from the aisles by paired columns.

Villa Brignole Sale (*open: 8am-7.30pm; January, October 8am-5.30pm; February 8am-6pm; March, September 8am-6.30pm; April 8am-7pm; November-December 8am-5pm*). This villa is also known as Villa della Duchessa di Galliera as a tribute to Maria Brignole Sale, who made some changes to the villa built between the 17th and 18th centuries and remodeled again in 1780 (*closed to the public*). The duchess also designed the layout of the grounds, which include an Italian garden in front of the villa and an immense (25-ha) **park*** behind.

Pines, holm-oaks and elms create an almost mountain feel, and the park is dotted with country cottages, marble statues and a small castle, around which deer and Tibetan goats graze. The climb continues to the **sanctuary of Nostra Signora delle Grazie**, preceded by a shady square with views over the Cerusa Valley. First mentioned in 1205, when it was dedicated to St. Nicolò, it was rebuilt in neo-Gothic style for the duchess of Galliera, who was buried here in 1888.

The centuries-old paper-making industry in the **Leira Valley** (the earliest mills date back to the 1500s), developed thanks to the plentiful supply of water and excellent ventilation. The history, machinery and methods of the industry is told at the *Centro di Testimonianza ed Esposizione dell'Arte Cartaria della Valle del Leira*, the paper museum housed in the 18th-century *Piccardo Paper Mill* (*visits by request, tel. 010638103*) at *Acquasanta* (elev. 165 m), part of the municipality of **Mele** (elev. 125 m, pop. 2,656). The 'holy water' of the place name comes from the *sanctuary of Our Lady of Acquasanta*, built (1683-1710) on the site of a medieval church; and the *thermal baths*, whose sulfur-rich waters are used in treating skin disorders. The long climb to the **Turchino Pass** (elev. 532 m) leads into the Valle Stura, a valley covered in chestnut woods. The first village is **Masone** (elev. 403 m, pop. 4,192), served by a turn-off on the A26 motorway, followed by **Campo Ligure** (elev. 342

A filigree vase, Campo Ligure

m, pop. 3,222), well known in Italy and abroad for its filigree craft tradition, the story of which is told in the *Museo della Filigrana* (*open: 3.30-6pm; Sat and Sun 9.30am-noon, 3.30-6pm; closed Mon*). **Rossiglione** (elev. 297 m, pop. 3,208), the last village before the border with Piedmont, stands at the junction with the provincial road that winds its way up into the Upper Orba Valley to **Tiglieto** (elev. 500 m). This hamlet is best known for the *Badia di Tiglieto*, Italy's oldest Cistercian monastery (1120), which stands in a beautiful leafy setting at the end of a country lane just after the bridge over the Orba. Now partly converted into a private home, it has a well-preserved Gothic *chapterhouse*, with a vaulted ceiling.

Back down at the coast, the charming little village of **Crevari** (elev. 82 m), is perched high up over the Via Aurelia just after Voltri at the end of the metropolitan district of Genoa. The last official village falling within the municipal boundary, however, is **Vesima** (elev. 50 m), which has a big pebbly beach.

The next real seaside resort along the coast is **Arenzano** (elev. 10 m, pop. 11,550), which also offers two beautiful green areas: the *pinewood* at Capo S. Martino and the park of the 16th-century (but much reworked) *Villa Pallavicini-Negrotto-Cambiaso*, now the Town Hall. Just the other side of the cape is **Cogoleto** (elev. 4 m, pop. 9,256), which also thrives on summer tourism. Just outside this resort, the Arrestra river marks the border with the province of Savona.

4.3 Western Genoa

4.4 The Val Polcevera, the Oltregiogo and the Val Bisagno
Drive through the area to the north and north-east of Genoa, approx. 110 km *(see map p. 106)*

This circular tour, which requires a car, explores the inland area, beginning at the Genoa West intersection of the A7 Genoa-Milan highway. Take state road SS 35 to Busalla, continuing briefly beyond Ronco Scrivia to visit Isola del Cantone and Castello della Pietra, before returning to the junction at Busalla with the SS 226, which follows the Scrivia Valley to Laccio and Torriglia, then back to Genoa on the SS 45. The urban sections of the tour are well served by public transport: bus no. 34 runs from the center of Genoa to the Staglieno cemetery, while no. 46 goes all the way to the Villa Imperiale of Terralba.

Val Polcevera
This valley has always been the main link between the Genoese coast and the Lombardy plains, a role that has been as good for the valley's economic growth as it has been harmful to its natural environment: the area has paid a high price for the large-scale industrial activities, mostly iron and steel making, which arrived here between the late 19th century and World War I. In the late 20th century industrial recession further disfigured the valley's townscapes, although it is still worth visiting for its various important monuments. One is the *church of the Certosa*, which stands at the end of Via S. Bartolomeo della Certosa, a street that crosses the busy *Via Canepari* (IV, D3). Built in 1297 by the Di Negro, it underwent many changes over the centuries. Note in particular the early 16th-century *main cloister** in the Tuscan style, with basket arches held up on marble columns.

The attention shifts from art to agriculture (grapes, olives, hemp cultivation) in the old borough of Garbo, where the *Museo di Storia e Cultura Contadina (open: 9am-noon and 2-5pm, Sun 9am-12.30pm and 2-5pm; closed Mon)* tells the story of local farming traditions. The museum, at no. 47 Salita al Garbo, is reached by continuing along Via Canepari to Piazza Durazzo Pallavicini, the center of the old town of Rivarolo, then turning right into Via Vezzani.
Across the river, Via al Boschetto leads to *Corso Perrone* (III, A1) and the 14th-century *church of*

San Nicolò del Boschetto, once part of a Benedictine monastery where the French king Louis XII stayed in 1507. The *campanile* of the original building survived the extensive changes made in the Baroque period. Inside are some fine *tombs* of the Doria and Grimaldi families (15th-17th cent.).

Sanctuary of Nostra Signora della Guardia*
(IV, B2; *open: 8am-noon and 2-7pm, Sun 8am-7pm*). The story of the most famous of the shrines to the Madonna in Liguria began on 29 August 1490, when the Virgin Mary is said to have appeared to a shepherd on the *Mt. Figogna* (elev. 804 m). The popularity of the shrine is testified to by the many votive offerings collected in a room on the left-hand side of the basilica, designed by Luigi Bisi (1866-90). This is a favorite destination for Sunday outings from Genoa, not least of all because of the spectacular **view** over the valley and the surrounding mountains; but also for the shrine, which is itself an unmistakable landmark.

A corner of old England survives near *Bolzaneto* (IV, C3-4), a populous suburb served by an exit from the A7 highway: **Villa Pinelli Gentile Serra**, which lies within the municipal boundaries of *Sant'Olcese* (IV, B-C4-5; pop. 6,157), is a 19th-century reconstruction in Tudor style of a residence from the previous century. Needless to say, the park was laid out (1850-59) as an English garden, and was the work of landscape painter Carlo Cubani: much neglected for years, the garden was restored and reopened to the public for the Columbus celebrations.

The northernmost part of the metropolitan district of Genoa is **Pontedecimo** (IV, B3), situated at the confluence between the Verde and Riccò rivers, which feed the Polcevera. The *parish church of San Giacomo* dates

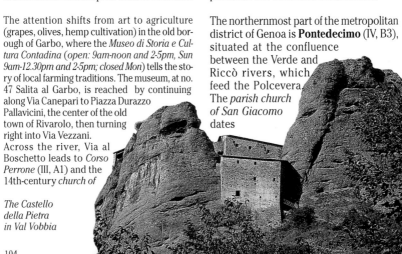

The Castello della Pietra in Val Vobbia

back to the 12th century, but was much altered thereafter.

The **Bocchetta Pass** (elev. 772 m), which tests the muscle power of those taking part in the annual *Giro dell'Appennino* cycle race (*second Sunday in June*), was up to pre-Roman times the main link with the Po Valley, a role it lost with the opening of the Giovi Pass (see below).
One place of interest along the way is **Campomorone** (IV, B3; elev. 118 m, pop. 7,668), a place known for its busy cultural life and research work. There are two museums in the 17th-century *Palazzo Balbi*, now the Town Hall: the *Museo Civico di Paleontologia e Mineralogia* (*open: 9am-noon and 2.30-5.30pm, Wed 9am-noon; closed Sat and Sun*), has an educational workshop dedicated to prehistoric times; the *Museo delle Marionette* (*open: 9am-noon and 2.30-5.30pm; closed Wed, Sat and Sun*), has an interesting collection of puppets, stage sets and related material. The town also boasts possibly Italy's only *Museo della Croce Rossa* (*open: Tue and Thur 3.30-5.30pm, Sat 3-6pm, Sun 10am-noon*), at no. 14 Via Cavallieri, which presents a collection of equipment and means of transport used by the local Red Cross.

The Giovi Pass
Napoleon understood the strategic potential of this crossing point, which is a good deal lower (elev. 472 m) and more accessible than the Bocchetta Pass. The Savoy household took advantage of the idea and in a matter of thirty years built a carriageway (1821) and railroad linking Turin with Genoa (completed in 1853), with a 3,250-m tunnel through the mountain. In 1932-35 the Genoa-Serravalle 'camionale' route was created, enlarged in the 1960s to become the A7 highway. After the industrial towns of *Busalla* (elev. 358 m, pop. 6,193) and *Ronco Scrivia* (elev. 334 m, pop. 4,667), the highway passes close to *Isola del Cantone* (elev. 298 m, pop. 1,561), the last town before the border with Piedmont, where the Vobbia river flows into the Scrivia.

The 13th-century **Castello della Pietra** (*open: Sun 10am-5pm; June, July, September Sat and Sun 10am-6pm; August Thur, Sat and Sun 10am-6pm*), is a beautifully atmospheric castle restored to its former glory in the late 20th century. This fortress, wedged between two ponderous rocky outcrops, once served as a formidable – and virtually impregnable – lookout over the bleak *Val Vobbia*, which now forms part of the **Antola Regional Nature Park**. This 7,680-ha protected area offers a wealth of different landscapes (woodland, mountain pasture, craggy precipices and tarns), with quite intact landscapes around *Mt. Antola* (elev. 1,597 m), the highest point of the Genoese Apennines: on a clear day the **view*** from the peak stretches from the Ligurian to the Piedmontese Alps and beyond to Valle d'Aosta. There are plenty of vestiges of the rural life lived by farming communities hereabouts, including the characteristic *casoni*, stone buildings used up to the mid-20th century during the haymaking and summer pasture season.

Savignone
The lush green valley in the upper Scrivia Valley in which this town lies (elev. 471 m, pop. 3,055) provided an inspiration for many late 19th-century landscape painters. Savignone's

Wildlife in the Antola Regional Park

present-day appearance as a quiet vacation resort belies the troubled past of this once bitterly-contested area. One reminder is the now ruined *Fieschi Castle* (13th cent.), which overlooks the town from high up on a rocky crag. The hamlet of *San Bartolomeo di Vallecalda* (elev. 394 m), situated on the SS 226, is the home of the *Archaeological Section* of the *Museo Storico dell'Alta Valle Scrivia* (*open on request: tel. 0109360103*); the museum's *Ethnological Section*, which offers eight itineraries in and around the valley, is at **Senarega** (elev. 723 m), a picturesque little town in the upper *Val Brevenna*.

The name of **Crocefieschi** (elev. 742 m, pop. 554), a village set in beautiful woodland that has made it a popular vacation resort, is a reminder of the feudal family that once held sway here.

Casella
Also accessible directly from Genoa by train, using the narrow gauge train of the

Genoa-Casella railway (constructed in 1923), this little town (IV, A5; elev. 410 m, pop. 3,106) has become something of a residential offshoot of the city itself. In addition, the little train, which winds its way through beautiful hills, stopping at quaint little stations on the way, is a firm favorite with day trippers and vacationers. Train enthusiasts looking for an authentic old-world experience can make the journey aboard two original 1929 carriages.

Montoggio

This village has earned its place in history as the scene of the conspiracy against Andrea Doria in the *Fieschi Castle* in 1547. But rural Montoggio (IV, A-B6; elev. 438 m, pop. 1,978) has more to offer than a ruined castle (destroyed after the failure of the plot). The *parish church of San Giovanni Decollato* boasts an important altarpiece decoration collection by 17th-century Genoese artists including Orazio

De Ferrari (*The Beheading of John the Baptist*) and Domenico Fiasella (*Refusal of Joseph's Gift in the Temple*).

Torriglia

A new, much straighter road (SS 45) continues east to what is often referred to as 'Genoa's Switzerland', because of its beautiful Alpine scenery. The immodest nickname for the area around the holiday town

The quiet shores of Brugneto Lake

of Torriglia (elev. 769 m, pop. 2,251) is not without foundation: in the winter months the Antola mountains are often capped with snow, and the town's ancient heart is huddled round the dramatic ruins of the *castle*.

Nearby is the *Brugneto Lake*, a reservoir created for the express purpose of supplying water to the city; the artificial lake that has been created is also attractive in its own right and now attracts visitors to its shores.

A road tunnel runs under the **Scoffera Pass** (elev. 674 m), beyond which the descent into the Val Bisagno begins. After *Bargagli* (elev. 341 m, pop. 2,622), we cross the municipal boundary back into the Greater Genoa area, through the districts of *Prato* (IV, D6) and *Struppa* (IV, C-D5-6).

San Siro di Struppa* (IV, D5; *open: 8.30am-6pm*). This church, surrounded by kitchen gardens and vineyards, is documented as early as 1025. It stands on the supposed birthplace of Saint Siro, the 4th-century bishop of Genoa. Two painstaking restoration schemes, in the 1920s and in the 1960s, restored the building's pre-Romanesque appearance, liberating it of the alterations made during the Renaissance and Baroque periods. The facade of the yellowish-gray sandstone church, preceded by a black and white checkered cobbled parvis, is in three parts, corresponding to the nave and side aisles, and is decorated with a series of blind arches in the upper part. The interior, whose columns have cubo-spherical capitals, has a beautiful 13th-century *holy water stoup* and a splendid **polyptych of St. Siro*** in the left-hand aisle: dated 1516, it has been attributed, though not with any certainty, to Pier Francesco Sacchi.

Val Bisagno

The river bed seems even too big for the Bisagno for much of the year, and yet with the arrival of the autumn rains it can often barely contain the force of Genoa's main river, so flooding is frequent, a situation not helped by the chronic lack of maintenance. The most violent episodes in recent decades were in 1970, 1992 and 1993. The last of these was fatal for the medieval *St. Agatha's Bridge* (of the 28 original arches only three remain on the left bank), formerly crossed by horticulturists, millers and shepherds bringing their valley produce to town. This is the origin of the term *bisagnini*, which is still used by the older Genoese people to refer to fruit and vegetable vendors.

The medieval **aqueduct**, a masterpiece of ancient civil engineering which was gradually added to between the 16th and 19th centuries, runs along the right bank of the Bisagno river, up from Via Burlando, near the Genoa-Casella railway station (see pp. 105-106), to the confluence with the Lentro, at *La Presa* (IV, D6).

Staglieno Cemetery* (III, A4; *open: 7.30am-5pm*). This enormous monumental Neoclassical complex, which is, regrettably, now in a rather derelict state, has long been considered as one of the Ligurian capital's main places of interest. To describe this burial place as a major tourist attraction is perhaps something of an overstatement – maintenance is evidently lacking and thefts of statues and other carved stonework all too commonplace – but it remains quite an awe-inspiring sight nonetheless, not least of all because of its beautiful woodland setting. The design of the cemetery by Giovanni Battista Resasco (1835-51) was based on plans by Carlo Barabino, who died a few weeks after approval of the project. The monumental entrance, on the west bank of the Bisagno, precedes a quadrilateral defined by an arcaded gallery in which the monumental tombs are placed. The circular *Suffragi Chapel* dominates the site from the side facing the mountain. Behind is the so-called *Regular Wood*, a large semi-circular space that continues as the *Irregular Wood*, whose sequence of avenues

The monumental Neoclassical complex of Staglieno Cemetery

The Genoa derby

The match between Genoa's two soccer teams Genoa and Sampdoria is always a major event in the city. The terraces of the Luigi Ferraris stadium (known to the Genoese simply as the 'Marassi') are awash with the reds and blues of the two teams' colors. And, with the exception of one or two rare episodes, things do not normally degenerate into the kind of violence so often seen at weekend soccer matches. Genoa is Italy's oldest team, founded in 1893 by a group of Englishmen who lived in the Ligurian capital; five years later it won the first football championship ever held in Italy. The team followed up this success by winning another eight trophies (the last one was in 1923-24) and in 1937 the *Coppa Italia*. But since then the 'Grifone', as the team is nicknamed, has added no other trophies to its collection, and has even had to suffer the humiliation of being relegated to Italy's *Serie C*, or third division. After the war, the only satisfaction for supporters of the 'rossoblu' (the nickname refers to Genoa's red and blue strip) was getting to the semi-finals of the UEFA Cup in 1991-92 and the splendid fourth place it achieved in the previous league championship. That season was indeed a golden one for Genoese football, and possibly unrepeatable, with Sampdoria getting its only league cup. This team, the 'blucerchiato' was created in 1946 out of the merger of Sampierdarenese and Andrea Doria. It has won the Italy Cup four times and a *Supercoppa*, as well as the only European trophy ever to have come to Genoa: the Cupwinners' Cup in 1990. These achievements are difficult to repeat, given the competition from the other multi-millionaire clubs. But there is still always plenty of excitement too look forward to when the derby comes round.

is reminiscent of north European cemeteries. The cemetery is particularly rich in funerary architecture and sculpture from the late 19th and early 20th centuries; among the most notable tombs are those of Giuseppe Mazzini (by Giovanni Battista Grasso, 1874-77).

On the opposite bank of the river is the *Marassi* district (III, A-B4-5), now best known for its detention center and the adjoining *Luigi Ferraris Football Stadium* (III, A-B4): redesigned by Vittorio Gregotti for the World Cup Championship in Italy in 1990.

Villa Imperiale di Terralba

This precious green area lies in the densely-populated district of *San Fruttuoso* (III, B5) that was overwhelmed by the haphazard postwar urban sprawl, but which this villa's English garden survived (the marble stairways and terracing suggest that the layout was originally Renaissance). The villa itself was built in the late 15th and early 16th centuries for Lorenzo Cattaneo, who had the honor of having as his guest the French king Louis XII, a visit recalled in the sculpted fleurs-de-lis on the corbels of the vaulted *vestibule*. Around 1560 the villa underwent a radical renovation, with the contribution of Luca Cambiaso, painter of the superb fresco cycle (**Rape of the Sabine Women***) on the vaulted ceiling of the salon on the piano nobile.

It comes as quite a surprise to find, so close to the city center, such a peaceful oak wood as the one that surrounds the **sanctuary of Nostra Signora del Monte** (III, B5): built in 1444, together with the adjoining Franciscan convent, on the site of a shrine mentioned as early as 1183. In 1654-58 the Saluzzo and Negrone families ordered the rebuilding of the church (*open: 6.15 am-noon and 3-7.45 pm*). The new building, designed by Giovanni Battista Ghiso, was based on a nave and side aisles, with a raised presbytery. The *chapel** below is exquisitely decorated with gilt stuccowork on the ceiling and marble walls and floor; the statue of the *Madonna del Monte* (15th cent.) on the altar is from the Siena school. Also from the 15th century is the polyptych (*Annunciation and Saints**) in the 3rd chapel of the left-hand aisle: formerly attributed to Giacomo Serfoglio, it is now thought to have been painted around 1466 by an anonymous Maestro dell'Annunciazione al Monte. The convent's refectory (*open on request, tel. 010505854*) has a *Last Supper* by Orazio De Ferrari (1641).

5 Savona and environs

Town and area profile

Some towns with relatively little to offer become major tourist destinations, while others are seen principally in terms of their commercial and manufacturing potential and as such are seldom given much prominence on the tourist map. Savona falls into this latter category: few people spend their vacation there, but none of those who do ever come away disappointed. Savona, even more than Genoa, seems to keep its treasures jealously guarded, revealing them only to those who are genuinely interested in them and prepared to dedicate some time to discovering them. The less discerning visitor, who merely happens to be in Savona, may well be put off by the docks and factory buildings (most of which are now disused) that still impinge rather unattractively on the historic center, and seem to overwhelm its many artistic and architectural treasures.

These industrial areas, which grew up after the last war, are now at the center of the debate as to what future form the post-industrial town should take: the choice is between developing the trading port aspect, creating a business center here and promoting tourism. Before the arrival of industry, Savona was a trading port and military stronghold, dominated by the massive presence of the Priamar fortress, and in the 19th century became a dignified town (with an almost Piedmontese atmosphere) laid out on a

regular grid pattern around the medieval core. Earlier in its history it had been a flourishing port: part-medieval, part-Renaissance, naval and mercantile, a place of crafts and commerce, its people divided between the nobility and the enterprising middle classes. Savona looked both to the sea (as the proud rival of Genoa) and landward, to the Po Valley: just beyond the Cadibona hill immediately inland from Savona was the easiest route in this area to the Po Valley, and thus an important means of communication with northern Europe.

The earliest records of the town speak of the see-sawing relationship between 'Savo' and 'Vada Sabatia' (or 'Vado') of the ancient Romans, the former settlement huddled on the hill around the early Priamar fortification, the latter lying on more open, flatter ground. While the imperial order lasted, Vado remained the more developed of the two, since it was more accessible and offered more opportunities for the development of the port. But in the early Middle Ages the Byzantines

Savona's busy port with the Leon Pancaldo Tower

preferred the strategy of defending the fortress. The town maintained its hegemony until 1528, the year in which it came under the political control of Genoa. Today the old division between Savona and Vado is still visible, but the ancient rivalry has now been replaced by a more constructive complementary situation. Vado can offer modern sea traffic with the infrastructures for good development of the docks, while Savona, squeezed into a narrower space, has become the center for other functions. The task of keeping alive the history of this ancient town falls to the 16th-century Priamar stronghold, now a center for cultural activities, and the ancient quarters close by.

The area around Savona described in this chapter comprises the coastal strip between Punta Invrea, to the east, and Capo di Vado, wedged in between the sea and the hills immediately inland (with the exception of the plain of Albisola and the plain between Savona, Quiliano and Vado Ligure) and the area behind, with the interesting Beigua Massif, the inappropriately named 'Desert' of Varazze (known for its abundance of water and lush vegetation), the wooded slopes of the Upper Teiro Valley, and the gentle hills of the 'Savona Wood', all areas of great environmental and natural interest. Further inland still are the more mountainous areas between Colle del Giovo, Dego and Carcare.

The third tour centers around the wonderful medieval town of Noli and the beautiful coastal and hill areas of Finale Ligure and the Manie Plateau, while the fourth and last tour goes from the seaside resorts of Pietra Ligure and Loano into the valleys that lead up to the Toirano Pass and the Melogno hill.

5.1 Savona

Walking tour of the town and two driving tours in the immediate surroundings *(see plan p. 113)*

This tour of **Savona** (elev. 4 m, pop. 63,102) begins at the Priamar fortress, where parking facilities are plentiful in the area in front of the historical edifice. We follow Corso Mazzini to the right beyond Piazza Mazzini to Piazza del Brandale at the inner harbor, where the two imposing 12th-century *Corsi* and *Guarnieri Towers* (or *Torri degli Scolopi*) mark one of the access points into the historical quarters. Via Orefici and Via Quarda Superiore lead from the Brandale Tower through the old town to the arcaded Via Paleocapa, Savona's more recent main thoroughfare, at whose seaward end stands the characteristic Leon Pancaldo Tower. In the other direction, Via Paleocapa leads to the *church of Sant'Andrea* and the oratory of the Risen Christ on the left, and (at the beginning of Via Mistrangelo on the right) the *church of San Giovanni Battista*.

Via Pia, an ancient street beginning at the oratory, runs back through the old town. At the other end, Via Sansoni and Via Vacciuoli lead to Piazza del Duomo, from which Via Aonzo leads to the Bishop's Palace and to Via S. Maria Maggiore, ending at Piazza Sisto IV (the Town Hall Square) and, on Via Manzoni, the almost hidden oratory of Our Lady of Castello. Corso Italia, finally, leads back toward the sea and the Priamar fortress.

After visiting the historic center it is worth heading north-west out of town along the river, to see the sanctuary of *Nostra Signora della Misericordia* and the ruins of *San Pietro in Carpignano*, to the south-west of Savona.

The Priamar Fortress* (C-D2; *open: Mon-Sat 7am-midnight; Sun and holidays 10am-midnight*). This enormous stronghold, built by Genoa as a garrison (work began in

Savona: Priamar Fortress

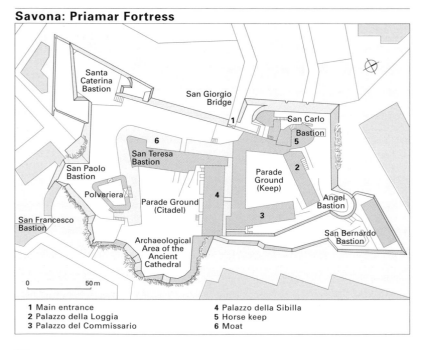

1 Main entrance	**4** Palazzo della Sibilla
2 Palazzo della Loggia	**5** Horse keep
3 Palazzo del Commissario	**6** Moat

1542), stands on the hill of the primitive settlement, destroyed along with the ancient 'castrum' and the first cathedral. It was altered several times (Giuseppe Mazzini was imprisoned here in 1830-31, when it was used as a prison), and after the most recent restoration turned into a major museum complex. It is, then, well worth a visit both as a work of military architecture in its own right (and the panoramic views it offers) and for its concentration of museums.

Pinacoteca Civica (*open: Mon-Sat 8.30am-1pm; Tue and Thur until 6pm; closed Sun and holidays*). This art gallery, housed on the 3rd floor of Palazzo della Loggia, offers a brief but comprehensive overview of Ligurian painting from the Middle Ages to the 18th century. The most interesting (albeit small) section is undoubtedly that devoted to the 14th and 15th centuries. It includes two splendid **Crucifixions*** by Donato de' Bardi and by Giovanni Mazone (the latter also painted the magnificent polyptych of the *Annunciation, Calvary and Saints**). The *Cinquecento* is less well represented, while the rooms dedicated to the 17th and 18th centuries have works by nearly all the artists encountered when visiting churches in the Genoa and Savona area (Domenico Fiasella, Bartolomeo Guidobono, Giovanni Stefano Robatto, Paolo Gerolamo Brusco, Giovanni Agostino and Carlo Giuseppe Ratti). Note in particular a *Resurrection* by Giovanni Battista Paggi and a *Christ Appearing to St. John* by Domenico Piola. The Ceramics Room has excellent works from the 16th century onward, from a local tradition well known beyond the region's borders.

Civico Museo Storico-Archeologico (*open: June-September, Tue-Sat 10am-noon and 4-6pm, Sun and holidays 4-6pm; October-May, Tue-Sat 10am-noon and 3-5pm, Sun and holidays 3-5pm; closed Mon*). This museum, on the lower floor of Palazzo della Loggia, is concerned mainly with the original Savonese settlement on the hill. Archaeologists have uncovered an interesting 5th/6th-century necropolis that forms part of the visit; no less interesting are the North-African floor mosaics (3rd-4th cent.). Other exhibits include Bronze Age items, an Etruscan bucchero (7th-6th cent. BC) and a Greek skyphos (5th cent. BC).

Roman amphora. Archaeology Museum, Savona

The other museum housed in Palazzo della Loggia, on the middle floor, is the **Museo d'Arte Sandro Pertini** (*open: 8.30am-1pm; closed Sun and holidays*), which holds around one hundred works of art collected by the former Italian president, a native of Savona, and bequeathed to the town by his widow. The collection includes works by Morandi, Sironi, Rosai, Moore, de Chirico, Guttuso, Miró, Vedova, Tápies, Fabbri and others.

The gloomy underground passages beneath the fortress lead, finally, to the **Museo Renata Cuneo** (*closed for renovation*), located in the San Bernardo bastion and with sculptures by the Savonese artist, whose work spans most of the 20th century. Two bronzes, *Man Asleep* (1931) and *Summer* (1939), are displayed in the entrance.

Savona: a room in the Sandro Pertini Art Gallery

Torre del Brandale (C2). This tower looks out over the square of the same name behind the old quay. It still bears vague signs of its medieval past, despite the major changes that were later made to it. Raised in the 12th century, the tower has medieval frescoes inside, while the front is decorated by a ceramic *Visitation*, a fine example of local craftsmanship. The big bell ('*a campanassa*') has given its name to the cultural association housed in the adjacent *Palazzo degli Anziani*, a 14th-century building with 17th-century facade.

Piazza Salineri. This square, which looks out over the sea, was the heart of the residential area in the Middle Ages. From this position high up over the docks, merchants and shipbuilders could conveniently keep watch over maritime traffic. What little remains of the former opulence of this area is concentrated in the nearby streets, namely *Via Orefici* and *Via Quarda Superiore* (note the fine doorway of the 15th/16th-century *palazzo* at no. 2).

The square is bordered by *Torre Ghibellina* (13th cent.) and *Torre Aliberti* (12th cent.), alongside which stands the badly-worn 16th-century *Palazzo Martinengo*. A tile in the wall next to the quaint *osteria* features the 'Tabella di Persepoli', a word game of obscure origin.

Palazzo Grassi Ferrero Doria Lamba. This elegant noble residence, which now houses the Chamber of Commerce, occupies the side of the square opposite the Ghibellina Tower, and is entered from no. 16 Via Quarda Superiore. This 12th-century building (rebuilt in the 1500s) has an interesting facade lower down on the side facing the sea (Via Quarda Inferiore). Inside are frescoes from the best Ligurian school of the 16th century, influenced by Perin del Vaga; they include the **Battle of Sennacherib**, by the Semino, at no. 32 Via Inferiore. It is worth asking the Chamber of Commerce staff to be allowed in to see the monumental staircase, beautifully frescoed and decorated up to the top floors.

Palazzo Del Carretto Pavese Pozzobonello (C2). The building at no. 7 Via Quarda Superiore (virtually unscathed by World War II bombing, which badly damaged much of the port area) is of medieval origin, and has a fine portal and vestibule. It houses the **Archivio di Stato**, a major archive of rare and ancient documents.

Torre di Leon Pancaldo (C2). This small, attractive tower by the sea, decorated with a statue of the *Madonna of Mercy*, is of 14th-century origin and takes its name from the Savona-born navigator who accompanied Ferdinand Magellan on his sea voyages, but who died tragically in 1537 on the Rio della Plata. On the seaward side a verse by Gabriello Chiabrera dedicated to the Madonna and in Latin (which coincides exactly with the Italian) reads: 'In this raging sea, this sudden storm, I beseech thee, oh guiding star'.

Via Paleocapa (C2). Savona's busy main thoroughfare, lined with elegant arcades full of shops, was laid out as part of a late 19th-century process of rationalization. This street was designed to provide a rapid link between the historic center and the train station, which once stood next to the Letimbro river (now the large empty space beyond Piazza del Popolo). Nos. 3 and 5 form the **Palazzo dei Pavoni**, whose facade, by Alessandro Martinengo, is beautifully decorated with peacocks and floral motifs (1912).

In the side street to the left stands the 18th-century *church of Sant'Andrea* (C2; *open mornings only*). The steps that now lead up to the entrance were added when the street level was lowered to create Via Paleocapa and the raised ground on which the church was built was flattened. The interior, with its visually attractive perspective, is decorated with 18th-century frescoes and paintings; in the sacristy is a statue of the *Madonna of Mercy* by Antonio Brilla and an icon of *St. Nicholas* from Constantinople.

The **Oratorio del Cristo Risorto** (C2; *open 4-6pm and Sun morning*), formerly the Augustinian church of the *SS. Annunziata*, was rebuilt in 1604. The lavishly-decorated interior has 18th-century frescoes; the majestic *Triumph of God and Angels* in the presbytery frames the statue of *Christ Risen*. Note also the 18th-century organ and two small paintings (*Flagellation* and *Crucifixion*) in the Nordic Gothic style (late 15th cent.). This oratory is famous for its three processional chests: the *Annunciation* by Maragliano, the *Lady of Sorrows* by Filippo Martinengo, and the *Deposition* by Antonio Brilla.

San Giovanni Battista (C2). This important church, on the opposite side of Via Paleocapa at the beginning of Via Mistrangelo, was built by the Dominicans in 1567, after the church of *San Domenico Vecchio* was demolished to make way for the Priamar fortress. The Baroque facade was added in 1735. The interior (with central nave and

A votive shrine in a picturesque corner of old Savona

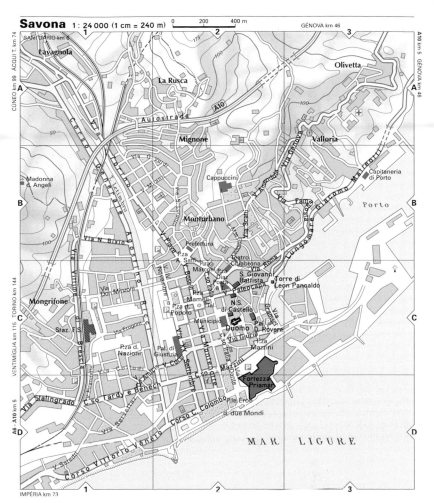

Savona 1 : 24 000 (1 cm = 240 m)

side aisles) has artworks from the 16th to 18th centuries: a *Glory of St. Dominic*, fresco by Paolo Gerolamo Brusco behind the facade; a statue of the *Madonna and Child*, by Tommaso Orsolino, in the chapel to the right of the high altar; two canvases by Carlo Giuseppe Ratti depicting scenes from the life of St. Dominic on either side of the presbytery; a *Nativity* by Antonio Semino in the chapel to the left of the high altar and, to its left, a *Madonna and Child with Saints* by Teramo Piaggio. The north aisle also has a *Madonna, St. Mary Magdalen and St. Catherine with the Image of St. Dominic* by Paolo Gerolamo Piola, a 16th-century wooden *Crucifix*, and, above the baptistery, a *Nativity of the Virgin* by Carlo Giuseppe Ratti.

The suggested detour beginning here crosses one of Savona's liveliest districts. Follow *Via Mistrangelo* to Piazza Diaz and the **Teatro Chiabrera** (B-C2), built in 1850-53 and named after the 17th-century Savonese poet Gabriello

Chiabrera. The theater's monumental neoclassical facade with two tiers of columns (Doric and Ionic) is topped by a tympanum with a large bas relief (*Gabriello Chiabrera Presenting the Poem Amadeide to Carlo Emanuele I of Savoy*).

On the corner between Via dei Mille (from Piazza Diaz) and Piazza Marconi, is the 18th-century **oratory of Ss. Pietro e Caterina** (C2) finely decorated inside with monochrome stuccowork. Note also the 17th-century painting in the apse (*Madonna and Child with St. Peter and St. Catherine*); Carlo Giuseppe Ratti painted the *Disputation of St. Catherine* (to the left of the entrance) and the four *Scenes from the Life of St. Peter* (on the piers supporting the dome); note also the two processional chests by Brilla, with another by Renata Cuneo.

From Piazza Marconi, Via dei Mille leads to Piazza Saffi, whose main building is the 1939 *Palazzo della Prefettura* (B2). The main road leading south from the square, *Via Boselli* (note the eccentric, late Art Nouveau *Casa Maffiotti*, at no. 4), meets Via Sormano. At no. 12 (on the corner with Via IV Novembre, C2), is the **Palazzo della Provincia**, the provincial administrative building designed by Pier Luigi Nervi (1964). If time permits, continue along Via dei Mille (see above) to *Via Poggi*, which leads up to the residential 'Villetta' district on the hill, with its villas and gardens. There is an interesting art gallery at no. 5 Via Ponzone: the **Quadreria del Seminario Vescovile** (*open to visitors on request*), with works from the 16th to 19th centuries, mainly by Ligurian painters, including Giovanni Battista Carlone, il Grechetto, Carlo Giuseppe Ratti and Paolo Gerolamo Brusco. There is also a *Holy Family*, which has been attributed (controversially) to Van Dyck.

Via Pia* (C2). This narrow, bustling street with its many shops and monumental buildings, was the main thoroughfare of old Savona, and is still very much the street it was in medieval times. Many of the buildings have beautiful slate doorways (15th-16th cent.) with sculpted lintels. The 16th-century *Palazzo Sormani* (no. 1) is decorated with historical scenes; *Palazzo Della Rovere-Cassinis* (no. 5) is a typical Ligurian Renaissance building. Beyond the picturesque old **Piazza della Maddalena** stands the 16th-century *Palazzo Pavese Spinola* (no. 26), with remains of frescoed grotesques in the vestibule, and beyond Palazzo Della Rovere (see below), just before the end of the street at the Brandale Tower (see p. 111), is *Palazzo Sansoni*, with a fine black and white facade and a 13th-century loggia (later walled in).

Palazzo Della Rovere (C2). This building, begun in 1495 by Giuliano da Sangallo at the request of Cardinal Giuliano Della Rovere (later Pope Julius II), is at no. 28 Via Pia. In 1673 it became a Clarissine convent, and was known as 'Palazzo Santa Chiara', but the splendid decorations inside were plastered over for religious reasons and are now lost. At the beginning of the 19th century it became a Napoleonic prefecture. All that remains of the magnificence of the original building is in the post office at the rear of the courtyard on the left: the 16th-century *frescoes* by Ottavio

Semino survived the rigors of convent life, but not the ill-advised addition of a false ceiling in modern times.

Duomo (C2). Via Sansoni and the curving Via Vacciuoli (*Palazzo Cerisola-Vacciuoli*, at no. 1, is a 15th/16th-cent. building with slate doorway and glazed tile vestibule), lead to the cathedral of *Santa Maria Assunta*, built 1589-1605 (with 19th-cent. facade). Inside, behind the facade, is a late 15th-century marble **Crucifix*** and *baptismal font* created out of a Byzantine capital, with sculpted transennae; note the interesting *Pulpit of the Evangelists* (1522) and the beautiful **carved wood choir*** (1500-15). In the chapel to the right of the high altar is an **Enthroned Madonna and Child with St. Peter and St. Paul***, a masterpiece by Albertino Piazza, and a 16th-century marble relief depicting the *Presentation of Mary in the Temple*. Note also the harmonious Mannerist complex in the 4th chapel on the left and, next to it, a 14th-century bas-relief of the *Assunta*. The sacristy has a large marble *relief* in the Gagini style. **Museo del Tesoro della Cattedrale** (*open on request; entrance in the cathedral or at no. 11 Via Manzoni*). Among the important paintings in the cathedral museum are a polyptych of the *Assumption and Saints* by Lodovico Brea (1495), a *Madonna and Saints* by Tuccio d'Andria (1487) and a Flemish *Adoration of the Magi*; there is also an interesting collection of silver and gold work and some English alabaster statues. The 15th-century cathedral *cloister*, with 21

Savona: the ceiling of the Cappella Sistina

marble statues of saints, leads to the **Cappella Sistina** (*open: Sat, 4-6 pm*) built by Pope Sixtus IV (the Savonese Francesco Della Rovere) in 1481-83, but redesigned in the Rococo style in the 18th century (when the organ was also built). The *cenotaph of the parents of Sixtus IV* dates back to 1483. Some original frescoes were discovered under the dome.

At no. 1 Piazzetta del Vescovado (along Via Aonzo) stands the 18th-century *Palazzo Vescovile*. Here are the apartments of Pius

VII, where the pope stayed from 1809 to 1812 and in 1814 after being arrested by Napoleon. Inside (*visits on the 2nd and 4th Friday of the month, entrance in Via Manzoni*) are period furnishings and works by Ligurian artists. The entrance to the *Curia* at no. 13 (red numbering) is surmounted by a marble relief with *St. George* (15th cent.).

Nostra Signora di Castello

(C2). This almost hidden oratory in Corso Italia (*open holidays only: 8-10am*) contains the monumental **Madonna and Saints****, a splendid late 15th-century polyptych by Vincenzo Foppa, completed by Lodovico Brea. Note also the processional chest of the *Deposition* by Filippo Martinengo (1795), the tallest in existence.

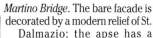

V. Foppa, Madonna and Saints. Oratory of Nostra Signora di Castello, Savona

Corso Italia

Corso Italia (C2). This long, straight road with its elegant shops is the second main thoroughfare (after Via Paleocapa) created during Savona's 19th-century expansion. On the part between Piazza Sisto IV and the sea, in Piazza Giulio II, is the imposing 19th-century *ospedale San Paolo*. A brief detour down Via Untoria leads to the 17th-century *church of San Pietro*, originally Carmelite, with a monumental facade and interesting elliptical plan; note the impressive polychrome marble partition between the high altar and the choir. Corso Italia ends in the municipal gardens adjoining the Priamar fortress (see pp. 110-111), in which stands the *tempietto Boselli*, an original gazebo dating back to 1785, named after its creator.

The immediate surroundings

There are two interesting things to see outside Savona: the *sanctuary di Nostra Signora della Misericordia* (from Piazza Aurelio Saffi, B-C2, drive out of town along Via Torino, A-B1, which follows the Letimbro river upstream) and, in the suburb of Legino, the remains of the *chapel of San Pietro in Carpignano* (from Corso Mazzini, C-D2 and, beyond the river, Corso Tardy e Benech, D1-2, take Via Stalingrado, D1).

San Dalmazio

San Dalmazio. This church, in the ancient suburb of *Lavagnola* (A1), is reached by turning right just before the 13th-century *San Martino Bridge*. The bare facade is decorated by a modern relief of St. Dalmazio; the apse has a **Madonna and Child with Saints***, a fine polyptych by Barnaba da Modena (1376), and to the right of the presbytery another good *polyptych* (also 14th cent.) of the Ligurian-Provençale school.

Santuario di Nostra Signora della Misericordia

Santuario di Nostra Signora della Misericordia. This shrine is in the hamlet of *Santuario* (elev. 96 m), 6.5 km north-west of Savona. The broad square before it offers an excellent perspective view of the complex: to the left, *Palazzo Pallavicino* and the old hospice, to the right the new hospice and (behind) Palazzetto Tursi; the fine Mannerist **facade** was designed by Taddeo Carlone (1610-11), who completed the original church built seventy years earlier. The interior, frescoed by Bernardo Castello (1610), has a range of artworks, most notably: in the 2nd chapel on the right, a *Nativity of Mary*, a masterpiece by Orazio Borgianni in the Caravaggio style; and, in the 3rd chapel, a *Presentation in the Temple* by Domenichino. The rich marblework before the crypt is by Giovanni Battista Orsolino; the 17th-century wooden *choir* is decorated with 19th-century intarsia; in the 3rd chapel on the left is a marble high-relief (*Visitation*) in an altar probably by Gian Lorenzo Bernini. *Palazzetto Tursi* houses the *Museo del Tesoro* (*open Sun, 3-6pm*), which displays gold and silver liturgical items, sacred furnishings, wooden sculptures, votive offerings etc.

San Pietro in Carpignano

San Pietro in Carpignano. The Legino depression beyond the Letimbro river is characterized by narrow country *creuze* (lanes), dry-stone walls and tower-houses. In the beautiful Piazza Legino stands the *parish church of Sant'Ambrogio*, which boasts a wooden sculpture by Maragliano depicting *St. Ambrose and Emperor Theodosius*. Near Quiliano turn inland along a short path to the poorly-preserved *chapel of San Pietro in Carpignano*, which has a fine 14th-century belltower. Built in the 11th century over an earlier ancient structure, and rebuilt in the 1600s, this complex is noteworthy both for its historical importance and beautiful setting.

5.2 Around Savona

Excursion to the north and west of Savona, 78 km *(see map p. 121)*

This extremely varied tour begins away from the busy coastal areas in the green hills inland from Savona, offering summer travelers a chance to retreat to the much cooler, higher ground away from the bustling seaside towns.

After visiting Varazze, Celle and Albisola Marina, which all lie along the Via Aurelia on the coast, we head inland along the SS 334 to Albisola Superiore, climb up to the Colle del Giovo, and continue a further 7 km to Sassello. Near the Giovo Pass, the road forks off (SS 542) to Pontinvrea and to Dego, where a brief detour along the SS 29 leads into Val Bormida, and, after another 7 km, to Piana Crixia. From Dego we continue south along the SS 29 to Carcare, then another 8 km to the west (along the SS 28 bis) to Millesimo. Finally, the SS 29 returns to Savona via Altare and Cadibona. This 78-km round trip (plus the short detours mentioned above) is all on good asphalted roads. Hiking enthusiasts will find many opportunities for walks along the way into the surprisingly unspoiled natural surroundings.

Varazze

This well-known seaside resort (elev. 10 m, pop. 13,844) is of late Roman origin and can be identified with the 'AD Navalia' mentioned in the 'Tabula Peutingeriana'. Jacopo da Varagine, who later became famous as the author of the "Golden Legend", was born here in around 1230.

The visit, from west to east, begins at the train station (see plan, A1), close to which stands the *church of Ss. Nazario e Celso*, with a Baroque facade and characteristic pebbled parvis (1902). Continuing parallel to the sea we come to the 16th-century **collegiate church of Sant'Ambrogio** (A2), with a 1914 facade and splendid Lombard *belltower** that was part of the earlier 14th-century church (note the paving of the square, created for the Lomellini family in 1759). Inside is an excellent polyptych by Giovanni Barbagelata with *St. Ambrose, Saints and Angel Musicians** (1500), and an *Annunciation* attributed to Francesco da Milano (1535); sculptures include a carved polychrome wooden statue of *St. Catherine of Siena* by Maragliano and, on the high altar, an *Assunta* by Francesco Schiaffino (1740).

Just behind the square, incorporated into the medieval ramparts, are the extensive and beautiful remains of an 11/12th-century Romanesque church also dedicated to St. Ambrose. Beyond the covered-over Teiro river, Via Ciarli leads to the *oratory of San Bartolomeo* (*open late Sat afternoon*), which has a fine polyptych (*Ecce Homo, Annunciation and Saints*) by Teramo Piaggio (1535), and, a little further on to the east, to the 15th-century *church of San Domenico*, in whose facade is lodged a cannon ball fired from a French ship in December 1746.

The 5-km seafront walk (or bicycle ride) along the **Lungomare Europa** is an opportunity to see a particularly beautiful stretch of the coast. It runs from just beyond San Domenico, along the now disused railroad track all the way to Invrea and Cogoleto. Numerous footpaths along the way head inland up to Mt. Beigua.

Another recommended excursion (ca. 8 km, possible also by car) leaves Varazze along the east bank of the Teiro river towards **Alpicella** (elev. 405 m), with a small archaeology museum in an

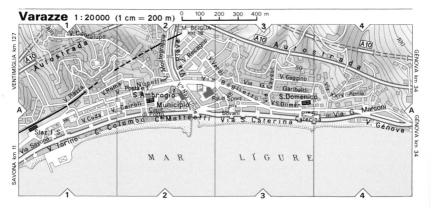

Varazze 1 : 20000 (1 cm = 200 m)

area covered with dense woodland cut through by roads and pleasant hiking paths. No less beautiful is the road which forks off to the right at Casanova and after approximately 9 km leads to the **convent del Deserto** (elev. 278 m), a hermitage built in the 1600s by the Discalced Carmelites, an order of barefooted friars. The complex is interesting for both its architecture and its superb shady setting among holm-oaks, beech trees and cypresses, through which an interesting 'botanical itinerary' has been traced.

Celle Ligure

This pretty and extremely well-preserved ancient fishing village (elev. 4 m, pop. 5,379) is a delight to explore. The main streets – the busy *Via Aicardi* and *Via Ghiglino* – end at the fine *belltower* of the Augustinian *church of Nostra Signora della Consolazione*. Take *Via Stefano Boagno*, which runs at right angles to the coast, inland along the covered Ghiare river, then cross the Via Aurelia and pass under the rail tracks, to reach the 17th-century **parish church of San Michele Arcangelo**, high up at the top of a flight of steps. Inside is an interesting 16th-century *Crucifix* with a cross in the form of a tree and, above the high altar, a superb polyptych of **St. Michael, St. Peter and John the Baptist***, by Perin del Vaga (1535); in the sacristy is a 14th-century marble tabernacle, a 16th-century slate *Crucifixion* and, in the archive, *St. Michael*, possibly the oldest processional chest in existence (1481). No one should leave Celle without visiting the panoramic **Bottini Public Park** (at the extreme west of the town), next to the age-old *Natta Pinewood*. Further on, in a place called *Pecorile* (elev. 117 m), stands the house in which Francesco Della Rovere, later Pope Sixtus IV, was born in 1414.

Albisola Marina

This popular little holiday town (elev. 8 m, pop. 5,594) is well known for its artistic ceramic-making activities, which flourished here in the 16th century and also in more recent times when craftsmen from Savona moved here. The *church of Nostra Signora della Concordia*, in a delightful modern cobbled square, has a processional chest by Maragliano and a *Nativity* in

Ceramics: past and present

This chapter of the guide describes the artistic ceramic heritage displayed in museums in the Savona area: special sections of the Civic Art Gallery in Savona itself, and of the Civic Museum at Finalborgo; Villa Faraggiana and the G. Mazzotti Factory-House-Museum at Albisola Marina; and Manlio Trucco Museum in Albisola Superiore. However, these brief descriptions do not do justice to an artistic output of which this area of Liguria is justly proud.

The ceramic tradition in the Savona area dates back to the 12th century; in Albisola ceramic art began to flourish from the 16th century on, thanks also to the deposits of red earth and white stone quarries inland which provided the raw materials. The crafted items were left to dry on the little town's broad beach, before being loaded onto ships to be transported to their far-off destinations.

The best-known Albisola ceramic decoration, in monochrome pale blue, began to become popular from the first half of the 17th century. The most sumptuous ornamental style was that decorated with historical scenes, known also as Baroque scenography, which developed at the end of the 17th century and took its inspiration from Genoese painting of the day. Scenes showed biblical, mythological, or historical figures moving against a background of castles and mountains.

Ceramic manufacture continues to this day in the Savona area, where various related cultural activities are also to be found. But perhaps the place that pays tribute most effectively to this illustrious tradition is the *Artists' Waterfront* at Albisola Marina, which was delightfully paved in ceramic stoneware mosaic in 1963 by various internationally-renowned painters and sculptors.

polychrome ceramic tiles (1576). The 18th-century **Villa Faraggiana***, which stands in a park on the north-east edge of the town (*open in summer*), is the home of the important museum of the same name, with

The elegant facade of Villa Faraggiana, Albisola Marina

sculptures by Filippo Parodi, polychrome majolica work and 19th-century furniture made by the English cabinet-maker E. T. Peters. To find out more about the town's ceramic-making tradition, visit the *Fabbrica-Casa-Museo G. Mazzotti* (*open: 10am-noon and 4-6pm*) at no. 29 Viale Matteotti.

Albisola Superiore
This town (elev. 10m, pop. 11,216), the center of a municipality stretching from the coast a good way inland, is dominated by the 18th-century *church of S. Nicolò*, which contains some fine sculptures, including a wooden *St. Nicolò* by Maragliano and, on the high altar, a *Glory of St. Nicolò* by Francesco Schiaffino. Also worth a visit is the *Museo Manlio Trucco*, a ceramic art museum with a small archaeological section.

Sassello
This cheerful little inland resort (elev. 405 m, pop. 1,772), noted for its cool, breezy climate in summer and its famous macaroons, or *amaretti* as they are known locally, was the first town in Liguria to be awarded the 'Orange Flag', the symbol of excellence created by the Regional Authorities together with Touring Club of Italy to promote tourism in inland Liguria. The little town has some particularly pretty corners, such as *Piazza Concezione*, with the 16th-century *church of the Immacolata Concezione*, and the area around the *church of the SS. Trinità*. The *Museo Perrando* (*open: Fri 3-5pm; Sat 10am-noon and 3-5pm*), in Via Perrando, has some beautiful paintings and local artifacts. Oth-

er sights worth seeing are the 18th-century complex of *San Giovanni Battista*, picturesquely situated on the edge of the town, and (a 15-minute walk from Via Perrando, past some typical rustic buildings) the *Bastia Soprana*, a medieval stronghold now almost completely ruined and overgrown.

Sassello is the headquarters of the Visitors' Center (Via G.B. Badano 45) for the **Mt. Beigua Regional Nature Park**, a 18,160-ha reserve established in 1985, which straddles the provinces of Savona and Genoa. The 1,287-m high mountain after which it is named is equidistantly situated (8 km as the crow flies) between Sassello and the coast (between Varazze and Cogoleto). The park, whose mountain pastures offer superb panoramic views, is crossed by many hiking paths and is interesting for its flora and fauna: birds of prey hover overhead, while roe-deer and wild boar are not an uncommon sight in the woods.

From Giovo Ligure to Dego
The health and holiday resort of *Giovo Ligure* (elev. 495 m) grew up around a 19th-century fortress.
Pontinvrea (elev. 425 m, pop. 814), the feudal domain of the Invrea marquises since 1607, was once famous for timber processing, mostly for the shipbuilding industry. At the center of the village stands the 17th-century *Palazzo Marchionale*.
Perched high up on a rocky spur, **Dego** (elev. 317 m, pop. 1,950), once the center of farming and forestry activities and later industrialized, also has ancient origins. Formerly the property of the Del Carretto family and the marquises of Monferrato, it was the home of a mint in the 14th century. High up to the north of the village stand the ruins of the *Del Carretto Castle*.

From Dego, take the SS 29 (*del Colle di Cadibona*) north, which after around 7 km comes to the scattered community of **Piana Crixia** (pop. 829). This area, a regional nature reserve, is interesting for its gully erosions, unique to this area in Liguria, and which to some extent anticipate the geography of the Langhe area further north in Piedmont. Before reaching *Molino* (elev. 267 m), the municipal center, a short road to the right with a small chapel leads to the tiny hamlet of *Borgo* (elev. 308 m), near which, on the landslide-prone slopes overlooking the Bormida di Spigno river, is the so-called **Fungo di Piana**: a huge mushroom-shaped mass of greenstone rock resting on a schistose column.

Carcare

Once an important intersection of the roads to Acqui and Ceva, this village (elev. 365 m, pop. 5,698) belonged to the Del Carretto family, to Spain and to Genoa by turns. Near the end of the village, on the west bank of the Bormida di Pallare river, stands the 19th-century *church of San Giovanni Battista*, a large brick building with a *Crucifix* by Anton Maria Maragliano in the apse. The SS 28 bis road leads north-west from Carcare 8 km up the Nanta river to the interesting village of **Millesimo** (elev. 429 m, pop. 3,350), which lies on the Bormida di Millesimo river. The oldest part of the village has maintained the typical ancient construction styles established in the 13th century under the Del Carretto family. It too came under Spanish control (17th century) before becoming Savoy property. It is dominated by the imposing *Del Carretto Castle* (1206) now being restored for use as a cultural center. Further on, the main road widens out into the arcaded *Piazza Italia*, laid out in the 16th century; together with the so-called *Torre*, an ancient tower-house built by the Del Carretto family in the 15th century over 14th-century foundations (now the municipal hall), this forms a small village complex that retains much of its old late medieval character. From the square, Via Ponte Vecchio leads through the beautiful area around the junction with Via Mazzini, with its medieval feel, to the **Ponte della Gaietta**. This ancient bridge, which dates back to the original 12th/13th-century settlement, creates a beautifully picturesque scene against the backdrop of houses and gardens along the river.

On the road that heads north out of Millesimo toward Cengio, turn left to reach the charming wooded area near the Bormida river that is the setting for the ancient parish **church of Santa Maria extra Muros**, of Romanesque origin greatly altered in the 15th century when the bell-tower was raised and frescoes painted in the presbytery.

Artistic glassware, for which Altare was once famous

Altare

Located midway on the road back to Savona, Altare is another interesting village of medieval origin (elev. 398 m, pop. 2,312) at the center of an extensive area of forest. Its importance in ancient times derived from its strategic position on a main road. It retains traces of the walls of the *castle* destroyed in the 17th century by the Spanish, while the 15th-century *church of the Assunta* has seen considerable change. The former *oratory of San Sebastiano*, in the upper part of the village, is the provisional home of the *Museo del Vetro (open: Mon-Fri 3-6pm)*, a museum documenting the ancient art of glassmaking for which Altare was once famous; the most important items are those made by the *Società Artistica Vetraria*, the glassmaking society founded in 1856, active until 1978.

5.3 Noli and Finale Ligure
Tour of the coast south-west of Savona and the nearby inland area *(see map p. 121)*

From Savona, a 25-km stretch of the Via Aurelia leads to Finale Ligure. This part of the coast (the scene of many important historical events) and the area immediately inland have been inhabited since earliest times: the first settlers were no doubt attracted by the favorable climate and environmental conditions, and by the many natural sheltered sites. Significant traces of prehistoric settlements and Roman roads survive, while the medieval towers and fortresses along the coast serve as reminders of the importance of fishing villages such as Noli, not only in terms of trade. The charm these villages still retain despite the speculative building of recent decades is only enhanced by the beauty of the natural surroundings. On the island of Bergeggi, for example, or on the Manie Plateau, visitors can leave their cars behind and rediscover an almost totally unspoiled natural environment.

Bergeggi

The name refers both to the panoramic village (elev. 110 m, pop. 1,175) that sits high up over the coast just south of Capo di

Vado, and to the tiny **Isle of Bergeggi***, off the rocky headland of Capo Maiolo.

This unusually conical islet, known for its wildlife (8 ha of rocky terrain covered in vegetation and a popular haunt of seagulls) has been a *Regional Nature Reserve* since 1985. It once had a lighthouse to mark the port of Vada Sabatia (remains of a circular tower from Roman times can still be seen), and in the late Middle Ages became the site of a monastery, as evidenced by the remains of two ancient churches.

Spotorno

Now overwhelmed by the arrival of mass tourism and unchecked property development, Spotorno (elev. 7 m, pop. 4,290) nevertheless has the typical layout of the ancient Ligurian fishing village, based around the main street parallel to the coast. The *church of the Assunta* (17th cent.) has paintings by Domenico Piola and Gregorio De Ferrari. A walk up the hill, through a relatively recently developed area, leads up to the 14th-century *Castle*, a huge quadrangular construction with a high curtain wall.

Noli**

This medieval port (elev. 2 m, pop. 2,884), one of the best preserved in the whole of Liguria, sits in the little bay between Capo Noli and the slopes of Mt. Ursino. The towers and castle that dominate the village from above create an extremely

Noli and its castle dominating the village

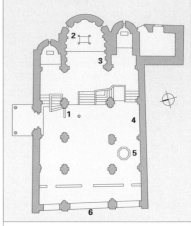

Noli: S.Paragorio

1 Romanesque ambo altered in 1889
2 Renaissance tabernacle
3 Bishop's chair (part-ancient)
4 Wooden Crucifix (12th cent.)
5 Baptismal font redesigned in 1889
6 Excavations from the Imperial Age

picturesque scene. The ancient 'Neapolis' grew up together with nearby Varigotti in Byzantine times, performing a defensive role against the Longobards and Saracen invasions. Following its involvement in the first crusade, Noli was granted political and commercial privileges and developed into an important seaport. It eventually broke free of feudal control by the Del Carretto family and became an independent republic with the help of Genoa, with which it formed a confederation (1202) in the fight against Pisa and Venice. Noli enjoyed not only the wealth brought by maritime trade, but also the protection of its ally Genoa, which used the little port as a shelter for its ships. This period of great security lasted until 1796-97, when Liguria was invaded by Napoleon's troops.

The Via Aurelia runs through the town (dividing it from the beach) as **Corso Italia**, which in summer becomes a busy promenade. This street was once lined with an uninterrupted arcade that served both as a public passageway and as a shelter for boats. The only surviving part is in the northern part near the *portici* and the *Loggia della Repubblica*, where some of the original cobblestones can still be seen. This porticoed section leads into the heart of the village, in whose narrow streets the houses are separated by the typical 'spacer' arches. To the right is the *Palazzo del Comune* (14th-15th cent.)

with mullioned windows on the seaward side and a twin-arched loggia on the opposite inland-facing facade. Its perfectly-preserved 13th-century tower has Ghibelline crenelations. Amid the many medieval houses and towers stands the 13th-century **cathedral of San Pietro**, whose Baroque transformations conceal a medieval structure; inside, in the apse, is a polyptych of the Lodovico Brea group depicting the *Enthroned Madonna and Child with Angels and Saints*, and a fine Roman *sarcophagus* used as the altar. A little further inland, *Piazza Morando*, with its lofty Torre del Canto, offers a beautiful view of the walls and the atmospheric remains of the Ursino castle (see below); at the southern end of Corso Italia, next to the medieval Arco del Portello, is *Casa Pagliano*, a 14th-century house much restored by Alfredo D'Andrade.

Noli's most important historic monument, beyond Casa Pagliano, is the **church of San Paragorio*** (*open: summer, Tue, Thur, Sat and Sun, 10am-noon; winter, Thur 10am-noon*), one of the best examples of Romanesque art in the whole of Liguria. The surviving construction, which was com-

pletely restored at the end of the 19th century, is thought to date back to the year 1000, but the original place of worship was probably founded in the 8th century, the period to which the Finale stone sarcophagi found near the church (now arranged on the left-hand side) belong. The facade and sides are decorated with blind arches and pilaster strips in the Lombard style. The interior (the entrance is on the left-hand side) has a central nave, two side aisles and a semi-circular apse facing the sea. The *ambo*, or pulpit, is from the Romanesque period, as is the wooden *crucifix*. The *bishop's throne* dates back to the 12th century; the frescoes are 15th century.

The climb up through the olive groves and terraced cultivations of Mt. Ursino leads to the ruins of *Noli Castle*. This Del Carretto fortification, built in the 12th century and later altered, stands in a particularly panoramic spot over the town and the coast. The imposing ancient walls on one side of the castle continue all the way down to the sea.

A few miles up the mountain above the castle, the road comes to a junction with the road to Voze. To the left (toward Finale Pia) the road

5.2 Savona province   5.3 Finale Ligure

crosses the **Manie Plateau***, directly above the stretch of coast between Noli and Finale Pia. This beautiful area of high ground, frequented since earliest times, bears traces of the old Roman and pre-Roman roads that diverted travelers away from the rocky slopes of the 'Malpasso' between Noli and Varigotti. The area is now to become part of the Finale nature park, designed to preserve a piece of landscape that is extremely interesting in terms of both its ancient human history and its flora and fauna. This "natural environment that has hardly changed at all over the millennia", to quote Italo Calvino, has the Finale area's largest cave: the **Arma delle Manie**, a large cavern containing traces of human life reaching as far back as Middle Paleolithic times. Numerous easy walking paths criss-cross the plateau, which forms a splendid terrace high up over the sea, immersed in the rich colors and scents of the Mediterranean *maquis* (scrubland), and the perfect place for hiking, cycling and riding tours, with plenty of opportunities to rest beneath the ilex and oak trees.

The beach at Varigotti

Rock-climbing in the inland area near Finale

Varigotti*

The next little village along the coast (elev. 5 m), the ancient point of access into Finale territory from the sea, is separated from Noli by the white limestone cliffs of Capo Noli and the Malpasso. Like Noli, Varigotti was a Byzantine center of defense against the Longobards, and an important port in the

area known today as 'Saracen Bay'. It was owned by the Del Carretto until it was covered over in 1341 by Genoa. The present-day village was built in the 14th century on the other side of Punta Crena. Annexed with the Marquisate of Finale to the Republic of Genoa and later to the Kingdom of Sardinia, it became part of the municipality of Finale Ligure in 1869. Its interesting, typically Ligurian flat-roofed houses face directly onto a good sandy beach over a mile long. The panoramically-situated *castle*, visible above Punta Crena, consists of the remains of the Byzantine 'castrum' and the later construction by the Del Carretto, destroyed by Genoa. On a sheer drop over Saracen Bay, reached by a footpath beginning to the north of the ancient village, stands the late medieval **church of San Lorenzo Vecchio** (*open Sun, 9am-2pm*), Varigotti's parish church until 1586, badly damaged during the last war and subsequently restored. The Roman and late medieval remains found in the church, including a precious 3rd/4th-century sarcophagus, have been moved to the Civic Museum in Finale.

Finale Ligure

Of the three once distinct villages that make up the now continuous conurbation (elev. 10 m, pop. 12,302), **Finale Pia** is encountered first when coming from Varigotti. The old village of Pia grew up around the **church of Santa Maria di Pia**, which already existed in 1170 as a chapel and was transformed in the 16th century as the abbey church of the adjoining Benedictine monastery; the Rococo facade was added during the 18th century, while the fine belltower retains the original Romanesque-Gothic appearance of the 13th/14th-century edifice. The Baroque interior has a 15th-century tabernacle (left wall) and beautiful 16th-century wardrobes in the sacristy. Behind the church is the 16th-century *abbey* with terracottas from the Della Robbia school, including a *Madonna and Child with St. Luke and St. John the Evangelists.*

From Finale Pia, the road that runs from Piazza di S. Maria along the east bank of the Sciusa river leads to the new district of *Calvisio,* and from here, along Vico Bedina (to the left just after the church) to the interesting ancient quarter (elev. 130 m): a group of typical old houses, or *casazze,* built from blocks of stone. Just before coming to this old district note the *church of San Cipriano,* redesigned in the Baroque period, but with a Romanesque belltower.

Further up the Sciusa valley river we come to the Verzi bridge, beyond which the road continues into the *Val Ponci* (take left at the first junction across the river). In Roman times, the road through this valley was an important artery, as can be deduced from the presence of no fewer than five **bridges*** dating back to the 2nd century, the period in which the emperor Hadrian ordered the restoration of the 'Via Iulia Augusta', originally laid out in the 13th century BC. The first of these, known as the *Ponte delle Fate,* and the third (*Ponte delle Voze*) are in an excellent state of preservation.

Finale Marina, now a busy seaside resort stretching along the coast (see plan p. 122), also has an ancient history. It came to prominence with the resumption of seafaring activities when the period of Barbarian invasions came to an end, and by the second half of the 16th century had become the center of commercial activity in the area. The historic center has a number of interesting 16th- and 17th-century buildings, while on the inland side of the Via Aurelia are the ramparts of the *Castelfranco,* built by the Genoese in 1365-67; after coming repeatedly under the control of the Del Carretto family, it was reinforced by the Spanish in the 17th century.

Finalborgo*, which has been spared the onslaught of mass urbanization thanks to its inland position, is the most interesting of the three parts into which Finale Ligure divides. Rebuilt by Giovanni I Del Carretto in the 15th century, after the destruction of the earlier *Burgus Finarii* during the war with Genoa, it was the capital of the marquisate and crucial to Spain's dominions in northern Italy. It was defended by a system of walls (well preserved) connected to the *castle of San Giovanni* above and by the two rivers enclosing the burgh, onto which the entrance gates opened. If anything can

An attractive old square of Finalborgo, the most interesting of the three parts into which Finale Ligure divides

be said to symbolize Finalborgo – whose ancient atmosphere can still be appreciated strolling through its streets and squares, with their historical buildings – it is surely the magnificent late Gothic belltower* of the **church of San Biagio**, erected over a tower in the walls. The church, now with a Baroque facade, has inside a *triptych* (1513) possibly by Bernardino Fasolo, a fanciful marble *pulpit*, by Pasquale Bocciardo, and a 1527 painting on wood (*Our Lady of the Rosary*) featuring members of the Del Carretto family. Near the 15th-century *Porta Testa*, in Piazza S. Caterina, stands the *convent of Santa Caterina*, founded in 1359 by the Del Carretto family, some of whom are buried in the church. In 1864 it was deconsecrated and used as a penitentiary until 1965. It has fine frescoes from the 14th and 15th centuries in the Olivieri Chapel. Note also the convent's two 15th-century cloisters, now the home of the **Civico Museo del Finale** (*open: summer 10am-noon and 3-6pm, holidays 9am-noon; winter 9am-noon and 2.30-4.30pm*), with prehistoric, Roman and medieval material found in the Finale area, and a ceramics section with exhibits ranging from earliest times through the Middle Ages to the modern age.

4 km inland from Finalborgo up the Aquila river valley lies the ancient hamlet of **Perti** (elev. 145 m), which boasts the late 14th-century *church of Sant'Eusebio*, with Romanesque crypt and attractive sail-vaulted belltower. A short drive across the hill from here stands the interesting **church of Nostra Signora di Loreto**, known also as the 'church of the five belltowers', an unusual Renaissance construction set among olive groves that repeats the design of the Portinari chapel in the *church of Sant'Eustorgio* in Milan. The actual village of Perti is situated near **Castel Gavone*** (elev. 172 m), also accessible on foot from Finalborgo along the 17th-century 'Beretta road' which passes close to the *Castel San Giovanni*, built by the Spanish in the 17th century. The superbly-situated Castel Gavone, thought to be late 12th century, was destroyed by the Genoese and rebuilt in the 1400s by Giovanni I Del Carretto. In 1713 it was

Castel Gavone, inland from Finalborgo

demolished by order of the Genoese Senate. The 15th-century *Torre dei Diamanti*, the only part left intact, is covered with rusticated stone in the Po Valley style; some of the frescoes that once decorated the tower are kept inside.

Inland from Finale Ligure and in the area of *Orco Feglino* (elev. 161 m, pop. 756), the 'Pietra di Finale' **rock-climbing practice walls*** have for the last three decades been an international rallying-point for rock-climbing enthusiasts. The white limestone walls of Monte Cucco, Rocca Perti and Boragni (to name just some of the best known) offer around 2,000 different free-climbing routes of all levels of difficulty, and attract tens of thousands of climbers from around the world.

3 km along the Via Aurelia west of Finale Marina, beyond the rocky spur of Caprazoppa, we come to **Borgio Verezzi** (pop. 2,233), which is really two villages in one: *Borgio* (elev. 32 m), on a low hill quite near the coast, and *Verezzi** (elev. 200 m), which overlooks the small plain around the Rio Bottasana. Despite the extensive building work that has gone on all around, the ancient centers of these two villages remain virtually intact, their old cobbled streets surrounded by gardens and olive trees. Verezzi, reached by a road whose twists and turns reveal superb views, is particularly well preserved and all the more charming as a result. For more than thirty years it has been the venue for a major international theater festival. Also worth visiting not far from the town are the **Borgio Verezzi Caves**, noted for their unusual filiform stalactites and Quaternary rock systems of great palaeontological interest.

5.4 Loano and environs
Circular tour, from Finale Ligure, approx. 70 km

After continuing a short way along the Via Aurelia to Loano, we continue 7.7 km inland to Toirano, from where a further 15.2 km of panoramic road leads between the imposing limestone crags of the Varatella river Valley up to the Toirano Col, the pass that connects this part of Liguria with the Po Valley. The old road on the other side of the col leads after 5 km to *Bardineto* (elev. 711 m, pop. 645), a village founded by the Del Carretto family and now a popular summer vacation resort (with 15th-cent. *oratory of the Assunta*). Another 6 km along the road that runs down the upper Bormida Valley to Millesimo lies Calizzano. Here we join the SS 490, which passes the Colle del Melogno (after 9 km), beyond which a further 16 km takes us back down to Finale Marina along the Val Maremola, dominated by Mt. Carmo, and the Pora Valley.

Pietra Ligure
This busy seaside resort and shipbuilding town (elev. 10 m, pop. 9,335) is one of the oldest settlements along the western Riviera. Its name derives from the ancient 'castrum Petrae', a Byzantine fortification built on the rocky spur on which a medieval *castle* (later remodeled) still stands. Owned by the diocese of Albenga in the Middle Ages, it was ceded in 1385 to the Republic of Genoa, which created an independent community here that remained her close ally. The old town, with its regular grid of streets running parallel to the sea, grew up to the south-west of the castle. It was partly rebuilt in the 16th century, but still retains medieval as well as 18th-century buildings. The ancient church was transformed in the Baroque period. The 'new town' dates back to the late 14th century. Note the 15th-century cusped belltower of the *oratory of the Annunziata*. More interesting still is the **church of San Nicolò da Bari**, built between 1750 and 1791, with a 19th-century facade; inside, is a painting of 1498 by Giovanni Barbagelata depicting *S. Nicolò Enthroned* and, in the chapel to the

right of the presbytery, *St. Anthony Abbot and St. Paul the Hermit* by Domenico Piola (1671). The seafront promenade was laid out in the 19th century with palm trees and gardens.

Loano
Like neighboring Pietra Ligure, Loano (elev. 4 m, pop. 11,111) is a popular bathing resort and summer vacation town. Of Roman origin, it was a feudal domain of the diocese of

5.4 Inland from Loano

Albenga, which in 1263 sold it to Oberto Doria. After a brief period in the hands of the Fieschi, it was returned to the Doria, who resided there (and endowed the town with monuments and works of art) until 1737, the year in which it became Savoy property. The town behind the palm-lined waterfront boasts some fine 16th-century buildings, including **Palazzo Comunale**, the municipal hall built for the Doria between 1574 and 1578 by a pupil of Alessi. Inside is an important fragment of a 3rd-century *Roman mosaic floor*. The building is also the home of the *Civico Museo Naturalistico*, a natural history museum with a remarkable ornithological collection. The nearby *church of San Giovanni Battista*, erected in 1633-38, has an anti-seismic iron dome, added after the 1887 earthquake.

Borgo Castello is the name of the walled medieval quarter beneath the *castle*: this building, which now appears as a sumptuous palace standing in its own grounds, was constructed in the 16th-17th century by Giovanni Andrea Doria over the remains of an earlier fortification.

A fifteen-minute walk away from here is the **convento di Monte Carmelo**, built between 1603 and 1608 for the Doria on a panoramic hill; inside the church are tombs of members of the Doria family up to 1793.

Toirano

This inland village (elev. 38 m, pop. 1,977), which sits between the Varatella and Barescione rivers, also has ancient origins. Originally a Roman settlement and subsequently a Byzantine fortified town, it became a feudal domain of the bishop of Albenga in the 12th century and in the second half of the 13th century passed, with Albenga, into the hands of the Genoese. Traces of the walls and defense towers survive in the old part, with its medieval houses and loggias; there is also a picturesque three-span stone *bridge* (14th cent.) over the Varatella river. The medieval **church of San Martino**, rebuilt in 1609, retains the sturdy 14th-century crenelated belltower, which formed part of the defense system. The main street through the village and its quaint old houses and craft workshops leads to *Palazzo Del Carretto*, with a walled-up medieval portico and Renaissance portal; its old stables now house the *Museo di Storia, Cultura e Tradizioni della Val Varatella (open: 10am-1pm, 3-6pm)*, an extensive collection of ethnographic material dedicated to olive-growing, viticulture and crop farming, together with an array of old costumes and craft implements. The building is also to house the new *Museo Preistorico della Val Varatella*, formerly at the Toirano caves.

1.5 km from Toirano, off the road for Bardineto, are the **Grotte di Toirano***, a group of caves in an impressive setting of white limestone rocks. Just beyond the parking lot is the entrance to the *Grotta della Basura* (or Witch's Cavern), of exceptional importance not only to speleologists, but also for the valuable prehistoric finds made there of material dating back to the Lower

Paleolithic. The route through the cave passes by some amazing formations of rock crystals, with traces of human prints, marks left by torches and bear claw marks. The Witch's Cavern is followed by the *Grotta di S. Lucia Inferiore*, a series of chambers with no prehistoric remains but some beautiful stalactites and stalagmites. The exit is on the opposite side under the *Grotta di S. Lucia Superiore*, which ends in a sheer drop over the valley.

The provincial road west out of Toirano leads (after 4 km) to **Balestrino** (elev. 371 m, pop. 503). This ancient village was the property of the monastery of San Pietro di Varatella before passing into the hands of the Del Carretto in the 14th century. The family were also the owners of the 16th-century *Palace-Fortress* semi-destroyed by the French in the late 1700s and restored in the following century: from its commanding position the whole valley could be kept watch over. The Romanesque *church of St. George*, near the cemetery, has 15th-century frescoes. Subsidence forced the inhabitants to move from the old feudal settlement at the foot of the castle onto higher ground, where a new parish church was built.

Calizzano

Del Carretto property until the 17th century, this little town (elev. 647 m, pop. 1,603) was subsequently owned by the Genoese, the Spanish and the Genoese again. The 14th-century tower (later the belltower) of the Romanesque *church of San Lorenzo* (rebuilt 1590-1630) was part of the now lost town walls. Near the church is the *oratory of San Giovanni Battista*, erected in the 17th century over the stables of the castle, which was also destroyed.

Colle del Melogno

Defended by fortifications of Napoleonic origin, this mountain pass (elev. 1028 m) once had enormous strategic importance. The two sides of the col are cloaked in some of the finest beechwoods to be found in Liguria, and are the ideal place to enjoy cool walks in the summer or the rich colors of the fall.

The spectacular Toirano caves

On the way back to Finale Ligure, it is worth making the brief detour to **Tovo San Giacomo** (elev. 80 m, pop. 2,132), which lies deep in the verdant landscape of the Val Maremola. The nearby hamlet of *Bardino Nuovo* (elev. 234 m) is the home of the *Museo dell'Orologio da Torre G.B. Bergallo*, the first of its kind in Italy: it displays an interesting collection of items (18th-20th cent.) connected with the traditional tower clock-making activities carried on here.

6 The Albenga valleys

Area profile

This area comprises the coast between Borghetto Santo Spirito and Marina di Andora, together with the valleys whose rivers flow down to this stretch of the sea. It is one of the most interesting and varied parts of the entire western Riviera, offering everything from beautiful seaside resorts and the beautiful historic town of Albenga to the quiet, ancient inland villages that lie along the main communication routes. The area is also one of great natural and environmental beauty, not least of all because of the Isle of Gallinara, now a regional nature reserve, and the mountains that rise up on the border with Piedmont to form the eastern part of the Ligurian Alps.

A view of Albenga and its towers in an old picture postcard

The geography of the area has been shaped to a large extent by the tributaries of the Centa river, a confluence of waterways that led to the formation of the Albenga plain in the Quaternary period as the broad gulf into which each river once flowed silted up. The plain was particularly prone to flooding, which influenced the way the area was settled. The Centa was indeed responsible for silting up the monuments of Albenga, and for the frequent evacuations of a populace threatened by malaria and advancing marshland. However, the river also made the plain extremely fertile: the Albenga countryside is still an area of intensive fruit and vegetable cultivation. The Lerrone, Arroscia, Neva and Pennavaira rivers, which all flow into the Centa, shaped the four valleys that gravitate on Albenga. They were each settled in a different way and developed their own distinctive character, much influenced by the fact that they were extensively used as important strategic communication routes between the vast expanse of southern Piedmont to the north and the sea. The ruins of medieval castles and defense walls show us today the main positions from which the roads heading inland were watched over and controlled.

6.1 Albenga and its plain
Walking tour of the town and two drives to nearby villages *(see map p. 135)*

This tour, the first of three in the area, begins with an exploration of the historic capital Albenga, one of the finest and architecturally richest towns in the region. There are three places worth visiting in the plain: S. Giorgio di Campochiesa, 4 km north of Albenga; Cisano sul Neva, 7.5 km to the northwest in the lower Neva Valley; and Villanova d'Albenga, 6.5 km to the west, on the south bank of the Arroscia river.

Albenga*

The origins of the town (elev. 5 m, pop. 22,642) date back to the 6th-4th century BC, when 'Albium Ingaunum' was founded, the

town of the *ingauno* people who were finally brought under Roman control in 181 BC. The typical 'castrum' layout of the Roman town, renamed 'Albingaunum', survives in the regular grid pattern. After its destruction by the Goths and Vandals, it was rebuilt at the beginning of the 5th century by General Constance, husband of Galla Placidia and future emperor. After the Longobard invasion and repeated Saracen attacks, Albenga became the capital of the marchland of King Arduino in the 11th century, when it enjoyed free commune status, and took part in the first crusade, thereby obtaining commercial and maritime privileges in the Levant. Between the 11th and 13th centuries it flourished, but in subsequent centuries, when it was caught up in fights over territorial possession in which feudal lords keen to assert their rights took part, it gradually lost its autonomy and eventually came under the control of Genoa (1251). The Middle Ages saw the rebuilding of the walls over those erected by Constance, and the construction of the public buildings that make Albenga the best-preserved historical center on the western Riviera. The change in the course of the Centa river to the south of the town (which led to the large-scale transformation of the local geography, and of agricultural and commercial activities) is thought to date back to this period. As the port silted up, the coast shifted further and further away from the town, and the inexorable decline of Albenga as a major sea power began.

Via Enrico d'Aste (see plan A1). This street, which corresponds to the eastern section of the *decumanus maximus* of Albingaunum, begins at the leafy Piazza del Popolo (along the old Via Aurelia). On the right is the *church of Santa Maria in Fontibus*, medieval in origin but much altered over the centuries. Opposite, stands the 13th-century *Torre Cazzulini*, which provides a foretaste of the beautiful architecture in the ancient heart of the town immediately beyond.

Piazza San Michele (A1). That this square was the hub of the civil and religious life of Albenga is demonstrated by the cluster of tower-houses, public buildings, and the cathedral itself. Together with the early-Christian baptistery and the other medieval buildings that line Via Bernardo Ricci beyond the square (see below), they form a quite charming monumental complex.
On the left, at the back of the square at no. 12 is the imposing **Palazzo Peloso Cepolla**, whose late 16th-century facade incorporates a 13th-century tower. The interior, decorated with 17th-century frescoes, houses the **Museo Navale Romano** (*open: summer 10am-*

Hunting scene. Palazzo Peloso Cepolla, Albenga

noon and 4-7pm; winter 10am-noon and 3-6pm; closed Mon*), which displays a collection of wine amphorae and the remains of a Roman ship that sank in the 1st century BC off the coast, along with archaeological finds from the Albenga area. On the same side of the square is the Town Hall, which incorporates (on the corner with Via Ricci) the 14th-century *Tower-House of the Malasemenza*.

Albenga: the monumental center

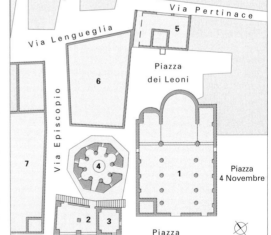

1 Cathedral
2 Palazzo Vecchio del Comune (Loggia)
3 Municipal Tower
4 Baptistery
5 Costa Tower-House
6 Palazzo Costa Del Carretto di Balestrino
7 Bishop's Palace
8 Malasemenza Tower-House (Town Hall)
9 Fieschi-Ricci House

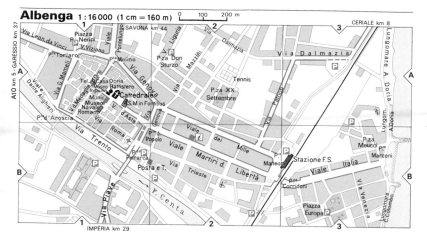

Albenga 1 : 16 000 (1 cm = 160 m)

A10 km 5–GARESSIO km 37

SAVONA km 44

CERIALE km 8

Piazza
P.ta Nenni
V. Viziano
P.za Torlaro
P.za Molino
P.za Don Sturzo
Via Liguria
Via Dalmazia
Via D a l m a z i a
Lungomare A. Doria
Via Leon.da Vinci
Viale
Viale
Pontelungo
Via Mazzini
Via Genova
Tennis
Via Patton
P.za XX
Settembre
Via G. Mameli
Viale Dante Alighieri
Casa Doria
Museo Battistero
Ingauni
Munic.
Museo
Navale
Romano
Cattedrale
S.M.in Fontibus
V. d'Asia
Via
Roma
P.za d'Aroscia
Via Trento
P.za Petrarca
P.za d'Aroscia
Viale
Roma
Viale
dei
Mille
Via
Trieste
Viale
Martiri d.
Libertà
Posta e T.
Viale
Italia
Via Piave
F. Centa
P.ta Maeton
P.za
Corridoni
Stazione F.S.
P.za Meucci
P.za
Marconi
Piazza
Europa
Via Venezia
Lungomare C.Colombo
IMPÉRIA km 29

Cattedrale* (A1). The cathedral of *San Michele* was built in the Middle Ages on the site of an early Christian church (5th cent.), and altered several times, as is apparent from the facade: the lower central section is Romanesque (11th cent.) while the two side portals are 13th century, and the central portal was added in 1669. The **belltower***, rebuilt between 1391 and 1395

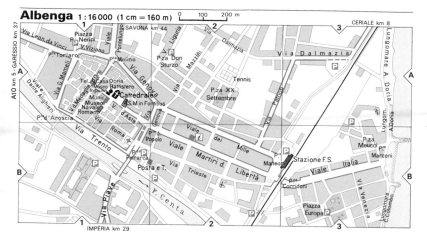

Albenga: the cathedral and its belltower

on the foundations of its Romanesque predecessor, is a fine late-Gothic structure. The interior, divided into a central nave with side aisles, has a monumental 19th-century *organ* with a 17th-century wind chest; the eastern aisle has a votive shrine from 1456; in the central apse is a 16th-century fresco of a *Crucifixion with Saints*.

The roof above the nave is decorated with 19th-century frescoes. Restoration work carried out in the 1960s brought to light some of the 13th-century structures and the remains of the late medieval apse and Carolingian crypt, part of which can now be seen beneath the presbytery.

Palazzo Vecchio del Comune (A1). This building, adjoining the baptistery to the left of the cathedral, forms, together with the **Torre Comunale** (on the corner of Via Ricci), a complex with a completely medieval flavor. It was built during the 14th century, but the large 13th/14th-century *Loggia Comunale* that extends out from the base of the tower now appears (on the Via Ricci side) in the form it acquired in 1421; the side facing the baptistery has Ghibelline crenelations and two steep flights of stairs to the upper level.

Inside is the **Civico Museo Ingauno*** (*opening times as Museo Navale in Palazzo Peloso Cepolla*), a varied collection of finds made in Albenga and environs from pre-Roman times to the Middle Ages, including stone tablets, mosaics, sculptures and some particularly interesting Roman ceramics.

Baptistery** (A1). Built in the first half of the 5th century by order of General Constance, this is the only example of late-Roman architecture to survive intact in Albenga and is Liguria's foremost early-Christian monument. It is entered from the Loggia Comunale down steps that descend to the level of the town in the 5th century, a mere one meter above sea level. This beautifully-preserved structure – ten-sided without and octagonal within – has quadrangular and semicircular niches on the

129

inside. The niches open onto the outside as a series of windows closed off by a series of superb sandstone **transennae*** pierced with typically Longobard stylized intertwined motifs; on the inside they are flanked by Corsican granite columns, with retrieved Corinthian capitals. The original dome, from the late ancient period, built with amphorae incorporated into the vaulting, was removed during restoration work in 1900 when it was erroneously believed to be a Renaissance addition. The interior also contains some interesting late medieval *tombs* with exquisite Longobard decorations; inside is an octagonal baptismal pool, and another rectangular basin, possibly used for the 'lotio pedum' that preceded immersion itself. One niche has a 5th/6th-century **mosaic** depicting the *Trinity and the Apostles in the Form of Doves*, the only extant work of Byzantine art in northern Italy outside Ravenna. In another niche is a Romanesque fresco of the *Baptism of Jesus*.

The charming little square behind the cathedral, whose apse has one-light windows and a gallery on 13th-century columns, is **Piazza dei Leoni***, so named after the three stone lions brought from Rome in 1608 by the Costa counts who owned the medieval houses. The most noteworthy of these houses is the one opposite the apse: it is surmounted by a *tower* with 12th-century stone base and an upper crenelated brick section; to the left is *Palazzo Costa Del Carretto di Balestrino*, a 1525 building whose vestibule has Roman epigraphs and a remarkable 16th-century coffered ceiling.

The passageway between this building and the baptistery leads to *Via Episcopio*, whose opposite side is entirely taken up by **Palazzo Vescovile**, an ensemble of medieval edifices (the oldest wing, on the far right, dates back to the 11th century; the tower in the left-hand corner is 12th century) that were joined together in the second half of the 16th century to form the bishop's palace. The building, which has 15th-century furnishings and frescoes, houses the **Museo Diocesano d'Arte Sacra** (*open: 10am-noon and 3-6pm; closed Mon*), a collection of ancient inscriptions, silver items formerly part of the cathedral treasury, Flemish tapestries and some notable paintings, including a *Last Supper* by Domenico Piola, an *Annunciation* by Domenico Fiasella and a good *Martyrdom of St. Catherine* by Guido Reni. The left-hand side of the palace, decorated with black and white bands and frescoed sections, faces onto Via Ricci.

Via Bernardo Ricci* (A1). Albenga's most picturesque street is lined on both sides with medieval houses; it is also one of the oldest, since it originally formed part of the Roman *decumanus maximus*. Opposite the junction with Via Episcopio (see above) at no. 16 is **Casa Fieschi-Ricci**, whose original 12th/14th-century appearance was restored in 1936 (the portal is Renaissance). Other houses of interest are the rear of Palazzo d'Aste at no. 6 (the front of the building is in Via Cavour, see below), which has a 14th-century *loggia* – and the **Casa-Torre d'Aste Rolandi Ricci**, at no. 2, a 14th-century tower-house restored to its original style in 1959-61, with 15th-century windows on the upper floor.

Via Medaglie d'Oro (A1). The *cardo maximus* of the Roman town is now a busy shopping street that retains a quaint old atmosphere. It runs north-east/south-west and intersects with Via Bernardo Ricci to form an historic crossroads, the so-called **Loggia dei Quattro Canti**, which includes the charming Gothic arcaded corner of Via Ricci (opposite the d'Aste Rolandi Ricci tower-house mentioned above) and a Romanesque arcade on Via Medaglie d'Oro, opposite which stands the *Lengueglia-Doria Tower-House* (13th-14th cent.), restored in 1936. Note also on the right-hand side of the street (no. 25) the leaning *Cepolla Tower*, a five-story medieval house. Leading off to the left along the south-west stretch of Via Medaglie d'Oro is **Via Cavour**, on which stands the main front (17th cent.) of **Palazzo d'Aste**, an important patrician residence (the staircase is lined with Roman and

Albenga: Piazza dei Leoni, the charming little square behind the cathedral

Renaissance busts) created by incorporating medieval houses still visible in Via Ricci. Via Cavour ends at Palazzo Peloso Cepolla in Piazza S. Michele.

A ten-minute walk along *Viale Pontelungo* (A1), the street that continues north out of town from Via Medaglie d'Oro along the old Via Aurelia (the main road into Albenga in Roman and medieval times) leads to the half-buried but nonetheless impressive **Pontelungo**, the old (probably 13th-cent.) bridge over the Centa river, before its course was deviated. Nothing remains of the hospice and church near the bridge, thought to have belonged to the Benedictine abbey of the Isle of Gallinara, but note

Villanova d'Albenga: a 'town in bloom'

opposite the 18th-century *sanctuary of Nostra Signora di Pontelungo.*

San Giorgio di Campochiesa. This beautiful Romanesque-Gothic church stands in an isolated position in the cemetery of Campochiesa. Built in the 12th century with the traditional nave and two aisles and enlarged two centuries later, it played an important role as the parish church for the entire area until the 17th century, when the prerogative passed to Campochiesa. Part of the right-hand nave and the belltower with two-light windows, destroyed in the earthquake of 1887, were rebuilt using original material in

1935-36. What makes the visit particularly interesting though, is the magnificent **Last Judgment*** fresco cycle in the apse (1446), that features, curiously, Dante, Virgil and other characters from the "Divine Comedy" – a fascinating testimony to the late-medieval Dantesque tradition in Liguria.

Cisano sul Neva

This fortified town (elev. 52 m, pop. 1,517) was founded in the 13th century by Albenga to protect its north-western territories. Some parts of the original quadrangular walls survive: they are made of river pebbles reinforced in the corners by local stone quoins. Part of the walls were used to build the 14th-century **belltower** adjoining the 17th-century *church of Santa Maria Maddalena*, which overlooks a pretty square. To the left, a street leads down to the most interesting part of the town. A few hundred yards along the river, near the cemetery, is the *church of San Calocero*, little of whose original Romanesque structure (11th cent.) survives.

Villanova d'Albenga*

This pleasant little town (elev. 29 m, pop. 1,941), which like Cisano was founded by Albenga in the 13th century as a fortified outpost, is arguably the most interesting in the Albenga plain, thanks both to its setting and to its interesting historical layout. It has a polygonal plan and is surrounded by walls with towers and gateways which survived completely intact until a few decades ago. The north-west section is the best preserved. The little alleyways through the town are particularly charming not only because of their strong medieval atmosphere, but because of the local custom of decorating doorways and windows with colorful flowers and plants. Just outside the walls is the small, beautifully-proportioned Renaissance building (circular in plan) of the **church of Santa Maria della Rotonda**. At the turn-off for *Albenga Airport* (opened in 1922 as a military airfield and now used for tourism and for the flower market; the **hippodrome** behind has for some years now been the venue for various national horseraces), stands the medieval **church of Santo Stefano in Cavatorio**, now surrounded by fields and cypresses, but formerly at the center of the town of Cavatorio, which disappeared with the foundation of Villanova. The church retains its 12th-century belltower and porch with capitals, probably carved by local master stonecutters from the nearby village of Cenova (see p. 133).

6.2 The Neva and Arroscia Valleys
Circular tour (on major roads) from Albenga to Garessio and Pieve di Teco, 97 km
(see map p. 135)

From the coast, the SS 582 (*del Colle di S. Bernardo*) leads up the Val Neva to Zuccarello, beyond which (15.2 km from the coast) a short detour to the right leads up a narrow winding and panoramic road to Castelvecchio di Rocca Barbena, while the main road winds its way a further 20.5 km up to the S. Bernardo Pass at 957 m (magnificent views) and on to Garessio in the Tanaro Valley. The SS 28 (*del Colle di Nava*) follows the Tanaro river upstream (in Piedmontese territory) to the Nava Pass (back in Liguria, and 23.6 km from Garessio). The road then descends to Pieve di Teco (10.2 km) and continues down through the Arroscia Valley (27.5 km, SS 453) back to Albenga.

Zuccarello*
This picturesque, elongated village (elev. 130 m, pop. 297) some of whose old walls are still intact, was founded in 1248 by the Clavesana, who made the castle above the feudal center of the valley. When the Del Carretto gained control of the area, they ceded the feudal dominion partly to Genoa and partly to the Savoy household, causing the outbreak of the so-called 'War of Zuccarello', which ended in 1625 with the Val Neva joining the Genoese Republic.

The road through the village, flanked by attractive medieval **porticoes**, links the two turreted *gateways* to which the walls running down the castle hill were connected. The defense of the opposite side of the town was through the river and its rocky bank, on which houses still stand (the most picturesque view is from the state road). The *parish church*, remodeled in the 17th century, has a fine old **belltower**, with an 12th/13th-century lower section and a 14th-century upper part, with local stone windows. From the northern end of the main street a path leads in twenty minutes to the impressive ruins of the castle. This was possibly the birthplace of Ilaria Del Carretto, who married Paolo Guinigi, lord of Lucca: this was the couple for whom Jacopo della Quercia sculpted the celebrated tomb (1408) in Lucca cathedral.

Castelvecchio di Rocca Barbena*
The Val Neva's oldest feudal center (elev. 430 m, pop. 197) sits high up on a rocky spur. The **castle**, built in around the 12th century and later modified, was originally the stronghold of the Clavesana family before passing to the Del Carretto. In the 1700s it served as a military fortress and is now privately owned. The town, perched on the two sides of a castellated rock, has an interesting circular layout, crisscrossed by tortuous streets. Note the typical Ligurian houses with their terraced roofs with little walls to collect the rainwater, and the pitched roofs typical of mountain areas, drying chambers and windows with plasterwork decorations:

Castelvecchio di Rocca Barbena dominated by its castle

traditional architectural features of the Neva and Pennavaira Valleys.

From Castelvecchio to Pieve di Teco
This section of the tour describes a broad semi-circle between the Neva and Arroscia river valleys, with much of the road following the course of the Tanaro river across the regional border in Piedmont. The main places of interest on the way are: **Garessio** (elev. 621 m, pop. 3,657), comprising three small villages, the first of which, *Borgo Maggiore*, has a number of noteworthy houses (some medieval) in the ancient *Via Cavour*; **Ormea** (elev. 736 m, pop. 2,054), an ancient small town – now a holiday resort – based around *Via Roma*, at the start of which stands the 15th-century *church of San Martino* (with 1397 frescoes in the apse); the **Colle di Nava** (elev. 941 m), a broad grassy depression

on the watershed noted for its honey and lavender production, and an excellent base for walks and hiking tours; and **Pornassio** (elev. 630 m, pop. 644), a collection of hamlets on the northern side of the upper Arroscia Valley with a 16th-century *castle* and the important **church of San Dalmazzo**, with a slender Romanesque belltower and 15th-century facade: in the lunette over the portal are frescoes attributed to Giovanni Canavesio; inside note the *polyptych of St. Blaise* (15th cent.), frescoes by Giorgio Guido da Ranzo, and others in the presbytery.

Another tiny hill village worth making the short detour to (3 km to the west along the road on the sharp bend between Colle di Nava and Pornassio) is **Cosio di Arroscia*** (elev. 721 m, pop. 302). This compact collection of houses (huddled together for protection against the harsh winters) and covered streets is one of the most charming rustic sights to be found anywhere in the Ligurian hills.

Pieve di Teco*

This little community (elev. 240 m, pop. 1,430), which grew up in the 14th and 15th centuries is another of western Liguria's attractive, well-preserved towns. Situated on the junction of some of the main 'salt routes' between Liguria and Piedmont, it soon became one of the cornerstones of the valley's feudal system. The Clavesana built a castle there (probably in the 12th century),

some remains of which survive on a spur of the mountain ridge. Another castle (destroyed in the 17th century) and the walls around the town were erected again by the Clavesana in the 13th century, until in 1385 the site passed into the hands of the Genoese, who made it the administrative center of the parish. Ever since the Middle Ages, the heart of the town has been **Corso Ponzoni**, bounded at either end by two pretty squares lined with medieval porticoes, beneath which fine doorways alternate with craftsmen's workshops. The **church of Santa Maria della Ripa**, the ancient church around which the town grew up, is 15th century in appearance (the period to which the belltower dates back). The grand **collegiate church of San Giovanni Battista** (1792-1806) has some good canvases including a *San Francesco di Paola* inconclusively attributed to Luca Cambiaso. Pieve di Teco is also noted for several ancient craft traditions such as shoe-making, and for its bread and cheese production. It also keeps alive some of the traditional sports associated with the Piedmont-Provence area such as elastic ball and skittles.

Making walking boots at Pieve di Teco

In the nearby Rezzo Valley, 6.5 km south of Pieve, is the tiny country village of **Cenova** (elev. 558 m), which boasts quite a collection of fine doorways with sculpted architraves, testifying to the important stone-cutting tradition that flourished here in the late Middle Ages, and produced the decorative material for buildings in many western Ligurian towns.

Rezzo (elev. 563 m, pop. 420), which lies 3 km further up the same valley, was a feudal dominion of the Clavesana, important in the Middle Ages for the links it provided with the Valle Argentina. 2.5 km outside Rezzo, on a hill overlooking the valley, stands the **Sanctuary of Nostra Signora del Sepolcro** (elev. 731 m), in a beautiful wooded setting. The outer structure is typical of 15th-century Ligurian mountain architecture, with a portico held up by stone columns and a belltower pierced with windows and topped by a spire. The interior has pointed arches decorated with black and white bands; note the *frescoes* by Giorgio Guido da Ranzo.

The road continues beyond Rezzo up into the hills, through chestnut and beech woods. The 15-km drive leads to the **Teglia Pass** (elev. 1,387 m), at the start of the descent into the Valle Argentina (see pp. 156-159), which has been traversed by man since earliest times.

The bridge over the Neva at Zuccarello

Church of San Pantaleo

This isolated place of worship, which is of considerable historical and architectural interest, stands on the valley bottom to the south of the state road, between Borghetto d'Arroscia and Ranzo; a single column stands in front of the entrance. The various phases of its construction are clearly visible: the early Romanesque stage, to which belongs one of the apses; and the 15th-century stage, which added the second apse and entrance porch, carved by the 'Cenova school' (1493) and decorated by 15th-century frescoes by local artists; the interior, which still has traces of frescoes from 1448 and other late medieval cycles, was transformed in the Baroque period into a single aisleless space topped by a dome.

6.3 The Bay of Alassio and Val Lerrone
Circular tour from Albenga along the coast and into the Val Lerrone, 63 km

The coastal part of the tour follows the Via Aurelia for 14.4 km from Albenga to Marina di Andora, taking in the well-known towns of Alassio and Laigueglia – two old fishing villages which since the 19th century have grown into major tourist resorts – and Capo Mele, a promontory marked by a naval lighthouse. From Marina di Andora we head inland to the restful hills of Val Merula, and then climb, along 23.4 km of provincial road, to the 677-m Ginestro Pass. From here, the 25.2-km descent along the provincial road back to Albenga, which begins quite steeply, passes through Val Lerrone, a valley dotted with small country villages and the remains of ruined castles.

Alassio*

This holiday resort (elev. 6 m, pop. 11,326), one of the finest on the western Riviera and the queen of the so-called 'Riviera delle Palme' (Savona province's palm-fringed coast), stands with its beautiful long beach of fine sand in the wide bay between Capo Santa Croce and Capo Mele. It began life as a fishing village in the 6th-7th centuries when a group of Milanese took refuge here after fleeing the Longobard invasion of the Po Valley. From 1303 it became the property of Albenga, from which it gained independence in the 16th century, and flourished thereafter. In the last two decades of the 19th century it was 'discovered' by English tourism, which turned it into one of the best-known resorts of this part of the Riviera, endowing it with many of the gardens and villas that now grace the hill behind the town.

Tourism clearly still dominates life in the town, offering a whole array of society events, cultural initiatives, and sports and recreational activities. But despite

Vacationing on the Riviera the way it used to be: a period photo taken at Alassio

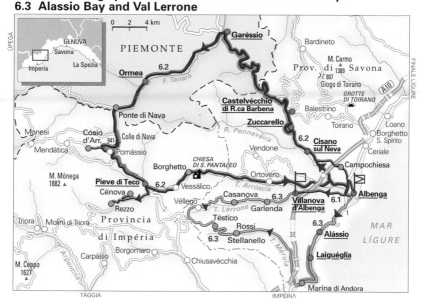

the fact that Alassio is crossed by the Via Aurelia and has seen a plethora of new buildings to cater for the hoards of tourists that descend on the town each summer, it still manages to retain the feel of an old Ligurian town in the so-called '**budello**', the narrow and busy *Via XX Settembre* (B2), parallel to the beach but divided from it by a row of buildings that face directly onto the sands. This animated street, as alive by day as it is by night, is still the commercial hub of Alassio. In nearby Corso Dante (B1-2) stands the **muretto**, a low wall containing the ceramicized autographs of famous personalities from the world of culture, art and show business since the 1950s, which is still a major attraction. One of the narrow lanes that crosses the 'budello' leads to the *Passeggiata Italia* (B1-2), the seafront promenade in the central part of the town offering good views of the bay. The **church of Sant'Ambrogio** (B1), on the Via Aurelia, was completely rebuilt during the 15th and 16th centuries over an earlier building; the 19th-century facade still has a Renaissance-style slate portal (1511) with *St. Ambrose*, *Christ and the Apostles*, and the *Everlasting Father*; the 1507 belltower, pierced with two- and three-light windows, is an example of late Romanesque-Gothic architecture; the Baroque interior with nave and side aisles has some interesting paintings dating from the 1500s and 1600s.

From Alassio, the road to Solva leads to the little Romanesque **church of Santa Croce** (C3), which stands on a panoramic site over the like-named cape; originally owned by the Benedictine abbey on the Isle of Gallinara, used as a refuge for wayfarers, it was repeatedly altered and restored, though the masonrywork, apse and left-hand side are from the original 11th-century building. The church is the starting point of the so-called *Archaeological*

Alassio's 'budello' crowded with tourists

Walk to Albenga: a footpath through the Mediterranean scrub that retraces the ancient Roman road.

Mt. Tirasso, which can be reached along a tortuous 8-km road beginning at the square in front of Alassio's train station (B1-2), is the site of the **sanctuary of the Madonna della Guardia**, built in the 17th century over a medieval castle, in a position

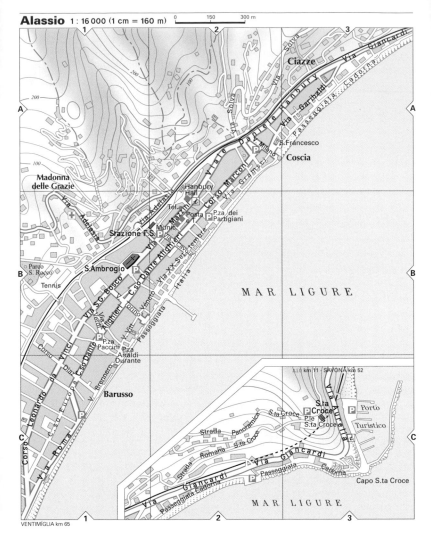

Alassio 1 : 16 000 (1 cm = 160 m)

0   150   300 m

Ciazze

Via Solva

Via Giancardi

Via Garibaldi

Via Cadorna

Passeggiata

S.Francesco

Coscia

Milano

Viale Daniele Hanbury

Corso Marconi

Via Gramsci

Madonna
delle Grazie

Hanbury
Hall

Via Adelasia

Via Mazzini

Tel.

Posta
e T.

P.za dei
Partigiani

Stazione F.S.

Munic.

Via Dante Alighieri

Via XX Settembre

Via Italia

S.Ambrogio

Pardo
S. Rocco

Tennis

Via S.G. Bosco

Torino

Via XX Settembre

Via Italia

Passeggiata

MAR LIGURE

Corso da Vinci

Leonardo da

Via Dante Alighieri

Corso Dante

Vittor.

Brennero

Veneto

P.za
Paccini

P.za
Airaldi
Durante

Barusso

Corso Diaz

Via Roma

S.ta Croce

Via Aurelia

Porto

S.ta Croce

P.le
S.ta Croce

Turistico

Strada   Panoramica   S.ta Croce

Strada   Romana   S.ta Croce

Via Giancardi

Passeggiata

Via Giancardi   Passeggiata Cadorna

Cadorna

Capo S.ta Croce

MAR LIGURE

a 10 km 11 · SAVONA / km 52

VENTIMÍGLIA km 65

that offers a wonderful *panorama** of the sea, the Lerrone and Arroscia Valleys and the Maritime Alps.

The motor-boat trips that run in summer from Alassio to **Isola Gallinara*** are to be recommended. Boats take tourists around the now privately-owned island, but may not normally moor there (*for further information contact: IAT Alassio, tel. 0182647027; Albenga Town Hall, tel. 0182541351*). The Isle of Gallinara, which is part of Albenga's municipal territory, is a regional nature reserve with flora and fauna of outstanding interest,

Divers discover Liguria's undersea world and its rich variety of marine life

136

including many endemic species, and beautiful grottoes on the southern side. In ancient times it was the home of a community of hermits, the first traditionally believed to have been St. Martin of Tours, who took refuge here between 356 and 360. In the early 8th century it passed into the hands of the Benedictine monks, who founded an abbey on the island. This religious community acquired extensive land holdings along the western Riviera and in Provence; the scant surviving remains of the monastery buildings have now been incorporated into a villa.

Laigueglia

This pleasant little seaside resort (elev. 6 m, pop. 2,307) still displays the typical layout of an ancient Ligurian settlement. Roman in origin, it was in the Middle Ages a fishing village dependent on nearby Andora. Coral fishing off its well-sheltered coast, and the growth of maritime trade helped it to flourish in the 16th century. At the start of the hill just behind the train station stands the imposing and attractive **church of San Matteo***, one of the most impressive Baroque edifices in the entire western Riviera, with a complex curving facade flanked by two belltowers with polychrome majolica domes.

The panoramic road that leads up the hill arrives after 3 km (by car or on foot) to **Colla Micheri*** (elev. 162 m), a quaint little country village set among the olive groves between the Laigueglia depression and Val Merula. This ancient village was restored and improved in the 1960s and '70s by the Norwegian ethnologist and navigator Thor Heyerdahl (see box). From the highest part of the town it is possible to see the castle of Andora (see below), which can be reached on foot, along the so-called Roman road, or by car.

Marina di Andora

This is the municipal center of the scattered community of **Andora** (pop. 6,636), and also its most populous part, corresponding to the old fishing village of Andora. One of the old look-out towers that

From the Kon-Tiki to Colla Micheri

When a 44-year-old Thor Heyerdahl visited Colla Micheri in 1958 it was love at first sight. The Norwegian ethnologist decided to restore the village and make it his second home, his first (and favorite) home being the high seas. "I feel a sense of peace here that reminds me of the ocean," he replied when asked why he chose Colla Micheri, adding, with a smile: "...of a calm ocean, I mean". The fearless Norwegian first came to the world's attention in 1947 when, together with five companions, he set out from the Peruvian coast on his famous balsawood raft. 101 days and 4,300 nautical miles later, the *Kon-Tiki* reached the Polynesian archipelago of Tuamotu, a legendary exploit demonstrating that the South Sea islanders may have come from South America and not from Asia, as had been assumed until then. After various adventurous archaeological expeditions to the Galapagos and to Easter Island, he went one step further in 1970, sailing the 3,270 miles from Morocco to Barbados on the papyrus boat *Ra II*; and in 1977-78 he sailed from the Persian Gulf to the Indian Ocean and the Red Sea (4,200 miles) on another papyrus vessel, the *Tigris*. What this iron-willed Norwegian octogenarian wanted to prove with his intrepid exploits (the ones mentioned here were only the most famous) was that our prehistoric ancestors were capable of fashioning oceanworthy vessels and that they were indeed pretty formidable continent hoppers. And one of the reasons why he was so keen to demonstrate this was the fact that he has always been a firm believer in the human race and the brotherhood of its peoples.

formed part of the Genoese defense system survives. The road along the Merula river comes to the so-called **Roman bridge**, with its ten spans, three of which are hump-backed. The bridge was actually built in medieval times over an older construction that made it possible to wade across the river to reach the Roman road between Colla Micheri and Andora castle.

Andora Castello*

This is the name commonly used for the isolated and highly atmospheric site (reached by a short road near the viaduct under the highway), on which stand the ruined remains of the **Castle of Andora** and the Romanesque-Gothic **church of Ss. Giacomo e Filippo***, one of the most important medieval complexes in the western Riviera. It passed from the Clavesana to Genoa in 1252 and life flourished there until the mouth of the Merula river became so marshy that the population moved to Laigueglia. The church is built in unfaced stone from nearby Capo Mele: the facade, with Gothic cornices and

small arches, has a basket-arch portal and a large five-centered arch that is the result of 1901 restoration work; note also the fine portal on the left-hand side and the beautiful apse. The interior, completely in unfaced stone, has sturdy round piers and octagonal pillars. The remains of the castle reveal both the parts dating back to the Clavesana period and the Gothic elements added under the Genoese. The early-Romanesque *church of San Nicolò*, at the entrance to the central part of the castle, is probably the community's original church.

Val Merula and Val Lerrone

The road that leads up the Merula Valley passes through an almost intact hillside environment, amid terraced olive plantations and dense woodland dotted with tiny rural communities. Among these are the typical country village of *Stellanello* (141 m, pop. 732), and **Testico** (elev. 470 m, pop. 206), which had a quite different history from the rest of the valley, since it belonged first to the Doria and then to the Savoy. Further up on the ridge, panoramic views extend to the Maritime Alps, as well as over the Merula and Lerrone Valleys, which are connected by the *Ginestro Pass* (elev. 677 m).

Val Lerrone also has a collection of scattered settlements, which grew up as farming communities. The medieval **Poggiolo Castle** in *Bassanico* (elev. 145 m), a hamlet that forms part of *Casanova Lerrone* (*private, closed to the public*), is a reminder of the importance of the Lengueglia family, who for a long period were lords of the valley. Further down near the Albenga plain, *Garlenda* (elev. 75 m) is well known for its sports and tourism activities, but above all as the home of the prestigious **Garlenda Golf Club**, which offers an 18-hole course designed by American architects John Morrison and John Harris without altering the landscape.

Andora castle

7 Imperia and environs

Area profile

Nearly eighty years since their fusion into one administrative unit (1923), Oneglia and Porto Maurizio continue
to function as quite distinct urban communities. And yet,
while the two halves of the provincial capital on the coast remain unyieldingly apart, the
area behind Imperia appears extremely unified in terms of landscape: the terraced hills
immediately inland form an almost uninterrupted sequence of olive groves, which since medieval times have been the main local resource. Attention has, as a result, traditionally turned away from the sea to the hills – higher up, the olive groves gradually give way to chestnut woods – leaving the area somewhat isolated from the major historical happenings around it. Not that this has hindered the development of the artistic
tradition in these parts. There are plenty of monuments, mostly from the medieval and
Baroque periods, to be found hidden away in the many picturesque mountain villages
and in the coastal towns themselves, although the latter have inevitably succumbed to
the more profitable cause of tourism.

Oil presses in the Imperia Olive Museum, and olive groves in the vicinity

7.1 Imperia
Walking tour through the town *(see plan pp. 140-141)*

The quite distinct separation between Oneglia and Porto Maurizio, the two small
towns that were brought together to form
Imperia (elev. 10 m, pop. 40,379) is not
only one of geographical distance: they also look totally different. Oneglia is a modern town that spreads out over the plain
at the mouth of the Impero river; Porto
Maurizio is a town rich in history that
clings to the hill high up over the sea. History has also kept them apart: between
1576 and 1797 they were separated by the
border between the Republic of Genoa
(which owned Porto Maurizio) and the Savoy Household, which would have liked
Oneglia to become their main port. The
plan never really came to fruition, but Oneglia remains the province's main port, de-

spite the fact that Porto Maurizio was the
main provincial town from 1860 to 1923.

Oneglia

Although the 20th century saw a growth in
industry alongside the traditional port and
olive-growing activities, Oneglia has never
lost its small-town atmosphere. This is best experienced in the central *Piazza Dante*
(A6), where the eclectic medieval-style facade of the former *Palazzo Comunale* (1890-
91) stands at no. 4. The almost contemporary *Palazzo del Tribunale* (1891-92) is in
Piazza De Amicis (A-B5-6), where Italian
writer Edmondo De Amicis was born (Oneglia's other famous son being Andrea Doria).
The many fishmonger's shops and *trattorie*
are tucked away under the characteristic

The long history of the olive

The museum created in 1992 in the Fratelli Carli establishment in Oneglia, possibly the only one of its kind in the world, examines everything from the production, transportation and trading of olive oil down the ages to the sacred associations attached to this typically Mediterranean plant. The exhibition sequence is in twelve sections spanning the history of olive oil from the most ancient times, when the oil of the fruit was used not so much as a food but for cosmetic and medicinal purposes. After the display of jars of perfumes and ointment receptacles, comes the section dedicated to the extraction and preparation of the oil. Here the mills, presses, filtering apparatus, and containers for storing and transporting the oil (goatskin bags, recepta-

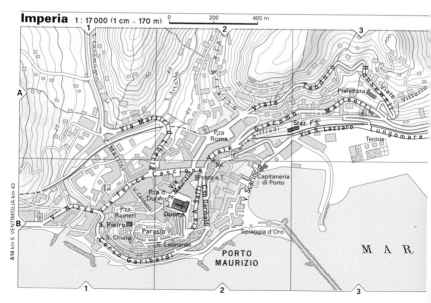

cles made of ceramic and horn and amphorae, including a mock-up of a Roman ship's hold where they were loaded), together with measuring and weighing equipment, explain (using modern audio-visual systems) the history of a culture that survived even through the darkest of the Dark Ages, when they provided those populations that cultivated them with a reliable resource. The last part of the exhibition is dedicated to the continuous-cycle olive processing system, which covers all the activities (from crushing the olives to remixing the fruit and extracting the oil) previously carried out in individual stages. Those unable to get to the museum in person, can admire the most interesting parts on the Internet, at *www.museodellolivo.com*.

CASA FONDATA NEL 1911

waterfront **portici** (arcades) of *Calata Cuneo* (B6). Behind them stands the **collegiate church of San Giovanni Battista** (B6), attributed to Gaetano Amoretti: this large-domed edifice, begun in 1739, has the traditional nave and two-aisle interior, divided by pillars. The marble *tabernacle* to the left of the presbytery is in the Gagini style (1516); the late 17th-century *Crucifix* in the 4th chapel of the north aisle

is attributed to François Lacroix (though its origins are possibly Genoese), while the first chapel has a *Madonna of the Rosary*, in the Maragliano school style.

Six millennia of olive cultivation are covered in the **Museo dell'Olivo*** (*open: 9am-noon, 3-6.30pm; fourth week in July to third week in August, 9am-noon, 4-7pm; closed Tue*), the olive museum (see box) in the Fratelli Carli oil-making plant in Via Garessio (A6).

Imperia 1 : 17 000 (1 cm = 170 m)

Porto Maurizio

In *Viale Matteotti* (A-B2-3-4-5) – the main road connecting Oneglia and Porto Maurizio to the west – stands Imperia's Town Hall (the 1932 *Palazzo Municipale*) and little else. Porto Maurizio itself, however, is full of history, with many of the surviving monuments dating back to the golden age under Genoese domination, when the town was the capital of the Vicariate of Western Liguria. The **Duomo** (B2) was started toward the end of this period but was not completed until the town had become part of the Kingdom of Sardinia (1781-1838). This cathedral, designed by Gaetano Cantoni on a grandiose scale in keeping with the dictates of the Neoclassical style, has a porch with eight Doric columns. The central-plan interior boasts a rich collection of 19th-century paintings, together with works from the demolished *parish church of San Maurizio* (see below), including a statue dated 1618 of the *Madonna of Mercy*, which is kept in the 2nd chapel on the right, and a *Crucifix* of Genoese origin, close to Maragliano in style, in the 3rd chapel on the left.

Imperia: a room in the Naval Museum of Ponente Ligure

Piazza del Duomo, laid out when the basilica was built, is also the home of the *Pinacoteca Civica* (open: 4-7pm; closed Mon) and, at no. 11, of the **Museo Navale Internazionale del Ponente Ligure** (open: Wed and Sat 3-7pm, June-September 9-11pm). Despite its limited display space, this museum of naval history offers some interesting insights into life on board ship.

Porto Maurizio's old quarter of stepped streets at the top of the hill is known as the **Parasio*** (B1-2), after the Genoese governor's palace ('Paraxu'). The late 20th century saw renewed interest in this district, which had been allowed to decay for a long period, an operation in which numerous foreign investors took part. It is reached from Piazza del Duomo by *Via Acquarone*, which leads to the 14/15th-century **Palazzo Pagliari**, with a pointed-arch porch. Higher up at the very top of the hill is *Piazza Chiesa Vecchia*, named after the old *church of San Maurizio*, demolished around 1838; this was also where the 'Paraxu' building once stood.

The three religious buildings on the seaward side of the Parasio district are all in the Baroque style. The 17th-century **oratory of San Leonardo** (B1-2) has a canvas by Gregorio De Ferrari (*Addolorata and Souls in Purgatory*) and two by Domenico Bocciardo (*Death of St. Joseph* and *Tobias Buries the Dead*); the *house* adjoining the oratory was the birthplace of the church's

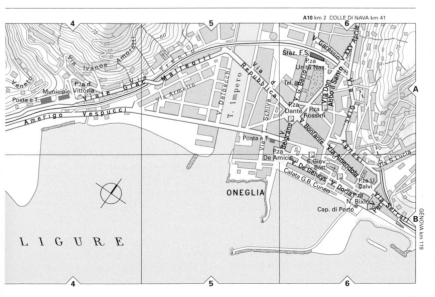

titular saint. The **convent of Santa Chiara** (B1) is of medieval origin (14th cent.) but was rebuilt in the 18th century. Inside are some important paintings (note the *San Domenico Soriano and the Madonna* by Domenico Fiasella and a *Madonna and Child with St. Catherine of Bologna* by Sebastiano Conca); hidden away at the rear of the convent is a majestic *porticato** with a spectacular view over the sea. The **church of San Pietro** (B1), belonged to a fraternity of merchants and is a 17th-century reconstruction of an earlier place of worship. It has a theatrical facade (1789) with three arches on paired columns and a small belltower created from a lookout tower; the cycle of paintings inside (*Life of St. Peter*) is by Tommaso and Maurizio Carrega.

Borgo Foce, at the estuary of the Caramagna river, has many fishermen's houses, as does **Borgo Marina**, reached by a pleasant *walk**. Here the old village is clustered around the little *church of San Giovanni Battista* (13th cent., remodeled in 1362), now deconsecrated and once annexed to a hospice of the Knights of Malta: a stone tablet reminds visitors that Petrarch stayed here in 1343 on his way to Avignon. Tourist activities are of course concentrated on the seafront. Most visitors arrive here from the sea: there are always plenty of boats (nearly all pleasure craft) moored in the little harbor.

Continuing along Via Nizza (B1) across the bridge over the Caramagna river, we come to the 17th century *Carmelite convent*, connected by a long flight of steep steps to the **church of Monte Calvario**, also 17th century. The *Madonna and Child* (French school) in the left-hand chapel dates back to the 1400s. There is a spectacular *panorama* from the square, with a view stretching all the way to Oneglia.

Artallo (elev. 92 m) is a pretty farming village 2 km to the north of Porto Maurizio, whose medieval layout remains almost completely intact.

A view of Porto Maurizio and the Parasio as it appears from the sea

7.2 Around Oneglia
A tour of the towns and villages along the coast and in the valleys, 42.5 km

This tour begins along the Via Aurelia northeast out of Oneglia to Diano Marina (5.5 km), San Bartolomeo al Mare and, 3 km further on, Cervo. The second part explores the inland area north of Oneglia, first along the SS 28 (*del Colle di Nava*) and then, after 13 km, heads west at San Lazzaro Reale along the provincial road toward Borgomaro, another 8.2 km to Ville San Pietro and a further 4.5 km to Conio. Back at Ville San Pietro, a particularly panoramic road offering beautiful views of the landscape cuts across the Maro Pass (after 4.2 km) and (3.6 km further on) the Colle d'Oggia, beyond which the road descends back down to the coast along the Valle Argentina (see pp. 156-159).

The coast

Diano Marina
This resort (elev. 4 m, pop. 6,267), which corresponds in part to the Roman town of 'Lucus Bormani' is separated from Oneglia by **Capo Berta**, a leafy promontory known for its beautiful villas. The town now forms a continuous conurbation with neighboring San Bartolomeo al Mare and Cervo (see below). Tourism has been the main activity in Diano Marina since the late 19th century, when the town was rebuilt following the disastrous earthquake of February 23, 1887. Nothing remains of the ancient town, once a major center for the oil trade, revenues from which gave the 'Communitas Diani' (the town and its inland satellite towns, see below) a certain autonomy as part of the Republic of Genoa. The history of the community is told in the *Museo Civico della 'Communitas Diani'* (*closed for restoration*) in Corso Garibaldi. On the same street stands the *church of Sant' Antonio Abate* (1862), built on a basilica-style plan with central nave and side aisles. It contains a number of paintings from the 17th-century Ligurian school.

The towns and villages that grew up in the Diano valley escaped attack from the Saracen pirates plaguing the coast. 2.2 km inland from Diano Marina lies **Diano Castello** (elev. 135 m, pop. 1,808), once the residence of the Clavesana marquises, who between 1033 and 1172 dominated the future 'Communitas Diani'. As well as retaining some of the medieval fortifications the town has a number of interesting churches: the Baroque *church of San Nicolò* was designed by Giovanni Battista Marvaldi (1699-1725); the *oratory of Santa Croce e San Bernardino*, at the end of Via Borgo is the result of 17th-century alterations, while the nearby churches of *San Giovanni Battista* (a 15th-century painting) and, in Via Martiri della Liberazione, *Santa Maria Assunta* date back to the 12th and 13th centuries (the latter was later remodeled).

4.4 km from Diano Marina, a minor road leads up to **Diano Borello** (elev. 194 m), where the late medieval *church of San Michele* stands. Much of this church was altered in the Baroque period, but the belltower is original, as is the fine ogival portal (1485) with 16th-century fresco. Inside are a polyptych (*St. Michael and Saints*) painted in 1516 by Antonio Brea, and a 16th-century painting on wood of the *Madonna della Provvidenza*.

After Diano Arentino, the road turns back toward the sea, and arrives – 12.4 km from Diano Marina – at **Diano San Pietro** (elev. 83 m, pop. 1,052). This little olive and fruit growing community is really two villages in one: in the

lower part stands the *church of Ss. Pietro e Paolo*, rebuilt in the Baroque style (except for the belltower) in the second half of the 18th century.

San Bartolomeo al Mare

Holiday homes line the stretch of the Via Aurelia that passes through this resort. To get a flavor of the ancient atmosphere of this town (elev. 26 m, pop. 3,074) cross the railroad to the site of the **sanctuary of the Madonna della Rovere**: a late-medieval edifice much altered between the 16th and 19th centuries. Inside, note the wooden *Crucifix* (15th cent.) at the end of the right-hand aisle and a 16th-century painting on wood (*Madonna and Child*) on the wall of the left-hand aisle. Another fragment of the medieval town is to be found around the *church of San Bartolomeo*, near the highway turn-off. This place of worship, again altered in the Baroque period, has in the apse a polyptych (*St. Bartholomew with Saints*) painted in the 16th-century by Raffaele and Giulio De Rossi.

Villa Faraldi (elev. 336 m, pop. 451), whose *parish church* has a Roman funerary tablet dating back to the 3rd century BC, is a picturesque medieval village set in beautiful countryside 7.2 km inland of San Bartolomeo a Mare.

7.2 The coast to the north-east and the Impero Valley
7.3 The Porto Maurizio valleys

Cervo**

This highly attractive seaside resort (elev. 66 m, pop. 1,261), which appears at its most picturesque at night, sits on a hill sloping gently down to the sea. Tourism has done little to mar the beauty of Cervo, whose history is very much bound up with that of its neighbor Diano Marina and which in medieval times was an important control point on the Via Aurelia. Testifying to this past are the remains of the *castle* at the highest point of the town, records of which go back to 1196. This much redesigned edifice is now the home of the *Museo Etnografico del Ponente Ligure* (*open: 9am-12.30pm, 3.30-6.30pm; summer 9am-12.30pm, 4-10.30pm*). From the stronghold, *Via Salineri* leads down to the splendid **church of San Giovanni Battista*** (1686-1734), rightfully considered as one of the best expressions of the Ligurian Baroque. Designed and begun by Giovanni Battista Marvaldi, it has a large stuccoed concave facade overlooking the sea; the belltower, added in 1771-74, was designed by Francesco Carrega.

The completely 18th-century interior boasts some remarkable *altars*, *stuccowork*, and *choirstalls*; a niche between the 2nd and 3rd altar on the right contains a polychrome wood sculpture (*St. John the Baptist*) by Marcantonio Poggio, while the *Crucifix* in the 4th altar on the left is attributed to Maragliano.

The nearby *oratory of St. Catherine* was built in the 13th century. Beyond the fine ogival portal, restoration work around 1959 eliminated the 16th-century additions, thereby reinstating the original architectural features. Further down toward the sea, note the slate portal of *Palazzo Morchio* (16th cent.), now the Town Hall, and the large portico of the 18th-century *Palazzo Viale*: the *frescoes* on the piano nobile are believed to have been painted by Francesco Carrega.

A millstone, an oil-press and other equipment are displayed at the *Museo dell'Olio 'U Gumbu'* (*open on request: tel. 0183408149*), in an oil-mill at no. 31, Via Matteotti.

Cervo, with the floodlit facade of the church of San Giovanni Battista

The Impero river valley

Castelvecchio di Santa Maria Maggiore

The main claim to fame of this little village (elev. 40 m), now a suburb of Imperia, is that of being the oldest settlement in the entire valley. Corso Dante leads up to the *church of Santa Maria Maggiore*, designed by Giovanni Battista Marvaldi (ca. 1680).

From **Pontedassio** (elev. 80 m, pop. 1,983), whose 19th-century *parish church of Santa Margherita* has a triptych (*St. Bartholomew between Sts. John the Baptist and Catherine*) painted in 1503 by Luca Baudo, the road leads after 2 km to **Bestagno** (elev. 245 m), which boasts the imposing ruins of a medieval *castle* and a fine late-Baroque *parish church* (1743-50). A variant of the same road leads (2.2 km) to **Villa Guardia** (elev. 257 m): the *church of the Madonna della Neve* dates back to 1590. Paintings on canvas and wood and wooden statues from the 15th to 19th centuries can be seen at the *Museo d'Arte Sacra Lazzaro Acquarone* (*visits on request: tel. 018352534*) in **Lucinasco** (elev. 499 m, pop. 283), reached by the road west from Chiusavecchia. 3 km from the village stands the late medieval *church of the Maddalena** in a quite unspoilt natural setting.

San Lazzaro Reale
The 'royal' part of the name of this village (elev. 170 m) is possibly a reference to the 'royal' road to Piedmont. Here, the Impero river is crossed by a *bridge* probably built in the late 1400s. The nearby *parish church*, rebuilt in 1647, has a 16th-century triptych (*Madonna and Child*) attributed to Pietro Guidi da Ranzo.

Borgomaro
The streets of this village (elev. 249 m, pop. 894), laid out in a regular grid pattern that is unusual for this area, have many slate portals. The square on the riverbank is dominated by the *church of Sant'Antonio*

(rebuilt in around 1675): the polyptych (*St. Nazario and St. Celso*) on the right-hand wall is by Giulio De Rossi.

Conio
This village (elev. 622 m), which lies close to the source of the Impero river, is clustered around the remains of the 13th-century *castle*, once the property of the counts of Ventimiglia. It was badly damaged during the last war, after which part of the building collapsed, and is now used to house exhibitions and other events. The *church of San Maurizio*, on the valley side of the town, has features dating back to the 11-12th centuries, such as the belltower.

7.3 The valleys of Porto Maurizio
A brief tour along the coast, and five short excursions inland *(see map p. 143)*

Five roads lead inland from this part of the Via Aurelia. This tour, from Porto Maurizio, begins on the SS 1 (the *Aurelia* itself), which after 2.5 km comes to the junction for Caramagna Ligure. A further 1 km inland from Caramagna, the road forks to the right to Montegrazie (5 km) and to the left to Molteo (3.5 km). After visiting these two villages we return to Caramagna Ligure and take another road north-west to Dolcedo (4.2 km), from where an 8 km drive returns to Porto Maurizio. Back on the Via Aurelia, we head south-west 5.5 km down the coast to the junction with the road that leads inland (5.5 km) to Civezza. The SS 1 continues to the coastal resort of San Lorenzo al Mare, where roads once again lead inland, to Pietrabruna (9.6 km) and Lingueglietta (6.2 km).

C. Braccesco, polyptych. Montegrazie, the parish church

from the nave by dark stone columns, are some of the most important works of art in the Imperia area: paintings by Pietro Guidi da Ranzo (*Passion of Jesus*), and by Gabriele della Cella (*Scenes from the Life of St. James*) in the left-hand aisle and its apse, and frescoes by Tomaso and Matteo Biazaci (*Last Judgment, Pains of the Damned, Scenes from the Life of St. John the Baptist*) in the right-hand aisle. The lower part of this well-preserved rural village is huddled around the *parish church*, a fine example of late-Baroque architecture (1754-64) by Domenico Belmonte. It contains a superb **polyptych*** by Carlo Braccesco (1478) originally in the sanctuary.

Montegrazie
The valleys behind the port are dominated by the **sanctuary of Nostra Signora delle Grazie ***, which lies 1 km to the south-east of the village (elev. 240 m). All that remains of the Romanesque building are the *chapel of the Visitation* and the lower section of the belltower. In the main building (mid-15th-cent.), whose aisles are divided

Molteo
Tradition has it that Antonie Van Dyck and noblewoman Paolina Adorno eloped to this medieval village (elev. 200 m). One other interesting historical detail is the fact that a border once divided the *Case Soprane* hamlet – Savoy property – from the rest of the community, which belonged to Genoa. The *church of San Bernardo*, begun in 1642, has a late 15th-century polyptych (*Madonna with Saints*), a *St. Isidore* by Gregorio De Ferrari, and a whole

The portal of the church of S. Tommaso, Dolcedo

picture gallery of Genoese and local works from the 17th and 18th centuries; it also boasted a painting traditionally attributed to Van Dyck (but by Jan Roos), until it was stolen in 1981.

Dolcedo

The community of Dolcedo (elev. 75 m, pop. 1,185) comprises five separate little hamlets centering around *Piazza*, where the main monuments are concentrated. One of the most interesting is the *Ponte Grande* (1292), the single-span bridge across the Prino river. On the right bank, the 17th-century *Loggia del Comune* – which conserves capacity measures dating back to 1613, the year in which Dolcedo achieved autonomy from Porto Maurizio – leads to the pretty little black and white cobbled square with the *church of San Tommaso Apostolo*. This church adjoins the neighboring buildings revealing only its facade, whose earliest feature is the black stone Gothic portal (1492); the rest is the result of Baroque transformations made in 1738. Works of art inside include a canvas by Gregorio De Ferrari (*Martyrdom of St. Peter of Verona*) and a 15th-century wood *Crucifix*.

Civezza

The hill village of Civezza (elev. 225 m, pop. 505), set among olive groves, is thought to have been founded by exiles from Venice, as the name of the *parish church of San Marco* (St. Mark's) suggests. The church was rebuilt in 1777-83 to a design by Domenico Belmonte. Note the layout of the street, based on a series of parallel thoroughfares that meet at either end of the village.

Pietrabruna

Named after the brown stone used for its buildings, this village (elev. 400 m, pop. 574) is interesting for the many oil-presses still to be found in its network of alleyways, which offer many a charming view. The Neoclassical *parish church of San Matteo* is 19th century; the *oratorio dell'Annunciazione* has a late medieval painting of the *Annunciation*.

Lingueglietta

The saying "the end justifies the means" might well be invoked to explain the alterations made to the 13th-century **church of San Pietro** in 1500, to defend the village (elev. 320 m) from Saracen attack. The church was provided with sentry posts, walkways and loopholes. And yet none of this interfered with the overall architectural effect of the church, which was heavily influenced by the Longobard Romanesque, and, unusually, has a sandstone slab floor. The picturesque village that stretches out beyond the fortified church has many attractive medieval corners, the best being in the alleyways laid out to join the different street levels and the main square, whose 14th-century *parish church* was built in three stages (13-14th cent., 15th cent., 1609-13).

A view of Sanremo

8 Sanremo and Valle Argentina

Area profile

For most Italians the name Sanremo (or San Remo, as it is officially written) means just one thing: 'the Festival', as if the town's only claim to fame were its much-publicized annual song contest. There is of course a lot more to the town. During the *belle époque* the natural beauty of the whole coastal area known as the 'Riviera dei Fiori' made it one of the favorite destinations of the Victorian middle classes. Elegant reminders of this age can be seen in the turn-of-the-century hotels, but also in the area's other great economic activity: floriculture. It was indeed the wealthy English with their passion for nature and gardens who laid the foundations for the local flower-growing industry, which made this western Riviera town world famous long before the song festival was conceived. An interesting indication of the importance of the business is the fact that Sanremo provides the flowers that decorate the Musikvereinssaal in Vienna for the New Year's Day Concert, another symbol of an age that came to an end with the Great War, but which to some extent continued in Sanremo and along the coast until World War II, the event that really did mark the end of high-class vacationing and the beginning of the more money-oriented business of mass tourism. Tourism is, however, still quite unknown in the verdant countryside behind Sanremo, an area which, despite the tortuous lie of the land, has

Il Casino di Sanremo

been populated since ancient times. Its long history from medieval to modern times is testified to by the multitude of hill villages dotting the landscape, some built on gentle slopes, others perched precariously high up on the ridges. The fairytale-like nature of the area has given rise to countless romantic and uncanny tales.

8.1 Sanremo
Walking tour of the modern quarters and the old town *(see plan pp. 150-151)*

The best place to leave the car at the start of this tour of **Sanremo*** (elev. 15 m, pop. 56,129) is in Piazza degli Eroi Sanremesi, or in the multistory parking lot in Via Asquasciati (B4). The tour follows Via Corradi (B-C4) and Via Calvi to Piazza S. Siro, in which

San Remo: cathedral of S.Siro

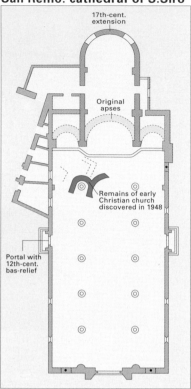

17th-cent. extension

Original apses

Remains of early Christian church discovered in 1948

Portal with 12th-cent. bas-relief

the cathedral, the baptistery and the oratory of the Immaculate Conception stand. It continues along the first stretch of Via Palazzo, then heads north into the oldest part of the town known as *La Pigna*, and up to the *sanctuary of the Madonna della Costa*. Back down in Via Palazzo, the walk continues to Piazza Colombo, before turning west along Via Matteotti, which ends at Piazza Battisti (C3), from which Corso Nuvoloni winds its way up to Corso degli Inglesi.

The 16th-century *Torre Ciapela* is known also as the Tower of the Saracens, because it was raised to defend the city from barbarian attack. On the southern side of **Piazza degli Eroi Sanremesi** (B4) stands a *Monument to Siro Andrea Carli*, a 19th-century mayor of Sanremo.

San Siro (B4). It took nearly fifty years, between the late 19th and early 20th centuries, to remove the Baroque additions and restore the cathedral's original Romanesque appearance. The building is believed to have been the work of the Comacini Masters, who erected the church in the 13th century on the site of an earlier place of worship. The shortage of stone in the area made necessary the use of yellow limestone from the Verezzo quarries, which adds to the sobriety of the facade, relieved by the porch in front of the main portal. There are two pseudo-porches, with pointed arch lunettes decorated with bas reliefs: the one on the right (*Enthroned Madonna between Two Saints*) dates back to the 15th century, the one on the left (*Paschal Lamb*) is 12th century.

The nave and side aisles are divided by octagonal piers and columns, and culminate in three apses, which were extended in the 17th century. The south aisle has a black *Crucifix* from the 15th century; on the high

---

The charming and colorful Pigna quarter, Sanremo

altar is a large *Crucifix** by Anton Maria Maragliano, while the 16th-century painting on wood (*St. Siro between St. Peter, St. Paul, John the Baptist and Romulus*) on the wall at the back of the choir is by Raffaele De Rossi. Other interesting works of art are the *pulpit* and *holy water stoup* in Brescia marble, sculpted in 1950 by Dante Ruffini.

To the left of the cathedral stands the **baptistery** (B4), originally a medieval church dedicated to John the Baptist, transformed to its new use in

sful choice, always attracting high numbers of participants. *For further information, contact: Sanremorally, tel. 0184577000, fax 0184663324, e-mail sanremorally@rosenet.it, or through the Internet at www.rally.sanremo.it.*

1576-1624; inside is a *Communion of Mary Magdalene* by Orazio De Ferrari. Opposite the west door of the cathedral is the **oratory of the Immacolata Concezione** (B3), built in the 15th-16th centuries, and remodeled in 1667. It has eight canvases (*Scenes from the Life of Mary*) by various painters, surrounded by a fine collection of polychrome marble.

Via Palazzo (B4), which probably runs along the course of the Roman Via Iulia Augusta, is connected by an arched passageway to *Piazza Nota*. At no. 1 of this square is the former Town Hall (1667); the nearby Piazza Cassini is dominated by the majestic facade of the *church of Santo Stefano* (1657-79): the *Madonna and Child with St. Anne and St. Francis* in the 2nd chapel on the right is by Domenico Piola.

La Pigna* (B3-4). The ancient name of the historic quarter of Sanremo (literally 'pine cone') derives from the geography of the land on which it grew up. The houses perched on this pointed hill create a system of concentric circles divided by a maze of alleyways, steep steps, arches and covered passageways. Although a little derelict now and surrounded by the modern buildings that have sprung up all around, it retains a quaint atmosphere. Entering through *Porta S. Stefano* (1321), we come to the so-called *Rivolte S. Sebastiano* steps that lead up to Piazzetta dei Dolori. From here, Via del Pretorio and Via Palma lead to the *church of San Giuseppe* (1666-84); the rounded-arch gateway of the same name (also known as the Porta della Tana) dates back to the 12th century.

149

Santuario della Madonna della Costa (A3).
A broad tree-lined avenue leads up to the
Madonna della Costa sanctuary, a symbol of
the town's autonomy: the original church, replaced by the present building in
1630, is thought by some to have been
built to celebrate the liberation of Sanremo
from Doria rule (1361). The interior is richly
decorated with marble and stuccowork; it
has a frescoed dome (*Assumption*), painted
in the 1700s by Giacomo Antonio Boni,
and three wooden *statues* by Maragliano,
who also sculpted the four figures around
the high altar, on which is a *Madonna and
Child* in the Barnaba da Modena style. Tradition has it that artists reproducing the face of the Virgin Mary would kneel down as
they painted almost in awe at the sight of
her tender countenance.

Damage caused by a French naval attack prompted the redesign in Rococo style of the *church of
Santa Maria degli Angeli*, on the corner between
Piazza Colombo (B4) and *Corso Garibaldi* (A-
B4-5). The visually striking interior, with a cen
tral nave and two side aisles, has a 16th-century
wood *Crucifix* in the 3rd chapel on the left.

Palazzo Borea d'Olmo (B4). In 1814 this
part-Mannerist, part-Baroque residence was
the scene of an unusual attempted pillage: it
was all the owners could do to fight off the
crowds that had amassed there to make off
with the furnishings of the rooms in which

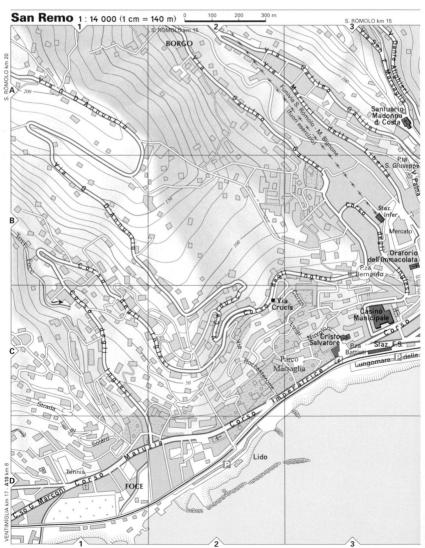

San Remo 1 : 14 000 (1 cm = 140 m)

150

Pope Pius VII had been received. The palace, with two *portals* on *Corso Matteotti* (B-C3-4) and Via Cavour decorated with late 17th-century sculptures (*Madonna and Child* and *John the Baptist*), is now the home of the **Museo Civico** (*open: 9am-noon and 3-6pm; Sun and Mon closed*). There are three sections: an archaeology collection, with finds from prehistoric to Roman times, a collection of 'Garibaldiana' (Risorgimento memorabilia) and an art gallery with paintings from the 17th to the 19th centuries.

The rooms of the Art Nouveau *Casinò Municipale* (C3), designed by Eugenio Ferret (1904-06) hark back to the days of the *belle époque*, though the effect is spoilt slightly by the less-than-tasteful additions to the casino made at the end of the 20th century. A little further on, in Corso Nuvoloni (C2-3), are the unmistakable onion domes of the *Orthodox Russian Church of Cristo Salvatore, Santa Caterina Martire e San Serafim di Sarov* (C3). The construction of this church, which was not consecrated until 1913, was encouraged by Russian Empress Maria Alexandrovna, who spent the winter of 1874-75 in Sanremo.

The life-size high-relief bronzes, by Enrico Manfrini, on the **Via Crucis** (C2) were positioned in 1990 at no. 374 *Corso degli Inglesi* (B-C-D1-2-3), an avenue lined with interesting Eclectic and Art Nouveau villas, such as the *Castello Devachan* (1890), now a residential hotel. This was the venue in 1920 for the conference to decide the future of the Middle East after the break-up of the Ottoman Empire.

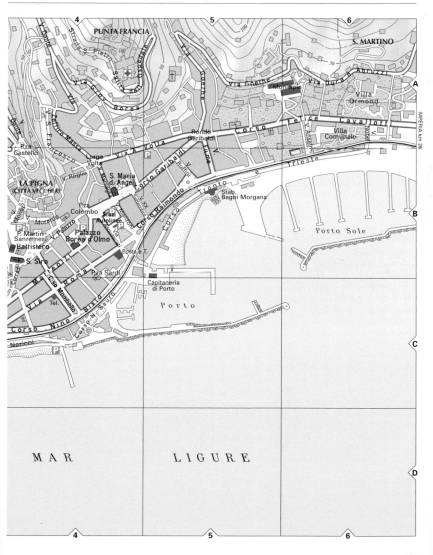

8.2 Three drives in the Sanremo area

Tours along the coast and into the horseshoe of hills behind the town *(see map p. 155)*

These tours take us into the immediate surroundings of the 'town of flowers'. Two of them, though short in terms of distance covered, take the best part of a day to complete. The first (approx. 30 km) covers the coastal resorts of Ospedaletti, Bordighera and Vallecrosia, before heading inland to visit Vallebona and Seborga. The second drive (65 km) leads up from Coldirodi to San Romolo, continuing toward the Ghimbegna Pass and, after calling at Bajardo, back down to the sea through the Valle Armea, with a final stop at Ceriana. The third tour, which can be completed in a few hours (around 10 km), is to the small coastal village of Bussana and Bussana Vecchia, the old town inland.

C. Monet, View of Bordighera. The Art Institute of Chicago

Ospedaletti

This little resort (elev. 5 m, pop. 3,564), named after the hospital thought to have been founded by the Knights of Rhodes in the 14th century, is set against a backdrop of verdant pinewoods and foothills of Mt. Bignone and Mt. Caggio. The tourist industry has done little to alter the elegance of the town, whose oldest quarters are particularly quaint.

Bordighera*

The successful novel "Doctor Antonio", written in English by Giovanni Ruffini, and published in Edinburgh in 1855, was what first attracted visitors from Britain to this Riviera resort (elev. 5 m, pop. 10,718). They were the vanguard of what by the last decades of the 19th century had for the standards of the time become a veritable invasion of tourists. Among the ranks of those who came to the 'town of the palm trees' to enjoy the sun and the sea, were also botany and archaeology scholars. One such scholar was the foun-

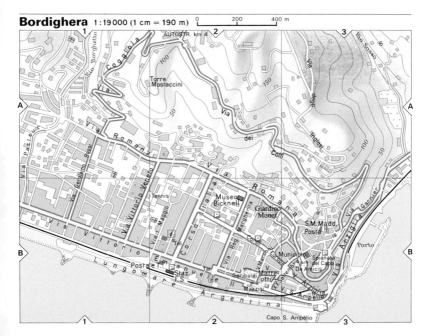

Bordighera 1:19 000 (1 cm = 190 m)

der of the *Biblioteca Clarence Bicknell*, now the **Clarence Bicknell Museum and Library** (B2; *open: 9am-1pm and 1.30-5.30pm, closed Sat and Sun*). On display inside are moldings of the rock carvings found in the Vallée des Merveilles (see p. 169), Roman funeral gifts, a herbarium and a butterfly collection. The museum is also the home of the *Mostra Permanente Pompeo Mariani* (*open: 10am-noon and 3-5pm, closed Sat and Sun*), a permanent exhibition of paintings dedicated to the Monza artist.

Via Romana (A-B 1-2-3), lined with elegant Art Nouveau hotels, leads to the attractive historic part of the town. In the heart of the old district is *Piazza del Popolo* dominated by the 17th-century **church of Santa Maria Maddalena** (B3), whose high altar has a group of *marble statues* by the workshop of Domenico Parodi (who drew on the model of his father Filippo) depicting Saint Mary Magdalene; note also the *oratory of San Bartolomeo degli Armeni* (late 15th cent.) and a *bell-tower* created in the 1700s possibly from an ancient lookout tower.

The nearby *Spianata del Capo* (B3), an esplanade offering superb views, leads down through a public garden to the *church of Sant'Ampelio*, near the cape of the same name (B3). This house of worship is believed to have been built (though the date is unknown) on the site where the hermit saint to whom it is dedicated lived and died. It has an early-Romanesque crypt (11th cent.), surrounded by architectural features added right up to the 19th century. The **Lungomare Argentina** (B1-2-3) borders the busy beach that stretches away to the west of the cape.

Vallecrosia

Like other towns on the Riviera, Vallecrosia (pop. 7,404) divides into two distinct parts: an inland community (elev. 43 m, 3 km from the coast), which retains some of its medieval urban fabric, and the seaside resort, which has suffered as a result of speculative building. Modern development also destroyed the olive groves that once surrounded the **church of San Rocco**, with a Romanesque apse (11th cent.) and a votive area inside dedicated to Apollo (1st cent. AD). In the hamlet of Garibbe, three train carriages dating back to 1910 house the *Museo della Canzone e della Riproduzione Sonora* (*open on request*), a museum of musical reproduction with old instruments, scores, records and phonographs.

Vallebona

This village (elev. 149 m, pop. 1,042), which has preserved its original layout almost intact, is entered from the *Porta Santa Maria* gateway. The 18th-century **parish church of San Lorenzo**, with a facade redesigned in 1841, retains the stone belltower of the earlier 13th-century church, and a fine slate portal (1478). Inside is a 15th-century painting on wood (*Eucharist, St. Lawrence and John the Baptist*). The frescoes in the nearby *oratory of the Disciplinati* (1780-81) are by Maurizio Carrega, as is the *Nativity of the Virgin* (1781-85).

Seborga

A new Monte Carlo in the Bordighera hills? The curious story of this little 'principality' (see box p. 154) is like something out of a film. As it awaits planning permission for gaming houses and the go-ahead for tax concessions, the main resources of the town (elev. 500 m, pop. 337) are mimosa and broom: it is still worth a visit, though, if only to admire the 17th-century *parish church of San Martino*, which faces onto the like-named square.

Flower-growing: one of Bordighera's main activities

The principality that was

It would hardly be an exaggeration to describe Seborga as the principality history left behind. On 20 January 1729, the territory was bought by Vittorio Amedeo II of Savoy in a deed that was never recorded in either the Savoy or the Sardinia Kingdom archives. And since this undoubtedly inadvertent omission was never made good, the existence of the tiny state, recognized in 1079 by the Holy Roman Empire, has been overlooked in all documents pertaining to the territory ever since, from the 1748 Treaty of Aix-la-Chapelle (which thus gave 'de facto' ownership to Genoa) to the Congress of Vienna, the establishment of the Kingdom of Italy and, more recently, of the Italian Republic. The question, which reads like something out a Pirandelli play, resurfaced in 1963, when the inhabitants of the 'ghost principality' once again asserted the independence that no formal document had ever removed. A prince was duly elected, followed by the drawing up of a constitution, which was renewed in 1995 in conjunction with the reopening of the Mint that originally issued coinage between 1666 and 1688. The monetary unit, then as now, was the *luigino*: a name derived from its fixed value of one quarter of the French *louis d'or* (the current exchange rate is six US dollars). Of course no one really imagines that Seborga's currency and stamps will ever have any more than souvenir value. Updates on any change in the principality's status can be obtained from the Palazzo del Governo, in Via della Zecca 7 (*tel. 0184223924, e-mail: seborga@masterweb.it; website: www.seborga.com*).

Coldirodi

This town (elev. 254 m), whose origins also date back to the Knights of Rhodes, is best known for the **Pinacoteca e Biblioteca Rambaldi***(*open: Tue and Thur to Sun 10am–noon; Tue, Fri and Sat also 3.30-6pm; closed Mon and Wed*). The collection of this art gallery and library, presented in a somewhat disorderly fashion (reflecting Rambaldi's original layout), centers around a *Madonna and Child* attributed to Lorenzo di Credi and canvases by Salvator Rosa (note in particular the *Temptations of St. Anthony*). There is also an interesting collection of works by 16th- and 17th-century Tuscan painters, north European landscape artists, and a curious collection of fakes thought to be by Guido Reni, Veronese and Rembrandt. Next to the art gallery stands the **church of San Sebastiano**, which has a *Pietà* and a *Via Crucis* by Maurizio Carrega, who also painted the frescoes in the presbytery of the preceding *oratory of Sant'Anna*, painted in 1768: the other pictorial cycles are thought to date back to the previous century.

Bajardo

This town (elev. 900 m, pop. 342), first mentioned by Greek geographer and historian Strabo, lies on the watershed between the Merdanzo Valley to the south and Bonda, to the north. At the beginning of the town is the *Pinacoteca Civica (open on request)* with canvases by local artist Antonio Rubino and other 20th-century paintings; the *oratory of San Salvatore*, in Piazza De Sonnaz, has an interesting polyptych (*Transfiguration*) painted in 1552 by Emanuele Macario and his assistants. Beyond the Porta dei Saraceni, *Via Portaro Piano* climbs through the old part of the town, dominated by the ponderous ruins of the **church of San Nicolò**, which was redesigned in the 15th century (when the *portal* and porch were added) and in the Baroque period. It was destroyed in the earthquake of 23 February 1887, which killed 202 townsfolk. The terrace behind affords a splendid *view** of the Maritime Alps.

On a clear day, the view from the peak of **Mt. Ceppo** (elev. 1,627 m) stretches all the way to Genoa. The mountain top can be reached on foot in three hours, or by car.

Ceriana*

The houses of this village (elev. 369 m, pop. 1332), perched high up over the upper Armea Valley, seem hewn out of the very rock on which they stand. Similar in layout to Pigna di Sanremo (see p. 149), Ceriana was first mentioned in Roman times as 'castrum Coelianae'. As well as being of great environmental interest it has some interesting monuments, beginning with the Romanesque **church of Ss. Pietro e Paolo** (12-13th cent., rebuilt between the late 15th and early 16th century), Ceriana's former parish church in the lower part of the village; its two right-hand *portals* were added in the early 1500s by stonecutters from Cenova. The interior is divided lengthwise by a wall, to divide male and fe-

male worshipers. Adjoining the church is the **oratory of Santa Caterina**, built 1736-37. Beyond the *Porta della Pena* gateway (12th-cent. or later) next to which is the 17th-century *oratory of the Visitation*, the road leads up to the top of the town: the main landmark here is the Romanesque belltower of the *church of Sant'Andrea*, which has Doric columns. The walk back down *Via Celio*, with its many picturesque corners, leads to the **parish church of Ss. Pietro e Paolo** (18th cent.), whose facade is flanked by two belltowers; the polyptych (*St. Peter, St. Andrew and St. Paul*) on the right-hand wall and the carved limewood *altar** in the sacristy both date back to the 1500s; an altarpiece depicting *St. Catherine between St. Martha and St. Magdalene* can be dated back to 1544.

Bussana

This town (elev. 70 m) played an important part in the history of the ice-cream cone: the first wafers were made here around 1910 in one of the bakeries after the 1887 earthquake

Bussana Vecchia: the 'artists' village'

destroyed ancient Bussana (see below). Great efforts were made to create a symbol of the town's rebirth: the *sanctuary of the Sacro Cuore*, begun in 1889, was finished 12 years later. The classical-style facade has an 1893 mosaic (*Christ the King*) and a lavishly monumental, aisleless interior. In the sacristy is the **Birth of John the Baptist** by Mattia Preti.

Bussana Vecchia

The once-abandoned alleyways of this former ghost village (elev. 201 m) have sprung to life again with the appearance of craft workshops, antique shops and artists' ateliers. There has been much talk about the restoration of part of this town, which began in the 1960s in a way that put commercial interests before historical and cultural considerations. Whatever the outcome, the sight of this ruined town, over a century after the earthquake, is a dramatic one; the only surviving monument is the belltower of the Baroque **church of the Sacro Cuore**.

8.3 The Valle Argentina
Inland tour from Arma di Taggia to Triora, 29.7 km excluding detours

This tour is worth doing just for Taggia and Triora, the towns that stand at the starting and finishing points. The first detour off the main road inland from Taggia, is a 7-km drive through the Val Carpasina, to visit Montalto Ligure and Carpasio. Almost at the end of the Valle Argentina is another detour (3 km) to Andagna and the *chapel of San Bernardo*. And once Triora has been reached, a final detour (10 km) should be made northwest to Realdo and Verdeggia, Alpine villages in an area that offers some exceptionally beautiful landscapes. Anyone intending to make the detours off the main route (from Ar-

The Argentina river

ma di Taggia, 7.7 km east of Sanremo, up the SS 548 to Triora) to some of the more out-of-the-way places mentioned (the upper Val Carpasina, the Pizzo and Teglia Passes, and the road north of Triora), is advised to use a four-wheel-drive vehicle, since these roads, closed for several months a year, include some long unsurfaced stretches.

Taggia**

Within the 16th-century walls of this town (elev. 39 m, pop. 13,630) on the Argentina river, lies a historic center that is as full of old-world charm as it is of exceptional works of art and architecture. One of the first, before entering the town proper, is the **convent of San Domenico*** (*open: 9.30-11.30am and 3.30-7pm; closed Sun*), which upon completion in 1490 became the focus of attention for the local school of painting. This ex-

L. Brea, Madonna del Rosario. Convent of San Domenico, Taggia

plains why the church (restoration work in 1935 restored the original Gothic forms) has what amounts to an entire art gallery inside: the main artist represented is Lodovico Brea, who painted the polyptychs in the 1st chapel on the right (*Madonna of the Rosary**), in the 3rd (triptych of *St. Catherine of Siena and Sts. Agatha and Lucy*), on the high altar (*Madonna of Mercy with Saints**) and on the altar to the left of the presbytery (*Baptism of Christ and Saints**, painted in collaboration with Antonio Brea). The two *organ doors* behind the facade are by another member of the Niçoise family, Francesco. Giovanni Canavesio painted the *frescoes* in the refectory and chapter-house, and the 1478 cusped triptych (*St. Dominic and the Doctors of the Church* in the lower sections, *Madonna and Child with Four Saints* in the upper sections) in the 4th chapel on the right. The convent is built around a 15th-century **cloister**, which has black stone columns (15th cent.) and lunettes with fresco remains (*Scenes from the Life of St. Dominic*) dating back to 1611-13. One of the most interesting works originally kept here, a splendid **Epiphany*** (1528-35) attributed to Parmigianino, has been stolen. The 16th-century reliefs above the main portal (*Pietà*) and on the left-hand side of the church (*Merciful Madonna*) can be traced to the stone-cutting school which once operated near the abbey. The visit to the historic quarters begins at the *Porta dell'Orso*, then along Via Lercari (note the Gaginesque *bas-relief* above the portal at no. 10) to Piazza Farini, in which the 17th-century *Palazzo Lercari* stands at no. 5. At no. 3 of the adjoining Via Curlo is the early 18th-century *Palazzo Curlo-Spinola*; the **parish church of Ss. Giacomo e Filippo**, situated in nearby Piazza Gastaldi, dates back to 1675-89. In the third chapel on the right inside the church is a canvas (*Sts. Anthony Abbot and Paul the Hermit*) by Luca Cambiaso and, in the chapel of the Body of Christ, a *Resurrection* by his father Giovanni (with Luca); note also the 1510 altarpiece (*Crucifixion with the Madonna and Saints*) in the first chapel on the right. A vaulted passageway leads off from the central **Via Soleri** (known as the *Pantan*) under *Palazzo Lombardi*: patrician palaces with porticoes and noble crests line the walk toward *Piazza della SS. Trinità*, which begins with the orange marble front of the *oratory of Ss. Sebastiano e Fabiano*. Also facing onto the square are the *oratory of the SS. Trinità*, the *church of Santa Caterina* and, on the right, the remains of a rampart that continues as far as the impressive sixteen-span **medieval bridge***: the last two spans are Romanesque; the others date back to different periods in the 15th and 16th centuries.

On the other side of the river, the 17/18th-century *Villa Curlo* marks the beginning of the footpath that leads seaward – in about ten minutes – to the ancient **church of San Martino**, rebuilt several times in its history: frescoes from various periods are to be found inside. Back over the bridge, turn right for the **church of Santa Maria del Canneto**, with an elegant cusped *belltower* and a portal by Gasparino de Lancia (1467), retrieved from the demolished church of Sant'Anna; Giovanni and Luca Cambiaso worked on the *frescoes* inside (1547), together with Francesco Brea. Through *Porta del Colletto*, the buildings facing onto **Via S. Dalmazzo** have elegant sculpted slate doorways; after *Porta Barbarasa*, pass under the *Torre Clavesana* (12-13th cent.) and up to the Santa Lucia quarter, the original settlement. The *church of Santa Lucia* is in an extremely poor state of preservation. Return back down Via S. Dalmazzo, and leave the old district through *Porta Pretoria* (or 'Parasio', a gateway opened in 1541). The visit ends along the Ciazzo and Orso ramparts.

Badalucco

The most picturesque corner of this village (elev. 179 m, pop. 1,289) is undoubtedly the *Ponte di Santa Lucia* (1548-51), a bridge with two asymmetrical arches and a *chapel* (1606). Also worth seeing are the **parish church of the Assunta e San Giorgio** (1682-93, remodeled in 1834), with an elegant Baroque facade and, inside, a wooden *Madonna* (purchased in Genoa in 1675), a *high altar* from the *church of San Siro* in Sanremo (1697), and two *angels*, from Rome, donated to the church in 1766. Opposite the church stands the 16th-century *Palazzo Boeri*, with a good loggia.

Originally occupied by a legendary temple dedicated to Diana, and later by the castle of the counts of Ventimiglia, the top of the hill overlooking the town is now dominated by the little 17th-century **church of San Nicolò**.

Just after Badalucco, stands the 18th-century *chapel of Nostra Signora degli Angeli*, which was faithfully restored after being badly damaged in the last war. The late-medieval three-span **bridge** over the Argentina is named after the chapel.

Montalto Ligure

Tradition has it that this village (elev. 315 m, pop. 430), which lies strategically on the hill overlooking the confluence of the Carpasina and Argentina rivers, was founded by two young newly-weds who escaped here to avoid the 'jus primae noctis' right exercised by the count of Badalucco. The upper part of the village is a maze of quaint

8.3 The Valle Argentina

alleyways, steps and vaulted passageways, suggesting that the original settlement served defense purposes.

At the top of the village stands the religious complex formed by the *parish church of San Giovanni Battista*, rebuilt in 1793, and the similarly Baroque *oratory of San Vincenzo Ferreri*, whose church stands over a vaulted passageway connecting to the lower level; its facade, dominated by the imposing belltower, is partly covered by the oratory, also built over a portico and entered at an even higher level. This miniature piazza brings together in a few square meters a section of facade, a belltower, a rectory and arcades. Inside the two religious edifices are some valuable works of art: the parish church has a *Via Crucis* by Maurizio Carrega, a *Martyrdom of St. Stephen* by Emanuele Macario, a *Resurrection* by Luca Cambiaso (1563), and a polyptych (*St. George*) painted in 1516 by Lodovico Brea and his assistants. Francesco Brea is thought to have painted the triptych (*Madonna and Saints*) kept in the oratory, where there is also an exquisitely carved *altar*.

The late-Romanesque **church of San Giorgio*** (14th cent.) stands in the village cemetery. Inside, note the 14th-century paintings and the central wall separating male from female worshipers.

Carpasio

Originally owned by the Lascaris family of Tenda and then the Savoy, this little mountain town (elev. 720 m, pop. 183) spreads out in a small, sunny depression. Note the many sculpted portals on the fronts of its slate-roofed houses, huddled around the **church of Sant'Antonino,** with belltower (slightly leaning) and Romanesque apse, which was spared the 18th-century Baroque transformations. On the facade of the adjoining *oratory* is a slate bas-relief (*Annunciation*).

Weapons, military supplies, photographs and documents from the Resistance movement are displayed at the *Museo Partigiano* (*open: Sat, Sun 10am-6pm and at other times on request, tel. 0183650755; closed November-March*) in the Costa di Carpasio locality.

Beyond the *Colle d'Oggia* (elev. 1167 m), continue toward San Bernardo di Conio, Rezzo and the Arroscia Valley (left), or toward Borgomaro (see p. 145), in the Impero valley (right).

Andagna

After taking a quick look at the village (elev. 728 m) with its customary parish church and oratory in an arcaded square, climb up to the **chapel of San Bernardo** to see the dual cycle of frescoes (1436) in the typical western Riviera and Niçois style. The *Passion* is depicted in the upper section, in sharp contrast with the *Domestic Virtues* and *Deadly Sins* below: the latter are crudely depicted, with the sinners being led on horseback toward the mouths of demons, in a representation typical of Gothic bestiaries.

The partly unsurfaced road leads up to the *Pizzo Pass* (elev. 1,390 m) and *Teglia Pass* (elev. 1,387 m), before descending to Rezzo.

Molini di Triora

In the late Middle Ages there were no fewer than 23 watermills along the Argentina and Capriolo rivers, hence the 'mills' in the name of this valley bottom town (elev. 460 m, pop. 734), once a hamlet of Triora and since 1903 a separate municipality. There are two main monuments in this village of relatively modern layout: the **parish church of San Lorenzo** (1486), rebuilt in the Baroque style in the 18th century, but still with Gothic portal and belltower, and inside a polyptych (*Santa Maria Maddalena between St. Martha and St. Catherine*) painted in 1540 by Emanuele Macario, together with a *St. Lawrence* on wood by Giovanni Runggaldier (1925); and the 15th-century **sanctuary of Nostra Signora della Montà**, which has 15th-century paintings (*Madonna, Crucifixion, Evangelists, Founders of the Religious Orders*); there is a good view of the town from the parvis.

The road up to *Colla di Langan* (elev. 1,127 m), with its many steep bends, leads into the Val Nervia (see p. 162).

Triora*

A dozen women were pitilessly burned at the stake following the celebrated witchcraft trials of 1587-89, whereafter Triora (elev. 780 m, pop. 427) was nicknamed the 'village of the witches'. In the following century, it withstood two attacks by Piedmontese troops (in 1625 and 1671), who were determined to conquer what since 1261 had been a Genoese stronghold.

Triora: the Museum of Witchcraft

The village of Realdo, perched high up on a rocky spur

Despite the damage done in 1944 during a vicious Nazi reprisal, the village has retained its original urban layout, including an elaborate defense system and the original system of pipes and fountains that brought water to all levels of the town.

On the way up to the town, note on the right the *church of the Madonna delle Grazie* (12th-13th cent.) and the remains of the *Colombara* (or *Poggio*) *Fort*. Further on, on the left, a road leads to the little 15th-century **church of San Bernardino***, with side portico held up on four pillars; the paintings inside (*Passion, Apostles, Last Judgment*) are also 15th century. Near the church stand the ruins of the *Sella Fort*, which together with the Colombara Fort withstood the Savoy attack of 1625.

The **Museo Etnografico e della Stregoneria** (*open: 3-6.30pm, November-March 2.30-6pm; Sat and Sun 10.30am-noon, 2.30-6pm*), at no. 1 Corso Italia in the town center, has a room dedicated to sorcery. A little further on, the **collegiate church of the Assunta** preserves the portal and belltower base of the original Romanesque-Gothic church; inside, as well as an exquisite **Baptism of Jesus*** painted in 1397 by Taddeo di Bartolo, are two early 15th-century paintings on wood (*Pietà* and *St. James*). The adjacent **oratory of San Giovanni Battista** (1694) has a marble portal and holy water stoup, an 18th-century wooden *statue* of John the Baptist, and a canvas (*Madonna and Saints*) by Luca Cambiaso and his assistants; the apse rests on columns clearly visible from the road below, which is lined with medieval houses and leads to *Porta Sottana*,

preceded by the like-named *fountain* (1480). Back in Piazza della Collegiata, *Via Cima* leads to the *church of San Dalmazio*, incorporated into the fabric of the town; little remains of the *fortress* of the same name, or of the nearby *Cabotina*, the presumed site of the witches' coven.

Also from Piazza della Collegiata, *Via Dietro la Colla* leads up to the *Soprana Fountain*, the oldest in Triora, near the round-arched *Porta Soprana*; the road ends at the ruins of the **castle** built by the Genoese in the 12th-13th centuries. Outside the town is the bulbous, polychrome *belltower* of the *church of Sant'Agostino* (1616, remodeled in the 18th century).

The Capponi family, forced into exile from their native Florence, built the *church of Santa Caterina* (1390), 1 km north of the town and now in ruins, though retaining its fine stone portal.

The partly unsurfaced road that leads north-west out of Triora and across the *Garlenda Pass* (elev. 1,461 m) and Colle *Garezzo* (elev. 1,801 m), continues toward Mendatica.

The high bridge (1959-60) over the deep Argentina river gorge, now used by bungee jumpers in summer, connects to the tiny village of *Cetta* (elev. 774 m). Continuing inland on the opposite side of the valley, the village of **Realdo*** (elev. 1,010 m), perched high up on a rocky spur, suddenly appears as if from nowhere. The scenery is similar around **Verdeggia** (elev. 1,092 m), which lies in the shadow of *Mt. Saccarello* (elev. 2,200 m), the highest peak of the Ligurian Alps.

9 Ventimiglia and the Ligurian Alps

Area profile

The westernmost section of the Riviera is a borderland with a great question mark over its future: in an increasingly barrier-free Europe what will become of a town whose economy has always relied heavily on border traffic? This dependence came about to a large extent when, thanks to the vagaries of history, Ventimiglia lost a chunk of its natural hinterland. Now, in today's ever more global age, it makes sense to take a new approach, and envisage collaboration agreements that go beyond frontiers which are no more than lines drawn on a map, leaving behind once and for all the days of bloody battles and interminable negotiations whose purpose was sometimes to shift the border no more than a few hundred yards. But until the much hoped-for trans-national exchanges become something more than crowds of Niçoises pouring into Italy to go 'shopping on the cheap', and long processions of Piedmontese vacationers clogging the 'Route Nationale' of Val Roia, the great challenge facing Ventimiglia – the descendant of the Roman *Albintimilium* and the even older *Albium Intemelium* – lies in its ability to convince its many 'just-passing-through' visitors to venture beyond the now deserted customs houses and look away from the maze of railroad tracks up

The Roman theater in Ventimiglia and a detail of the Arione mosaic in the thermal baths

to the rocky spur to which the medieval town clings, as they embark on the first stage in a supra-national journey into the past that takes in the Balzi Rossi caves, where humanity once had to fight for its very survival, and, across the border to the Trophée des Alpes, that great symbol of *pax romana*. To complete the visit to the area there are the beautiful landscapes of the Roia and Nervia Valleys, where the scenery is mountainous but the air is still redolent of the sea.

9.1 Ventimiglia
Walking tour through the medieval and modern town *(see plan p. 162)*

This tour of the town (elev. 9 m, pop. 26,788) begins in Piazza della Costituente (A1-2), on the west bank of the Roia river, and heads down the panoramic Via Biancheri (A-B1-2) to the Colla walk, where it is advisable to leave the car. Entry into the historic center is through Porta Nuova; after the visit to the cathedral and baptistery, Via al Capo (A-B1-2) leads to the esplanade of the same name, which affords a spectacular view stretching from Bordighera to Menton. A little way below is the *oratory of San Giovanni*, whose Baroque bell-tower was lopped off by a missile during World War II. Back at the cathedral, Via Garibaldi leads into Via Appio and down to the *church of San Michele*. We now take the car and return to Piazza della Costituente

to park again before visiting the modern town, which is also connected to the other side of the Roia river by a footbridge.

Cattedrale dell'Assunta* (A1). The 'grandeur' of Ventimiglia around the year 1000 is seen in its cathedral, built on the site of a Carolingian church and much altered and enlarged over the centuries. The south side and facade are 11th-century Romanesque (a portico and pseudo-Gothic porch were added to the facade after 1222); the upper part of the belltower (12th cent.) was altered in the Baroque period and remodeled again in the 19th century. The three apses and the lantern are 13th century; the 16th-century north chapels, while interrupting the architectural unity of the whole, give the interior a greater sense of space. The only works of art are the *Assumption* by Giovanni Carlone in the first chapel of the north aisle, and a Byzantine *pulvino* (5th-6th cent.), used as a holy water stoup; the *crypt* preserves part of the early medieval (8th-10th cent.) church. Behind the cathedral is the octagonal **baptistery**, which, like the *Assunta*, dates back to the 11th century (the ceiling is 16th century). The majestic *baptismal pool* dates back to the 12th-13th century; the basin in a niche bears an inscription dated 1100.

Via Garibaldi (Al). The main thoroughfare through the medieval town is lined with a series of noteworthy buildings. At the beginning, on the left, is the *Vescovado*, or Bishop's Palace, preceded by the 15th-century **Loggia del Parlamento o dei Mercanti**: a part of the portico, with two ogival arches on low quadrangular pillars, was demolished in the 19th century to make way for the *Teatro Civico*. This Neoclassical building is now the home of the **Civica Biblioteca Aprosiana**, Liguria's oldest library (1648) which boasts an important collection of manuscript and incunabula. Continuing along Via Garibaldi, we see on the left a succession of 16th-century noble palaces – most of them redesigned in the 19th century – with hanging gardens to the rear on the level of the *piano nobile*, in the Genoese style. On the right, note the Baroque facade of the *Neri oratory*, which has frescoes by Maurizio and Tommaso Carrega (1784-86). A little further on, on the left, is the deconsecrated *church of San Francesco*, which flanks the street as far as the ponderous *Porta Nizza* (Al).

A float in the Ventimiglia 'Flower Battle'

Ventimiglia: cathedral of the Assunta

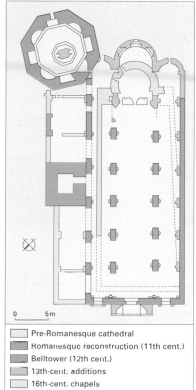

	Pre-Romanesque cathedral
	Romanesque reconstruction (11th cent.)
	Belltower (12th cent.)
	13th-cent. additions
	16th-cent. chapels

The *Forte dell'Annunziata* (A1, off map) started life as a convent (16th cent.), then became a Savoy fortress, and is now an exhibition center: no. 41 Corso Verdi (A-B1-2), is the entrance to the **Museo Archeologico Gerolamo Rossi** (*open 9am-12.30pm and 3-5pm, Sun 10am-12.30pm; closed Mon*). As well as material excavated from the Roman site of *Albintimilium* (see below), the museum has archaeological collections from the late 19th and early 20th centuries, with funerary gifts, ancient glassware, sculptures and an extensive collection of carved inscriptions.

The walk from Porta Nizza to **Forte San Paolo** is difficult but well worth the effort. Built by the Genoese in 1222, it was much altered in later centuries (the quadrangular plan is oriented to the four cardinal points). Here, too, is *Porta Canarda*, the gateway built into a massive 13th-century tower and restored in 1880. It is possible to continue by car to the ruins of **Castel d'Appio**, a castle on a site that was already fortified in Neolithic times and subsequently occupied by a Roman *castrum*. The name is a reference to consul Appius Claudius, who in 185 BC vanquished the local tribes. Of the stronghold, rebuilt by the Genoese in the 13th century, two five-sided towers and a large water cistern remain.

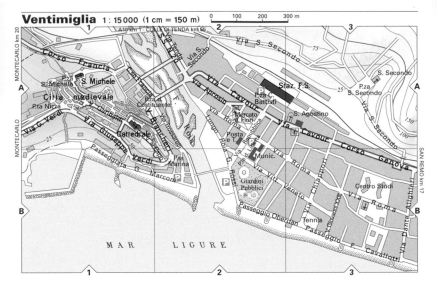

San Michele (A1; *open: Sun 10.30am-noon*). This partly derelict Romanesque church faces onto a square high up over the Roia Valley. Built around 1100 on the site of a 10th-century chapel, it was first altered in the late 12th century (when the apse, belltower and nave were built), and again in 1564 following earthquake damage; in 1885 an interpretative restoration of the facade was carried out. The *crypt* has retrieved Roman elements and a milestone from the time of Caracalla.

The modern part of Ventimiglia is abuzz with commercial activities, aimed mainly at the French shoppers who pour into the town at the weekend. The neo-Gothic *church of Sant'Agostino* (A3) has a precious 15th-century *Crucifix* and a painting by Raffaele De Rossi (*St. Augustine between John the Baptist and St. Anthony Abbot*).

The small but well-preserved **theater** (21 meters in diameter) is the most interesting part of the excavations of the Roman *Albintimilium*, on the eastern outskirts of the modern town (B3, off map). This arena, built at the end of the 2nd century with stone blocks from La Turbie, has two entranceways; the one on the right survives virtually intact.

9.2 Val Nervia

From Ventimiglia to Pigna, 20.3 km excluding detours *(see map p. 167)*

A stretch of just over 20 kilometers, as the crow flies, between the sources of the Nervia river, on the slopes of Mt. Pietravecchia (elev. 2,040 m), and the sea. Along the entire course of this fast-flowing river is an unusual combination of Alpine and Mediterranean flora: the *maquis* reaches up well beyond the 1,000 meter line, touching the woods of silver fir. For those not content simply to admire the natural beauty, there are also plenty of artistic treasures and excellent food and drink in Val Nervia to make the visit worthwhile: the valley's vineyards produce the celebrated Rossese di Dolceacqua enjoyed by Napoleon. All of this in a context in which farming life is still very much alive, a situation reflected in the way the valley has been settled, with little towns dotted along its length and verdant valleys leading off to the sides.

Camporosso and Dolceacqua are the first towns on this charming tour, followed by a 6-km detour to Val Barbaira to Rocchetta Nervina. Back in Val Nervia, we call in at Isolabona, which in turn leads to a 9-km detour along the Rio Merdanzo, to see Apricale and Perinaldo. From Isolabona, the main valley road leads on up toward Pigna, from where two roads branch off, to Castel Vittorio (2 km) and Buggio (4 km).

Camporosso

This little inland town (elev. 25 m, pop. 4,999), which has always been the most populous in Val Nervia, thanks to the flat, fertile, and easy-to-farm terrain, was long fought over by the house of Savoy and Genoa, the latter taking control finally in 1686. The considerable demographic growth in the second half of the 20th century brought about some inevitable changes to the town's structure, whose old center nevertheless still retains some attractive corners. The main monument is the 15th-century *parish church of San Marco* (more work was done on the building in 1505-18 and in the 18th century); inside are three 16th-century polyptychs, by Lodovico Brea (*Martyrdom of St. Sebastian*), Agostino Casanova (*Madonna with St. Julian and St. Bernard*) and Stefano Adrechi (*St. Peter, Paul and Other Saints*) respectively. Also in Piazza Garibaldi is the *oratory of the Annunziata*, preceded by an original flight of steps with a double curving balustrade. In the cemetery, the **church of San Pietro** has, on the right, an 11th-century apse and belltower, and some 15th-16th century frescoes.

Dolceacqua*

The name of this town (elev. 51 m, pop. 1,940), literally 'freshwater' (after a Roman-Ligurian latifundium), is a little misleading considering its present-day reputation as a producer of one of Italy's most celebrated wines. The exquisite Rossese is a must for connoisseurs of course, but there are also plenty of other reasons for

Dolceacqua's high-quality Rossese wine

visiting the town. The *church of San Giorgio*, in the cemetery, still has part of the original Romanesque structure on the facade and base of the belltower. The graveyard also affords the best single view of the town, dominated by the castle built between the 12th and 14th centuries by the Doria family. A spectacular, daringly-engineered **bridge** (15th cent.) crosses the Nervia river, uniting the Borgo and Terra districts. The latter is the oldest of the two and has a layout based on concentric semicircles connected by a maze of alleys and covered passageways that remind us of its former defensive role. The Baroque *church of Sant'Antonio Abate* has a polyptych (*St. Devota*) by Lodovico Brea, dated 1515; opposite the church, the *Olive-Press Monument* remembers Pier Vincenzo Mela, who invented the olive oil extraction process in the early 1700s. For a medieval experience, climb to the **castle**: this fortress, abandoned after bombing during the War of Austrian Succession in 1745, suffered further damage during the 1887 earthquake.

Rocchetta Nervina

This Y-shaped village (elev. 235 m, pop. 282) lies at the point where the Rio Coe flows into the Barbaira river, and is connected to the provincial road by two hump-backed bridges. This picturesque locality (note the 16th-century *portal* of the Baroque *church of Santo Stefano*), is the starting point for numerous hikes into the surroundings, well served by comfortable and modern mountain refuges.

Isolabona

Another town (elev. 106 m, pop. 691) on two rivers: this time at the point where Rio Merdanzo joins the Nervia, giving rise to the 'island' in the name of the village. In an effort to defend its exposed side, the Doria built a castle (13th-14th cent.), of which only the large quadrangular *keep* survives.

Just outside the village, the **sanctuary of Nostra Signora delle Grazie** has a facade with 17th-century porch and, inside, some *frescoes* from the previous century; the little *church of San Giovanni Battista*, inside the cemetery, is medieval.

Hikers stop to enjoy the splendid views from the Melosa Col

The medieval town of Dolceacqua

Dolceacqua, a little town dominated by the ruins of the Doria castle, straddles the Nervia river, with two bridges connecting the two sides. The hump-backed Ponte Vecchio, the older of the two, is a daring 15th-century construction with a single 33-meter span. The medieval part of the town on the left bank of the river, known as "Terra" and with a layout based on a series of concentric circles, was designed with defense purposes in mind. The *church of Sant'Antonio Abate*, built in the 15th century along the southern side of the walls surrounding the town and later transformed in the Baroque style, is still linked to the adjoining palace by a private pas-

Church of San Giorgio

15th-century
hump-backed bridge

sageway for the Doria family. Across the river to the west, the more recent quarter of Borgo has a linear layout following the course of the river. Here, at the entrance to the town, stands the *church of San Giorgio*, an ancient pagan temple that later became a Christian church; it was the first collegiate church of Dolceacqua.

The Doria castle, a defense structure dating back to the 12th century, was built in stages around the original circular tower. In 1400 a rampart and square towers at the sides were added, with further enlargements made in the following two centuries, when the castle took on the character of a noble palace. The building was seriously damaged after the surrender of 1754, and destroyed by the earthquake of 1887.

Palazzo Doria

Church of
Sant'Antonio Abate

Left bank leading to "Pontagno", an open area by the river where the townspeople and authorities once gathered for meetings.

Apricale

This village (elev. 273 m, pop. 579) which is *apricus*, or south-facing, is known as the 'village of the artists' because of the many wall paintings, which only add to its picturesque charm. The main square, **Piazza Vittorio Emanuele***, has the late-medieval *church of the Purification of Mary*, redesigned in the 18th century, and the *oratory of San Bartolomeo*, which has an interesting polyptych (*Madonna and Child with Saints*) dated 1544, and a *St. Anthony Abbot*, from the 1620s; in summer, this area – onto which face the ruins of the *castle* (housing a permanent local history exhibition and temporary art exhibitions) – is the scene of the Elastic Ball Tournament, an ancient game still quite popular in the inland area behind Imperia. To the right of the oratory, the interesting *Via Cavour* leads toward the cemetery, the site of the 13th-century *church of Sant'Antonio Abate*, which has a Baroque facade and contains paintings dating back to the 15th century.

In the Middle Ages, religious buildings could also become fortified positions. One reminder of this, below the town, is the ponderous *church of Nostra Signora degli Angeli*, which has no facade and a polygonal apse; inside are 15th-18th century frescoes.

The countryside north of Apricale is the setting for the atmospheric remains of the *church of San Pietro in Ento* (11th cent.), whose aisleless interior ends in a semi-circular apse.

Perinaldo

The most famous native son of this little town (elev. 572 m, pop. 860) is Gian Domenico Cassini, court astronomer to Louis XIV. The busy life of this scientist, who was also an eminent biologist, is recorded in the *Museo Gian Domenico Cassini* (*open: 8.30am-13.30pm, closed Sun*), in the Town Hall. Also in *Piazza del Municipio* stands the *church of San Nicolò* (1495), redesigned in the Baroque style in the 18th century. Note the slate work over the door (*Agnus Dei*) from the previous building, the antependium (*Ecce Homo*) dated 1465, and a *Madonna and the Souls in Purgatory* attributed to Bartolomeo Gennari. The road that leads from here to San Romolo offers a splendid *panorama* over Apricale, Bajardo (see p. 154) and the verdant surroundings.

Pigna*

Although this town has the same name and a similar layout to the old quarter of Sanremo (see. p. 149), tradition has it that this rural Pigna (elev. 280 m, pop. 1,015) was actually named after the fir-tree forests that once surrounded the town. On the valley side, the majestic ruins of the 12th-century **church of San Tommaso** mark the original site of the settlement, which later moved onto higher ground to make it easier to defend. The new location did not, however, prevent Pigna from passing under the control of different rulers: first the counts of Ventimiglia and of Anjou and from 1388 the house of Savoy, which – except for a brief period of Genoese domination (1625-33) – held onto the town until the unification of Italy. Restored after being damaged in World War II, the 15th-century *Loggia della Piazza Vecchia* is the starting-point of the tour of the attractive historic center. It continues with the **parish church of San Michele*** (1450), rebuilt by Comacin master Giovanni de

G. Canavesio, Passion of Christ, detail, fresco. Church of San Bernardo, Pigna

Lancia in a style that marks the transition between Gothic and Renaissance. The facade has a pseudo-porch with bas relief (*St. Michael and the Dragon*) in the lunette and a magnificent **rose window** possibly by Giovanni Gagini: the tracery radiating out from the central Agnus Dei represents divine salvation triumphing over earthly things, symbolized by floral motifs in the new Renaissance style; the stained glass windows depict the Twelve Apostles. The interior, with its round and octagonal piers, has a 15th-century *Crucifix* and, in the presbytery, a monumental **polyptych of St. Michael***, a masterpiece by Giovanni Canavesio (1500): its 36 sections show the clear influence of the Brea brothers, who toned down the style of the Piedmontese artist's earlier works.

This style is exemplified in the frescoes (**Passion of Christ***, 1482) kept in the little *church of San Bernardo*, inside the cemetery; the once-detached frescoes were painstakingly restored and recently rehung.

9.2 Val Nervia

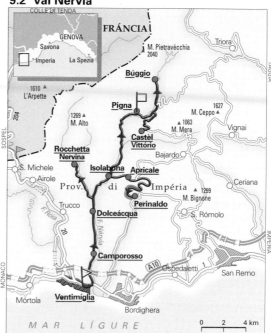

Before leaving the town, it is worth climbing up to *Piazza Castello** to admire the slate portals of the doorways and enjoy the splendid view over to Castel Vittorio (see below).

The *Gouta Gorge*, set in beautiful unspoiled natural surroundings, lies at the end of a scenic 14-km road that winds its way north-west from the junction just before Pigna. From here it is possible to follow the system of Neolithic *castellari* (fortified terraced heights) and after another 30 km return to Ventimiglia.

The border between the Savoy and Genoese dominions ran across the *Lago Pigo Bridge*, rebuilt after the last war. The nearby **church of Santa Maria di Lago Pigo**, documented from 1227, was rebuilt first in the 15th-16th centuries (to which the 1512 *portal*, reused for the facade, belongs) and in the 18th century redesigned in the Piedmontese Baroque sanctuary style, with two belltowers on the facade.

There are more exceptional views from the road that crosses the *Langan Col* (elev. 1,127 m) continuing to the artificial lake of Tenarda and on (after 20.4 km) to the *Melosa Col* (elev. 1,540 m). The road beyond the pass is unsurfaced, and suitable for four-wheeled drive vehicles only; alternatively it is possible to leave the car and follow the 'Alpine Trail' created between the wars that leads from the *Rifugio Grai* mountain hut to Mt. Toraggio (elev. 1,973 m).

Castel Vittorio

In 1862 this village (originally called Castelfranco) changed its name to honor unified Italy's first king – and possibly to be pardoned for its century-long loyalty to Genoa. The walls that once defended the village (elev. 420 m, pop. 418) are now part of the structure of the houses, and the only gateway still visible is the *Porta Communis*, decorated with the Genoese crest. The Baroque *parish church of Santo Stefano* is decorated – unusually for a church – with friezes of bucranes, grotesques, cornucopias, and cannon; in 1727 the tower bells were stolen by the village's arch-rival Pigna.

Buggio

Tradition has it that three thieves from Languedoc founded this still totally rural village (elev. 410 m) in the upper Val Nervia. The ground floors of the houses opening onto alleyways that have never seen motor traffic are still used as cowsheds, and the fields still have the characteristic little constructions in which cheese is left to mature. The most unusual feature, though, is the **Piazza***, built over the main street, which passes along a small bridge below. The village also has the only *church* dedicated to *San Siagrio*, bishop of Nice in the Carolingian period.

9.3 Val Roia
From Ventimiglia to Tende, in Italy and in France

After the slight adjustments made to the Franco-Italian border after World War II, a large stretch of this tour, along the SS 20 (*del Colle di Tenda*, the N204 in France) and through the Roia Valley, now passes through French territory. After Airole (12.8 km from Ventimiglia), the road crosses the Fanghetto border and, 23.8 km from Ventimiglia, arrives at Breil-sur-Roya (Breglio in Italian), after which come the ravines of Saorge (Saorgio) and a short detour to Fontan. The N204 continues through the Bergue and Paganin Gorges, and, 39.8 km from Ventimiglia, Saint-Dalmas-de-Tende (San Dalmazzo di Tenda), the starting-point for two excursions, one into the Vallée des Merveilles (Valle delle Meraviglie), the other to Brigue (Briga Marittima). From Tende (Tenda), the road passes through the Colle di Tenda tunnel and back onto Italian soil. 18.5 km further north is the town of Limone Piemonte.

Airole

This village (elev. 149 m, pop. 519) has an elliptical structure with concentric circles, in common with many towns in western-most Liguria. Probably of medieval origin, for more than a century and a half (1273-1435) it came under the jurisdiction of the monks of the Carthusian monastery of Pesio. The *church of Ss. Filippo e Giacomo*, redesigned in the Baroque style in the 1700s (now with a 19th-century facade), is also thought to date back to medieval times.

The last little town before the Fanghetto border is **Olivetta San Michele** (pop. 273), which is really two separate villages: San Michele (elev. 139 m), near the junction with SS 20 and the provincial road to Olivetta (elev. 292 m), the other half of a town that lies in a beautifully wild natural setting. The Olivetta road continues for 9 km on the other side of the border to **Sospel** (Sospello, elev. 349 m). This town, well known to motor racing enthusiasts (special preliminary trials for the Monte Carlo rally are held at the Col du Turini) received the schismatic bishops of the anti-Pope of Avignon between 1380 and 1421. The now Baroque *cathedral of St-Michel* still has a Romanesque belltower; inside note the polyptych (*Immacolata*) by Francesco Brea and a triptych (*Pietà*) attributed to Lodovico Brea. The houses facing onto the Bevera river are a picturesque site, as is the medieval *bridge* with its central tower.

9.3 Val Roia

Breil-sur-Roya (Breglio)

One look at the map is enough to understand the strategic importance of this village (elev. 286 m), situated at the junction between the N204 and the departmental Route 220 to Nice. As a result of its position it was much fought over by the counts of Ventimiglia and the house of Anjou (12th-13th cent.) and subsequently by the Piedmontese and the French, the latter finally taking possession in 1860. Note the interesting belltower of the 18th-century *church of Santa Maria in Albis* (1663-99), with its colored ceramic dome.

The strategically important town of Breil-sur-Roya was fought over for centuries

Saorge (Saorgio)

In the Middle Ages it was considered virtually impregnable, but by the 14th century its castle was forced to endure an attack by a besieging army; an episode that was repeated in 1794, when the troops of Massena – among whose ranks was the young Napoleon Bonaparte – entered the town without striking a blow. Olive groves and Mediterranean *maquis* temper the steep slope that surrounds the town (elev. 520 m), a maze of alleys, steps and covered passageways that wind their way in amongst the old stone houses. Note the 15th-century *parish church of St-Sauveur*, redesigned in the Baroque style in 1718, and the church (also Baroque) of the nearby Franciscan monastery, preceded by a portico. Records dating as far back as 1092 mention the Romanesque **Madonna del Poggio** (*closed to the public*) in the south of the village. The slender *belltower* is 12th century.

Spectacular, colorful schistose walls line the **Gorges de Bergue** and the **Gorges du Paganin** along the road to **Saint-Dalmas-de-Tende** (San Dalmazzo di Tenda, elev. 696 m), whose name refers to a monastery founded in the 11th century by the abbey of Pedona: it was rebuilt in 1850 and is now private property.

Vallée des Merveilles*
(Valle delle Meraviglie)

As well as offering beautiful Alpine scenery, this 'Vale of Marvels' (*visitor information: tel. 0033493047371*), which forms part of the *Parc National du Mercantour*, is famous for its countless **stone carvings** dating from the late Neolithic to the Iron Age, which have come to light on the slopes of Mt. Bego (elev. 2,872 m), carved into the rock by transhumant shepherd communities at between 1,900 and 2,700 m. Although most are of animals, some depict weapons, scenes from everyday life and other symbolic and religious subjects.

La Brigue (Briga Marittima)

The area around this little town (clev. 765 m) on the Levenza rivers is a paradise for anyone keen on hiking and mountain biking (a sport known in French as VTT, or 'Vélo-Tout-Terrain'). Tourist activities have not, however, spoilt the medieval charm of the town, dominated by the remains of a feudal castle and until 1947 part of Italy, a fact recalled by the inscription in Italian on the facade of one of the two Baroque *oratories* that flank the grand **church of St.-Martin**. This 15th-century Gothic edifice contains parts of an earlier place of worship (the portal on the right-hand side dates back to the 13th century; the belltower appears to be late Romanesque) and later additions (the Renaissance portal on the facade was added in 1576). The interior has important paintings of Ligurian-Provençal origin (15th-16th cent.), namely an *Adoration of the Christ Child* attributed to Lodovico Brea and a triptych (*Madonna della Neve with St. Nicholas of Bari and Louis of Toulouse*) painted in 1507 by Sebastiano Fuseri.

On 12 October 1492 (the historic day of the discovery of America) Giovanni Canavesio completed the remarkable cycle of **frescoes**** on the walls of the **sanctuary of Notre-Dame des Fontaines** (Madonna del Fontan, 3.8 km from Briga; *open on request, tel. 0033493043607*), a masterpiece of the school of painting active in the late Middle Ages in the Maritime Alps area. The Pinerolo-born artist painted the *Last Judgment* behind the facade, the *Passion of Jesus* on the side walls and the eleven scenes (including the *Nativity of Mary*, the *Presentation of Jesus* and the *Purification of the Virgin*) on the arch around the choir, which was frescoed (seven sections dedicated to the *Death of Mary*, and the *Evangelists*) in 1452 by another late 15th-century artist, who also painted the *Fathers of the Church* in the intrados.

Tende (Tenda)

In today's single-currency, barrier-free Europe, we might almost smile at the idea that this village (elev. 816 m) should have been so bitterly fought over at the end of World War II, were it not for the bloody episodes preceding the plebiscite that sanctioned the handover of the town to France in 1947. This was nothing new for a town whose strategic position had since medieval times made it a fiercely contested territory. The ruined castle of Ventimiglia-Lascaris (destroyed in 1692 by French Field-Marshal Nicolas de Catinat and now the local cemetery) testifies to these events. 19th-century fountains, wooden balconies and slate doorways line the walk through the streets, squares and steps of the old quarter, perched on the western side of the valley. From *Place de la République*, which overlooks the N204, Rue de France and Rue Cotta lead to the **church of Nôtre-Dame de l'Assomption**, built between the 15th and 16th centuries over the ruins of a church dedicated to St. John: the majestic *portal* in local green stone, finished in 1562, is by the Varensi brothers of Cenova. The square-section *belltower* ends in a hemispherical dome covered in ceramic scales.

Housed in a modern building outside the town, the **Musée des Merveilles** (*open: 10.30am-5pm; 1 May-15 October 10.30am-6.30pm, Sat 10.30am-9pm; closed Tue*) has rock carvings from Mt. Bego, along with other finds from prehistoric to Roman times.

9.4 From Ventimiglia to La Turbie
The westernmost Riviera to the Côte d'Azur, 25 km *(see map p. 172)*

This tour, which also passes through what is now French territory, ends at the imposing remains of the trophy erected during the reign of Augustus, near present-day La Turbie. The tour first takes in two important sights on the Italian side of the border: the first is to Mortola Inferiore (6 km from Ventimiglia), home of the famous gardens of Villa Hanbury; the second is to the Balzi Rossi, a site of exceptional importance because of the prehistoric remains found in the caves there. The proposed route passes along the coast-road variant of the Via Aurelia from Ventimiglia toward the Ponte San Ludovico frontier post. In France, the tortuous but panoramic 'Grande Corniche' road leads high up over Monaco to La Turbie.

Giardini Hanbury**

Two brothers, Thomas and Daniel Hanbury, among the many English people who fell in love with this part of the Riviera in the 19th century, laid out this fine botanical garden (*open last Sun in September to 31 October and from last Sun in March to 14*

Giardini Hanbury: the villa (above) and a detail of the bronze dragon fountain from Kyoto, Japan

The dawning of mankind, just by the border

Foreigners entering Italy at the Ponte San Ludovico border get quite an unexpected introduction to the country; Italians heading to the Côte d'Azur get the opportunity to visit a unique feature of their country before they leave. In the mid-19th century anthropologists began to dig in the six caves along the limestone wall known as Balzi Rossi, located along the stretch of coast between the French border and the little village of Grimaldi in the municipal area of Ventimiglia. No major finds were made, however, until 1873, when the skeletons of two children were found in what thereafter came to be known as the 'Infants Cave'. Eleven years later, human remains came to light in the 'Barma Grande' cave, in which another three burial sites were found in 1892-94: all dating back, like those previously found, to the last stage of the Würm Glaciation

(29,000-16,000 years ago), a dating confirmed by the rock carvings discovered in the mid-1970s on the walls of the Caviglione cave. A slightly earlier fragment of a 'Homo Erectus' hipbone was found in the Cave of the Prince, together with various tools demonstrating man's presence here since the Upper Paleolithic (40,000-85,000 years ago). This archaeological legacy, which is of inestimable value, has on several occasions come close to being destroyed by so-called industrial civilization: beginning with the damage caused by the building of the Genoa-Nice railroad and continuing with World War II: the worst to suffer were the finds in the Barma Grande, which at the time were still housed there.

June, 10am-5pm, from 1 November to the last Sunday in March 10am-4pm, closed Wed; and from 15 June to last Sun in September 9am-6pm) around the villa of the same name, begun in 1867. As well as species typical of the Mediterranean and traditional Ligurian cultivations, the garden boasts a remarkable variety of exotic plants, which grow luxuriantly thanks to the exceptionally mild climate and the fact that the gardens slope down southward to the sea, and are thus sheltered from the cold north winds. The lower section of the garden is crossed by the ancient Via Iulia Augusta: a stone tablet placed here by Thomas Hanbury serves as a reminder that Dante, Niccolò Machiavelli and Pope Pius VII all passed along this way.

Balzi Rossi*

A stone's throw from the border with France we are catapulted back to prehistoric times. This promontory, still in Italy by just a few hundred meters, is famous for the extraordinary finds made in the caves and now exhibited, in part, at the **Museo Preistorico dei Balzi Rossi** (open: 9am-

7pm, closed Mon), entered from the parking lot opposite the Ponte San Ludovico border. The museum presents fossils of animals typically found in warm climates (elephants, hippopotami, rhinoceros) found in the oldest deposits, and remains of marmots and reindeer which lived during the Würm glaciation; the human remains displayed have mostly been dated back to the Upper Palaeolithic, when the caves were used as burial chambers. The most important exhibit, now in a new display (1993), is the *triple grave* found in 1892 inside the *Barma Grande cave*, with the remains of an adult and two adolescents together with extensive funeral gifts. A walkway connects to the caves, which have the only *rock carvings* of this kind from the Upper Paleolithic ever found in northern Italy.

Augustus and the *pax romana* in the Alps

"To the Emperor Augustus son of Caesar the divine (...), under whose auspices the entire people of the Alps, from the Adriatic to the Mediterranean were brought under the authority of the people of Rome". This opening dedication inscribed on the base of the Trophée des Alpes monument at La Turbie is followed by the list of the 45 populations so subjected after putting up strong resistance to the Roman legions, whose duty it was to guarantee the absolute safety of the land routes to the provinces north of the Alps. One of these was the Via Iulia Augusta, opened by Octavian, which headed toward Gaul. It was decided that a monument to Alpine victory would be erected at the highest point overlooking this road. The trophy is almost the only one of its kind (another was put up at Adam Klissi, in present-day Romania, to celebrate the conquest of Dacia). It was turned into a watchtower after the fall of the Empire, and in the 12th and 13th centuries its mighty walls gave shelter to the inhabitants of La Turbie during the fierce wars between the Guelphs and the Ghibellines. And the structure of the monument remained virtually intact until 1706, when Louis XIV, who had been obliged to return it to Savoy, ordered that it should be blown up: the explosion spared only the ponderous central section. It was not until 1905 that restoration of the trophy began: after the interruption of World War I, the work was eventually finished in 1932-33 thanks to funds supplied by American magnate Edward Tuck.

La Turbie

This huge monument erected by Augustus to celebrate peace in the Alps was designed to be seen from a great distance. Indeed the **Trophée des Alpes*** (*open: 10am-5pm; 1 April-20 June 9.30am-6pm; 21 June-20 September 9.30am-7pm; closed Mon*), built between the 7th and 6th centuries BC, can be seen quite clearly from as far away as Roquebrune. The original monument, which was 50 m high and 36 m across, had a Doric colonnade over the base with statues of the generals who fought in the Alpine campaigns. Above was a majestic dome topped by marble statues of the emperor with two prisoners. The *epigraph* with the names of the 45 subjected Alpine peoples on the side facing the mountains, the largest surviving Roman inscription, is of great ethnographic value. Opposite the monument the small *Musée Edward Tuck* (named after the American who financed the 1932-33 restoration scheme) has a scale model of the monument as it was originally designed, and tells the eventful story of how it was stripped of its statues in the Middle Ages and used as a fortification. The nearby terrace offers a superb *panorama** of the coast from Bordighera to Esterel, and a spectacular view over the principality of Monaco; on very clear days it is also possible to make out Corsica on the horizon.

After visiting the monument, it is worth spending some time in the delightful historic center of La Turbie (elev. 480 m) to see the **church of St.-Michel**, rebuilt in 1777 with a concave facade: inside note the painting (*St. Magdalene*) by Jean-Baptiste Van Loo and, at the back of the nave, a 16th-century *St. Catherine of Siena*.

9.4 From Ventimiglia to La Turbie

10 Portofino and Tigullio

Area profile

There is something particularly enchanting about Mt. Portofino, the famous rocky headland that separates two beautiful bays – Golfo Paradiso and Golfo del Tigullio – in a part of eastern Liguria that offers such an incredible variety of different scenery in such a small space. It is clear from the map that this piece of land jutting out into the sea is something of an anomaly on the otherwise more or less straight Ligurian coastline. The steep, craggy western part gradually flattens out toward the eastern side, where the coast takes the form of a series of inlets with corners of great beauty. The rough geographical layout has also influenced the climate and landscape of the area: on the sides facing the sea things are distinctly Mediterranean, with grassland, *maquis*, ilex and pines, while the northern part of the promontory has a much more continental feel, with its woodlands of chestnut and walnut trees, hornbeam and oak.

Charming Portofino in a 1950s picture postcard

Human intervention has added further variety, most notably in the form of olive groves and orchards. Man has, alas, also been the cause of the forest fires that have done such damage to the natural environment of the Portofino promontory, and prompted the setting up (1986-1995) of a regional park covering the southern section of the promontory, to which the protected marine area was joined in 1998.

The inaccessibility of the coast (landslides are not uncommon) has, however, saved the area from the uncontrolled building work that has transformed so many other parts of the region, ensuring that the rich historical heritage – much of it dating back to medieval times – has not disappeared under concrete. By contrast, the towns along the more habitable stretches of the coast delight visitors with their charming rows of tall, narrow and colorful houses, the beautiful and authentic expression of a maritime civilization that has now given way to a quite different lifestyle.

Camogli gets a pounding during a sea-storm

10.1 Camogli and Mt. Portofino

A series of tours – by car, by boat and on foot – of the headland and along the coast
(see map p. 178)

These short tours, offering plenty to see and do, pass through some of the most beautiful scenery on the eastern Riviera. The 3.5 km drive from Camogli to Ruta traverses an area of villas and their lush flower and vegetable gardens set against the backdrop of Mt. Portofino. A turn-off from the Via Aurelia just before the tunnel leads to the little village of San Rocco (2 km); while a private road among pines and chestnut trees climbs to Portofino Vetta (2 km), the mountain top from where walks lead to Punta Chiappa and San Fruttuoso. These last two places can also be reached from Camogli by boat: an option worth considering especially in summer, when the build-up of traffic on the Via Aurelia makes the car more of a hindrance than a help: parking becomes a headache, and the excursion can easily end up being a complete waste of time, especially given the inflexibility of the local traffic police.

Camogli*

This town (elev. 32 m, pop. 5,790), which the narrow shoreline has forced to develop upward rather than outward, has some extremely tall buildings (some over six stories high), with a network of alleys, steps and covered passageways in between. The result is one of the most charming examples of coastal architecture on the eastern Riviera, with the brightly-colored fronts of the houses lining the shore and forming a backdrop to the large rocky prominence known as 'Isola' (or island, a reminder that it was once separated from the mainland), which together with the 'Priaro' district behind forms the original town that grew up around the fishing port. The 'Isola' is the site of the town's two main monumental buildings: the **basilica of Santa Maria Assunta**, built in the 12th century but much expanded and altered up to the 19th century, when the neoclassical facade was added behind the black and

---

The Submerged Christ

"As a man of the sea, I too wanted a sacred figure to turn to, such as an Alpine mountaineer might have on a mountain top (…) and I saw in my mind's eye the statue that would be, in the blue translucent water of the deep sea, in the midst of the decorative flora and the darting fauna, in that primordial, solitary silence; a floating figure, born of the waters, its arms reaching upward, both invoking and embracing, slender and luminous in form, beautifully proportioned and with intense religious expressiveness". Italian scuba diving pioneer Duilio Marcante had made a dive to find solace after the shock of a dear friend's death. He resurfaced with an idea that came to fruition on 22 August 1954, when the bronze statue of the Redeemer designed by Guido Galletti was submerged in the waters of San Fruttuoso. It immediately became a symbol of the visceral links between the people of Camogli and the sea, which had always been the source of the town's wealth but also the cause of so much tragic loss of life. A ceremony to remember the victims of the sea is held on the last Sunday in July, culminating in the laying of wreaths at the feet of the underwater statue. The event attracts large crowds: most watch from boats with underwater viewing equipment, but large numbers of divers also turn out for the occasion (although the figure of Christ is venerated at all times during the year). Since the creation of the Portofino Marine Reserve (1999), it is now possible to dive in the area in organized groups only. For further information contact *The European Diving Center of Santa Margherita Ligure (tel. and fax 0185293017)*.

The 'padellata': Camogli's fried fish festival

white cobbled parvis. The interior, richly decorated with marble and gilt stuccowork, has ceiling *frescoes* by Nicolò Barabino and Francesco Semino. The adjoining **Castel Dragone** (*closed to the public*) also dates back to medieval times, its single tower dominating the ponderous walls; like the church, this stronghold was rebuilt at various times in its history.

The coffee shops, pubs and ice-cream parlors that line **Via Garibaldi** are a good place from which to enjoy the fine views over Golfo Paradiso and Monte Portofino. On the other side of Piazza Schiaffino begins Via Ferrari, where a modern building (no. 41) houses the **Museo Marinaro Gio Bono Ferrari** (*open: 9-11.45am and 3-5.40pm; Wed, Sat and Sun 9am–noon; closed Tue*). Though presented in a somewhat haphazard fashion, this collection of models, nautical instruments, shipping equipment, flags and historical documents of the age of sail is an extremely valuable legacy of the unquestioned importance of the Camogli fleet during the 'golden century'. Between the Napoleonic Wars and World War I over 2,900 vessels were rigged here. One room in the *Biblioteca Nicolò Cuneo*, a library adjoining the museum, has finds from the prehistoric settlement found at Rio Gentile.

The walk (about 90 minutes) to the tiny fishing village of Punta Chiappa is demanding but scenically rewarding. The footpath heads south-east out of Camogli, following the course of the Rio Gentile as far as the village of *San*

Rocco (elev. 221 m) whose *parish church* (1863) also affords a superb view. To the right of the parvis begins the descent to Punta Chiappa. On the way we come to the **church of San Nicolò di Capodimonte** (elev. 97 m), records of which date back to 1141. Built by monks of the Congregation of San Rufo, it retains in the apse section the original Romanesque structure, reinstated by restoration work in 1925-26 and 1971; the marble *high altar* is probably as old as the church itself. The last part of the walk descends steeply to Porto Pidocchio, a mooring place for boats, and on to **Punta Chiappa** (elev. 18 m). Here, a stele with a *Stella Maris* (or 'starfish') mosaic adorns the rocky spur that towers up behind the little village.

The splendid monumental complex of **San Fruttuoso di Capodimonte**** in the small seaside hamlet of **San Fruttuoso**** (elev. 25 m) was reinstated to its former splendor after restoration work in 1986-88 by FAI (Italy's National Trust). By far the most convenient way to reach this out-of-the-way place is by boat (approximately 30 minutes from Camogli), since the alternative is the difficult path down from Portofino Vetta (a 75-minute walk). The first landmark to appear when arriving by sea is the *Andrea Doria Tower* (1562), situated on the cape between the two inlets in the bay. The bishop of Tarragon Prospero settled here in the 8th century, after fleeing his native Spain to escape the Moors, and founded a chapel to house the ashes of St. Fructuosus (the first patriarch of the Spanish town) and of the deacons Augurius and Eulogius. The presence of Benedictine monks here is documented from the 10th century, when the central part of the **church** was built, with a *dome* later incorporated into the octagonal *tower*, and the lower part of the **cloister**: the upper part was added two centuries later, thanks to a generous donation from Empress Adelaide of Burgundy. In the 13th century the

San Fruttuoso Bay area

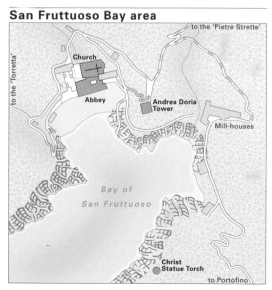

Abbey of San Fruttuoso di Capodimonte

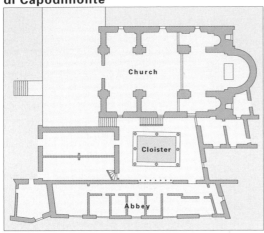

area. In the 17th century the upper cloister was rebuilt; in 1861 the Doria household bought the whole complex, now in a state of dereliction made considerably worse by the 1915 flood. After an initial restoration scheme in 1933, which recreated the abbey's two tiers of three-light windows, the property was bequeathed to FAI in 1983.

As well as attracting many tourists and sunseekers, San Fruttuoso is also popular with scuba divers, who are attracted in particular by the *Cristo degli Abissi* (Submerged Christ), a bronze statue by Guido Galletti (1954) which stands offshore, eight fathoms down (see box).

Doria family financed the construction of the **abbey** (*open: 10am-3.45pm, closed Mon; May-September 10am-6pm*), in exchange for the right to use the adjoining crypt as the family burial place: between 1275 and 1305 eight *tombs* were installed there, made of white marble and gray stone, a chromatic pattern common to many churches of the time in the Tyrrhenian

The abbey and beach of San Fruttuoso

Ruta

The scattered houses of this little village (elev. 254 m) stand among the pine and chestnut trees at the junction of the roads and paths that cross the Portofino promontory. The 17th-century *parish church of San Michele*, just above the Via Aurelia, is not to be confused with the Romanesque *church of San Michele* (13th cent.), which was restored in the early 20th century after a long period of neglect, and stands on the road to San Martino di Noceto.

Portofino Vetta

The elegant hotel complex built here in the early 20th century (and refurbished for the new millennium) commands spectacular views all around. Mt. Portofino's panoramic 'peak' (elev. 416 m) is the starting-point for a number of different walks through the 4,660-ha **Parco Naturale Regionale di Portofino****.

10.2 The Bay of Tigullio
From Ruta to Portofino and Zoagli, 24.5 km *(see map p. 178)*

This tour, which winds its way along the Bay of Tigullio, takes in holiday resorts famed the world over. From Camogli, we head east along the Via Aurelia as far as the little town of San Lorenzo della Costa, just after which a turn-off to the right offers splendid views of the bay as it leads down to Santa Margherita Ligure (6.5 km). From here the SS 227, one of the most panoramic in the whole of Italy, leads after 5 km to Portofino. In the other direction, the coast road passes San Michele di Pagana and Rapallo (3 km), and back to the Via Aurelia toward Zoagli (5 km).

San Lorenzo della Costa

On the right-hand side of the state road stands the *parish church* of the town (elev. 192 m), built in the 13th century but much altered thereafter. Inside is a splendid triptych* (the central panel depicts the **Martyrdom of St. Andrew**; the side panel has the **Wedding at Cana** and the **Raising of Lazarus**) in the 3rd chapel on the left, a work from the Flemish school (1499); note also the *Martyrdom of St. Lawrence* in the presbytery, by Luca Cambiaso.

Santa Margherita Ligure*

This busy seaside town (elev. 13 m, pop. 10,689), whose waterfront bars and cafés fill up with young vacationers in summer, also conserves brightly-colored houses that recall its fishing village past. The elegant Art Nouveau hotels, on the other hand, are a reminder of its early fortunes as a tourist resort in the late 19th and early 20th centuries. Tourism boomed again after the last war, although the spread of new buildings was more contained here than elsewhere. The town did not come into being until the 19th century, with the unification of the old villages of Pescino and Corte, the latter situated on what is now the tourist marina; the original name of Porto Napoleone was dropped after Bonaparte's fall, the inspiration for the new name coming from the *parish church of Santa Margherita d'Antiochia* (B2), which has come down to us in its present form thanks to the work of Giovanni Battista Ghiso (17th cent.). Continuing to the right of the church we come to the **Villa Durazzo Municipal Park** (B2; *open: 9am-7pm, October-March 9am-5pm*), divided into an Italian garden filled with exotic plants, and a wilder English garden. The park's **Villa*** (B2; *open: 9am-6pm, October-March 9.30am-12.30pm and 2.30-4.30pm; closed Mon*), attributed (controversially) to Galeazzo Alessi, was built in the years immediately following 1560. The square-plan building has ashlarwork and moldings around the windows that punctuate the four stories. The interior is filled with marble and majolica, stuccowork, tapestries, Murano glass and chinoiserie; the art gallery has works by Domenico Piola and Giovanni Andrea De Ferrari. On the seaward side of the park, which also contains

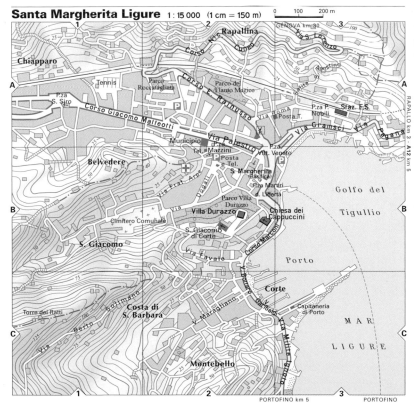

Santa Margherita Ligure 1 : 15 000 (1 cm = 150 m)

the *Villa del Nido* and *Villa San Giacomo* (both 19th century), the 17th-century *church of San Giacomo di Corte* (B2) with its light-colored facade stands in a scenic position overlooking the bay; the frescoes inside are by Nicolò Barabino. Steps lead down to the *oratory of Sant'Erasmo* (the patron saint of sailors), also 17th century, like the *church of the Cappuccini* (B2), in whose confessional hall stands a 12th-century statue (**Enthroned Madonna***) from the Provençale school. Opposite the church are the remains of the *castello*, built in a record six months in 1550.

San Michele di Pagana (elev. 5 m) is a little seaside village with the typical row of colorful houses along the shore. Its 17th-century *parish church* has a *Crucifixion** by Antonie Van Dyck, and a *Nativity* attributed to Luca Giordano.

Completely restored in the late 20th century, the former *Benedictine abbey of San Gerolamo della Cervara* (*open on request, tel. 800652110*), was built in the second half of the 14th century on the high ground behind Punta Pedale. Further on, a Gothic-style *castle* (1626), now a private home, marks the beginning of the bay of **Paraggi***   (elev. 5 m), whose little sandy beach is washed by crystal clear water.

Portofino**

The sight of Portofino so enchanted the Wehrmacht official who had been instructed to bomb the bay to prevent the munitions depot from falling into allied hands, that he did not have the heart to carry out the order, responding instead to the pleas of an elderly German noblewoman who begged him to spare the village. The headland and little bay of Portofino (elev. 3 m, pop. 574) whose tall, narrow, pastel-colored houses frame the harbor, is one of the most famous views in Italy. Less well known are the origins of the village, records of which date back to the imperial age, when it was known as *Portus Delphini*. The central part of the village still has the regular grid of streets laid out in Roman times. In the 12th century, after a long period during which it depended on the abbey of San Fruttuoso, Portofino passed under the jurisdiction of Genoa, which retained control thereafter. Leave the car in the Piazza della Libertà carpark (B1; parking elsewhere is reserved for residents only) and take *Via Roma* down to the sea; the 14th-century *oratory of Nostra Signora Assunta*, on the right, with a fine sculpted slate portal (1555), is now used as an exhibition center. The road ends at Piazza Martiri dell'Olivetta (B2), or *piazzetta* as it is more commonly known. Under the porticoes, which form the backdrop to the little harbor, are shops, boutiques, restaurants and ice-cream parlors. At the rear of the piazzetta, on the left, note the *church of San Martino*, whose facade faces onto the SS 227 road: built in the Romanesque Lombard style in the 12th century, it acquired its present-day appearance in the 19th century. The *church of San Giorgio* (C2), which occupies a splendid panoramic position on the isthmus connecting the promontory to the mainland, was rebuilt after the last war (1950); inside are what are reputedly relics of Saint George. On the promontory itself

10.1 Camogli and Mt. Portofino
10.2 Tigullio Bay

178

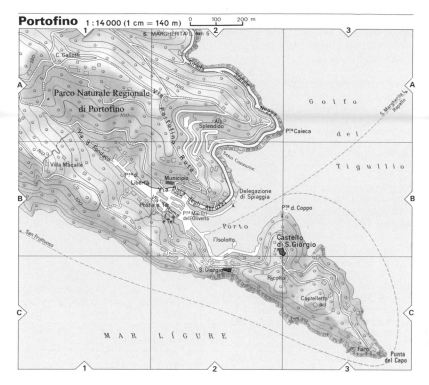

stands the **castello di San Giorgio** (B2-3; *open: 10am-6pm, November-March 10am-5pm; Closed Tue*), a medieval fortress redesigned in 1554-57 and in the 17th and 18th centuries, and transformed in 1870 into the private residence of Yeats Brown, the British consul in Genoa. The visit ends with the traditional walk to the lighthouse at *Punta del Capo* (C3).

Rapallo*

This is the most populous town in the Tigullio area (elev. 5 m, pop. 29,344) and – thanks to its bathing establishments, marina and other modern amenities (golf, riding stables, tennis and many other sports facilities) – one of the most prestigious vacation resorts in eastern Liguria. The Art Nouveau hotels that line the **Lungomare Vittorio Veneto** (B2-3) serve as a reminder of Rapallo's early days as an elegant tourist center. The waterfront promenade ends opposite the **castello** (B3), built in 1551 by Comacin master Antonio de Carabo. Linked to the main-

land by a thin strip of land, this little castle was restored in 1960 and is now used for temporary exhibitions. On the other side of *Piazza Garibaldi* (B3), *Via Mazzini* and Via Magenta lead to the **church of Santo Stefano** (A2), which is recorded as early as 1155, although the present building is the result of 17th-century renovation work. The nearby *Civic Tower* was built in 1473; the *oratory of the Bianchi* (A-B2-3) is 17th century. At the end of Via Mazzini, note the elegant neoclassical front of the *parish church of Ss. Gervasio e Protasio* (B2), also of medieval origin (consecrated in 1118) but remodeled between the 17th and 20th centuries; it has

The Vittorio Veneto seafront promenade at Rapallo

179

a noticeably leaning belltower (1753-57). The visit of the town ends at the so-called *Ponte di Annibale* (B2), a bridge dating back to the early Middle Ages.

The late 18th-century *Villa Tigullio*, inside the *Casale Park* (B3), houses the *Biblioteca Internazionale Città di Rapallo* and the **Museo del Merletto** (*open: 3-6pm, Thur 10am-noon; Sun by request, tel. 018563305; closed Mon*), a museum of lace-making from the 16th to 20th centuries with examples of lace-pillows and other utensils, lacework designs and samples, period clothing and furnishings.

The **sanctuary of Nostra Signora di Montallegro** (elev. 612 m) can be reached by cable car or by driving out of the town, along Via Fratelli Betti (A3). Turn right after the hamlet of **San Maurizio di Monti** (elev. 290 m), whose *parish church* (redesigned in the 19th-20th cent.) has an *Apparition of the Madonna Odigitria* attributed to Bernardo Strozzi. The sanctuary lies a total of 11 km from Rapallo. The *panorama* from the parvis is spectacular. The elaborately neo-Gothic facade of the shrine, built in 1557, is by Luigi Rovelli (1892-96). Inside are hundreds of votive offerings; the frescoes on the apse semidome (*Apparition*) were painted by Nicolò Bara-

Damask weaving in Zoagli

bino, while the altarpieces in the 1st altar on the right (*Visitation*) and the 1st altar on the left (*Pietà*) are by Giovanni Battista Carlone and Luca Cambiaso respectively.

Zoagli

This little resort (elev. 17 m, pop. 2,474), where life is much quieter and friendlier than in bustling Rapallo, has a centuries-old tradition of velvet and damask manufacture. The town still shows the scars of the heavy World War II bombing it suffered because of its vicinity to the railroad viaduct, the main target of allied air raid attacks; the *parish church of San Martino*, built in 1725 to a design by Antonio Maria Ricca, was also badly damaged during the war. The beauty of the natural surroundings does, however, do something to compensate for man's destructive powers: the *walk* cut into the sheer cliff face offers some marvelous views of the whole bay. In the town's own little bay, some four fathoms under water, stands the *Madonna del Mare,* a statue sculpted by Marian Hastianatte (1996).

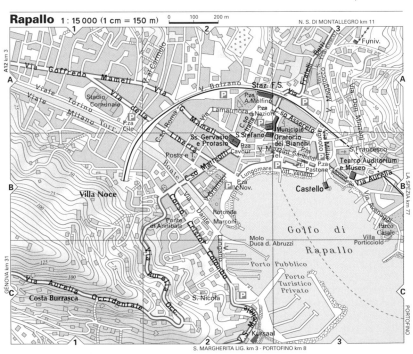

Rapallo 1 : 15 000 (1 cm = 150 m)

11 The Chiavari area

Area profile

Such is the importance of Chiavari there have been proposals to make it the main town of its own province, which would be the region's fifth. The town lies to the west of the Entella river estuary, at the confluence of the Graveglia, Fontanabuona and Sturla Valleys: the latter two provided relatively easy links with the Po Valley across the mountains (the Sturla Valley leading into the Aveto Valley). The vicinity of the valleys helps to explain why there has been an important settlement here since prehistoric times: a large Iron Age necropolis (8th-7th cent. BC) was found in 1959 to the west of the present town. Chiavari was officially founded on 19 October 1178, when a consular decree from the Republic of Genoa approved what amounted to a development plan for the town, establishing the construction of four streets with buildings running parallel to the sea, to be cut across at right angles by a series of smaller streets, creating a regular grid pattern. Chiavari, with its own system of defense walls (demolished in the 18th century), soon rose to prominence, and in 1332 became the seat of the vicariate of the eastern Riviera, more or less the area considered in this chapter, which remained under its jurisdiction – as part of Genoese domination – until the end of the 18th century. In 1646 Chiavari was officially designated as a town, the first in eastern Liguria. It prospered until the early 19th century, after which its fortunes changed, and the recession in manufacturing and farming activities that hit the whole area provoked mass emigration to the Americas, especially to Rio de la Plata. Tourism, which for many coastal areas was a main source of income as early as the late 1800s, did not really flourish here until after the last war, bringing about rapid growth, some of it governed by the all-too-frequent speculative criteria. But the local economy is not only based on summer tourism: the Chiavari area also boasts a highly competitive industrial furnishing industry, which has developed out of traditional craft activities, most notably 'Campanine' chairs.

11.1 Chiavari*
Walking tour of the town, and a short excursion by car *(town plan p. 182)*

The visit of the town (elev. 5 m, pop. 28,086) begins at Piazza Mazzini (A2), and continues west along Via Martiri della Liberazione. At the junction with Viale Millo (A1-2) we turn right and come to Piazza S. Giacomo. To the left of the church of *San Giacomo di Rupinaro* is the start of Via Raggio, which continues beyond Piazza S. Giovanni as Via Ravaschieri, crossing Piazza della Fenice – characterized by the ogival arcades of the 13th-century palace known as the Palazzo dei Portici Neri – and ending at Piazza Matteotti (A2), in

A view of Piazza Mazzini, Chiavari

which Palazzo Rocca stands. From here, Corso Garibaldi (B2) and Via Vinelli lead toward Piazza Nostra Signora dell'Orto, the square in which the Town Hall, the cathedral, and the Bishop's Palace stand.

Piazza Mazzini (A2). Every morning (except Sundays) this square comes to life with a colorful fruit and vegetable market.

181

Towering above is the neo-Gothic *Palazzo di Giustizia* (designed by Giuseppe Partini in 1886), whose construction necessitated the demolition of the 1404 citadel. All that remains of the stronghold is a sturdy square *tower*, squeezed in between the Palace of Justice and the Town Hall behind. Elegant marble balconies add grace to the severe front of the 17th-century *Palazzo Torriglia*, on the corner with Via Cittadella.

The **church of San Giaco-mo di Rupinaro** dates back to the 7th century and is the oldest in Chia-vari; the present building, however, is the result of al-terations completed in

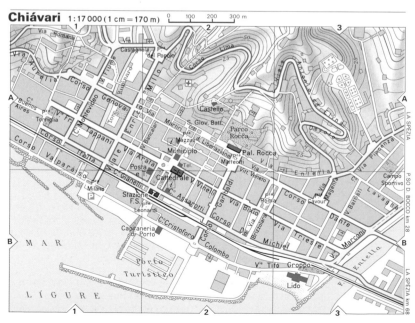

The typical "Campanina" chair back

1637; the belltower is 18th century and the modern facade was added in 1938.

The square in front of **Palazzo Marana**, at no. 36 Via Raggio, was opened up to accommo-date coaches. Built in 1730, the building has a linear facade with a marble balcony above the majestic doorway, behind which is a large, light-filled vestibule.

San Giovanni Battista (A2). This church, with a 1935 facade, was founded in 1332, but the present building is the result of the redesign by Bartolomeo Bianco and An-drea Vannone in the 17th century; the belltower dates back to 1557. Inside are a *Crucifix* by Anton Maria Maragliano on

the high altar, two altarpieces by Orazio De Ferrari (*St. Peter Receives the Keys*) and Domenico Fiasella (*Ecstasy of St. Joseph*), in the 2nd and 3rd altars on the right respectively.

The Economic Society for Agriculture, Trade and the Arts, at no. 15 Via Ravaschieri, has a *Li-brary*, one of Liguria's largest, with 70,000 vol-umes. The society, found-ed in 1791, comprises three permanent exhibitions (*open on request, tel. 0185 363275*): the **Museo Stori-co**, with an important col-lection of *Risorgimento* memorabilia; a **Picture Gallery**, whose works in-clude a *Descent from the Cross* from the school of Quentin Metsys and a *Connoisseur's Chamber* by Frans Frencken II; and, at no. 1 Via Ravaschieri, the *Museo Garaventa*, given over entirely to the works of sculptor Lorenzo Garaventa.

Palazzo Rocca (A2). Now an exhibition center, this was originally the residence of the Costaguta marquises, built by Bar-tolomeo Bianco in 1629 and enlarged in the following century for the Grimaldi with the addition of the two side wings; the *park* behind the building (*open: 7am-7pm*) was laid out in the same period. The door-way at no. 4 Via Costaguta marks the en-trance to the *Museo Archeologico per la Preistoria e Protostoria del Tigullio* (*open:*

Chiávari 1:17 000 (1 cm = 170 m)

J. Roos, Still Life with Dog and Game. Palazzo Rocca, Chiavari

1841-1907), and the new interior: a central nave with two side aisles divided by piers and sumptuously decorated with marble and gilt stuccowork. The *St. Joseph* in the 3rd chapel on the right is by Orazio De Ferrari, while Maragliano sculpted the three wood groups in the south transept (*Crucifixion and Addolorata, Temptation of St. Anthony Abbot*) and in the north transept (*St. Francis Receives the Stigmata*).

Adjoining the cathedral to the right to form a continuous front in the direction of the train station (B1-2), are *Palazzo Vescovile* and the *Seminario*, the 19th-century Bishop's Palace and Seminary. The former houses the *Museo Diocesano* (*open: Wed and Sun 10am-noon*), whose most important works are a 14th-century *painting on wood* from the Barnaba da Modena school and a processional baldachin *canopy lining* embroidered in colored silk and gold thread, made in China in the late 16th-century.

Heading west out of town toward Zoagli (see. p. 180), the Via Aurelia passes by the *sanctuary of Nostra Signora dell'Olivo*, which took on its present appearance in the 1600s. After around 5 km, a secondary road leads up to the **sanctuary of the Madonna delle Grazie** (elev. 177 m) from which there is a fine view; the church, built at the end of the 14th century, is decorated with an elaborate but badly preserved cycle of 16th-century frescoes. They comprise *Scenes from the Life of Christ* painted in 1539 by 'local boy' Teramo Piaggio and, behind the facade, the grand *Last Judgment* by Luca Cambiaso (1550). Note on the tabernacle of the high altar a wooden statue of the *Madonna delle Grazie*, in the Flemish style.

9am-1.30pm; closed Mon and 2nd and 4th Sun of the month), whose most interesting exhibits are the finds from an Iron Age necropolis. Most of the paintings in the **Pinacoteca Civica** at no. 2 (*open: Sat and Sun 10am-noon and 4-7pm*) are from the Genoese Baroque school (B. Strozzi, D. Fiasella); the collection was enlarged with the addition of the paintings formerly displayed in Palazzo Torriglia.

The Costaguta family also commissioned Bartolomeo Bianco to build the *church of San Francesco* (1630), now a culture center.

Cattedrale di Nostra Signora dell'Orto (A-B2). Originally a sanctuary, it was built in 1613-33 to house an image of the Madonna that became an object of veneration after the plague of 1493. It was redesigned in 1823, resulting in the imposing porch (Luigi Poletti,

---

11.2 From Chiavari to Moneglia
The south-easternmost stretch of coast in the province of Genoa, 20.5 km *(see map p. 187)*

The first stop on this tour, Lavagna, is divided from Chiavari by nothing more than the Entella river. An almost perfectly straight stretch of the Via Aurelia leads to Cavi, and on to Sestri Levante. Because of the heavy traffic along this section of the coast at the weekends and in summer the narrow, winding but scenic provincial road that hugs the coast between Sestri Levante and Moneglia (11 km) is best avoided: the narrowness of the tunnels originally dug for the Genoa-La Spezia railroad line (which was later moved inland) necessitates an alternating, traffic light-controlled one-way system, which can mean long delays, although the

magnificent view at the end of the tunnels makes the wait worthwhile.

Lavagna
The typical local black slate quarried near here and used to make school blackboards (the Italian word for blackboard is, in fact, *lavagna*) is the main claim to fame of this town (elev. 6 m, pop. 13,087), on the east bank of the Entella, although its main source of income is now tourism, an industry that has brought with it the occasional unlovely building between the sandy beach and the surrounding olive-, pine-, and chestnut-cloaked hills. Owned in

A cake fit for a... village

Once upon a time in a little Ligurian fishing village, there lived a young count who was to be married to a beautiful noblewoman from Siena. To celebrate the event, he decided to prepare a cake so big there would be a piece for everyone in the village. And so it was: on 14 August 1230 in Lavagna, the wedding took place between Count Opizzo Fieschi (older brother of Sinibaldo, the future Pope Innocent IV) and Bianca de' Bianchi. Whatever the size of that wedding cake – the chronicles of the day do not furnish such details – it can hardly have been much bigger than the 1,500-

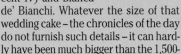

kilo creation made each year for the re-evocation of the wedding. Thousands of townsfolk take part in the event, which as well as the tasting of the colossal confection, includes a pageant in medieval costume through the old streets of Lavagna. After flag-throwing displays, dances and jousting tournaments comes the proclamation of the wedding, followed by a spirited 'pairing-off' game, in which all present busily embark on a highly amusing search for their 'kindred spirit'. Anyone who fails in the enterprise, however, still gets a slice of the Gargantuan cake!

around 1000 by the counts of Lavagna (from where the Fieschi hailed), the town is medieval in layout, its two main streets – *Via Roma* and *Via Dante*, which run at right angles to one another – lined with colorful buildings. In *Piazza Marconi*, at their crossroads, stands the **collegiate church of Santo Stefano**, on a site that has been occupied by a church since the 10th century. The present Baroque design (1653) features an impressive facade, two bell-towers, staircase and cobbled parvis.

Follow Via Dante to Piazza S. Caterina Fieschi Adorno. Via Nuova Italia leads to the *oratory of the SS. Trinità*, redesigned in the 18th century, with a fine 15th-century slate portal; the *church of Nostra Signora del Carmine*, behind, has also been much altered in its history.

A truly panoramic road climbs from Viale Mazzini (which starts opposite the train station) after about 4 km to the 17th-century **church of Santa Giulia di Centaura** (elev. 254 m), where the *view* stretches from Portofino to Sestri Levante. This church, with a light-colored facade, has an exquisite wooden Byzantine *Crucifix* in the 3rd altar on the left.

Sestri Levante *

This seaside resort (elev. 10 m, pop. 19,682) enjoys the privilege of having two beautiful bays thanks to the promontory (known as the 'island') which stretches out into the sea to create two of the most picturesque views on the entire Riviera. To the north is the *Baia delle Favole*, literally 'Bay of Fables', a name coined by none other than

The beautiful 'Bay of Silence' set against the colorful houses of Sestri Levante

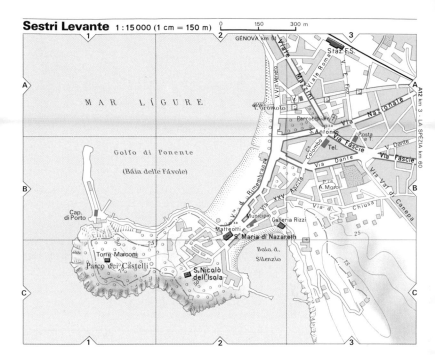

Sestri Levante 1:15 000 (1 cm = 150 m)

Hans Christian Andersen, who stayed in Sestri Levante in 1833. Even prettier is the **Baia del Silenzio***, on the opposite side, its small beach framed by a backdrop of pastel-colored houses. The isthmus in between is occupied by *Piazza Matteotti* (B2), in which stand the 17th-century *Palazzo Durazzo Pallavicini*, now the Town Hall, and the **basilica of Santa Maria di Nazareth** (1604-16), whose 1840 facade has a Neoclassical porch. The Baroque interior has a wooden *Crucifix* (12th cent.) and two canvases by Domenico Fiasella (*Pentecost**) and Lazzaro Tavarone (*Madonna del Carmine with St. Lawrence and St. John the Baptist*), in the 4th and 2nd altars on the left. To the left of the basilica, *Via Penisola di Levante* leads up to the promontory, passing alongside the sad remains of the *oratory of Santa Caterina* (1578), destroyed in a 1944 air raid: fifty years later a *statue* of the saint was placed among the ruins together with a commemorative plaque. Immediately beyond is the apse of the **church of San Nicolò dell'Isola** (C2; *closed for restoration*), built in 1151; the facade, with a pseudo-porch portal, is 15th century; the belltower, with pyramid-shaped spire, has a belfry with paired windows. At the highest point of the adjoining *Grand Hotel dei Castelli Park* (C1-2; *closed to the public*) stands the *Marconi Tower* (C1), where the inventor of radio telegraphy carried out the first experiments with short-wave signals.

Back in Piazza Matteotti, *Via XXV Aprile* (B2-3) and Via Palestro lead through one of the most attractive parts of the town to Vico Macelli, in which the 17th-century *church of San Pietro in Vincoli* stands. Though rather dilapidated looking from the outside, it does contain some good artworks: notably a group of wooden sculptures by Anton Maria Maragliano (*Martyrdom of St. Catherine of Alexandria*) in the 1st chapel on the right; the *Christ at the Column* in the 2nd chapel on the left is by Luca Cambiaso. Nearby, at no. 8, Via dei Cappuccini, is the *Galleria Rizzi* (B2-3; *open: April and October Sun 10am-1pm; 1 May-19 June and 11-30 September Wed 4-7pm; 20 June-10 September Fri and Sat 9-11pm*), with a collection of paintings and sculptures from the 15th to 18th centuries.

The next little town in the bay beyond Punta Manara, the promontory south of Sestri, is **Riva Trigoso** (elev. 6 m), where seaside tourism lives somewhat uncomfortably alongside the ship-building industry that grew up here from 1898.

Moneglia
Like so many towns on the Riviera, Moneglia (elev. 4 m, pop. 2,691) has in the last few decades seen a gradual shift from traditional fishing activities to seaside vacationing. This is the birthplace of Luca Cambiaso, who is thought to have painted the

Adoration of the Magi on the right-hand wall of the *church of San Giorgio* (1396, redesigned in 1704), adjoining which is a 15th-century *Franciscan cloister*. At the opposite end of the town, a magnificent cobbled *parvis** literally paves the way to the *parish church of Santa Croce*, another medieval church converted to the Baroque style (1726); a marble slab on the right bears the date of 1290 and two chain links from the port of Pisa serve as a reminder of Moneglia's involvement in the Battle of Meloria, which led to the destruction of the Tuscan maritime republic. The church takes its name from the Byzantine *Crucifix* in the 4th altar on the left, found on the beach after a shipwreck; the *Immacolata* in the 3rd altar

Fishermen in Sestri Levante at the turn of the 20th century

on the right is by Anton Maria Maragliano, and the sacristy has a *Last Supper* by Luca Cambiaso.

To the left of the church note the frescoes (13th-18th cent., poorly preserved) on the interior walls of *oratory of the Disciplinati*, founded in the 10th century.

11.3 From Chiavari to Santo Stefano d'Aveto
A tour into the Apennines, through the Sturla and Aveto Valleys, 58 km

Just a few miles inland, away from the hustle and bustle of the coast, Liguria is a very different place. The Sturla Valley is one of those out-of-the-way places which, though an important transit route in ancient times, is virtually unknown to the masses of vacationers hurrying down to the coast. And yet it is an area of great natural beauty, as is its continuation, the Valle d'Aveto, a valley that modern tourism has now discovered, especially in the Santo Stefano area.

This tour heads inland from Chiavari along the SS 225 to Carasco (6 km), and then onto the SS 586, which follows the Sturla river up to Borzonasca (10 km). After the village, the road begins to climb the tortuous 16 km toward the Forcella Pass (elev. 876 m), the watershed between the Sturla and Aveto basins. The road continues through beautifully scenic Apennine country, with its broad areas of pastureland bordered by fir and beechwoods, to Rezzoaglio (11 km), where a turn-off to the right takes us the final 15 km to Santo Stefano d'Aveto.

Borzonasca
This village (elev. 167 m, pop. 2,070), on the left bank of the Sturla, is surrounded by hills cloaked in dense chestnut woods. Although Borzonasca only became important from 1805, when the carriage road to Chiavari was opened, its origins are much older, as suggested by the *chiesuola*, the little

medieval church at the end of Via Raggio (the street that leads off from the square with the 17th-century *church of San Bartolomeo*, to the left of the bank); the facade of the little building, which has a sail-vaulted belltower, bears a slate bas-relief (*God the Father Among the Heavenly Host*) and a stone slab dated 1460.

Slate is also the material used for the 1554 *portal* of the *oratory of San Rocco*, at the junction with the provincial road that leads 7 km up the Penna river valley to **Prato Sopralacroce** (elev. 563 m), famous for its iron-rich water springs. From here, an unsurfaced road continues to the *Rifugio Prato*

Borzone Abbey

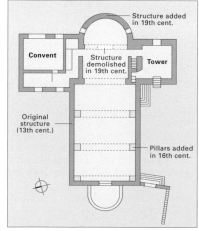

Cabanne

In recent decades a number of vacation homes have appeared in amongst the old rural buildings in this farming and stock-rearing village (elev. 809 m). The 18th-century *church of San Bernardo*, with its fine stone belltower, is easily located. Its main works of art are two paintings (*Descent from the Cross** and *Resurrection**) to the sides of the presbytery, attributed (the former inconclusively) to Giovanni Lanfranco. Until 1861 they were kept in the church of Santa Maria di Castello in Genoa (see p. 57).

Rezzoaglio

The name of this little town (elev. 700 m, pop. 1,341) in the upper Aveto Valley comes from the Latin *Rusagni*, or 'land of the lamb', a name that indicates the sheep-rearing activities carried on here in ancient times. It was for a long time a feud of the Della Cella household: its position on the main road between Val Fontanabuona and the Piacenza area ensured a certain amount of trading activity. The *parish church of San Michele*, rebuilt in 1929, retains its slender Baroque *belltower*; on the left-hand side of the church, a partly cobbled road leads down to the medieval *bridge* over the Aveto.

Mollo (elev. 1,498 m), a mountain refuge set in some beautiful, almost Alpine scenery.

Unspoiled scenery and more also awaits those who venture up the road to Prato Sopralacroce, which after 3 km arrives at **Borzone Abbey*** (elev. 355 m), set in a silent valley. A lofty, centuries-old cypress tree only adds to the charm of the complex, which, according to the stone slab walled into the eastern side of the tower, comes down to us in the form established in 1244 by abbot Gherardo da Cogorno. Almost the only one of its kind in Liguria, the abbey is in the style of the Lombard school, as seen in the gray stone and brick walls of the church and tower. The interior is marred somewhat by the 1834 alterations to the roof over the nave, part of a process that also opened up the apse, which contains, on the left, a sculpted slate *tabernacle* (1513).

The two side altars are Baroque: note the twisted columns of the one on the left.

Beyond the village of Magnasco, a minor road leads up 2.5 km to the *Lago delle Lame* (elev. 1,043 m), a lake whose forest setting is part of the 11,509-ha **Aveto Regional Nature Park**. The western slopes of Mt. Aiona (elev. 1,695 m), with its collection of little glacial lakes, is another protected area that forms the *Agoraie di Sopra and Moggetto State Nature Reserve*: access is possible only by permission of the regional branch of the Italian Forestry Department (*tel. 010566831*).

Santo Stefano d'Aveto

This village (elev. 1,012 m, pop. 1,284) in the shadow of Mt. Maggiorasca (elev. 1,799 m), has to some extent succeeded in becoming the mountain retreat of the Genoese (there is usually enough snow in winter to make the cross-country skiing trails here worthwhile), but it is best known as an inland summer vacation resort. As a result it is mostly modern in appearance, though some ancient remains survive, most notably the ponderous ramparts of the 13th-century **castle of the Malaspina**, who ruled over the town from 1164 to 1495. Rising up opposite the fortress is the *belltower* of the old parish church, now an oratory; the new

Winter wonderland in Val d'Aveto

church, finished in 1929, has on its high altar a canvas (the *Madonna of Guadeloupe*), traditionally thought to have hung on the main mast of Andrea Doria's galley.

There are superb views along the 16 km of road from Santo Stefano d'Aveto that skirts Mt. Tomarlo (elev. 1,602 m) and Mt. Chiodo (elev. 1,602 m), and briefly crosses over into the neighboring Emilia region before beginning the descent, back in Liguria, toward the *Mt. Penna Forestry Hut* (elev. 1,387 m), the starting point for many excursions of the Penna mountain area (elev. 1,735 m).

11.4 From Chiavari to Varese Ligure and Brugnato
A tour through the Graveglia and Vara Valleys, 63 km

The first part of this tour, which is of exceptional artistic and historical interest, takes us to San Salvatore dei Fieschi, one of the most important monumental complexes in eastern Liguria. The tour then continues into the Graveglia and Vara Valleys (the latter in the province of La Spezia), which are interesting primarily for their beautiful scenery.

From Chiavari we head up to one of the more inland bridges over the Entella river, the *Ponte della Maddalena*, beside which stands the sanctuary of Nostra Signora del Ponte, then turn left toward San Salvatore di Cogorno, the village famed for its connections with the Fieschi family and for the

basilica complex there (3 km). After Panesi, we turn right to begin the climb into the Graveglia Valley, which includes a detour to Reppia (15 km), in the northern part of the valley (reached from a turn-off to the left). Further east, at the Biscia Pass on the border with La Spezia province, we begin the descent down the Vara Valley, with a short detour to Cassego in the north, and to Varese Ligure (23 km). From here we head south down the SS 523 to San Pietro Vara (5.6 km) then left onto SS 566 and down to the provincial road for Brugnato (16.4 km). Here, the A12 highway can be accessed for a rapid return (34.5 km) to Chiavari.

11.4 From Chiavari to Varese Ligure and Brugnato

(map)

The **Ponte della Maddalena** is the oldest bridge across the Entella river. Its construction was ordered by Ugone Fieschi after the collapse of its Roman predecessor, and was completed before 1210. In 1428 another four arches were added to the original thirteen; the bridge was repeatedly altered thereafter, until 1887. At the eastern end of the bridge stands the **sanctuary of Nostra Signora del Ponte**, a 1492 enlargement of a chapel built 50 years earlier. Reconstruction work in 1898-1903, however, left very little of the original construction: frescoes remain on the facade (*Madonna of Mercy*) and on the wall behind it (*Massacre of the Innocents*), both attributed to Lorenzo Fasolo.

San Salvatore dei Fieschi

Overwhelmed now by the somewhat disorderly collection of modern buildings that have swallowed up what was once a rural neighbor of Lavagna (see p. 183) but now forms part of one big conurbation, this village (elev. 38 m) still retains its beautiful old square to which the monumental basilica complex forms the backdrop. Despite the vicinity of new vacation homes and hypermarkets, the impression is one of being whisked away in time and space, to a place whose sacred atmosphere is heightened by the unexpected silence of the *piazza*.

The square is named after Pope Innocent IV, who in 1245 began the construction of the **Basilica dei Fieschi****, a project that was completed seven years later by his nephew Ottobono Fieschi (the future Pope Adriano V). The bulky pointed tower, with its four-light windows, is the main architectural feature of the building, which is basically Gothic in style, as seen in the white marble and gray slate striped facade and the large marble rose window, but also with stylistic features from the Romanesque tradition, such as the row of arches along the upper part of the front and along the central nave. The fresco on the lunette above the portal is attributed to Barbagelata (*Christ on the Cross with the Madonna, St. John, Pope Innocent IV and Ottobono Fieschi*). The interior, whose central nave and side aisles are divided by square-section capitals, seems to be immersed in a rarefied gloom relieved by the four openings (two one-light windows, a round window and a cross-shaped opening) on the apse wall. Opposite the basilica stands the 18th-century *church*, also dedicated to San Salvatore; it is flanked to the right by the **Palazzo Comitale**, built by the Fieschi around 1252: though in a poor state

of repair (the building was devastated by the Saracens in 1567, and subsequently much altered), it still retains the white and dark stripes of the upper section, and the ogival arches (walled up) of the portico below.

After **Frisolino** (elev. 129 m), a small village with a number of rustic houses made with unfaced stone, a detour off the provincial road leads up from *Piandifieno* (elev. 212 m) to the village of *Nascio* (elev. 380 m). The road then continues to *Cassagna* (elev. 432 m) and across the *Cambiaso Bridge** (1766), with a picturesque arch spanning a gorge over 50 meters deep.

Reppia

The old part of this village (elev. 491 m), set amidst verdant pastureland, has quite a number of vaulted passageways. The 18th-century *parish church of Sant'Apollinare*, re-

Pesto sauce and 'corzetti', Varese Ligure's round pasta specialty

stored in 1903, is interesting for its fine 16th-century triptych (*St. Apollinaire between St. John the Baptist and St. Lawrence*).

Prato and Arzeno are the last places on the way up to the *Biscia Pass* (elev. 892 m). Across in Val di Vara, the first villages encountered are Codivara and Comuneglia. From the latter a rather tortuous secondary road leads up to **Cassego** (elev. 700 m), interesting for its *Museo della Tradizione Contadina* (*open on request, tel. 0187843005*), a museum that documents in particular the production of milk, corn, vines and wood. The provincial road continues the 8 km through quite unspoiled woodland to the Bocco Pass (elev. 956 m). Heading in a south-easterly direction from Cassego the road leads down the valley to Varese Ligure (10 km).

Varese Ligure

The Val di Vara's largest town (elev. 353 m, pop. 2,468), and also the most interesting in the inland area of La Spezia province, is known principally for the **Borgo Rotondo*** (see box) and now also its cheese-making activities. There are, though, several other things of interest to look out for. *Piazza Marconi* has two sharply-contrasting features: the walls of the *Fieschi castle* (15th-century) and the **church of Ss. Teresa d'Avila e Filippo**

Garibaldi, the central axis of the so-called 'Borgo Nuovo' (New Town), lead to Piazza Mazzini, where a vaulted passageway leads to *Ponte Grecino*, the bridge built in 1515 across the Crovana river.

San Pietro Vara

This village (elev. 293 m), set among vineyards on the confluence of the Vara and Torza rivers, centers around the 16th-century *parish church* (which did not escape later alteration) with an unusually red-colored facade; the triptych (*St. Peter Enthroned between St. Paul and St. John the Baptist*) behind the high altar is by Luca Cambiaso.

Brugnato

Highway exits can change life in the area drastically: the opening of the exit of the A12

highway in the late 20th century prompted the growth of numerous industrial and commercial activities around this little town (elev. 115 m, pop. 1,183), which after World War II was still a farming village. The 'pincer-shaped' historic center is reached through the medieval *Porta Sottana* and *Porta Soprana*, the arch of the latter frames the Baroque facade of the *oratory of San Bernardo*. In the central square, Piazza S. Pietro, stands the ancient *parish church of Ss. Pietro, Lorenzo e Colombano*: originally built as a sort of cemetery basilica near an early Christian necropolis, it was rebuilt in the 8th century and elevated to the status of Benedictine abbey. The present building, erected between the 11th and 12th centuries, was altered at various stages in its history: the facade in particular dates back to the 1700s. The adjoining *Palazzo Episcopale*, (bishop's palace), was built on the site of a medieval monastery in the century before.

Neri (17th century), built in the shape of a Greek cross with an elegant Baroque facade, twin belltowers and dome. Inside is a *Madonna and Child with St. Giovannino and St. Francesco Saverio* on the left-hand altar by Gregorio De Ferrari, who also painted the two works in the first altar (*Ecstasy and Stigmata of St. Francis*) and the second altar on the right (*Liberation of St. Peter*) of the *parish church of San Giovanni Battista* (1648; the porch was added in 1929), reached from Via Colombo and Via della Chiesa; note also the fine 17th-century wooden *choir*. Again from Piazza Marconi, Via Umberto I and Via

12 La Spezia, the Cinque Terre and easternmost Liguria

Area profile

The area described in this chapter has never really formed a clear-cut unit: in its checkered history towns rose and fell and geographical difficulties made communications difficult, favoring the independence of the individual parts.

Indeed this lack of uniformity goes back to the most ancient times, when the area known as Lunigiana with its 'statue-stele' civilization rarely made its presence felt down on the coast. In Roman and early medieval times Luni was a major river port and early episcopal seat. But the gradual silting up of the harbor and the greater safety of land routes after the defeat of the Longobards favored the growth of settlements further inland, and the rise of the new town of Sarzana. A new powerful merchant class set itself up against the bishop-counts, the rich holders of landed property, and this eventually brought about the demise of the Luni bishopric. The area whetted the appetites of

The church of San Pietro perched on the rocks over the sea at Portovenere

Genoa, Parma, Pisa, Lucca, and in the 15th century even Aragon. But the Genoese prevailed, and their supremacy brought some commercial benefits, although economic growth was not really stimulated until after 1808, when Napoleon declared the bay a military port and La Spezia a maritime prefecture. New building methods made it possible to create stronger sea walls to replace the medieval harbor and its narrow lanes, which relied on natural protection. La Spezia became the first military port of the fledgling Kingdom of Italy: the construction of the imposing Arsenal and more rational urban-planning in the late 19th century destroyed what was left of the medieval fabric and created the town we see today.

Fortunately, these extensive urban design and architectural changes were limited to La Spezia itself: the areas inland and along the coast retained their ancient appearance. More recently, the relative lack of sandy beaches and the general inaccessibility of the area have prevented the seaside villages from the flood of concrete that so radically changed other parts of the coast in the late 20th century. As a result, the coast around La Spezia can still be enjoyed for its great natural and environmental interest.

12.1 The Bay of La Spezia
A walking tour through the town and two coastal drives *(see map p. 196)*

Interestingly, and a little oddly, the province's main town has fewer attractions than the surrounding area – the famous 'Bay of the Poets' – and so is only marginally touched by the flow of tourists who above all come to see the coast that was immortalized in the romantic verse of Byron and Shelley, and later frequented by various generations of intellectuals who, according to the vogue of the day and developments in mass tourism, colonized the well-known haunts (Portovenere,

Lerici, San Terenzo), then moved on to the small fishing villages (Bocca di Magra), and most recently to the hidden hill towns (Montemarcello). What puts many tourists off La Spezia, as is so often the case, is the very thing that turned it from a small town into a large prosperous one: the huge changes brought about by the creation of the Arsenal and the arrival of the Navy. And yet there are some very pleasant surprises for those who do take the trouble to visit La Spezia: for example

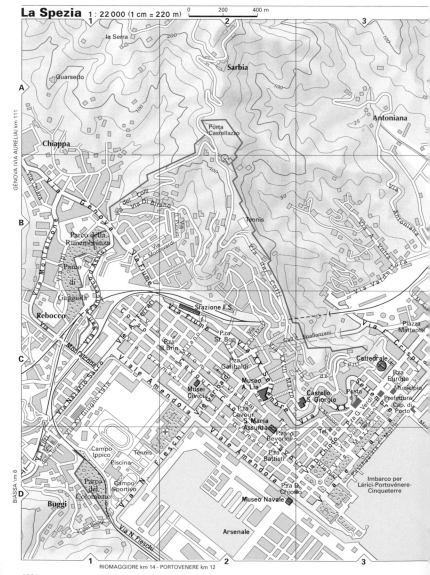

La Spezia 1 : 22 000 (1 cm = 220 m)

the extremely rich Amedeo Lia Museum, inaugurated in 1996, which now ranks as one of Italy's finest art collections; the climb to the impressive and now carefully restored castle of St. George; and the stroll along the lively, orderly seafront promenade.

P. B. Shelley

La Spezia

This walking tour of the provincial capital of La Spezia (elev. 3 m, pop. 96,320) begins at Corso Cavour, close to the train station, and continues in the direction of the sea, with brief detours to the town's main monuments. Worth visiting just out of town are the church of Santo Stefano di Marinasco and the church in Biassa, where a belvedere also offers a superb view over the bay.

Corso Cavour (C-D1-3). This long thoroughfare, created as part of the 'Expansion Plan' drawn up in 1862 (and which did away with most of the medieval town) is perhaps the part of La Spezia that best sums up the 19th-century desire to create here an

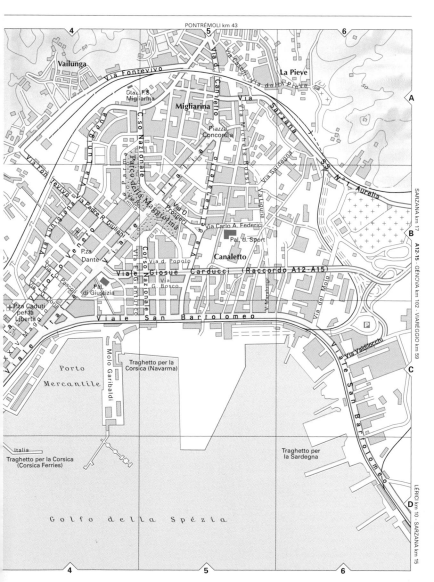

elegant, orderly town center, despite the noticeable lack of any special features that would give it character. The most noteworthy works of architecture along the avenue are the *church of Nostra Signora della Salute* (1900), in Piazza Brin; *Palazzo Crozza*, at no. 251, now the Municipal Library, in front of the Civic Museums (see below); and the **church of Santa Maria Assunta** (D2), in Piazza Beverini. This 15th-century church (originally founded in the 13th century) was extensively remodeled in the 20th century. Note in the far left aisle an exquisite polychrome terracotta work by Andrea della Robbia depicting the *Coronation of the Virgin*.

Museo Civico Giovanni Podenzana

(C2). At no. 9 Via Curtatone is the entrance to this museum complex which, since the recent transfer of the archaeology section to the castle of San Giorgio, divides into two parts (*open: 8.30am-1pm; closed Mon*): a natural history section (palaeontological and mineralogical collections from the inland areas of La Spezia province), and an important ethnographic section displaying costumes, everyday utensils and farming equipment used by the people of Lunigiana.

Museo Civico d'Arte Antica, Medievale e Moderna Amedeo Lia* (C2). The painstaking restoration of the 17th-century Paolotti convent (*open 10am-6pm; closed Mon*), aimed at turning the complex into a functional exhibition center, has created a worthy backdrop for the exceptional works of art donated by collector Amedeo Lia to the town of La Spezia, including a collection of 13th- and 14th-century paintings described by art critic Federico Zeri as one of Europe's most important private collections. Also on show in the 13 rooms are liturgical items from various periods, medieval ivories, stained glass fragments, a rare collection of miniatures, medals, rock crystals fashioned in Milan, and Venetian glass, as well as a selected series of archaeological finds from around the Mediterranean.

Each section features some truly exceptional works that represent some of the finest examples of the various artistic genres, but

mostly paintings. There are masterpieces by Paolo di Giovanni Fei, who kept the Siena school alive in the 14th century (*Annunciation*), by Giovanni Bellini (*Nativity*, an early work), by Sebastiano del Piombo (*Birth of Adonis*, an early work on wood influenced by Giorgione), by Pontormo (*Self Portrait**, a tempera painting on terracotta that has become the museum's symbol), and by Titian (*Portrait of a Gentleman**, one of the artist's best works of portraiture). Other works include a *Descent from the Cross* by Lippo di Benivieni, *St. John* by Pietro Lorenzetti, a *Madonna and Child with Saints*, probably by Sassetta, and *St. Martin and the Pauper*, which has been attributed to Raphael.

The museum also has a collection of Renaissance, Mannerist and Baroque *bronzes**.

The Paolotti Convent faces onto *Via del Prione*, a street that reminds us of the old medieval layout of the town as it winds its way through the now regular grid system of streets. This road, now closed to traffic, has become a fashionable shopping boulevard.

Castle of San Giorgio (C3). The original 13th-century fortress was gradually demolished and the castle was rebuilt in 1371, then enlarged in the 17th and 18th centuries. The importance of this imposing edifice, which occupies a splendid position overlooking the town and the entire bay, has now been acknowledged with the meticulous (and much-needed) restoration that was completed recently. The important *Archaeology Collection* (*open: summer 9.30am-12.30pm, 5-8pm; winter 9.30am-12.30pm, 2-5pm; closed Tue, 1 Jan, 24 and 25 Dec*), recently transferred here from the Museo Civico Formentini, is best known for its nineteen anthropomorphic sandstone **statue-stelae** fashioned by the ancient people of Lunigiana in the Bronze and Iron Ages. The collection also contains interesting material excavated at ancient Luni (see p. 206),

Statue-stelae from Lunigiana. Castle of San Giorgio, La Spezia

remains from the Ligurian necropolises in the southern part of the province and other items, from private donations.

Arsenale (D2). La Spezia's military arsenal was one of the first major public works carried out after the unification of Italy. Its construction transformed the town's socio-economic situation in a matter of decades, as well as radically altering its appearance. The design of this industrial and military complex was by Domenico Chiodo, who also masterminded the urban redevelopment of the town. Badly damaged during the last war, the arsenal was later rebuilt with careful attention to historical accuracy. To the left of the monumental entrance is the **Naval Museum** (*open: 9am–noon, 2-6pm; Mon, Fri 2-6 only; Sun 8.30am-1.15pm*). The old original collection consists of material collected by Emanuele Filiberto of Savoy from the Arsenal of Villafranca (Nice) in the 16th century, together with memorabilia from the Battle of Lepanto. The museum's most important exhibits are 28 *figureheads* from ancient sea vessels.

Seafront promenade (D3). This long pedestrian area bordered by trees and flowers is where the townspeople gather on sunny days to walk, talk, play cards and read. It affords good views over the celebrated bay and to the Apuan Alps of Tuscany beyond. It runs parallel to the first part of *Viale Italia*, a beautiful long avenue with palms, pine trees and oleander. A colorful sea festival known as the *Palio del Golfo*, a rowing race between the 13 maritime villages that border on the bay, is traditionally held in the waters off the promenade on the first Sunday in August. At the junction with Via Diaz (the seaward continuation of Via del Prione),

The Arsenal

La Spezia's Arsenal – a 165-ha space comprising seven miles of roads, mooring basins and docks equipped also to accommodate submarines – still dominates the townscape, whether seen from the sea or the hills behind. Its presence here is indeed the very reason for the growth of the town, which gradually developed in response to the construction of the great military complex, a concrete, tangible symbol of the colossal modernization efforts made by Italy, in keeping with the highest ideals of the *Risorgimento*. The Arsenal and Royal Navy of the Kingdom of Sardinia were moved from Genoa to La Spezia following a royal decree of 1849 at the insistence of Cavour (although Napoleon too had had the idea to build an arsenal at La Spezia). The design was commissioned to Domenico Chiodo (1823-70), son of Agostino Chiodo, a soldier of rank who distinguished himself in the siege of Peschiera, became Minister of War and of the Navy in the Gioberti Cabinet (1849) and for a short period was prime minister of the Kingdom.

Because of its importance as a historical piece of industrial archaeology, it has been decided to open the doors of the Arsenal (hitherto only open to visitors on the feast days of St. Joseph, 19 March, and St. Barbara, 4 December), with guided tours now available at weekends (*for further information and bookings contact the local tourist office, tel. 0187745627*).

An array of naval exhibits at La Spezia's Naval Museum

stands the *Centro Salvador Allende*, a lively cultural center where debates and symposia are held; beyond the pier is *Piazza Europa* (C3), the heart of the modern town, surrounded by La Spezia's main public buildings. It is dominated by the new *cathedral of Christ the King*, designed by Adalberto Libera and opened in 1975.

Two brief excursions lead to the ancient but remodeled **church of Santo Stefano di Marinasco**, which has a 13th-century *Madonna and Child* by Nino Pisano, and to **Biassa**, a picturesque hill town (elev. 315 m) whose *belvedere** gives a magnificent view over the entire town of La Spezia and the Bay of the Poets. The most interesting works of architecture are the *church of St. Martino* which, despite many transformations, has retained its Romanesque appearance, and, on higher ground outside the town, the remains of the 13th-century *castle of Coderone*, a Genoese outpost against Pisa.

SESTRI LEVANTE SESTRI LEVANTE

LEVANTO

Pignone

*Parco reg.
Montemarcello-
-Magra*

Bolano

T O S C A N A

T.Aulella

Aulla

A15

*Parco nazionale
delle
Cinque Terre*

Gravéglia

Prov. 330 di

La Spézia

S. Terenzo
Monti

Marinasco **LA SPÉZIA**

Vezzano
Lígure

Fosdinovo

*Parco
regionale
delle Alpi
Apuane*

Corníglia

Manarola

Biassa

Baccano

Sarzana

Ortonovo

Carrara

Golfo della Spézia

370

Campíglia

530

S. Terenzo

Lérici

Ameglia

A12

Fiascherino

le Grázie

Portovénere

I. Palmária

Tellaro

**Bocca
di Magra**

Montemarcello

Marina
di Carrara

I. del Tino

I. del Tinetto

0 2 4 km

MASSA

VIARÉGGIO

GENOVA

Savona

La Spezia

Imperia

M A R   L Í G U R E

Marina
di Massa

Toward Portovenere
12.3 km excursion with detour to Campiglia

This tour follows the SS 530 road from western La Spezia down the coast to the end of the Portovenere peninsula. Just out of town, immediately before Marola, a minor road leads up the hill to Campiglia.

Campiglia

This is not only a charming village (elev. 389 m) with an old world atmosphere, but also an excellent vantage point from which to enjoy spectacular views of the surrounding scenery. The walks that begin here are superb too, most notably the long descent (down 2,090 steps) through the vine-covered territory of **Tramonti** overlooking the sea to the tiny hamlet of Schiara. Other walks from Campiglia lead to Portovenere (see below) and Riomaggiore (see p. 200).

Le Grazie

This fishing village turned seaside resort on the other side of the peninsula has an elegant waterfront promenade and a small marina. The village is graced by the *church of Santa Maria delle Grazie*, once part of the former *monastery of the Olivetani*, which has an early 16th-century fresco depicting the *Crucifixion*.
Inside the church note the remarkable Tuscan school painting on wood of *St. Margaret*

of Cortona, also early 16th century.
A little further on, at the Varignano inlet preceding the Bay of Portovenere, are the interesting remains of the *Roman Villa of Varignano*, with an antiquarium.

Portovenere**

The blend of art and nature, and the beautifully picturesque sequence of colorful houses divided by narrow alleyways create a magic that is never spoiled by the crowds of tourists who flock here in summer. One of the best views of the ancient part of this little fortified town (elev. 8 m, pop. 4,348) is from the promenade down at the harbor, which is closed to traffic and extends along the promontory. The backdrop is a solid wall of tall houses that are entered from both sides (the boat depots were reached from the marina; the workshops and living quarters from the main street behind). The monotony of this long row of buildings is relieved by the typical brightly-colored fronts; in between are the extremely steep stepped and vaulted walkways known as *capitoli*, over which a system of trap doors and slits in the walls helped make the town easier to defend.
The 'monumental' entrance to the ancient town is through an ancient *gateway* bearing a Latin inscription "Colonia Januensis 1113", a reminder that in the 12th century this site was fortified by Genoa as a major defense outpost against Pisa. Note the Genoese measures of capacity (1606) to the

left of the gate. From here, the town's narrow main street, *Via Capellini*, leads up to the open space from which a flight of steps leads up to the **church of San Pietro**, situated on the very tip of the promontory. In ancient times this was the site of a temple to Venus, the goddess after whom the settlement that later grew up here was named (*Venere* in Italian). The church has a particularly interesting architectural history: an early Christian building made of Pal-

The Isle of Tino, one of three off Portovenere

maria black marble (6th cent.) was extended in the 13th century with a Gothic style addition featuring the typical Genoese bands, and a sturdy belltower designed for defense purposes: the resulting church became the focal point of the walls. Running around the church is a Romanesque *loggetta* with graceful arches that frame the splendid coastline from the Muzzerone cliffs and the Ferale rock, all the way to Punta Mesco.

Returning toward Via Capellini, beyond the steps on the left that lead down to the sea and the *Grotta Arpaia Cave* (also known as Byron's Cave), keep to the left and continue on up to the late **church of San Lorenzo** (built by the Genoese in the 12th century). The original structure has been much altered down the ages, often following damage by cannon fire. The fiercest attack was by the Aragonese in 1494, who destroyed the campanile (the present belltower was built immediately after the first was lost) in a battle that marked the end of Portovenere's importance. Inside, a 15th-century marble altarpiece from the Florentine school contains a small parchment painting of the *White Madonna*. Legend has it that the image was brought here from the sea in 1204 and on 17 August 1399 was miraculously transformed into its present 14th-century form. On this night each year, the miracle is remembered in a beautiful torchlight procession.

The street leads up from the church to the *castle*, the imposing, mostly 16th- and 17th-century stronghold that dominates the town.

The islands

Palmaria**, the largest of the three islands just across the narrow strait, is traditionally visited by boat from Portovenere. The highlight of the tour of this rugged island is the *Blue Grotto*, accessible only from the sea, while another interesting cave, or *Grotta dei Colombi*, can be reached (with difficulty) by land only. Finds dating back to the Mesolithic period were made here. Palmaria, along with the much smaller **Tino**** and **Tinetto****, which is little more than a rock (these two lesser islands are now a military zone), was colonized by Benedictine monks. On the island of Tino, open to visitors only on 13 September (on the occasion of the feast of Saint Venerio, a local hermit), stand the remains of the 11th-century *abbey of San Venerio*. In 1998 the three islands and Portovenere were added to UNESCO's list of World Heritage Sites.

Toward Lerici and Bocca di Magra
26.5 km excursion with detours to Fiascherino, Tellaro and Ameglia

The 10-km road from La Spezia to Lerici, passes through **San Terenzo**, where Shelley and Byron were staying at the time of the tragic boat trip during which Shelley drowned (a multimedia museum dedicated to the lives of Percy Bysshe Shelley and his wife Mary is currently being created in the ancient, but poorly-preserved *castle of San Terenzo*). From Lerici, a panoramic coast road leads to Fiascherino and Tellaro, while the parallel inland road on the hill (reached only by returning to Lerici) leads after 9.5 km to Montemarcello, and after another 7 km to Bocca di Magra. Ameglia lies at 5.5 km from Montemarcello and 3.5 km from Bocca di Magra.

Lerici

Although the town is now overrun with visitors, and construction work here has not always been of the highest quality, this town (elev. 10 m, pop. 11,284) still retains some of the atmosphere that made it such a popular destination for tourists back in the Romantic period. Particularly charming are the network of narrow streets and steps in the old part of the town and the imposing **castle***, in a fine position overlooking the promontory. Built by the Pisans in the 13th century, it was later enlarged and fortified by the Genoese, who added the pentagonal tower (16th cent.) and the outer walls (17th cent.). As one of the most complex and best preserved military complexes in the whole of Liguria it is well worth a visit; of particular interest is the 13th-century *chapel of Sant'Anastasia*, in Ligurian Gothic style. The rooms and courtyard house the **Geo-Palaeontological Museum** (*closed Mon; open: November-March 9am-1pm, 2.30-5.30pm, Sunday and holidays 9am-6pm; September, October, and April-June 9am-1pm, 3-7pm, Sunday and holidays 9am-7pm; July, August 10am-1pm, 5pm-midnight*). This is a spectacular journey of discovery of the age of dinosaurs, with fossils, elaborate dioramas and robotized versions of ferocious predatory anthropoids. One room in the museum has an earthquake simulation illustrating the nature and effects of seismic phenomena.

Lerici has two main religious buildings. The **Oratory of San Rocco**, in Corso Marconi, has a 14th-century belltower with 16th-century *bas-reliefs*; inside is a fine 16th-century painting on wood of *St. Bishop Martin, St. Christopher, St. Sebastian and St. Roch* on the high altar; and a *Madonna della Salute*, an original painting on slate (16th. cent) in the left-hand aisle. The 17th-century **church of San Francesco**, in Via Cavour,

The coast near Tellaro

is noted for its fine altarpieces, nearly all from the Genoese school; the sacristy leads to the *oratory of San Bernardino*, which has a marble *triptych* with lunette by Domenico Gar (1529); Bernardino da Siena is traditionally believed to have held a sermon from the small black slate pulpit.

The drive out of town along the road to Tellaro follows a beautiful unspoiled stretch of coastline, noted for its crystal clear waters and lush vegetation. Here, between *Punta di Maramozza* and *Maralunga*, is an **Underwater Archaeological Park** containing remains of a Roman trading ship.

Fiascherino and Tellaro

These two coastal villages are set in beautiful, unspoiled surroundings best enjoyed by boat (the popularity of the area in summer makes parking extremely difficult,

and the beaches – especially the ones at Fiascherino – are often crowded). Tellaro (elev. 10 m) has all the features of the perfectly preserved, picturesque Ligurian seaside village, complete with church overlooking the sea and a short walk that winds its narrow way between the houses and the rocky shore.

Montemarcello

The name of this village (elev. 266 m), high up on the hill and with beautiful views of the Bay of La Spezia and the sea down to Versilia in northern Tuscany, comes from the Roman consul Marcellus, who defeated the Ligurian population in the area. Despite its hilltop position, the layout is not concentric but designed on the grid pattern of the original Roman 'castrum'. The colorfully-painted houses, which enliven the sleepy streets and are surrounded by lush vegetation, are another unusual feature of a hill town, and a reminder of the vicinity of the coast, where color is commonplace. Montemarcello has for years attracted high-class tourism, and been frequented by prosperous, discreet intellectuals, mostly from Milan. Montemarcello's beautiful natural surroundings make up the southern part of the *Montemarcello-Magra Regional Nature Park*, characterized by typically Mediterranean flora and fauna. It is crossed by various well-signposted footpaths, some of which lead all the way down to the sea.

Ameglia*

This small town (elev. 89 m, pop. 4,447), panoramically situated high up on the hill, retains sections of the ancient crenelated walls and other architectural features of the old fortifications. At the highest point stands the *Palazzo Comunale*, or Town Hall, housed in what was previously a Renaissance-style *podestà* building and, before that, a castle, mentioned by Otto I in 963.

Bocca di Magra

This coastal locality on the west bank of the Magra river estuary has a pleasant riverside walk, at the end of which is a small beach. Being a natural harbor, Bocca di Magra has in recent years become almost exclusively a mooring place providing all the necessary services and expert assistance (berthed yachts abound). In the 20th century Bocca became an important part of Italian cultural life, particularly in the 1940s and 1950s when it became the favorite holiday destination of famous Italian writers Elio Vittorini, Salvatore Quasimodo, Cesare Pavese, Emilio Gadda, as well as publisher Giulio Einaudi (son of Italian president Luigi Einaudi) and painter Ernesto Treccani.

12.2 The Eastern Riviera
Two tours from La Spezia: to the Cinque Terre, and to Deiva Marina *(see map p. 203)*

This stretch of coast, known as the *Riviera Spezzina* (after the main town of La Spezia) runs from the promontory of Montenero to the border with the province of Genoa before Moneglia. It is best known for the *Cinque Terre*, the 'five lands' that punctuate the most rugged and inaccessible part of the coastline, to the north of which, beyond Levanto, the shore takes on a more typically Ligurian character, with generous beaches and generally more space for the development of tourist facilities. Arguably the best art treasures are to be found at Levanto, the largest coastal town, which makes this stretch of Liguria not only a place of vacation but also one with cultural appeal – an excellent way to round off the visit to the Cinque Terre.

The Cinque Terre**
From La Spezia to Monterosso al Mare, 51.8 km

A visit to Italy's famed 'five lands' (Riomaggiore, Manarola, Corniglia, Vernazza and Monterosso), which in 1998 joined UNESCO's list of World Heritage Sites, takes us into what is one of Italy's best preserved areas, in terms of both the history of its people and its natural scenery. The hard work that has always been done in the often hostile environment around these isolated little villages still bears its fruits. Take, for example, *sciacchetrà*, the strong, sweet wine produced here. Although all are accessible by road, use of the car is definitely to be discouraged, for both ecological and practical reasons: parking is impossible in summer and many of the roads operate an alternating one-way system, making even short journeys interminable. And the rail service from La Spezia is excellent: trains run frequently, all day, to all five villages. Many, however, insist that the best way to really get to know the Cinque Terre is on foot, along the sometimes strenuous but well-organized footpaths that offer some truly breathtaking views, and the scents of the Mediterranean carried on the breeze.

Vineyards high up over the sea at Manarola, one of the 'Cinque Terre' (just visible in the background)

Riomaggiore

The main street is the final part of the now covered-over *Rivus Major*, the river that gave its name to the village (elev. 35 m, pop. 1,881). It is bordered on each side by rows of tall, narrow houses. The charm of Riomaggiore, a frequent theme in the paintings of Telemaco Signorini, has been enhanced by recent restoration work, which has uncovered the medieval arches previously hidden by mid 20th-century constructions. Monuments include the *church of San Giovanni Battista* (1340), with neo-Gothic facade (the fine rose window is original, however). Riomaggiore lies at the center of a protected area which, among other things, regulates underwater activities in seas that have some of the richest marine life in Italy. The two areas open to scuba divers are the well-known Punta di Montenero, to the south, and Punta del Mesco, to the north. Riomaggiore is now the headquarters of the recently set up **Cinque Terre National Park**. A panoramic walk leads up to the remains of the *castle* (15th-16th cent.); a more difficult climb leads up to the *sanctuary of the Madonna di Montenero* (elev. 341 m, also accessible by car or using the rack-and-pinion 'wine train' usually used to transport grapes), built on a hill overlooking the village and the sea. At Torre Guardiola, on the Montenero promontory, an *Environmental Awareness Center* has recently been set up, comprising a botanical sequence teaching visitors about Mediterranean *maquis*, a lookout post for bird-watchers and an innovative 'writing itinerary', designed to encourage visitors to put down on paper their observations and stories about the natural environment.

Riomaggiore is also the starting point for the most famous (and often most crowded) walk in the 'Cinque Terre', the so-called **Via dell'Amore*** (Lovers' Walk), which was hewn out of the rocky coast in the 1920s. As it winds its way through interesting geological formations, it offers beautiful panoramic views out to sea, and leads, after about half an hour to the next village, Manarola.

Manarola

This uniquely picturesque village (elev. 70 m) perches on a huge rocky prominence overlooking the sea, and slopes steeply down to a tiny harbor. The cluster of colorful houses fill the space originally occupied by a castle, destroyed in 1273, whose remains have been incorporated into the present-day village. The view from a distance is a truly memorable one. Higher up, stands the **church of San Lorenzo** (or church of the Nativity of Mary), built in

The 'Lovers' Walk' between Riomaggiore and Manarola

1338. The Gothic facade has a *rose window* by Matteo and Pietro da Campilio; inside are three 15th-century works: a *bas-relief of St. Lawrence* (formerly in the lunette of the portal), a triptych, and a polyptych. Winter visitors might be interested to know that from December to Epiphany a charming *Christmas crèche* is displayed on the hill above Manarola. The figures used in the nativity scene, which is beautifully lit up at night, are made using recycled materials.

Volastra (elev. 340 m), whose name derives from the Latin *Vicus Oleaster* (village of olives) is a small village high up in a panoramic position on the hill, about an hour's walk from Manarola but accessible also by car. Nearby is the *sanctuary of Nostra Signora della Salute* (12th cent.), a Romanesque building with Gothic decorations.

Corniglia

This charming village is rather different from the other four. It is situated about a hundred meters above the waves that pound against the small headland on which it lies, and has more the atmosphere of a hill town than that of a fishing village, though the panorama is no less spectacular for that. 365 steps lead down to the train station and the sea. Corniglia has always been a farming village, with close links to the surrounding hills, known especially for wine-growing traditions stretching back over 2,000 years: amphorae bearing the name 'Cornelia' were found during excavation work at Pompeii. The *church of San Pietro*, remodeled in the Baroque style, has a Gothic portal and rose windows.

Vernazza

This next village (elev. 3 m, pop. 1,131) has the only tourist port in the 'Cinque Terre', situated at the mouth of the now covered-over Vernazzola river around which the medieval settlement developed. The richness of its architecture testifies to the good fortunes of the village, which has always been wealthier than its neighbors because of the easier access from the sea (the excellent local wine was already being traded in Roman times). Vernazza is dominated by two bulky Genoese lookout towers and the beautiful Ligurian Gothic **church of Santa Margherita d'Antiochia**, unusually designed on two levels. Its position is also unusual: the apse rather than the main facade faces onto the *piazzetta* by the port, the center of life in the village lined with the familiar colorful houses.

Vernazza, the only one of the 'Cinque Terre' with a port

The *sanctuary of the Madonna di Reggio*, built in the 11th century and partly remodeled, is about an hour's walk up from Vernazza, or can be reached by car.

Monterosso al Mare

The most westerly of the Cinque Terre (elev. 12 m, pop. 1,643) divides into two quite distinct parts. The old village, which suffers from the passage of the rail line between the houses and the fine beach, offers the same characteristic atmosphere found in the other four, with narrow alleys leading up the hill. The modern seaside resort of **Fegina**, on the other hand, is a more typical holiday spot, but an elegant one with a long-standing tradition. Among its most famous visitors were the Genoese Montale family, whose son Eugenio, winner of the 1975 Nobel Prize for Literature, derived the inspiration for some of his best-loved poems here. The old part of

Monterosso has two particularly interesting churches. The *parish church of San Giovanni Battista*, on the little main square, has the typical Gothic facade with horizontal bands, and a magnificently worked rose window. Note in the lunette of the portal the 18th-century *Baptism of Jesus*, the loggia facing the sea at the back of the church, and the fine campanile (a converted lookout tower). The **church of San Francesco** (1619), higher up on the hill and with an adjoining Capuchin convent, has some important paintings: a *Crucifixion* (believed by some to be by Van Dyck), a *Derided Christ* by Bernardo Castello, *Veronica* by Bernardo Strozzi, *St. Jerome in Penitence* by Luca Cambiaso and a *Pietà*, possibly by the same artist.

A brief excursion leads to the *hermitage of Santa Maddalena*, with the remains of the Romanesque complex in a beautiful verdant setting.

Further up stands the **sanctuary of the Madonna di Soviore** (accessible by car); the walk to the shrine was once a Via Crucis, but the stations of the cross along the way have now nearly all disappeared. Note on the portal of the church a fine bas-relief of *Our Lady of Sorrows*.

A steep climb leads up to **Punta del Mesco**, with the ruins of the *church of Sant'Antonio*; it offers a magnificent panoramic view.

From Pignone to Levanto and along the coast to Deiva Marina
A drive from La Spezia to Deiva Marina, 60.2 km *(see map p. 207)*

This tour begins on the SS 1 (Via Aurelia), which heads north-west out of La Spezia. After 13.8 km, a turn-off to the left just after Pian di Barca leads to **Pignone** (elev. 189 m, pop. 665), an old hill village with characteristic alleys around the *church of Santa Maria Assunta*, now with an 18th-century appearance, but built in the 14th century over an earlier Romanesque building. The nearby hamlet of *Casale* (elev. 176 m) is the starting-point for *Trail no. 51* run by the Italian Hikers' Club CAI. This ancient and recently-revived mule-track leads through impressive countryside marked along the way by ancient bridges and old stone buildings, all the way to Levanto. The provincial road from Pignone to Levanto is 17.4 km. Down at the coast the tour continues north-west to Bonassola, and from there to Framura along a road parallel to but not on the sea. To reach Deiva Marina, the last place on the tour, the road winds inland 5.3 km, where it meets the provincial road leading down to Deiva from the highway.

Levanto

Although the fourth largest town in the province with a large sandy beach (a rarity in Liguria), this pleasant town (elev. 3 m, pop. 5,788) retains an air of elegance that has, at least in the central area, withstood the large-scale holiday-home construction work that began to hit the entire Ligurian Riviera in the late 1960s, and has continued virtually unabated since. This is explained by the relative seclusion of the town – a tortuous thirteen-kilometer road separates Levanto from the highway – and by its illustrious past, first under the Da Passano marquises and then as a free Commune, which from 1229 came under the control of the Republic of Genoa.

The visit begins at *Piazza Cavour*, once the cloister of the 17th-century convent of the Poor Clares, a building now used as the Town Hall; a passageway to the left leads from the square to Via Vinzoni. Turning right into this street we come to *Via Guani* (again to the right), with old houses that are only partly restored. The arch that opens up on the left-hand side of the street is the beginning of a steep flight of steps, a favorite haunt of the local cat population, known as the *Salita Madonna della Costa*, at the top of which stands the ancient *church of Santa Maria della Costa*, now

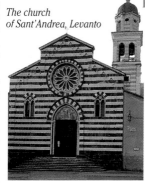

The church of Sant'Andrea, Levanto

rather dilapidated but decorated with a 16th-century bas-relief in the portal depicting *St. George and the Dragon* of the Gagini school. A little further on is the *oratory of the Confraternita di San Giacomo* (with a 16th-century wooden *statue of St. James* inside and a *Crucifix* by Maragliano). From here, the Salita S. Giacomo leads down to *Piazza del Popolo*, with a fine *loggia* of 1256 (partly remodeled).

Alongside the composite *Casa Restani*, Via Emanuele Toso leads off to the **church of Sant'Andrea**, built in the 13th-century

Gothic style and added to in the 15th century. The elegant black and white striped facade has an 18th-century rose window and a frescoed lunette (badly worn) depicting the *Coronation of the Virgin*. Inside, note on the left the venerated *Crucifix* (known as the black cross because of its color before recent restoration), and to the right of the entrance a fine late 15th-century tombstone, which rests on a modern metal support.

Next to the parish church is the *Permanent Exhibition of Material Culture*, illustrating through a large number of period items the way in which Levantese farmers used to work, with other exhibits relating to everyday life in days gone by. Finally, it is worth making the climb to the castle. Along the way is the best-preserved part of the ancient town walls, including the 1265 clock tower.

An interesting sight to see on the way to Bonassola is the **convent of the Annunziata**, whose facade has a 16th-century bas-relief of the *Annunciation*. Inside there are some fine paintings, including the *Miracle of St. Diego* by Bernardo Strozzi (1620), *St. George and the Dragon* by Pier Francesco Sacchi and, in the refectory, *Supper at Emmaus* by Giovanni Battista Casone (1641); the two convent cloisters are particularly graceful.

Bonassola

This small village (elev. 6 m, pop. 1,009) is both a popular seaside resort and an elegant vacation spot with exclusive villas that blend beautifully into the surrounding leafy hills overlooking the Mediterranean. The fishermen of Bonassola, faced with the perennial dangers of the sea (once rendered all the more perilous by the threat of attacks by pirates), created one of the first forms of insurance ever recorded in Italy. As early as 1569, they set up an indemnity fund for villagers who fell victim to marauding Turks. The large collection of votive offerings, now collected in the *church of Santa Caterina*, date back to this period. The parish church also has an original painting by Antonio Discovolo entitled *Pious Women at the Foot of the Cross* (1924), a remarkably expressive work, and, in the sacristy, a *St. Francis* by Bernardo Strozzi.

A pleasant and popular walk just over half a mile along the sea leads to the tiny

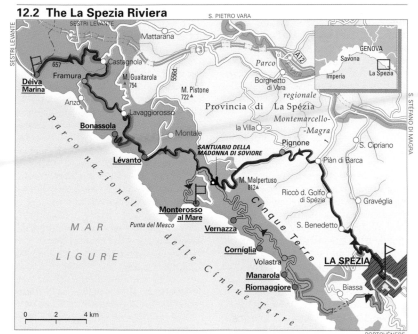

Madonna della Punta chapel, built onto the cliff and particularly charming at sunset.

Continuing by car toward Deiva, the locality of *Costa* (elev. 289 m, a hamlet belonging to the town of **Framura**, pop. 802) has the medieval **church of San Martino de Muris**. Though much remodeled, it is nevertheless remarkable for its three apses and belltower (once a lookout tower), once attached to the church but now separated from it; inside is a baptismal font and *Madonna of the Rosary with St. Dominic and St. Charles* by Bernardo Strozzi. At Anzo, which is also in Framura, stands the *chapel of Nostra Signora della Neve* (1342), in the Ligurian Gothic style, decorated with ogival arches.

Deiva Marina

This seaside resort (elev. 15 m, pop. 1,495), which started life as an inland settlement and gradually spread to the sea, still has a rather disjointed appearance. The part nearest the shore has little to offer other than a fine, well-equipped beach, while the original core boasts two old towers and the beautiful parvis of the *church of Sant'Antonio Abate*. A little way inland, at the hamlet of *Piazza* (elev. 185 m), stands a parish church with an even more beautiful parvis, whose decorative pattern is repeated on the belltower. Further on, the graceful *chapel of the Assunta* has a rustic 15th-century bas relief. Continuing toward Framura and Bonassola, a panoramic hill has a richly-scented pinewood that conceals the remains of the feudal complex of the Da Passano marquises, destroyed by the Genoese in 1180. The atmosphere of the site with its old abandoned stones among the trees is truly magical.

The nearby hamlet of *Castagnola* (elev. 287 m) is dominated by the **church of San Lorenzo**, with an impressive facade. Inside is a *Descent from the Cross* by Luca Cambiaso (1575).

12.3 Sarzana and Lower Lunigiana
The town of Sarzana; two excursions to Luni and Santo Stefano di Magra *(see map p. 207)*

The beautiful, broad and in places still untamed Magra river flows down 62 km from the mountains to the sea. It has a dual history: on the one hand it generated the morphologically varied but culturally quite homogeneous region known as Lunigiana, and on the other it served as the dividing line between the regions (in antiquity separating Liguria from Etruria). Today it is itself divided, straddling two provinces in different regions: it rises in the Tuscan province of Massa-Carrara (which administers the middle and upper valley) before veering southeast into Liguria's La Spezia province, which begins at Santo Stefano di Magra. The name Lunigiana derives from the ancient thriving city of Luni, which ceased to exist in the early centuries of the second millennium, without any other settlement of this or any similar name growing up in its place. The inhabitants of Luni retreated to the hills a few miles inland and, accustomed as they were to city life, brought a taste for urban decoration to their new towns. The most important was Sarzana – the place of origin of the Buonaparte family (the spelling was changed to Bonaparte after Napoleon) – soon the main town of lower Lunigiana.

Sarzana

Situated on the eastern part of the Magra river flood plain, this town (elev. 21 m, pop. 20,055) quickly developed after the nearby ancient city of Luni fell into decline. In the 13th century the first walls were erected to ward off attack from the powerful neighbors to which Sarzana was subjugated: Pisa, Lucca and Florence and finally the Republic of Genoa (1562), whose domination lasted for three centuries. Though badly bombed during the last war, the architectural and urban features of the past have survived in the town center, which still corresponds to the ancient heart of Sarzana.

The visit follows the thoroughfare that is the urban section of the ancient Via Francigena – the route taken by pilgrims to Rome – which corresponds to present-day Via Bertoloni and Via Mazzini, from Porta Parma in the north-west to the Neoclassical Porta Romana in the south-east. Along the road are the town's main squares and their monuments, including the house and tower (no. 28) that belonged to the Buonaparte family (which moved to Corsica in 1529). The tour ends at the imposing citadel and the *church of San Francesco*, just outside the northern walls.

Piazza Matteotti (A-B1-2). This elegant square is lined with 17th- and 18th-century buildings that have been much changed over the centuries. At the center stands the *Procellaria*, a monument to the war dead by Carlo Fontana (1934). The 16th-century *Palazzo Comunale*, or Town Hall, on the south-west side separates the square from the smaller Piazza Luna.

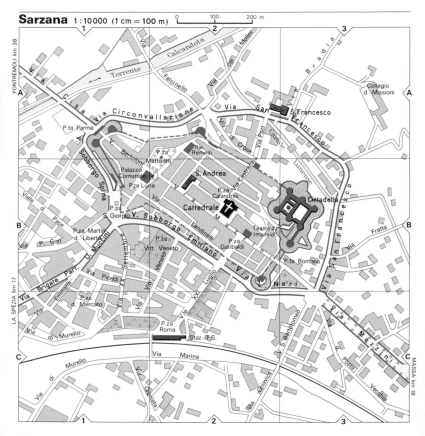

Sarzana 1:10000 (1 cm = 100 m)

Sarzana's 'Attic on the Street' antiques market

The elegant arcaded courtyard inside this building has crests, stone tablets and other architectural fragments from the ancient town of Luni.

Sant'Andrea (B2). This church is the result of the radical transformation in 1579 of an ancient Romanesque church (of which the fine paired window on the facade survives). The unusual portal has profane decorations (two caryatids), suggesting that it came from a civil home. The belltower is the result of a 14th-century reworking of a lower tower.

Cattedrale* (B2). The cathedral, consecrated to the Assunta, forms the luminous backdrop to the square dedicated to Sarzanese Pope Nicholas V (1447-55). Built in 1204, after the bishop's see was moved here from Luni, it was remodeled. The various additions and alterations are clearly seen on the facade: the splayed portal, intricately-worked marble rose window and the fine crenelated belltower with four rows of windows date back to the 14th century; the mosaic in the lunette is modern; the trilobate arches framing the gable roof were added in 1479, and the statues that top the facade are 18th century. The main work in the majestic, classical-style interior is the **Cross of Maestro Guglielmo*** (1138), a fine painting by the Tuscan artist, in the chapel to the left of the high altar. There are also two marble relief altarpieces by Leonardo Riccomanni: in the south transept the *Purification** (1436), and in the north transept the *Coronation** (1432); also by Riccomanni is the *Assunta*, at the back of the presbytery near the painting by Francesco Solimena with *St. Clement Pope and Saints*; in the 3rd chapel on the left is an *Annunciation with Saints* (1722), by Giuseppe Maria Crespi.

Cittadella (B2-3). The citadel was built over the destroyed Pisan fortress by order of Lorenzo il Magnifico between 1488 and 1492, and was designed by Florentine military architects including Giuliano da Sangallo, Francesco di Giovanni ('il Francione') and Luca del Caprina. This rectangular edifice has six round bastions at the corners and on two sides and is surrounded by a broad moat.

San Francesco (A2-3). This much remodeled church was founded in the 12th century. One of the finest works of art inside is the *Tomb of Guarnerio degli Antelminelli**, the son of Castruccio Castracani who died as a child in 1322. It is the work of Giovanni di Balduccio (1324-28).

Leave the town by Porta Romana (B-C3) and, after a short distance, take the road on the left that leads (2 km) to the **Fortezza di Sarzanello**, the fortress built by Castruccio Castracani around 1322 but remodeled in the 15th century and later by the Genoese.

The road that continues up beyond the fortress eventually leads to the junction with SS 446. Turn left and continue up to **Fosdinovo** (elev. 500 m, pop. 4,267), a hill village (in the neighboring Tuscan province of Massa-Carrara) that is particularly interesting for its urban layout and architecture. The domination of the Malaspina has left its mark here, especially in the restored *castle* (13-14th cent.), now a private residence but open to visitors.

From Sarzana to Luni
17 km excursion

Take the road that heads south-east out of Sarzana from Porta Romana, the Via Aurelia. After 5.6 km, a turn-off to the left soon leads up to Castelnuovo Magra. Return to the Aurelia (the left-hand fork on the way down), and take the next turn-off

The fortress of Sarzanello

to the left (at the crossroads) to Ortonovo, just before which a road off to the right leads to the tiny village of Nicola. Take the road back down toward Dogana, and cross the Aurelia to reach the archaeological area of Luni, where the tour ends.

Castelnuovo Magra

The importance of some of the works of art in the parish church only adds to the interest of this hill village (elev. 181 m, pop. 8,022), with its relatively complex urban layout in a beautiful setting. Some of the buildings have fine doorways, especially in Via Dante. Castelnuovo Magra is known to have existed since the 11th century, when a considerable number of inhabitants from Luni moved here from their rapidly declining city. The exiled Dante worked in the 13th-century *castle* (remodeled in the 15th century) at the service of the Malaspina. The **parish church of Santa Maria Maddalena** has a 19th-century facade, but has otherwise maintained its late-Renaissance structure. The paintings inside include a *Calvary* (on wood) attributed to Pieter Brueghel the Younger, and a *Crucifixion* attributed to Van Dyck.

The quiet, well-preserved hilltop village of **Nicola*** (elev. 181 m) is reached after a short but steep climb, away from the bustle down nearer the coast. It is designed around a fine piazza with an 18th-century church (of ancient foundation) and is surrounded by walls that are still partly visible. The view stretches from the marble-streaked Apuan Alps, across the wooded hills and olive groves down to the broad sweep of the Versilia coast and away to the open sea.

At the very top of the hill stands the ancient village of **Ortonovo** (elev. 283 m, pop. 8,393), much of whose walls remain; just before, note the *sanctuary of the Madonna del Mirteto*, built in the 1500s on the site of the supposed bleeding of the *Image of the Madonna Addolorata*, kept in the church in a late 18th-century ornamental temple. In the lunette of the central portal is an interesting *Madonna and Child with Sts. Joachim and Anne*, in the Michelangelo style.

Luni

In ancient times Luni was a rich, important city and thriving port after which the entire region of Lunigiana was named. Founded in 177 BC, it prospered under Rome, and

withstood even the most destructive invasions, but declined when the port silted up irretrievably in the 11th and 12th centuries and with the arrival of malaria. Abandoned by its people, Luni was first reduced to a simulacrum of a city (Petrarch used it to exemplify the transitory nature of human fortunes), then became an empty expanse dotted with ruins. Today it is an archaeological area *(open: 9am-7pm; closed Mon)*, noted mainly for the remains of its great **amphitheater** (which could seat 5,000 spectators), just outside the town. Within the excavated area is the **Museo Archeologico Nazionale***, which displays some of the finds made here, including two draped, headless *statues* and a series of *portraits* from the Julio-Claudian period. Some of the material has been organized into thematic sections in the archaeological area near the remains of some buildings.

From Sarzana to Santo Stefano di Magra on the border with Tuscany
22 km circular tour

Leave Sarzana from Piazza S. Giorgio along the road for La Spezia. Immediately after the river take the road to Lerici (first left), and after a short distance make the short detour (along a narrow winding road to the right) up to **Trebiano** (elev. 162 m), a hill village dominated by the imposing ruins of an ancient castle. Continuing north along the west bank of the Magra, the road leads to

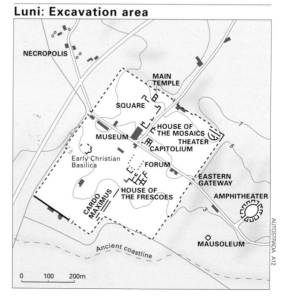

Luni: Excavation area

NECROPOLIS

MAIN TEMPLE

SQUARE

MUSEUM

HOUSE OF THE MOSAICS

THEATER

CAPITOLIUM

Early Christian Basilica

FORUM

CARDO MAXIMUS

HOUSE OF THE FRESCOES

EASTERN GATEWAY

AMPHITHEATER

MAUSOLEUM

Ancient coastline

0   100   200m

AUTOSTRADA A12

Arcola, and further on to Vezzano Ligure. After crossing the bridge over the river further up still, the road heads back east to the junction with the SS 62 (*della Cisa*). Turn right here for Santo Stefano di Magra, from where the main SS 62 road leads conveniently back to Sarzana.

Arcola

This village (elev. 70 m, pop. 9,956) is best viewed from the high ground opposite, from where the buildings appear as a compact, uniform whole huddled around the top of the hill. All that remains of the castle, demolished by the Genoese, is a five-sided tower; in its place stands the *Municipio* (1885), built in the medieval style. One particularly interesting feature of the village is *Piazza della Parrocchiale*, which blends the rural character of the surrounding houses with a solemnly impressive though now rather dilapidated flight of steps with balustrade.

Vezzano Ligure

This village (elev. 271 m, pop. 7,447) is divided into an upper and a lower part. The layout of Vezzano Superiore, not surprisingly, follows the contours of the hill on which it sits, while *Vezzano Inferiore* has an interesting ring-shaped layout. Note in this lower part the ruined Romanesque *church of Santa Maria*, at the cemetery, and, in the heart of the village, the 17th-century *church of the Assunta*, which has a wooden *Pietà* attributed to Maragliano. At the cemetery in *Vezzano Superiore*, note the Romanesque *belltower*, which is all that remains of the *church of San Siro*, and, beyond the gate, the *oratory of Sant'Antonio*, with a rustic architrave depicting the saint with his hooded brothers at prayer. The main paved street of the upper village has an attractive *well*. Further up are the ruins of the *castle*,

12.3 Lower Lunigiana

[Map of Lower Lunigiana showing locations including Barbarasco, Agnino, Càlice al Cornoviglio, Aulla, TOSCANA, Bolano, Caprigliola, S. Stéfano di Magra, Parco regionale d. Alpi Apuane, Fosdinovo, Vezzano Ligure, Arcola, Sarzana, Castelnuovo Magra, Trebiano, Ortonovo, Nicola, Parco regionale Montemarcello-Magra, Lérici, Dogana, LUNI, Portovénere, Tellaro, Í. Palmária, Bocca di Magra, Marina di Carrara, MAR LÍGURE. Inset map showing GENOVA, Savona, La Spezia, Imperia. Scale: 0 2 4 km]

the leafy open space in front of which affords an exceptional **view** over the confluence of the Vara and Magra rivers.

Santo Stefano di Magra

This ancient fortified trading town (elev. 50 m, pop. 8,216) preserves interesting vestiges of the past, including the walls and

Bocca di Magra, against the backdrop of the Apuan Alps

original regular urban layout. The historic part is a mixture of medieval and 16th-century elements (note in particular the fine gray sandstone doorways). The main monumental building is the Baroque *church of Santo Stefano* (1749-76).

Itineraries

Walking and cycling in Liguria

A region with such a long, virtually unbroken sequence of mountains and sea stretching hundreds of kilometers, is clearly ideal for outdoor pursuits. The backbone of the region's network of hiking routes is the **Alta Via dei Monti Liguri** (High Ligurian Mountain Trail), which runs for over 400 km all the way from *Ventimiglia* to the *Vara Valley*. As it winds its way along the watershed of the Alpine-Apennine chain, it offers views not only down to the Riviera, but also to the Po Valley and the peaks of the Alps beyond. It is the ideal way of coming into contact with inland Liguria's many faces, such as those parts of the Ligurian landscape described by writer Riccardo Bacchelli as "something distressful, fierce and desperate in human tenacity, which attacked and ate into those crags, creating steps and terraces up to the most incredible heights, work that involved a frightful amount of effort".

The High Trail also passes through three of the region's main parks (the Ligurian Alps, Beigua, and Aveto). It is equipped with mountain refuges and connected to the coast by numerous other trails that often follow the path of ancient trading routes between the ports and the Po Valley, such as the celebrated 'salt route'. One other important route here is the **Via dei Feudi Imperiali** (Imperial Feudal Way) which, though not yet completely equipped as a hiking trail, runs from *Genoa* through the former enclave of the *Vobbia and Borbera Valleys* granted to Ludovico il Moro by Emperor Maximilian I in 1495 in return for transit taxes.

An excellent service that can be used in connection with this excursion is provided by the Genoa-Casella railway, a beautiful tourist train that has somehow survived the transport cutbacks.

Walking and cycling in Liguria

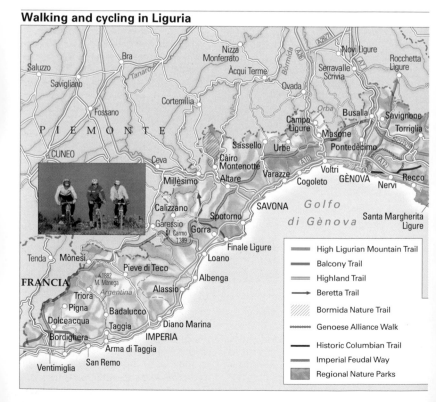

High Ligurian Mountain Trail
Balcony Trail
Highland Trail
Beretta Trail
Bormida Nature Trail
Genoese Alliance Walk
Historic Columbian Trail
Imperial Feudal Way
Regional Nature Parks

One of the many historical itineraries is the **Strada Beretta** (Beretta Road), the ridgeway connecting *Finale Ligure* to the province of *Alessandria* and *Milan*, created in 1666 by the engineer Gaspare Beretta to facilitate relations between Spanish-controlled Lombardy and the domains of the Finale Marquisate. Today most of the road can be covered on foot from *Finalborgo* to the *Val Bormida*.

Also in this valley lie the **Bormida Nature Trails** that pass through various local protected areas, including the *Bric Tana* and *Langhe di Piana Crixia parks*, *the Adelasia Reserve*, the *Monte Camulera Wilderness*, and the *Rocchetta Cairo Protected Area*. The **Sentiero Terre Alte** (Highland Trail) is a walk in three stages, connecting the High Trail to the coast at *Borghetto Santo Spirito* and passing through the beautiful landscape of the *Loano* area.

Anyone who finds the High Trail a little too far away from the coast might be interested in one of the many, less demanding coastal paths, whose attraction lies in the unique blend of nature, history and culture they offer. One of these, the **Sentiero Verdeazzurro** (Verdeazzurro Trail), organized by Liguria's Unioncamere, runs the entire length of the *eastern Riviera* and

——	Verdeazzurro Trail
——	CAI Trail 1
/////	Fontanabuona Trails
——	Canoeing and kayaking (Argentina, Orba, Lavagna and Vara Rivers)

covers 140 km in ten stages; **Cai Trail 1** connects the *Cinque Terre* and the recently-instituted national park; the seven-part **Sentiero Balcone** (Balcony Trail) at Liguria's westernmost extremity joins *Sanremo* to the *French border* where it links up with the French 'balcony route' (GR 51) to *Marseilles*; the **Sentiero Arcobaleno** (Rainbow Trail), another route through *Ingauno* country, connects *Ventimiglia* with *Ospedaletti*. Other hikes through various parts of the region have more of a cultural flavor to them. One particularly interesting one is the network of trails in the *Fontanabuona Valley* north of *Rapallo*, which comprises: the **Itinerario dei Sette Passi** (Seven Passes Hike), along major historic footpaths; the **Itinerario dei Feudi Fliscani** (Fliscan Feuds Hike), along the ancient road to *Torriglia*; the **Sentieri della Valsangiacomo** (Valsangiacomo Trails), which form part of the slate museum project and retrace the old mule-tracks connecting the slate quarries to the ports. Christopher Columbus was the inspiration for the **Sentiero Storico Colombiano** (Historic Columbian Trail), along the old mule-track connecting *Fontanabuona* to *Nervi*, and possibly used by the great navigator's ancestors when they moved to Genoa. An important route in the *Genoa area* itself is the **Percorso Genovese del Cammino dell'Alleanza** (Genoese Alliance Walk), recently established by the Italian Hiking Federation (FEI), which circles the *Bisagno Valley* and includes the *City Wall Park*. The FEI has also been involved in the setting up of the **Percorsi dell'Alleanza** routes in the *Magra river area* in the *Montemarcello Regional Park*. Liguria's protected nature areas also run special theme tours. Among these, the **Self-guided Nature Tours** through the *Portofino Park* consist of three routes that bring together all natural and man-made aspects of Mt. Portofino, the natural border area between the continental and Mediterranean environments. The natural environment can also be enjoyed on the **Sentiero Brugneto** (Brugneto Trail), in the *Mt. Antola Nature Park*, and the **Sentiero Botanico di Ciae** (Ciae Botanical Trail) at *Sant'Olcese*, near Genoa.

Conditions are ideal in Liguria for canyoning, and sports involving the use of canoes and kayaks are catching on fast here. The best rivers are the *Argentina* in Imperia province in the west, the *Orba* in the north-eastern part of Savona province, the *Lavagna* in Fontanabuona Valley, and the *Vara river* near La Spezia (see also 'For extreme sports enthusiasts', p. 38). Finally, a brief mention of some of the opportunities for mountain biking in the region on inland Liguria's old cart roads and forest trails. Although the differences in level makes them quite demanding, they provide a satisfying opportunity to explore the area within a reasonable distance of the seaside resorts and train stations, which offer a Train+Bike service. The **Magra and Montemarcello Nature Park** has organized a special riverside biking route on the banks of the *Magra* and *Vara*.

For further information: *Associazione Alta Via dei Monti Liguri, c/o Centro Studi Unioncamere, Via San Lorenzo 15/1, Genova, tel. 0102471876, <http://www.lig.camcom.it> http://www.lig.camcom.it; Itinerari Escursionistici del Savonese - Riviera delle Palme, Apt Riviera delle Palme, Viale Gibb 26, Alassio, tel. 018264711, <http://www.italianriviera.com> http://www.italianriviera.com; Federazione Italiana Escursionismo, Via La Spezia 58r, Genova, tel. 010463261; Sentieri della Fontanabuona, Comunità Montana Fontanabuona, Piazza Cavagnari 7, Cicagna, tel. 018592212; Sentieri del Parco di Portofino, Ente Parco di Portofino, Viale Rainusso 1, Santa Margherita Ligure, tel. 0185289479, <http://www.parks.it/parco.portofino>http://www.parks.it/parco.portofino.*

The silent towns

The silent towns

Off Liguria's well-beaten tourist track, the green of the hills that rise up so rapidly into mountains is dotted with little patches of color: what we might call the 'silent towns'. As we travel along the roads through inland Liguria, perhaps retracing the old salt routes, there always seems to be something, however small, waiting round the corner to attract our attention. History and popular culture are interwoven in a context in which nature still reigns supreme: and the result is something quite remarkable.

Take, for example, **Ceriana**, a little town in the Armea Valley, not far from Sanremo. The road cuts through the green surroundings as it rises up from the coast to a bare mountain. After a bend we suddenly come across this ancient medieval town built over the remains of a Roman villa, following the contours of the land, and forming a collection of houses, churches and oilpresses still in use, surrounded by a curtain wall. What strikes the visitor as an inextricable maze of streets and alleys is a voyage of discovery with seemingly never-ending examples of a surprisingly rich local art.

The town of Ceriana is one of the most interesting examples of this perfectly-preserved world apart, within easy reach of the sea. But across the whole of Liguria countless little rural towns and villages on the *Adagio di Liguria* trail never fail to delight those who take the time and trouble to visit them and savor their history, culture, crafts and their food and drink.

This itinerary, which is more conceptual than cartographic (hopping as it does from valley to valley), begins at Dolceacqua, just inland from Ventimiglia, almost on the border with France. A town whose two parts are separated by the Nervia river and connected by its single-span medieval bridge, it is another world unto itself, nestling beneath the Doria castle. The cellars are redolent of Dolceacqua's famous quality wine, Rossese. All around there are countless tiny villages to discover. **Apricale**, sits atop a hill surrounded by olives, with castle, old houses, alleys and stone steps; **Pigna** has a set of concentric alleys and narrow passageways; **Realdo** is an old mountain town overlooking a precipice; **Triora** is the village of the witches (whose

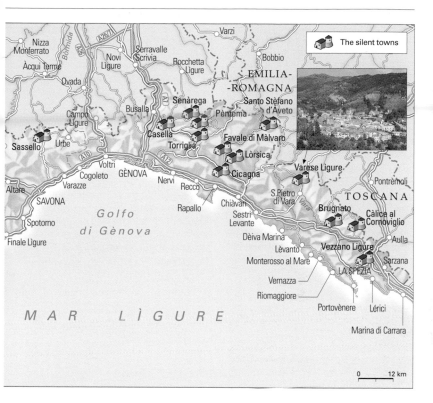

The silent towns

story is told in the ethnographic museum there), and is still a slightly spooky place to be; **Bussana Vecchia** has been given a new lease of life by the international community of artists who have come to settle in a town razed to the ground by an earthquake in the late 19th century.

Calizzano lies in a verdant depression in the upper Bormida Valley surrounded by beechwoods amid gently rolling hills. The houses of the old town (laid out in a regular grid pattern typical of fortified settlements) still show signs of the existence of walls connecting the town to the castle. The chestnut woods around Calizzano make it a major mushrooming area, the exquisite *porcini* variety being the subject of a famous annual festival. **Bardineto** lies in a strategic position in the same valley, at a junction of roads to Piedmont and the coast. A few bends to the south, it is worth stopping off at **Castelvecchio di Rocca Barbena**, a feudal town whose houses are arranged in concentric circles under the crag topped by the Clavesana castle.

The landscape between Savona and Genoa provinces is dominated by the Beigua massif. To the north-west of the mountain lies **Sassello**, the town which invented the 'orange flags of excellence' and which delights visitors not only with its fine ancient town in lush green surroundings, 17th-century buildings, medieval structures and examples of industrial archaeology, but also with its soft, wonderfully fragrant *amaretti* (macaroons), and flavorful mushrooms.

One of the nicest ways of traveling inland from Genoa is by the Casella railway, which offers some quite breathtaking views as it cuts its way into the heart of the Ligurian Apennines, through the Val Bisagno into Valle Scrivia. The terminus is **Casella** itself, a town in an exceptionally green valley: not to mention the 17th-century Palazzo dei Fieschi in the main square. **Torriglia**, which lies at an altitude of 770 meters, is the center of what has been referred to as 'Swiss Liguria'. The nearby village of **Pentema** seems enchanted: its stone houses ranged one against the other on the mountainside. A little further north-west is Val Brevenna, whose many hamlets form a kind of openair museum of popular architecture: each village tells of the hard life of its farming folk: **Senarega**, for example, is an almost perfectly preserved medieval village.

211

The roads that wind their way inland from the Golfo del Tigullio lead through the various valleys – Val Fontanabuona, Val Graveglia, Val d'Aveto – to any number of ancient, isolated little towns and villages: **Santo Stefano d'Aveto**, with its fine historic center and 13th-century castle is situated just under Mt. Maggiorasca; and from **Cicagna** in Fontanabuona, known for its slate-quarrying, it is worth driving up the side valley to **Favale di Malvaro**, and to historic Lorsica with its old mill. Val Graveglia, which leads up from Cogorno, is a beautiful wooded vale (the so-called 'valley of the mills') full of unspoiled villages.

Down in La Spezia province, time really does seem to have stood still in the towns and villages that dot the countryside. In some places, the past blends beautifully with the present and future. No visitor to Val di Vara should miss the Borgo Rotondo (Round Town), the innermost part of **Varese Ligure**, with its typical porticoes and buildings facing onto the circular piazza and the Fieschi castle, but Varese Ligure (the first municipality in Europe to be awarded ISO 140001 environmental certification) is also the chief town of the so-called 'organic valley' because of its exclusively organic production of cheese, meat and other produce. Near the highway turn-off is the historic town of **Brugnato**, a former bishop's see. Another 'must' for those walking the High Ligurian Mountain Trail is **Calice al Cornoviglio**, a feudal town clinging to the mountain, and dominated by a 16th-century castle. Finally, **Vezzano Ligure** is a spectacular old hilltop town just a mile or two outside La Spezia, overlooking the Val di Magra, whose plain stretches away to the south and the border with Tuscany.

Food and wine specialties

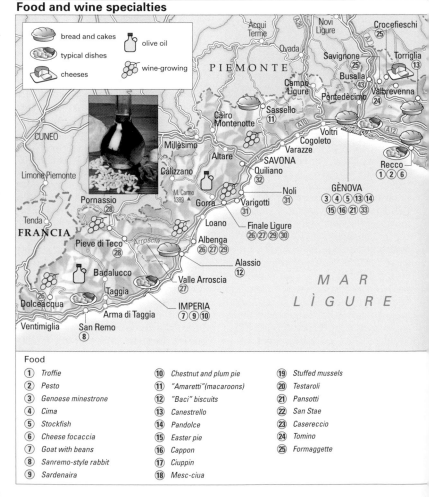

Food

① Troffie	⑩ Chestnut and plum pie	⑲ Stuffed mussels
② Pesto	⑪ "Amaretti"(macaroons)	⑳ Testaroli
③ Genoese minestrone	⑫ "Baci" biscuits	㉑ Pansotti
④ Cima	⑬ Canestrello	㉒ San Stae
⑤ Stockfish	⑭ Pandolce	㉓ Casereccio
⑥ Cheese focaccia	⑮ Easter pie	㉔ Tomino
⑦ Goat with beans	⑯ Cappon	㉕ Formaggette
⑧ Sanremo-style rabbit	⑰ Ciuppin	
⑨ Sardenaira	⑱ Mesc-ciua	

From seafood to mountain fare: traditional local specialties that never fail to surprise

Pride of place among the region's 'culinary capitals' is *Recco*, famous not only for its cheese **focaccia** (see p. 99), but also for its **troffie**, the spindle-shaped pasta that also comes in a tasty chestnut flour variety, and which is typically accompanied by the celebrated Ligurian **pesto** dressing, made from basil, cheese, garlic, oil and pine nuts. The best season to sample the sauce is in winter, when the basil used is the paler hothouse-or balcony-grown variety (stronger-tasting basil from the garden is better suited to tomato-based sauces). Pine nuts do not, however, feature in the recipe for **pesto** used in the all-vegetable **minestrone alla genovese**. Another Genoese delicacy is the so-called **cima**,

a veal roll stuffed with egg, cheese, chopped giblets and vegetables (the latter to be found especially in the western Riviera version of the dish) and stockfish, which entered the Genoese diet in the 19th century, especially in one variety known as '*ragno*', the Italian word for spider but actually a dockyard corruption of the name of the Norwegian supplier 'Ragnar'. The culinary specialties of the province of Imperia are dominated by two meat courses (**goat's meat with beans**, typical of the inland area behind *Ventimiglia*, and *Sanremo rabbit*, in a dressing of onion, garlic, rosemary, pine nuts, olive oil and white wine) and by **sardenaira**, much loved by Andrea Doria and therefore known as **pizza all'Andrea**, although it bears little resemblance to the traditional Neapolitan pizza. Then there are the various sweetmeats, such as chestnut and plum pie, another typical mountain valley recipe. Liguria boasts quite a big confectionery industry: the **amaretti** *di Sassello* (Sassello macaroons), which have links with neighboring Piedmont, originated in the mid-19th century; similarly successful after World War I were the famous **baci** *di Alassio*, literally 'Alassio kisses', made from hazel nuts, egg and cocoa. Another very popular Ligurian sweetmeat is the **canestrello**, whose origins are claimed by both *Genoa* and *Torriglia*: this excellent breakfast or tea-time pastry is pale in color, a guarantee of its fragrance and 'melt-in-the-mouth' texture. Liguria's traditional Christmas cake is **pandolce**, traditionally served with a sprig of bay leaf; the list of ingredients spares no expense: orange water, 'zibibbo' (a small sweet grape) and candied citron, a rich array that reminds us of Genoa's age-old links with the Levant. Strictly home-grown, on the other hand, are the vegetables (spinach, artichokes and zucchinis) and eggs used to make the **torta pasqualina**, a savory pie traditionally eaten at Easter time. No one should leave Genoa without sampling **cappon magro**, a combination of fish and other seafood boiled with vegetables, once the food of the poor and now considered a delicacy, like **ciuppin**, a simple fish soup whose origins go back to *Sestri Levante*, and *La Spezia*'s **mesc-ciua**, prepared with cereals and other kinds of corn that spilled out of the sacks being loaded and unloaded at the docks. *La Spezia* is also famous for its **stuffed mussels alla Vecchia Spezia**: the sauce often contains hot *peperoncino* (chili pepper). From nearby

Wines

㉖	Rossese	㉟	Bianchetta
㉗	Pigato	㊱	Ciliegiolo
㉘	Ormeasco	㊲	Musaico
㉙	Vermentino	㊳	Cinqueterre white
㉚	Lumassina	㊴	Sciacchetrà
㉛	Mataosso	㊵	Marea
㉜	Buzzetto	㊶	Albachiara
㉝	Coronata white	㊷	Grappolo
㉞	Moscato	㊸	Beer

Lunigiana, come **testaroli**, prepared in two different varieties, typical of the *Sarzana* area and *Varese Ligure* respectively: the ideal dressing for this pasta dish is walnut sauce, usually used for Genoese **pansotti**. Because of the limited amount of pastureland, Liguria's cheese production is much more limited; varieties worth trying, however, are **San Stae** from *Santo Stefano d'Aveto* (the only Ligurian cheese with the DOP, or protected origin mark), **Casereccio** from *Gorreto* and **tomino** from the *Val Brevenna*. *Bonassola*, *Crocefieschi* and *Savignone* all make **soft cheeses** that are eaten fresh or matured in oil. **Pian del Vescovo, Costa Marina, Monte Bernardo, Bricco Arcagna, Villa Torrachetta** and **Le Petraie** are colorful local names that mean little outside Liguria – except to wine experts. Ligurian wines are indeed a treat for the palate: no fewer than 20 have been awarded the coveted DOC (controlled-origin) mark. Perhaps the finest is the **Rossese** of *Dolceacqua*, in which connoisseurs trace a hint of blackberry, red currant and pine resin. The vineyards that line the *Nervia Valley* yield an excellent **Vermentino**. Another white wine is the **Pigato** of the *Arroscia Valley*; at *Pieve di Teco* and *Pornassio* wine lovers should try the dry red **Ormeasco**, with its subtle cherry-cum-blackberry flavor.

At Albenga, in the province of **Savona**, **Vermentino**, **Pigato** and **Rossese** are bottled, a trio of wines found also in *Finale Ligure*, together with **Lumassina**, a white wine still awaiting the DOC appellation but no less deserving for that: the name derives from the fact that it was traditionally served as an accompaniment to a special local snail dish (*lumache* in Italian), while in *Noli* and *Varigotti* it is known by the name of **Mataosso**, and in *Quiliano* as **Buzzetto**. A wine worth sampling in *Genoa* is **Coronata white**. In eastern Liguria, the *Sestri Levante* vineyards produce high-quality **Vermentino**, **Moscato** and **Bianchetta**, the **Ciliegiolo** rosé and the unusual **Musaico** red. Excellent red and white wines are also produced on the hills above *Levanto*, and further along the coast on the difficult terrain of the *Cinque Terre*, the hard work done over the centuries has paid off with the celebrated **Sciacchetrà** (pronounced 'shac-e-trà') an amber-colored wine with a hint of apricot. On the border with Tuscany, the hills of *Luni* produce another kind of **Vermentino**, together with another three whites (**Marea**, **Albachiara** and **Grappolo**), which few non-connoisseurs are familiar with. Anyone who prefers beer to wine will want to try the local blonde and red varieties – from the bottle or draught – at the *Busalla* brewery.

Liguria: one big open-air gym

The Garlenda golf course, near Arenzano

Liguria is the ideal place to practice outdoor sports. **Water sports** feature prominently, of course: the region boasts some 60 yacht clubs, including the prestigious Italian Yacht Club (YCI), founded in 1879 and the country's oldest. The YCI, based in *Genoa* (at the Duca degli Abruzzi marina) and *Portofino*, was the base for Italy's participation in the 1987 America's Cup. **Scuba divers** are also well catered for, thanks to the many diving centers and the fact that the seabed already reaches considerable depths just a few meters out from the coast. The best underwater views are at the *Cinque Terre* and

on the *Portofino Promontory*, although the creation in 1999 of the Marine Reserve has limited access to organized and specially-authorized groups only. **Rowing** is another popular water sport, with regatta fields at *Sanremo*, *Savona*, *Genoa/Pra*, *Santa Margherita Ligure*, *La Spezia*, *Sarzana*, and on *Lake Osiglia*. For those who like to go at a faster pace, *Savona* is something of a center for **speed-boating** (trials for the world offshore championships are held here), while *Genoa* and *Andora* offer the best opportunities for enthusiasts of the latest high-speed water sport: **jet skiing**, to which *Alassio* and *La Spezia* respond with the ever-popular and no less spectacular **water-skiing**. But water sports are not limited to the coast. Inland, many rivers offer sporting attractions: the *Argentina*, *Orba*, *Teiro* and *Vara* to name just a few. **Kayaking** is popular and, where possible, **canyoning**. For the increasing numbers of extreme sports enthusiasts there is also **bungee jumping** on the seemingly endless eight-second drop from the Loreto bridge near *Triora*. The sheer rock walls in the *Argentina Valley* attract many **free-climbing** enthusiasts, who also have at their disposal what has become something of a mecca for rock climbers, a kind of open-air rock gymnasium at *Finale Ligure*, offering over 1,500 routes; other sequences can be found at *Albenga*, *Sestri Levante* (at Lastre di Riva and Punta Manara), *Cogoleto* (near the hamlet of Sciarborasca) and *Muzzerone*, in addition to which there are two artificial training grounds at *Cogoleto* and in the Genoa suburb of *Borzoli*. Opportunities for **traditional mountaineering** are more limited, although the slopes of *Mt. Pietravecchia* and *Mt. Toraggio* have something for the most demanding mountaineers. A couple of localities (*Monesi* and *Alberola*) are equipped with **skiing facilities**, although the season is inevitably short because of the climate and vicinity of the sea; the same goes for the **cross-country skiing** circuits around *Colla Melosa*, *Calizzano* and *Santo Stefano d'Aveto*. On the other hand the mildness of the Ligurian climate means that riding stables in the region are nearly always open and **horse-riding** routes practicable, the most interesting opportunities being in the provinces of *Genoa* (as well as Genoa itself there are riding centers at *Busalla*, *Campo Ligure*, *Carasco* and *Rapallo*) and *Savona* (at *Albenga*, *Albisola Superiore*, *Celle Ligure*, *Ferrania*, *Finale Ligure* and *Loano*); the scenery for riders in the *Cinque Terre* is truly spectacular. The **mountain-bike** is another ideal way of discovering the region's natural beauty; the most difficult course in Liguria is probably the one in the *City Wall Park*, a few minutes' drive outside the center of *Genoa* (or half an hour for those prepared to pedal their way up), and it is no coincidence that the 'MTB Genoa Cup' qualifying rounds for the Italian mount-biking championship are held here. The park also has two **keep-fit paths** (there are another two high up above *La Spezia* and one at *Sassello*), together with an **archery ground**, while anyone looking for a more modern kind of target practice can check out the **shooting-range** in *Rapallo*, complete with armored tunnel; similar amenities are on offer in *Genoa*, *Sanremo*, *Savona*, *Chiavari* and *La Spezia*. *Rapallo* also has one of three **18-hole golf links** in the region (the others are at *Garlenda* and *Sanremo*), with **nine-hole links** available at *Arenzano* and *Lerici*, all of them open all year round. Of course summer is the only time for beach sports: as well as **beach volleyball**, **beach soccer** is growing in popularity, as is **water-polo** in the sea, a discipline with a guaranteed future in a region that has done so much to ensure Italy's continuing success in the sport.

Literary and culture parks in a border region

The links between geography and literature are many: there are innumerable descriptions of clearly identifiable landscapes, and the reading of a poem and contemplation of a beautiful view are emotional experiences. There is often a quite evident relationship between the biographical haunts of writers and their artistic output: both Montale and Caproni began with two collections of poetry that were unquestionably set in the region. This stylistic device is shared by many Ligurian artists. The idea of the literary park derives from the desire to make the most of such fundamental links as the coming together of celebrated artistic individuality and the natural and cultural environments of a particular historical period, the literary, pictorial, musical, cinematic echoes of specific geographical areas, and the new place they are taking up in the collective psyche. Confirmation of interest in the

Sculptor Arturo Martini

idea came with the European Community's Global Subsidy in December 1997.
Back in the 18th century Liguria was already exerting an irresistible charm on refined travelers making the Grand Tour: the places that would go on to become major tourist capitals in the modern world soon saw English yawls and schooners at anchor in their bays. Poets and painters fleeing the gray climes of the North paved the way for a high-class kind of tourism that intermingled with the fabric of the local culture, giving rise to an artistic and intellectual map with deep local roots, one that soon became an integral part of its identity. In the 19th century Claude Monet spent in weeks in *Bordighera*, painting no fewer than forty canvases – mostly landscapes – and Guy de Maupassant moored his yacht Bel Ami off *Portofino*. In the early 20th century the poor tormented Nietzsche took refuge in the *Cinque Terre*, while Anna Maria Ortese moved to *Rapallo* for the last twenty years of her life.

A sequence of seven **parchi culturali** runs across the whole of Liguria. These parks were sponsored by the region's Culture and Tourism Department to promote quality tourism throughout Liguria. The **Parco Culturale Riviera dei Fiori e delle Alpi Marittime** (*Cooperativa Liguria da Scoprire, tel. 0183290213, e-mail liguriadascoprire@libero.it*) spreads over an area extending historically to the *Nice* area and ranges from the beaches of *Sanremo* and *Bordighera* in Imperia province to the snow-capped *Maritime Alps*. It is an area of great scenic, historical and artistic charm. The various cultural itineraries on offer here include the one devoted to Italo Calvino in Sanremo, the **Parasio tour** in *Imperia* and routes that wind their way from *Diano Marina* to *Porto Maurizio*, and from *Bordighera* to *Taggia*. The Sasso oil-making industry represents the happy coming together of culture and nature: contributors to its magazine "La Riviera Ligure" included some of Italy's leading early 20th-century writers and poets: Pascoli, Pirandello, Sbarbaro, Ungaretti, Saba and more besides; many of these articles are reprinted in the *Itinerari Letterari e Pittorici della Riviera dei Fiori*. The **Parco Culturale Riviera delle Palme** - *Savona* (*Apt Liguria delle Palme, tel.*

0182882383, Società Savonese di Storia Patria, tel. 019 811960, e-mail lunardo@pn.it-net.it) offers both historical tours – the city of the Popes, the Napoleonic Wars, the Partisan Resistance Movement – and archaeological and palaeontological excursions; this interdisciplinary project includes art (Arturo Martini) and literature, from Chiabrera to Boine. Meanwhile the **Parco Culturale Giorgio Caproni** (*Edizioni San Marco dei Giustiniani, tel./fax 0102474747*), further inland in the *Trebbia Valley*, is of course dominated by its main protagonist. The poet's study will be rebuilt in the *sanctuary of Montebruno* and a writing workshop set up. The itineraries in the valley are both literary and historical (particular attention is dedicated to testaments of material culture) and take place in a charming and quite unspoiled natural setting. Beloved of artists from all over the world and every period in history–from Dante and Petrarch to Manzoni, Nietzsche, Lamartine, Valéry, Andersen, Capote, Kandinsky and Pound – *Tigullio Bay* is one of the most beautiful parts of the whole region, its scenic attractions now heightened by the creation of the **Parco Culturale del Golfo di Tigullio** (*Associazione Pagina 98, tel./fax 0185234492, e-mail pcadema@tin.it and sitessi@tin.it*), while

'among falcon and seagull nests', along 'the path I took one day / like a restless dog; it laps the torrent, / climbs up among the rocks' against the ever-changing colors of the sea. The *Bay of Lerici* is the world famous *Golfo dei Poeti*. It was from here that Shelley set sail, never to return: Byron cremated his body on the beach at Viareggio, on a funeral pyre that took its inspiration from heroic canons of classical literature: the emotion felt by Mary Shelley is shared by anyone looking out over the bay today. The **Parco Culturale Lerici – Golfo dei Poeti** (*Comune di Lerici – Settore Politiche Sociali – Carlo Oliva, tel./fax 0187966831, www.comune.lerici.sp.it, e-mail pubblist@iclab.it*) comprises a geographical area stretching from *Lerici* to *Tellaro* and to *San Terenzo*, in whose castle a multimedia culture center dedicated to the Shelleys is to be created. D.H. Lawrence and Virginia Woolf also stayed here, and Mario Soldati made his retreat here.

Where Liguria gradually gives way to Tuscany, beneath the portentous ridges of the Apuan Alps, we find, finally, the **Parco Culturale Val di Magra e Terra di Luni** (*Laboratorio di Arte Contemporanea della Lunigiana, Gabriella Bertone, tel. 0187624668, Carla Sanguineti, tel. 0187600317, e-mail carlasanguineti@tin.it*). Many traces of ancient and even more remote civilizations have been found in this valley; however, the itinerary also includes nature and gastronomic tours. Those writers who from the Middle Ages to the present day traversed this ancient communication route between the Po Valley and the sea recorded their impressions. Their writings are collected together in *Su e giù per la Val di Magra. In vacanza con gli scrittori*, published by Agorà Edizioni, La Spezia.

the **Parco Letterario Eugenio Montale** dedicated to Nobel prizewinner Eugenio Montale (*Adriana Beverini, tel. 018721223, e-mail adriana2@libero.it and vanicella@yahoo.com*), centers around *Monterosso*, where the Montale family of the 'distant summers' has its home. Among the terraces high up over the sea, the poet's verses accompany visitors

The marinas: modern structures and charming surroundings where the world of the sea meets that of the land

Sailing enthusiasts really are spoilt for choice in Liguria: there are no fewer than 61 ports of call along the region's coast, offering berths for 16,000 vessels (with more planned for the coming years), catering fully or partly for pleasure craft. Some of them have become such a familiar part of the scene they are virtually landmarks in their own right, as deserving of a place in tourist guide books as the scenery or the historical sights. Undoubtedly the most famous of them all is the little harbor of **Portofino**, where luxury yachts and powerful motor boats, aboard which the rich and famous (and even the royal) can occasionally be spotted, has become an integral part of the view of Italy's richest

seaside town. The nearby marinas of **Camogli** and **Santa Margherita Ligure** are every bit as much a part of the town, while in **Rapallo**, the Porto Turistico Internazionale (376 berths) offers first-class amenities, as do the 290,000-m^2 Cala dei Genovesi marina in **Lavagna**, which has mooring facilities for as many as 1,455 vessels, and can accommodate boats measuring up to 50 meters; the 459-berth marina at **Chiavari**; and the 280-berth Porto Antico marina in **Genoa**, created during redevelopment of the port area for the Columbus celebrations in 1992, and, curiously, with exactly the same capacity as Genoa's other mooring facility, the Ma.Ri.Na. Service, opposite the International Trade Fair.

The 590-berth Capo San Donato marina at Finale Ligure

The vicinity to the fair is explained by the fact that the marina was originally purpose-built to accommodate vessels presented at Genoa's International Boat Show, held in October, for the duration of which the marina is closed to private vessels.

La Spezia's marina, the 439-berth Porto Lotti, is located at San Bartolomeo Pagliari. Because of the naval port here, navigation in the Golfo dei Poeti is subject to various military restrictions, which also penalizes the marinas at nearby **Lerici** and **Portovenere**. The beautiful little harbor at **Vernazza** is the only mooring facility in the Cinque Terre: the tiny basin still fills with fishing boats, which make a truly picturesque sight against the backdrop of the village's colorful houses.

Porto Bello is the name of the marina at

Loano that is currently undergoing a major overhaul. When the refurbishment and enlargement program is completed in 2002, the number of mooring places will have increased from 471 to over 1,000, and offer new modern amenities for vessels berthed there. In the province of Savona, high-capacity, well-equipped marinas are to be found at **Andora** (700 berths), **Alassio** (420 berths), **Finale Ligure** (the 590-berth Capo San Donato marina), and at **Varazze**, whose marina has room for 256 boats, including vessels that measure over 25 meters in length.

The big yachts can also be accommodated at Portosole, the main 465-berth marina opposite the Municipal Villa Park in **Sanremo**, a town that also offers the much smaller Capo Pino Marina for 20 boats. 190 boats can find room at the marina and canal port of nearby **Arma di Taggia**, while the Marina degli Aregai, east of **Santo Stefano al Mare**, has berthing facilities for no fewer than 945 boats. Slightly smaller (477 berths), but arguably more charming scenically is the Imperia Mare marina at **Imperia**: it is located behind Borgo Marina, whose architecture reveals its fishing village origins, behind which rises up the Parasio, the picturesque old district on the hill of Porto Maurizio.

Liguria's marinas

Alassio (420 berths) 📩 t. 0182 642516

Andora (700 berths) 📩 t. 0182 88331

Arenzano (165 berths) 📩 t. 010 9125172

Arma di Taggia (190 berths) 📩 t. 0184 476222

Bordighera (287 berths) 📩 t. 0184 266688

Camogli (287 berths) 📩 t. 0185 770032

Chiavari (459 berths) 📩 t. 0185 3161

Diano Marina (270 berths, 320 in summer) 📩 t. 0183 404757-497757

Finale Ligure (590 berths) 📩 t. 019 601697

Foce della Magra (1,640 berths) 📩 t. 0187 28580

Foce della Magra-Marina 3B (150 berths) 📩 t.0187 673391

Genova-Duca degli Abruzzi (470 berths) 📩 t. 010 2411

Genova-Marina Fiera (503 berths) 📩 t. 010 580760-594200

Genova-Sestri Ponente (1,000 berths) 📩 t. 010 2411

Imperia-Porto Maurizio (477 berths) 📩 t. 0183 61555

La Spezia-Porto Integrato Lotti (439 berths) 📩 t. 0187 524218

La Spezia-Porto Turistico (400 berths) 📩 t. 0187 2858

La Spezia-Seno delle Grazie (810 berths) 📩 t. 0187 28580

Lavagna (1,455 berths) 📩 t. 0185 312626

Lerici (1,309 berths) 📩 t. 0187 967346

Loano (471 berths) 📩 t. 019 669727

Monterosso al Mare-Porto di Levante (12 berths) 📩 t. 0187 817319

Monterosso al Mare-Porto di Ponente (45 berths) 📩 t. 0187 28580

Portofino (253 berths) 📩 t. 0185 269040

Portovenere (80 berths) 📩 t. 0187 900618

Rapallo (517 berths) 📩 t. 0185 50583

Rapallo-Porto Turistico Internazionale (376 berths) 📩 t. 0185 6891

Sanremo (465 berths) 📩 t. 0184 505531

Santa Margherita Ligure (700 berths) 📩 t. 0185 287029

Santo Stefano al Mare (945 berths) 📩 t. 0184 486748

Savona (293 berths) 📩 t. 019 386656

Sestri Levante (454 berths) 📩 t. 0185 41295

Varazze (256 berths) 📩 t. 019 95919

Vernazza (105 berths) 📩 t. 0187 821147

The telephone number given is that of the licensee who runs the marina or, in cases where there are several licensees, of the port authority concerned (Maritime Department, Harbor Office, Beach Committee etc.).

Information
for travelers

Where to eat, where to stay, other tourist attractions

The figurehead of a 17th-century galleon in Genoa's old port

Other places: hotels, restaurants, curiosities. Addresses, opening times

This town-by-town compendium of recommended hotels, campsites and holiday camps (together with hostels and tourist boards) indicates the official star classification provided for by the Italian law of 17th May 1983. Restaurants are classified using the traditional Touring Club symbols (on the basis of price, comfort, service and elegance): ⍦⍦⍦ luxury; ⍦⍦ excellent; ⍦⍦ very good; ⍦⍦ good; ⍦ inexpensive.

Some hotels, restaurants, farmhouses and museums listed in this section of the guide offer reductions to TCI members. A complete list of these establishments and institutions is given in an illustrated booklet supplied with the member's pack. Hotels and restaurants which have this arrangement with TCI are also listed in *Guida Alberghi e ristoranti*, the Touring Club Directory of Hotels and Restaurants updated annually and on sale in bookshops, where they are marked with a special symbol. Members who hire cars from Hertz are given favorable rates; for information and bookings call toll-free from Italy on 800868016 (or by mobile phone on 0248233668), specifying the special TCI member's code.

The information given on these pages has been carefully checked before going to press. Nevertheless, since the details given are subject to variations, readers are advised to make a further check before departure. All suggestions and observations are welcome.

Alassio

Page 134 ✉ 17021

ℹ *APT Riviera delle Palme,* Sede Amministrativa Viale Gibb 26, tel. 018264711, fax 0182644690. *IAT Alassio,* Piazza della Libertà 5, tel. 0182647027, fax 0182647874.

Hotels, restaurants, campsites and holiday camps

⍦ **Ambassador.** Corso Europa 64, tel. 0182643957, fax 0182645972. 47 rooms. Facilities for disabled. Air conditioning, elevator; garage, private beach. This extremely pleasant, elegantly-furnished hotel with its characteristic salons and comfortable rooms offers high-quality amenities and a fine restaurant (C1).

⍦ **G.H. Diana.** Via Garibaldi 110, tel. 0182642701, fax 0182640304. 51 rooms. Facilities for disabled. Air conditioning, elevator; parking facilities, garden, indoor pool, private beach. A particularly comfortable hotel by the seashore, with a large terrace and garden; swimming-pool with whirlpool bath (A3).

⍦ **G.H. Beach.** Via Roma 78, tel. 0182643403, fax 0182640279. 89 rooms. Facilities for disabled. Air conditioning, elevator; parking facilities, garden, open-air pool, private beach. A modern, comfortable hotel with piano bar, solarium-terrace and panoramic restaurant (C1).

*** **Beau Sejour.** Via Garibaldi 102, tel. 0182640303, fax 0182646391. Seasonal. 51 rooms. Elevator; parking facilities, garden, private beach. A well-established hotel with a long tradition; regular customers enjoy the special treatment of the family-run establishment (A3).

*** **Enrico.** Corso Dante 368, tel. 0182640000, fax 0182640075. 32 rooms. Air conditioning, elevator; parking facilities, private beach. Right in the center of town, overlooking the Municipal Gardens; lively, much-frequented restaurant (B2).

*** **Lamberti.** Via Gramsci 57, tel. 0182642747, fax 0182642438. 25 rooms. Air conditioning, elevator; parking facilities, garden. A pleasant, simply-designed place to stay, quietly situated very near the sea (A2).

*** **Majestic.** Corso L. da Vinci 300, tel. 0182642721, fax 0182643032. 77 rooms, 76 with own bath or shower. Air conditioning, elevator; parking facilities, private beach. A newly refurbished establishment for a relaxing stay by the sea, thanks among other things to the long experience of the family who run it (C1).

*** **Savoia.** Via Milano 14, tel. 0182640277, fax 0182640125. 35 rooms. Facilities for disabled. Air conditioning, elevator; parking facilities, private beach. A modern seafront establishment with comfortable rooms (A2).

** **Badano sul Mare.** Via Gramsci 36, tel. 0182640964, fax 0182640737. 18 rooms. Elevator; parking facilities, private beach. A comfortable, centrally-situated hotel right by the sea that benefits from the long experience of the family who run it (A2).

⍦⍦ **Palma.** Via Cavour 5, tel. 0182640314. Closed Wednesday, and for a period in November. Air conditioning. Ligurian and Provençale cuisine - fish. A delightful, elegant restaurant that pays careful attention to every detail, from the table settings and expertly-organized wine cellar to the selection of bread and cheeses. Massimo Viglietti keeps a careful watch over proceedings in the dining-room while mother is busy in the kitchen preparing her light but exquisitely-flavored Ligurian recipes, such as ravioli with marjoram and pullet, zucchini and crawfish soup, angler fish with dill, and rabbit with thyme. To follow, a range of delicate puddings and delicious cinnamon sherbet (B2).

¶¶ **La Scogliera.** Passeggiata Ciccione, tel. 0182642815. Closed Monday, and mid-October to mid-December. This restaurant with a large terrace overlooking the sea offers good Ligurian cuisine in a perfect seaside atmosphere; also with its own bathing establishment offering nautical sports (C1, off map).

△ **Monti e Mare-International Resort - P.V.** *** Via Aurelia, km 619.5, tel. 0182643036, fax 0182645601. All year.

🚗 Services and car hire

Hertz. Corso Dante 70, tel. 0182643382.

Albenga

Page 127   ✉ 48102

ℹ️ *IAT Albenga,* Viale Martiri della Libertà 1, tel. 0182558444, fax 0182558740.

🏨 Hotels, restaurants, campsites and holiday camps

*** **La Gallinara.** Via Piave 66, tel. 0182 53086, fax 0182541280. 25 rooms. Elevator. An elegant, comfortable hotel situated away from the center, with marine-style decor and traditional furnishings (B1, off map).

¶¶ **Antica Osteria dei Leoni.** Via M. Lengueglia 49, tel. 018251937. Closed Sunday evening, Monday, for a period between October and November, and in March. Air conditioning. Two elegant dining-rooms in a period building with cross-vaulted ceilings; kitchen on view offering traditional Ligurian seafood as well as inland dishes (A1).

¶¶ **Minisport-Il Pernambucco.** Viale Italia 35, tel. 018253458. Closed Wednesday (in winter), and for a period in October. Air conditioning, parking facilities, garden. Set in a park providing sports and recreational facilities, this pleasant, modern restaurant run by Luciano Alessandri (in the dining-room) and his wife Ivana (in the kitchen) offers the best in local traditional cuisine (B3).

△ **Delfino.** Regione Vadino, Via Aurelia 23, tel. ** 0182555085, fax 018251998. Seasonal.

△ **Green Village - P.V.** Regione Burrone, Viale Che ** Guevara 14, tel. 0182559248, fax 0182554396. Seasonal.

🏛 Museums and cultural institutions

Civico Museo Ingauno. Piazza S. Michele 12, tel. 018251215. Closed Monday. Open: 10am-noon, 4-7pm; winter 10am-noon, 3-6pm.
Museo Diocesano di Arte Sacra. Via Episcopio 5, tel. 018250288. Closed Monday. Open: 10am-noon, 3-6pm.
Museo Navale Romano. Piazza S. Michele 12, tel. 018251215. Closed Monday. Open: 10am-noon, 4-7pm; winter 10am-noon, 3-6pm.

⚖️ Arts and crafts

Sommariva Ancient Olive Press. Via Mameli 7, tel. 0182559222.

🌲 Nature sites, parks and reserves

Gallinara Isle Regional Nature Reserve Authority. C/o Town Hall, Piazza S. Michele 17, tel. 0182541351.

Albisola Marina

Page 117   ✉ 17012

ℹ️ *IAT Albisola,* Corso Ferrari, Passeggiata a mare, tel. 0194002008, fax 0194003084.

🏨 Hotels, restaurants, campsites and holiday camps

☆ **Garden.** Viale Faraggiana 6, tel. 019485253, fax 019485255. 34 rooms. Facilities for disabled. Air conditioning, elevator; parking facilities, garden, open-air pool, private beach. Centrally situated near the beach, the recent, air-conditioned establishment is fully soundproof and equipped with all modern conveniences.

¶¶¶ **Mario-Ai Cacciatori.** Corso Bigliati 70, tel. 019481640. Closed Wednesday, and for a period in September. Air conditioning. Ligurian cuisine. Overlooking the sea with attractive Art Nouveau windows and a large panoramic terrace.

🏛 Museums and cultural institutions

Fabbrica Casa Museo Giuseppe Mazzotti 1903. Viale Matteotti 29, tel. 019489872. Open: 10am-noon, 4-6pm. Also point of sale.
Villa Faraggiana. Via Salomoni 117, tel. 019480622. Closed Tuesday, October-March. Open: 3-7pm.

⚖️ Arts and crafts

Ceramiche San Giorgio. Corso Matteotti 5 r., tel. 019482747. Artistic ceramics.
Porcù Mario. Via dei Ceramisti 46, tel. 019481780. Sculpture workshop.

Albisola Superiore

Page 118   ✉ 17011

ℹ️ *IAT Albisola,* Corso Ferrari, Passeggiata a mare, tel. 0194002008, fax 0194003084.

🏨 Hotels, restaurants, campsites and holiday camps

*** **Park Hotel.** At Albisola Capo, Via Alba Docilia 3, tel. 019482355, fax 019482355. Seasonal. 11 rooms. Air conditioning, garage. A modern, comfortable establishment not far from the beach run by a family with a long experience.

☕ Cafés and pastry shops

Clipper Pub. Corso Mazzini 137, tel. 019480679.
La Taverna di Mu. Via Colombo 65, tel. 019488529.

🏛 Museums and cultural institutions

Museo della Ceramica "Manlio Trucco". Corso Ferrari 193, tel. 019482741. Closed Sunday. Open: 10am-noon; on other days by prior arrangement.

⚖️ Arts and crafts

A cantin-a. Via Poggi 19, tel. 01949262. Production and sale of wines.
Casa dell'Arte. Via Colombo 91, tel. 019484714. Artistic ceramics.
Sandro Soravia. Via Colombo 13, tel. 019485202. Artistic ceramics.
Studio Ernan. Corso Mazzini 77, tel. 019489916. Artistic ceramics.

🚶 Local guides and excursions

Luceto Riding Club. Via Borace, tel. 019480036.

Altare

Page 119   ✉ 17041

ℹ️ *Pro Loco Altare,* Via Roma 69, tel. 019584391.

🏨 Hotels, restaurants, campsites and holiday camps

¶¶ **Quintilio.** Via Gramsci 23, tel. 01958000. Closed

Sunday evenings, Monday and in July. Ligurian-Piedmontese cuisine in a historic establishment with a pleasant atmosphere; reasonably priced.

🏛 Museums and cultural institutions

Museo del Vetro. Piazza S. Sebastiano 1, tel. 019584734. Open: Monday-Friday 3-6pm; on other days by prior arrangement.

⚖ Arts and crafts

Soffieria Artistica Amanzio Bormioli. Via Paleologo 16, tel. 01958254. Glass-making.

Ameglia

Page 198   ✉ 19031
at Montemarcello, 5 km
ℹ *IAT (seas.), Via Nuova 48, tel. 0187600324.*

🏨 Hotels, restaurants, campsites and holiday camps

*** **Paracucchi-Locanda dell'Angelo.** Viale XXV Aprile 60, tel. 018764391, fax 018764393. 37 rooms. Air conditioning, parking facilities, garden, open-air pool. A modern establishment with luminous, comfortable rooms set in the relaxing, leafy environment of Piana di Luni, catering for both vacationers and business people.

*** **River - P.V.** Locality Armezzone, Via Falaschi 23, tel. 018765920, fax 018765183. Seasonal.

at Bocca di Magra, km 4   ✉ 19030
♟ **Lucerna di Ferro.** Via Fabbricotti 126, tel. 0187601206. Closed Monday evenings and Tuesday, December and January. Parking facilities. Ligurian and Tuscan cuisine - fish. Modern, recently-refurbished establishment; the summer terrace over the water offers views of the Magra river estuary and the Apuan Alps; run by a family with a long, well-established tradition.

at Fiumaretta di Ameglia, 4 km
♟♟♟ **Locanda delle Tamerici.** Via Litoranea 106, tel. 018764262, fax 018764627. Closed Wednesday lunchtime (excluding July and August), Tuesday and from Christmas to 6 January. Air conditioning, parking facilities, garden. Romantic setting on the beach a stone's throw from the sea; Ligurian and traditional cuisine of a surprisingly high standard, thanks to the expert, but modest chef Mauro.

🚶 Local guides and excursions

Centro ippico Corte di Camisano. Via Arena 1, tel. 018765323. Excursions on horseback.

Andora

Page 137   ✉ 17020
ℹ *IAT Andora, Via Aurelia 122/a, Villa Laura, tel. 0182681004, fax 0182681807.*

🏨 Hotels, restaurants, campsites and holiday camps

*** **Moresco.** Via Aurelia 96, tel. 018289141, fax 018285414. 35 rooms. Elevator. Well situated on the eastern seafront promenade (access to the beach) with pleasant, functional rooms.

♟♟♟ **Casa del Priore.** Via Castello 34, tel. 0182684377. Closed Monday, and January to mid-February. Parking facilities. Ligurian cuisine. An elegant vaulted restaurant in the medieval town and outdoor area in summer.

♟ **La Palma-da Mario.** Viale Mazzini 34, tel.

0182684794. Closed Monday (in low season), and for a period in November. Air conditioning, garden. Comfortable, modern restaurant run by Mario Vottero. A good selection of local dishes as well as Tuscan and Sicilian specialties; wood-oven pizzeria.

Apricale

Page 166   ✉ 18030
ℹ *Tourist Board, Via Roma 1, tel. 0184208641.*

🏨 Hotels, restaurants, campsites and holiday camps

♟ **Capanna-da Baci.** Via Vittorio Veneto 9, tel. 0184208137. Closed Monday evenings, Tuesday (except in August) and for a period in December. Garden. Ligurian cuisine - fresh pasta, mushrooms. In the historic center, large covered verandah and shady garden (age-old chestnut trees), with panoramic view of the valley.

Àrcola

Page 207   ✉ 18030
ℹ *IAT (seas.), Via Valentini 197, tel. 0187986559.*

⚖ Arts and crafts

Vivaio Salvatore Trio. Via Aurelia Nord 32, tel. 0187986005. Plants.

Arenzano

Page 103   ✉ 16011
ℹ *IAT, Lungomare Kennedy, tel. 0109127581.*

🏨 Hotels, restaurants, campsites and holiday camps

☆ **Grand Hotel.** Lungomare Stati Uniti 2, tel. 01091091, fax 0109109444. 110 rooms. Facilities for disabled. Air conditioning, elevator; parking facilities, garden, open-air pool, tennis, private beach. A completely refurbished early 20th-century building situated on the waterfront near the harbor, offering a wide range of recreational and keep-fit facilities; "La Veranda" is the name of the busy restaurant.

*** **Ena.** Via Matteotti 12, tel. 0109127379, fax 0109123139. 25 rooms. Meublé. Elevator; parking facilities, garden, private beach. An elegant, beautifully refurbished 19th-century waterfront villa; the cellar houses the "Osteria degli Archi" restaurant, run independently of the hotel.

*** **Poggio Hotel.** Via di Francia 24, tel. 0109135320, fax 0109135321. 40 rooms. Facilities for disabled. Elevator; parking facilities, garden, open-air pool. The tranquillity of the countryside within easy reach of the sea, ideal for business meetings and receptions; linked to the separately run "La Buca" restaurant.

♟ **Parodi.** Via Romeo 30, tel. 0109126637. Closed Tuesday (except in August), and for a period in October. Air conditioning. Ligurian and traditional cuisine. Spacious, attractively and comfortably furnished; also a pizzeria.

⚽ Sport

Golf Tennis Club della Pineta. Via del Golf 2, tel. 0109111817.

⚖ Arts and crafts

Florliguria. Via Francia 31, tel. 0109133836. Flowers.
Vetreria Arenzanese (glass-making). Via Pian Masino 25, tel. 0109111726.

Arma di Taggia

Page 218 ⊠ 18011
ℹ️ *IAT*, Villa Boselli tel. 018443733.

🏨Hotels, restaurants, campsites and holiday camps

⁂ **Vittoria Grattacielo.** Via S. Erasmo 1, tel. 018443495, fax 0184448578. 77 rooms. Facilities for disabled. Air conditioning, elevator; parking facilities, garden, private beach. Large complex equipped with a wide range of facilities; open-air seawater pool.

🍴 **Conchiglia.** Via Lungomare 33, tel. 018443169. Closed Wednesday, and for periods in November and June. Air conditioning, sophisticated Ligurian cuisine. An elegant waterfront restaurant in an old pink fisherman's house with vaulted ceiling and simple furnishings. Excellent fresh fish, comprehensive wine list, impeccable service.

Bajardo

Page 154 ⊠ 18031
ℹ️ *Pro Loco*, c/o Town Hall. Via Roma, tel. 0184673054.

🏛 Museums and cultural institutions

Pinacoteca Civica. Via Roma 58. Visits by prior arrangement, tel. 0184673054.

Bergeggi

Page 119 ⊠ 17042
ℹ️ *IAT Bergeggi* (seas.), Via Aurelia, tel. and fax 019859777.

🦅 Nature sites, parks and reserves

Regional Nature Reserve Board. C/o Town Hall, Via De Mari 28, tel. 019257901.

Bogliasco

Page 98 ⊠ 16031
ℹ️ *Pro Loco*, Via Aurelia 106, tel. 0103470429.

🏨Hotels, restaurants, campsites and holiday camps

🍴 **Il Tipico.** At San Bernardo, Via Poggio Favaro 20, tel. 0103470754. Closed Monday, and for periods in January and August. Air conditioning. A spacious room decorated in nautical style with a splendid panorama of Paradise Bay, traditional cuisine prepared with imaginative flair.

Bonassola

Page 202 ⊠ 19011
ℹ️ *IAT*, Via Fratelli Rezzano, tel. 0187813500, fax 0187813529.

🏨Hotels, restaurants, campsites and holiday camps

*** **Delle Rose.** Via Garibaldi 8, tel. 0187813713, fax 0187814268. 27 rooms. Elevator. Near the beach, modern, functional, suites also available; meticulously run by a family.

🛖 **La Francesca.** Locality La Francesca, tel.
⁂ 0187813911, fax 01878139108. All year.

Bordighera

Page 152 ⊠ 18012
ℹ️ *IAT*, Via Vittorio Emanuele II 172-174, tel. 0184262322.

🏨Hotels, restaurants, campsites and holiday camps

⁂ **G.H. del Mare**. Via Portico della Punta 34, tel. 0184262201, fax 0184262394. 107 rooms. Facilities for disabled. Air conditioning, elevator; parking facilities, garden, open-air pool, tennis, private beach. Large complex overlooking the sea, spacious roof garden always in bloom. Extremely comfortable (suites available), efficient congress service, new keep-fit and beauty center (A3, off map).

*** **Astoria.** Via T. Tasso 2, tel. 0184262906, fax 0184261612. 24 rooms. Elevator; parking facilities, garden, private beach. Refined atmosphere, beautiful furnishings, set in a fine garden with palm trees and flowers (A2).

*** **Bordighera & Terminus.** Corso Italia 21, tel. 0184260561, fax 0184266200. 26 rooms. Elevator. Pleasant hotel with an ancient tradition, quietly situated, not far from the sea and the train station; evening meals served outdoors in summer with barbecue (B2).

🍴 **La Via Romana.** Via Romana 57, tel. 0184266681, fax 0184267549. Closed Wednesday, Thursday lunch, and for a period in October. Air conditioning. Mediterranean cuisine - fish. Arriving at this sumptuously elegant restaurant along the "Via Romana" is part of the treat. Great care and expertise is lavished on the fish specialties. Meticulous, professional service; excellent wine list (A2).

🍴 **Carletto**. Via Vittorio Emanuele 339, tel. 0184261725. Closed Wednesday, for a period in July and between November and December. Air conditioning. Refined Ligurian cuisine - John Dory with duck's liver and braised onions. Elegant and sophisticated, with large windows. Seafood specialties with occasional concessions to Provençale cuisine; a wide range of fine wines (B1, off map).

🍴 **La Reserve.** Via Arziglia 20, tel. 0184261322. Closed Sunday evenings and Monday in low season, and in November. Parking facilities. A restaurant with a beautiful atmosphere with plenty of light thanks to the large window overlooking the sea. During the warmer months the typical Ligurian seafood and inland dishes are served out on the fine terrace (B3).

🍴 **Piemontese.** Via Roseto 8, tel. 0184261651. Closed Tuesday, and for a period between November and December. In summer, Ligurian cuisine (mostly fish); in winter, traditional Piedmontese fare (B1).

🛖 **Baia la Ruota.** Via Madonna della Ruota 34,
⁂ tel. 0184265222, fax 0184262290. All year.

🍷Cafés and pastry shops

Bar John Silver. Via Vittorio Emanuele II 229, tel. 0184260476.
Graffiti Pub. Via Vittorio Emanuele II 122, tel. 0184261590.

🏛 Museums and cultural institutions

Biblioteca Museo Clarence Bicknell. Via Bicknell 3, tel. 0184263694. Closed Saturday and Sunday. Open: 9.30-13, 13.30-16.45.
Mostra Permanente Pompeo Mariani. Via Romana 39, tel. 0184263601. Closed Saturday and Sunday. Open: 10am-noon, 3-5pm.

🎭 Shows and other festivities

Salone dell'Umorismo. Cartoons and Humorous Writing Competition and Exhibition; last week in July and throughout August.

⚖️Arts and crafts

Berro Porcellane e Cristallerie. Via Vittorio

Emanuele 50, t. 0184260687. Porcelain and crystalware.

Borgio Verezzi

Page 124   ✉ 17022
ℹ️ *IAT Borgio Verezzi* (seas.), Via Matteotti 158, tel. and fax 019610412.

🏨 Hotels, restaurants, campsites and holiday camps

🍴 **Doc.** At Borgio, Via Vittorio Veneto 1, tel. 019611477. Closed Monday, variable holiday closure. Parking facilities, garden. Sophisticated Ligurian cuisine. In an early 20th-century villa with traditional furnishings and a large garden, an "authentic" establishment serving carefully prepared local seasonal dishes.

🏃 Shows and other festivities

Theater Festival. A variety of shows and plays; in July and August.

Borzonasca

Page 186   ✉ 16041
ℹ️ *Pro Loco* (seas.), Piazza Severino 1, tel. 0185340433.

🐟 Nature sites, parks and reserves

Aveto Regional Nature Park Authority. Via Marré 75/A, tel. 0185340311, e-mail parco.aveto@comunic.it.

Busalla

Page 105   ✉ 16012
⚖️ Arts and crafts

Fabbrica Birra Busalla. tel. 0109640161. Brewery that makes and sells beer.

🐟 Nature sites, parks and reserves

Antola Regional Nature Park Authority. Via XXV Aprile 17, tel. 0109761014, e-mail antola@libero.it.

Calizzano

Page 126   ✉ 17020
ℹ️ *IAT Calizzano* (seas.), Piazza San Rocco, tel. 01979193.

🏨 Hotels, restaurants, campsites and holiday camps

🍴 **Msè Tutta.** Via Garibaldi 8, tel. 01979647. Closed Monday, variable holiday closure. Ligurian cuisine. Delightful locanda with a homey feel, where Maria Grazia serves her refined, exquisite dishes prepared fresh every day following the seasonal patterns: spinach beet, mushrooms, nettle and borage ravioli, roast goose. Excellent sweets and a good choice of wines recommended by Alessandro.

⚓ **Laghetti - P.V.** Via Carisciano 12, tel. 01979659, fax 01979175. Seasonal.
**

⚖️ Arts and crafts

Barberis funghi. Via Pera 40, tel. 01979642. Mushrooms.

Camogli

Page 174   ✉ 16032
ℹ️ *IAT,* Via XX Settembre 33, tel. 0185771066.

🏨 Hotels, restaurants, campsites and holiday camps

₊₊* **Cenobio dei Dogi.** Via Cuneo 34, tel. 01857241, fax 0185772796. 107 rooms. Meublé. Facilities for disabled. Air conditioning, elevator; parking facilities, garden, open-air pool, tennis, private beach. This comfortable hotel, once a doge's palace, is beautifully situated between a large park and the sea; views over Paradise Bay.

** **La Camogliese.** Via Garibaldi 55, tel. 0185771402, fax 0185774024. 16 rooms. Meublé. Parking facilities. A friendly, family-run establishment overlooking the sea; independently-run restaurant in the immediate vicinity.

🍴 **Rosa.** Largo Casabona 11, tel. 0185773411, fax 0185771088. Closed Tuesday, for a period between January and February, and in November. Ligurian cuisine. Art Nouveau villa with terrace and verandah-cum- winter garden, with excellent views over Paradise Bay. Truly fresh meals thanks to the plentiful supply of local fish.

at San Rocco, 6 km   ✉ 16030
🍴 **La Cucina di Nonna Nina.** Via Molfino 126, tel. 0185773835. Closed Wednesday. Air conditioning. Liguria's famous traditional cuisine, in a little town. One dish not to miss: "trofie" (spindle-shaped pasta) with nettles, pesto and quail.

🚗 Services and car hire

Trasporti Turistici Marittimi Golfo Paradiso. Via Scalo 3, tel. 0185772091 (boat rides to Punta Chiappa and San Fruttuoso).

🏛 Museums and cultural institutions

Museo marinaro Gio Bono Ferrari. Via Ferrari 41, tel. 0185729049. Closed Tuesday. Open: 9-11.45am, 3-5.40pm; Wednesday, Saturday and Sunday 9am-noon.

at San Fruttuoso
Abbazia di S. Fruttuoso di Capodimonte. Via S. Fruttuoso 12, tel. 0185772703. Closed Monday. Open: 10am-3.45pm; May-September 10am-6pm.

🏃 Shows and other festivities

Fish Festival. Distribution of pan-fried fish; second Sunday in May.

at Punta Chiappa
"Stella Maris" Festival. Procession of boats; first Sunday in August.

at San Fruttuoso
Submerged Christ Ceremony. Flowers laid at the feet of the submerged statue; last Sunday in July.

Campo Ligure

Page 103   ✉ 16013
ℹ️ *IAT* (seas.), Via della Giustizia 5, tel. 010921055.

🏛 Museums and cultural institutions

Museo della Filigrana (Filigree Museum). Via della Giustizia 5. Closed Monday. Open: 3.30-6pm; Saturday and Sunday 9.30am-noon, 3.30-6pm.

⚖️ Arts and crafts

Bongera Filigrana. Via Saracco 1, tel. 010921067.
F.P. Fabbrica Filigrana. Via Don Minzoni 47, tel. 010920850.

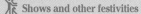

Il Gioiello. Via Saracco 29, tel. 010921176 (filigree work).
Rizzo Filigrana. Via Saracco 23, tel. 010921172.

 Local guides and excursions

Prato Rondanino Riding Center. Via Valle Ponzema Superiore 90, tel. 0109270068.

Campomorone

Page 105   ☒ 16014

🏛 Museums and cultural institutions

Museo Civico di Paleontologia e Mineralogia. Via Gavino 144, tel. 010781630. Closed Saturday and Sunday. Open: 9am-noon and 2.30-5.30pm, Wednesday 9am-noon.
Museo della Croce Rossa Italiana (Red Cross Museum). Via Cavallieri 14, tel. 010783694. Open: Tuesday, Thursday 3.30-5.30pm; Saturday 3-6pm; Sunday 10am-noon.
Museo delle Marionette (puppets). Via Gavino 144, tel. 010781630. Closed Wednesday, Saturday and Sunday. Open: 9am-noon, 2.30-5.30pm.

Camporosso

Page 162   ☒ 18030
ℹ️ Pro Loco, Corso Repubblica, tel. 0184288037.

🏨 Hotels, restaurants, campsites and holiday camps

🍴 **Gino.** At Camporosso Mare, Via Braie 10, tel. 0184291493. Closed Tuesday (Monday in July and August), and periods in February and between June and July. Parking facilities. Ligurian and traditional cuisine. Classy, professional family-run restaurant; wide range of Italian and French wines. Evenings only in July and August (except Sunday); lunchtime only September to June (except Saturday).

⚖ **Helios - P.V.** At Camporosso Mare, Via Dante Alighieri 1, tel. 0184251762, fax 0184256330. All year.
**

🌲 Farm holidays

Il Bausco. Locality Brunetti, tel. 0184206013. Accommodation in two farmhouses. Bike trips; sale of oil, wine, fruit and vegetables.

⚖ Arts and crafts

Foresti. Via Braie 223, tel. 0184292377. Production and sale of wines.

Carpasio

Page 158   ☒ 18010

🏛 Museums and cultural institutions

Museo Partigiano (history of partisan movement). Costa di Carpasio. Closed November-March. Open: Saturday, Sunday 10am-6pm; by prior arrangement, tel. 0183650755.

Castelnuovo Magra

Page 206   ☒ 19030
ℹ️ IAT, c/o Town Hall, tel. 0187675394.

🏨 Hotels, restaurants, campsites and holiday camps

🍴 **Armanda.** Piazza Garibaldi 6, tel. 0187674410. Closed Wednesday, from Christmas to 6 January, and for a period in June. Air conditioning. Ligurian

cuisine - mushrooms. Typical trattoria with just one room and a few tables, but the menu is excellent: most customers are keen to return.

⚖ **Ippotur.** At Molicciara, locality Molino del Piano, tel. 0187674592, fax 0187674592. All year.
***

🌲 Farm holidays

Cascina dei Peri. Via Montefrancio 71, tel. 0187674085. Vacation in the hills among olive groves, orchards and bougainvillea. Swimmingpool. Sale of d.o.c. wine and extra-virgin olive oil.

🏛 Museums and cultural institutions

Enoteca Pubblica della Liguria e della Lunigiana (Public Winery). Palazzo Ingolotti, Via V. Veneto 1, tel. 0187675394, fax 0187670102.

 Local guides and excursions

Colline del Sole riding stables. Via Olmarello, tel. 0187671660/03383594302.

Celle Ligure

Page 117   ☒ 17015
ℹ️ IAT Celle Ligure, Via Boagno, Palazzo Comunale, tel. 019990021, fax 0199999798.

🏨 Hotels, restaurants, campsites and holiday camps

🍴 **L'Acqua Dolce.** Via L. Pescetto 5/A, tel. 019994222. Closed Tuesday, and Wednesday lunchtime; variable holiday closure. Air conditioning. Sophisticated cuisine. An elegant restaurant with a warm atmosphere in an early 19th-century waterfront building; light, meticulously prepared dishes, including many fish specialties; good selection of Italian wines.

🌲 Farm holidays

at Sanda, 4 km
Colombo. Via Camprevi 18, tel. 019993120. In the hills amid olive groves. Seasonal farm produce; walks and excursions organized.

⚖ Arts and crafts

Ceramiche Il Tondo. Via Arecco 35, tel. 019993651. Artistic ceramics.
D'Aquino Luigi. Via Aicardi 33, tel. 019994002. Paintings and ceramics; miniature ceramic houses.
Enocolumbus. Via degli Artigiani 96, tel. 019993436. Wines.

 Local guides and excursions

Riding stables. Via Bolano 14, tel. 019994245.

Ceriale

     ☒ 17023
ℹ️ IAT Ceriale, Piazza Nuova Italia 1, Palazzo Comunale, tel. 0182993007, fax 0182993804.

🏨 Hotels, restaurants, campsites and holiday camps

⚖ **Il Paese di Ciribì.** Via Privata Le Caravelle, tel. 0182992411, fax 0182992411. Seasonal.
**

🦅 Nature sites, parks and reserves

Rio Torsero Regional Nature Reserve. C/o Town Hall, Piazza Nuova Italia 1, tel. 0182990024.

🎡 Amusement parks

Le Caravelle. Via S. Eugenio 51, tel.

0182931755/931991, fax 0182931471, e-mail info@lecaravelle.com, website www.lecaravelle.com. Open: 3 June-3 September 10am-7pm, holidays in July and August 10am-10pm. The only aqua fun park in Liguria.

Ceriana

Page 154   ☒ 18010
ⓘ *c/o Town Hall*, Corso Italia 141, tel. 0184551017.

🏃 Shows and other festivities
Holy Week. Procession with sacred medieval and baroque chants.
Earth music. Traditional world music. First weekend in September.

Cervo

Page 144   ☒ 18010
ⓘ *IAT ,* Piazza Santa Caterina 21, tel. 0183408197.

🏨 Hotels, restaurants, campsites and holiday camps
🍴 *San Giorgio.* Via A. Volta 19, tel. 0183400175. Closed Tuesday lunchtime in July and August, and for periods in January and between November and December. Air conditioning. Ligurian cuisine. Attractive restaurant, with food served on terrace overlooking the sea in summer; excellent fish and mushrooms dishes. Apartments available.
ⓜ *Capo Mimosa - P.V.* A Capo Mimosa, Via
** Aurelia 1, tel. 0183408155, fax 0183408156. All year.

🏛 Museums and cultural institutions
Museo Etnografico del Ponente Ligure (Ethnography Museum). Piazza S. Caterina 2, tel. 0183408197. Open: 9-6.30pm; summer 9am-12.30pm, 4-7.30pm, open evenings by prior arrangement.
Museo dell'Olio "U Gumbu" (Oil Museum). Via Matteotti 31, tel. 0183408149. Visits by prior arrangement.

🏃 Shows and other festivities
International Chamber Music Festival. July and August.

Chiavari

Page 181   ☒ 16043
ⓘ *IAT,* Corso Assarotti 1, tel. 0185325198.

🏨 Hotels, restaurants, campsites and holiday camps
*** *Monte Rosa.* Via Marinetti 6, tel. 0185300321, fax 0185312868. 70 rooms. Elevator; garage. In the medieval center, elegant ancient building with busy restaurant (A2).
*** *Torino.* Corso Colombo 151, tel. 0185312231, fax 0185312233. 33 rooms. Meublé. Garage. Modern waterfront hotel, with comfortable rooms (B2).
🍴 *Lord Nelson Pub.* Corso Valparaiso 25, tel. 0185302595, fax 0185310397. Closed Wednesday (except in July and August), and for a period in November. Traditional cuisine - fish. A restaurant in a 19th-century building with an old English nautical atmosphere. Good verandah overlooking the sea; suites available upstairs (A1).

🍴 *Armia.* Corso Garibaldi 68, tel. 0185305441. Closed Wednesday, and for a period in November. Ligurian cuisine - grilled meat. A restaurant near the roundabout at the seaward end of the street, with a small dining-room upstairs and a larger room below; traditional cuisine (B2).

☕ Cafés and pastry shops
Caffè Defilla. Corso Garibaldi 4, tel. 0185309829. Ice-cream and pastries in a shop dating back to 1883.

🏛 Museums and cultural institutions
Biblioteca della Società Economica. Via Ravaschieri 15, tel. 0185363275. Closed Sunday and Monday. Open: 9am-noon, 3-6pm; Saturday 10am-noon. Visits to the art gallery by prior arrangement.
Museo Archeologico per la Preistoria e la Protostoria del Tigullio. Via Costaguta 4, tel. 0185320829. Closed Monday and 2nd and 4th Sunday of the month. Open: 9am-1.30pm.
Museo Diocesano. Piazza Nostra Signora dell'Orto 7, tel. 0185314651. Open: Wednesday and Sunday 10am-noon.
Museo Garaventa. Via Ravaschieri 15, tel. 0185324713. Visits by prior arrangement, Saturday 10am-noon.
Museo Storico. Via Ravaschieri 15, tel. 0185324713. Visits by prior arrangement, Saturday 10am-noon.
Pinacoteca Civica (Art Gallery). Via Costaguta 2, tel. 0185365404. Open: Saturday and Sunday 10am-noon, 4-7pm.

⚖ Arts and crafts
Fratelli Levaggi. Via Parma 469, tel. 0185383092. Hand-made chairs.
S.A.C. Via Bancalari 60, tel. 0185305551. Hand-made chairs.

🏛 Markets and fairs
Antiques show-sale. Every second weekend of the month in Via Martiri della Liberazione.

Cogoleto

Page 103   ☒ 16016

🏨 Hotels, restaurants, campsites and holiday camps
🍴 *Gustin.* Piazza Stella Maris 7, tel. 0109181925. Closed Wednesday, and for a period in February and November. Parking facilities, garden. This spacious hotel by the sea and with garden boasts a long family tradition; the restaurant serves beautifully-prepared Ligurian cuisine, with a good selection of wines.

Deiva Marina

Page 203   ☒ 19013
ⓘ *IAT,* Lungomare Colombo 1, tel. 0187826136.

🏨 Hotels, restaurants, campsites and holiday camps
*** *Caravella.* Via Colombo 1, tel. 0187815833, fax 0187825551. 21 rooms. Private beach. An old train station building transformed into a comfortable hotel right by the sea.
*** *Clelia.* Corso Italia 23, tel. 0187815827, fax 0187816234. 24 rooms. Elevator; parking facilities, garden, open-air pool, private beach. Typical Ligurian building in a leafy setting near the sea, with comfortable rooms: the food is prepared by the owners themselves. Outbuilding with holiday apartments.

Diano Marina

Page 142   ✉ 18013
ℹ *IAT*, Piazza Martiri della Libertà 1, tel. 0183496956.

🏨 Hotels, restaurants, campsites and holiday camps

★⚑ **Bellevue et Méditerranée.** Via Ardoino 2, tel. 01834093, fax 0183409385. 70 rooms. Facilities for disabled. Elevator; parking lot and garage facilities, open-air pool, private beach. A tastefully furnished hotel right by the sea; the elevator leads to the private beach.

★⚑ **G.H. Diana Majestic.** Via degli Oleandri 15, tel. 0183402727, fax 0183403040. Seasonal. 82 rooms. Facilities for disabled. Elevator; parking lot, garage, open-air pool, private beach. This quiet hotel, which opens directly onto its own beach and is thus ideal for children, is set in grounds filled with age-old olive trees; the rooms have sea-view balconies.

★★★ **Caravelle.** Via Sausette 24, tel. 0183405311, fax 0183405657. Seasonal. 58 rooms. Elevator; parking lot, garage, garden, open-air pool, tennis, private beach. Modern, well-equipped hotel in a leafy setting right by the sea.

★★★ **Golfo e Palme.** Viale Torino 12, tel. 0183495096, fax 0183494304. Seasonal. 41 rooms. Elevator; parking facilities, garden, private beach. Modern, comfortable, professionally-run hotel, pleasantly situated by the seashore.

⊩⊩ **Caminetto.** Via Olanda 1, tel. 0183494700. Closed Monday, and for a period between January and February. Parking facilities, garden. Ligurian cuisine. Not far from the train station; lunch is also served on the verandah (sea specialties).

⚑⚑ **Edy - P.V.** Via Diano Calderina, tel. 0183497040, fax 0183494680. All year.

⚑⚑ **Marino - P.V.** Via S. Novaro 3, tel. 0183498288, fax 0183494680. All year.

🏛 Museums and cultural institutions

Museo Civico della "Communitas Diani". Corso Garibaldi. Closed for restoration.

🏃 Shows and other festivities

Corpus Christi Flower Display. Procession through the flower-decked town center.

Dolceàcqua

Page 163   ✉ 18035
ℹ *IAT*, Via Barberis Colomba 3, tel. 0184206666.

🏨 Hotels, restaurants, campsites and holiday camps

⊩⊩ **Gastone.** Piazza Garibaldi 2, tel. 0184206577. Closed Monday evening and Tuesday, variable holiday closure. Garden. In the shady square opposite the Doria castle, a journey of discovery into the unknown delights of this valley's Ligurian specialties; good selection of wines.

🌲 Farm holidays

Rifugio Alta Via. Regione Pozzuolo, Strada La Colla-Gouta. tel. 0184206754. Accommodation in the rooms of a stone house with panoramic view. Wine, oil and honey sold.

Terre Bianche. At Arcagna, tel. 018431426. Accommodation in an ancient farmhouse with excellent panoramic view. Walks and horse riding; wine, oil and preserves sold.

⚒ Arts and crafts

Cantina del Rossese. Via Roma 33, tel. 0184 206180. Production and sale of the local wine Rossese.

Finale Ligure

Page 122   ✉ 17024
ℹ *IAT Finale Ligure*, Via S. Pietro 14, tel 019681019, fax 019681804.

🏨 Hotels, restaurants, campsites and holiday camps

★⚑ **Punta Est.** Via Aurelia 1, tel. 019600611, fax 019600611. Seasonal. 39 rooms. Elevator; parking facilities, garden, open-air pool, private beach. Exclusive but friendly hotel (an 18th-century villa and a modern building) in its own grounds high up over the sea (A3).

★★★ **Internazionale.** Via Concezione 3, tel. 019692054, fax 019692053. 32 rooms. Parking facilities, private beach. Pleasantly situated on the seafront promenade, equipped with all modern conveniences, this hotel is guaranteed to provide a pleasant stay at any time of the year (B1).

★★★ **Miramare.** Via S. Pietro 9, tel. 019692467, fax 019695467. 35 rooms. Facilities for disabled. Air conditioning, elevator; private beach. A refined, professionally-run waterfront hotel, with a bright, modern interior (B2).

⊩⊩⊩ **Ai Torchi.** At Finalborgo, Via dell'Annunziata 12, tel. 019690531. Closed Monday (in winter), Tuesday (except in August), and for a period between January and February. Ligurian and traditional cuisine - fish. Elegantly situated in an old (16th century) olive mill. (B1, off map).

⊩ **Osteria della Briga.** At Le Manie, tel. 019698579. Closed Tuesday and Wednesday, January. Parking facilities, garden. This restaurant, in a leafy setting, shows another side of Ligurian cuisine, since it specializes in grilled meat (A3, off map).

⚑⚑⚑ **Eurocamping Calvisio - P.V.** Locality Calvisio 37, tel. 019600491, fax 019601240. Seasonal.

⚑⚑ **San Martino - P.V.** At Varigotti, Via Manie 32, tel. 019698250, fax 019698698. All year.

🏠 Youth hostels

Wuillermin. Via Generale Caviglia 46, tel. 019690515. Open mid-March to mid-October.

🏛 Museums and cultural institutions

Civico Museo del Finale. Cloisters of Santa Caterina, tel. 019690020. Closed Monday and in January. Open: 9am-noon, 2.30-4.30pm; June-September 10am-noon, 3-6pm; Sunday 9am-noon.

🏃 Shows and other festivities

Marquisate Festival. Race and historical pageant; second Sunday in July.

Framura

Page 203   ✉ 19014
ℹ *IAT* (seas.), Via Setta 41, tel. 0187823004.

🏨 Hotels, restaurants, campsites and holiday camps

⚑⚑ **Valdeiva - P.V.** Locality Ronco, tel. 0187824174, fax 0187825352. Annual.

at Fornaci, 12 km   ✉ 19013
★⚑ **Lido.** tel. 0187815997, fax 0187816476. Seasonal. 12 rooms. Parking facilities, garden, private beach. This small, but meticulously-run hotel near Deiva Marina could hardly be nearer to the sea.

🌲 Farm holidays

at Castagnola, 4 km
La Caprarbia. Le Fosse, tel. 0187824282.

Apartments and rooms in a villa with arcades and terraces; tents and mobile homes welcome. Vegetables and honey sold.

Garlenda

Page 138   ☒ 17033
🛈 *IAT Garlenda* (seas.), Via Roma 4, tel. 0182582114.

🏨🍴 Hotels, restaurants, campsites and holiday camps

⁣ **La Meridiana.** Via ai Castelli 11, tel. 0182580271, fax 0182580150. Seasonal. 34 rooms. Facilities for disabled. Elevator; parking facilities, garden, open-air pool. Near the tourist airport in a charming country setting that is a golfer's paradise. All comforts provided, sports and cultural events. Traditional fare served with style and expertise.

✓ Sport

Golf Club Garlenda. Via del Golf 7, tel. 0182580012.

Genoa

Page 43   ☒ 16100
🛈 *Regional Tourism Promotion Board "in Liguria"*, Palazzo Ducale, Piazza Matteotti, tel. 0105308201, e-mail info.inliguria@liguriainrete.it.
APT Genova, Via Roma 11, tel. 010576791, website www.apt.genova.it, e-mail aptgenova @apt.genova.it.
IAT, Cristoforo Colombo Airport, Via Pionieri e Aviatori d'Italia, tel. 0106015247.
IAT, Palazzina S. Maria, Via al Porto Antico, tel. 010248711.
IAT, Porta Principe Train Station, Piazza Acquaverde, tel. 0102462633.
IAT, Cruise Terminal, Stazione Marittima (seas.), Ponte dei Mille, tel. 0102463686.
Touring Viaggi. Palazzo Ducale, Piazza Matteotti, tel. 0105955299.

🏨🍴 Hotels, restaurants, campsites and holiday camps

⁣ **Bristol Palace.** Via XX Settembre 35, tel. 010592541, fax 010561756. 133 rooms. Meublé. Facilities for disabled. Air conditioning, elevator; parking facilities. An elegant (and now refurbished) 19th-building in the heart of the city, with pleasant comfortable rooms. Suites available (II, D4).

⁣ **Britannia.** Via Balbi 38, tel. 01026991, fax 0102462942. 83 rooms. Meublé. Air conditioning, elevator; parking facilities. Efficient and extremely comfortable, just 50 yards from the terminal. The hotel offers fourteen highly elegant suites available. (II, B2).

⁣ **City.** Via S. Sebastiano 6, tel. 01055451, fax 010586301. 64 rooms. Meublé. Air conditioning, elevator; garage. Centrally situated, refurbished, modern and extremely comfortable, this hotel offers several comfortable suites and congress facilities; linked to the independently-run "Le Rune" restaurant (I, C3).

⁣ **Jolly Hotel Plaza.** Via M. Piaggio 11, tel. 01083161, fax 0108391850. 142 rooms. Facilities for disabled. Air conditioning, elevator; parking facilities. Offers the same high standard of service as comfort as all hotels belonging to the chain. With Villetta di Negro restaurant (II, C4-5).

⁣ **Jolly Marina.** Via Gramsci, tel. 800-017703. 140 rooms. Facilities for disabled. Air conditioning,

elevator; garage. Situated in the charming docks area of the Old Port, overlooking the Aquarium, an ultra-modern, high-tech establishment, inaugurated in 2000, with views of the cruise liners leaving and arriving in the busy port (II, C3).

⁣ **Moderno Verdi.** Piazza G. Verdi 5, tel. 0105532104, fax 010581562. 87 rooms. Facilities for disabled. Air conditioning, elevator; garage. This very friendly hotel outside Brignole train station offers an extremely high standard of comfort and meeting rooms; in operation since 1926, it has some fine communal rooms and a small inner patio (II, D6).

⁣ **Novotel Genova Ovest.** Via Cantore 8/C, tel. 01064841, fax 0106484844. 223 rooms. Facilities for disabled. Air conditioning; parking facilities, open-air pool. This modern, strategically located complex with comfortable bedrooms and also meeting rooms caters for both business guests and families. The "La Terrazza" restaurant offers Ligurian and other types of cuisine (III, B2).

⁣ **Savoia Majestic.** Via Arsenale di Terra 5, tel. 0102464132, fax 010261883. 120 rooms. Facilities for disabled. Air conditioning, elevator; parking facilities. Near Porta Principe train station, the Old Port and the sea terminal. Modern, comfortable rooms, suitable for meetings and congresses (II, A2).

⁣ **Sheraton Genova.** Via Pionieri e Aviatori d'Italia, tel. 01065491, fax 0106549004. 284 rooms. Facilities for disabled. Air conditioning, elevator; parking facilities. A recently-built hotel near the airport, offering extremely comfortable rooms and suites, multi-functional congress center, busy Il Portico restaurant (I, B1, off map).

⁣ **Starhotel President.** Corte Lambruschini 4, tel. 0105727, fax 0105531820. 193 rooms. Facilities for disabled. Air conditioning, elevator; garage. Situated in the new business district, next to Brignole train station, a modern, functional complex which offers business clientele executive rooms with fax and modem access; busy La Corte restaurant (II, D6).

⁣ **Torre Cambiaso.** Via Scarpanto 49, Pegli, tel. 010665236, fax 0106973022. 46 rooms. Facilities for disabled. Air conditioning, parking facilities, garden, open-air pool. Situated on the Pegli hills overlooking the sea and set in leafy grounds complete with ornamental lake and grottoes, it combines the charming atmosphere of the ancient noble residence it once was with the modern facilities and services that make it ideal also for receptions and meetings (III, B1, off map).

*** **Alexander.** Via Bersaglieri d'Italia 19/r, tel. 010261371, fax 010265257. 35 rooms. Meublé. Air conditioning, elevator; parking facilities. In a panoramic area with a fine view over the port, a traditional Genoese meublé hotel offering a good standard of overall comfort (II, B2).

*** **Europa.** Vico delle Monachette 8, tel. 010256955, fax 010261047. 38 rooms. Meublé. Air conditioning, elevator; parking facilities. A stone's throw from Porta Principe train station, this meublé hotel has its own private parking lot and a panoramic terrace (II, B2).

*** **Galles.** Via Bersaglieri d'Italia 13, tel. 0102462820, fax 0102462822. 20 rooms. Meublé. Facilities for disabled. Air conditioning, elevator; parking facilities. Opposite the maritime station, a modern, well-equipped and comfortable hotel run with care and attention to detail (II, B2).

*** **Metropoli.** Piazza Fontane Marose, tel. 0102468888, fax 0102468686. 45 rooms. Meublé.

Air conditioning, elevator; parking facilities. In the heart of the city within easy reach of the Aquarium and the Opera House, this meublé hotel caters for guests in town for business or pleasure (I, B3).

*** *Viale Sauli.* Viale Sauli 5, tel. 010561397, fax 010590092. 56 rooms. Meublé. Air conditioning, elevator; parking facilities. A well-equipped, comfortable meublé hotel, located in the area between downtown Genoa and Brignole train station (II, D5).

ℍℍ *Antica Osteria del Bai.* Via Quarto 12, Quarto dei Mille, tel. 010387478, fax 010392684. Closed Monday, and for periods in January and in August. Air conditioning. This historic establishment, elegant and refined, occupies a splendid waterfront location. Gianni Malagoli offers the best Ligurian fish and seafood dishes (III, C6, off map).

ℍℍ *Edilio.* Corso De Stefanis 104, tel. 010880501. Closed Monday, and for a period in August. Air conditioning, parking facilities. Ligurian and Piedmontese cuisine. Close to the Luigi Ferraris soccer stadium, it has two well equipped communal rooms for its sporting and other clientele (III, A4).

ℍℍ *Gran Gotto.* Viale Brigata Bisagno 69/R, tel. 010564344. Closed Saturday lunchtime, Sunday, and for a period in August. Air conditioning. Refined Ligurian cuisine. This ancient osteria, (the name "gran gotto" refers to the big tankard on the old sign) is a refined establishment in which Sergio, Paolo and Riccardo Bertola continue the tradition of gourmet food and drink for which they are so well known (II, E6).

ℍℍ *La Bitta nella Pergola.* Via Casaregis 52, tel. 010588543. Closed Sunday evening, Monday, and for periods in January and August. Air conditioning, parking facilities. Elegant, nautical atmosphere; flavorful, beautifully presented food; extensive wine list and choice of desserts; private dining room available; a eritifs and appetizers offered (II, F6).

ℍℍ *Saint Cyr.* Piazza Marsala 4, tel. 010886897, fax 010815039. Closed Sunday and Saturday lunchtime, Christmas-New Year and for a period in August. Air conditioning, parking facilities. Ligurian and Piedmontese cuisine. This restaurant, with its three charming wood-paneled rooms, has a long, well-established tradition (II, C5).

ℍℍ *Zeffirino.* Via XX Settembre 20, tel. 010591990, fax 010586464. Air conditioning, parking facilities. Ligurian and traditional cuisine. This restaurant near the Ponte Monumentale is famous for the Genoese pesto one of the Belloni brothers prepares for the Pope or for personalities from the world of show business and politics (II, D5).

ℍ *Baldin.* Piazza Tazzoli 20/r, Sestri Ponente, tel. 0106531400. Closed Sunday, Monday evening, and for periods in January and August. Air conditioning. Traditional establishment serving fresh fish, mushrooms and truffles; good choice of homemade desserts and cheeses (III, B2, off map).

ℍ *Bruxaboschi.* Via F. Mignone 8, S. Desiderio, tel. 0103450302. Closed Sunday evening, Monday, from Christmas to 6 January and in August. Parking facilities, garden. Ligurian cuisine - fish. Here, where the city ends and the mountains begin, the attention turns to mushrooms and other fruits of the land (III, B6, off map).

ℍ *Cicchetti 1860.* Via Gianelli 41/r, Quinto al Mare, tel. 0103200391. Closed Monday, Tuesday, and in August. Air conditioning. Ligurian cuisine. Typical Genoese osteria: traditional furnishings, traditional cuisine (III, C6, off map).

ℍ *Da Toto-al Porto Antico.* Ponte F. Morosini Sud 20, tel. 0102543879. Closed Monday evening. Air conditioning. An elegant establishment near the Aquarium, at the tip of an ancient, recently-restored pier; in summer food is served in the outside pile-built, covered verandah. Exquisite fish and seafood dishes (II, C3).

ℍ *Genio.* Salita S. Leonardo 61/r, tel. 010588463. Closed Sunday, and in August. Genoese cuisine. Characteristic restaurant which has revived some of the old local dishes (II, D4).

ℍ *Rina.* Mura delle Grazie 3/r, tel. 0102466475. Closed Monday, August. Air conditioning. The friendly owner of this, the oldest restaurant in Genoa, has been serving good Ligurian cuisine based on the freshest of fresh fish since 1945. A favorite haunt of personalities from the stage, screen and world of business (I, E1).

ℍ *Santa Chiara.* Via Capo S. Chiara 69/r, tel. 0103770081. Closed Sunday, for a period in August, and from Christmas to 6 January. Ligurian and traditional cuisine. Typical old fisherman's house by the sea with terrace, where the friendly owner Luigi Lombardi has been serving his specialties for over thirty years (III, C5-6).

ℍ *Toe Drue.* Via Corsi 44/r, Sestri Ponente, tel. 0106500100. Closed Sunday, Saturday lunchtime, and for a period in August. Air conditioning. Ligurian and traditional cuisine. Early 20th-century osteria, now a characteristic establishment, that takes its name from the tables of a Lombard convent; fish is served regularly, but in season the menu also includes terragne with mushrooms, truffles and game (III, B1, off map).

ℍ *Torre del Mangia.* Piazza Montano 24/r, Sampierdarena, tel. 0106469569. Closed Sunday evening, Monday, and in August. Air conditioning. Tuscan and traditional cuisine - mushrooms, fish. A typical Tuscan restaurant transported to Liguria, offering the culinary traditions of its region of origin, such as Tuscan grilled meat (III, B1).

ℍ *7 Nasi.* Via Quarto 16, Quarto dei Mille, tel. 0103731344. Closed Tuesday. Parking facilities. Ligurian and traditional cuisine. A pleasant establishment with a nautical atmosphere overlooking the sea, panoramic terraces, swimming-pool and beach (III, C6, off map).

ℍ *Al Veliero.* Via Ponte Calvi 10/r, tel. 0102465773. Closed Monday, for a period in January, and between August and September. Air conditioning. Ligurian cuisine - fish. Restaurant in nautical style that serves meals with all the care and attention of the family-run establishment (I, B1).

ℍ *Enoteca con Cucina Sola.* Via C. Barabino 120/r, tel. 010594513. Closed Sunday, and for a period in August. Air conditioning. Ligurian and traditional cuisine. A winery and restaurant where the typical, beautifully prepared dishes are accompanied, of course, by a good glass of wine (II, E6).

🏕 ** *Caravan Park La Vesima - P.V.* At Voltri, locality La Vesima, S.S. Aurelia at km 547, tel. 0106199672, fax 0106199686. All year.

🏕 ** *Villa Doria.* At Pegli, Via al Camp. Villa Doria 15 N, tel. 0106969600, fax 0106969600. All year.

🏕 ** *Villa Masnata.* At Creto, tel. 010830187 9, fax 010803311. Seasonal.

The city

🛏 **Youth hostels**
Genova. Via Costanzi 120, tel. 0102422457. Open 22 January-22 December.

Services and car hire

Cooperativa Battellieri del Porto di Genova. Calata degli Zingari, tel. 010265712. Boat tours of the port, boat hire.
Genova-Casella Railway. Via alla Stazione per Casella 15, tel. 010837321, website www.ferrovia genovacasella.it, e-mail fgc@ferroviagenovacasella.it (service also with period passenger cars).

 Cafés and pastry shops

Bar Berto. Piazza delle Erbe 6 r., tel. 0102758157. Art Nouveau café with tables outside.
Bar Gelateria Balilla. Via Macaggi 84 r., tel. 010542161. Elegant, early 20th-century café and ice-cream parlor.
Caffè degli Specchi. Salita Pollaiuoli 43 r. "Scent of a Woman" was filmed here; no-smoking room inside.
Caffè Il Barbarossa. Piano di S. Andrea 23 r., tel. 0102465097. Hundreds of different varieties of tea.
Caffetteria Orefici. Via XX Settembre 152, tel. 0102472859 and Via Orefici 25 (standing room only). Delicious flavored coffees.
Confetteria Pasticceria Klainguti. Piazza di Soziglia 98 r., tel. 0102474552. *Zena* cake specialty.
Confetteria Pasticceria Mangini. Via Roma 91 r., tel. 010564013. With tables outside.
Confetteria Romanengo. Via di Soziglia 74 r., tel. 0102474574. Founded in 1780, the shop makes sweets, candied fruit, chocolate, and preserves.

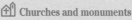 Museums and cultural institutions

Aquarium. Old Port, Ponte Spinola, tel. 0102481205. October-February, closed Monday. Open: 9.30am-7pm; Saturday and Sunday 9.30am-8pm.
Galleria di Palazzo Bianco. Via Garibaldi 11, tel. 0102476377. Closed Monday and holidays. Open: 9am-1pm; Wednesday and Saturday 9am-7pm; Sunday 10am-6pm.
Galleria di Palazzo Rosso. Via Garibaldi 18, tel. 0105574700. Closed Monday and holidays. Open: 9am-1pm; Wednesday and Saturday 9am-7pm; Sunday 10am-6pm.
Galleria Nazionale di Palazzo Reale. Via Balbi 10, tel. 0102710272. Open: 9am-7pm, Sunday-Tuesday 9am-1.45pm.
Galleria Nazionale di Palazzo Spinola. Piazza Pellicceria 1, tel. 0102477061. Closed Monday. Open: 9am-7pm, Sunday 2-7pm.
Museo Biblioteca dell'Attore (Actor's Museum). Viale IV Novembre 3, tel. 010586681. Closed Saturday and Sunday. Open: 9am-1pm; Monday 2-7pm.
Museo Civico di Storia Naturale Giacomo Doria. Via Brigata Liguria 9, tel. 010564567. Closed Monday and holidays. Open: 9am-12.30pm, 3-5.30pm; Friday 9am-12.30pm.
Museo d'Arte Contemporanea di Villa Croce. Via Ruffini 3, tel. 010580069. Closed Monday. Open: 9am-7pm; Sunday 9am-12.30pm.
Museo d'Arte Orientale Edoardo Chiossone. Villetta Di Negro, Piazzale Mazzini 1, tel. 010542285. Closed Monday and Wednesday. Open: 9am-1pm.
Museo dell'Accademia Ligustica di Belle Arti. Largo Pertini 4, tel. 010581957. Closed Sunday and holidays. Open: 9am-1pm.
Museo del Risorgimento. Via Lomellini 11, tel. 0102465843. Closed Monday, Wednesday and Sunday. Open: 9am-1pm.
Museo del Tesoro di S. Lorenzo. Cathedral of San Lorenzo, Via Reggio 17, tel. 0102471831. Closed Sunday. Open: 9am-noon, 3-6pm.
Museo di S. Agostino. Piazza Sarzano 35 r., tel.

0102511263. Closed Monday. Open: 9am-7pm; Sunday 9am-12.30pm.
Museo Etnografico Castello d'Albertis. Corso Dogali 18, tel. 010280104. In preparation.
Museo Nazionale dell'Antartide Felice Ippolito. Old Port, Palazzina Millo, tel. 0102543690. Closed Monday. Open: 9.45am-6.15pm; Sunday 10am-7pm; June-September 2-10pm.
Pudiglione dcl Mare e della Navigazione. Old Port, Magazzini del Cotone, tel. 0102465422. Closed Monday. Open: 10.30am-6pm, Saturday and Sunday 10.30am-7pm; October-February 10.30am-5.30pm, Saturday and Sunday 10.30am-6pm.
Palazzo del Municipio - Council Room. Via Garibaldi 9, tel. 0105572223. Visits by prior arrangement.
Palazzo Doria Pamphily - Andrea Doria Apartments. Via S. Benedetto 2, tel. 010255509. Open: Saturday 3-6pm; Sunday 10am-1pm; on other days by prior arrangement.
Palazzo San Giorgio. Via Frate Oliverio, tel. 0102412754. Open: Saturday 10am-6pm; on other days by prior arrangement.
Presepe del Santuario della Madonnetta. Salita della Madonnetta 5, tel. 0102725308. Open: 9.30-11.30am, 3-6pm; by prior arrangement.

 Churches and monuments

Auditorium of Sant'Agostino. Piazza Negri. Visits by prior arrangement, tel. 0102511263.
Casa di Colombo. Vico Dritto di Ponticello. Open: Saturday and Sunday 9am-noon, 3-6pm; on other days by prior arrangement, tel. 0102465346.
Cathedral of San Lorenzo. Via Reggio 17, tel. 010265786. Open: 8am-noon, 3-7pm; Sunday and religious holidays 8am-12.15pm, 4-7.15pm.
Church of SS. Annunziata del Vastato. Piazza della Nunziata. Open: 7-11.30am, 4-6.30pm; Sunday and religious holidays 7.30am-noon, 4.30-6.45pm.
Church of San Siro di Struppa. Via alla Chiesa di San Siro di Struppa, tel. 010809000. Open: 8.30am-6pm.
Church of Santa Maria di Castello. Salita di S. Maria di Castello 15, tel. 0102468772. Open: 9am-noon, 3.30-6.30pm.
Cimitero di Staglieno (Cemetery). Piazzale Resasco, tel. 010870184 . Open: 7.30am-5pm.
Convent of Nostra Signora della Consolazione. Via della Consolazione, tel. 010561922. Visits by prior arrangement.
Convent of S. Maria di Castello - Sale dei Ragusei. Salita di S. Maria di Castello 15, tel. 0102549511. Visits by prior arrangement.
Porta di Sant'Andrea. Piano di S. Andrea. Open: Saturday and Sunday 9am-noon, 3-6pm; by prior arrangement, tel. 0102465346.
Sanctuary of Nostra Signora del Monte. Salita Nuova di Nostra Signora del Monte 15, tel. 010505854. Open: 6.15am-noon, 3-7.45pm.

Shows and other festivities

Regata delle antiche Repubbliche marinare (Old Sea Republics Regatta). Race between four rowing boats representing Amalfi, Genoa, Pisa and Venice, ending in the basin between Ponte Andrea Doria and Ponte dei Mille. Third Sunday in May, every four years.
Teatro Carlo Felice. Passo del Teatro 4, tel. 010589329. Opera, classical music concerts.
Teatro della Corte. Via E. Filiberto Duca d'Aosta 19, tel. 0105342200. Stage plays and cabaret.
Teatro della Tosse in Sant'Agostino. Piazza Negri 4, tel. 0102470793. Stage plays.

Teatro di Campopisano. Piazza di Campopisano 4, tel. 0102511772. Theatrical performances and cabaret.

🎺 Sport

Ice-skating Porto Antico (seas.). Ice rink in the old Port area, Ponte Parodi, tel. 0102461319. Open October-April.

⚖️ Arts and crafts

Antiquariato Rubinacci. Via Garibaldi 7, tel. 0102474091. Antiques bought, sold and auctioned.

Argenteria Brizzolari. Piazza di Soziglia 104 r., tel. 0102474309. Silverware.

Bottaro. Piazza delle Scuole Pie 3/A r., tel. 0102477752. Crystal glass and artistic windows.

Cioccolato Viganotti. Vico dei Castagna 14 r., tel. 0102514061. Chocolate production.

Corderia Nazionale. Via Gramsci 53 r., tel. 0102465929. Nautical rigging.

Galleria Imperiale. Piazza Campetto 8, tel. 0102510086. On the ground floor of the 16th-century Palazzo di Giovanni Vincenzo Imperiale. Antiques.

Libreria Antiquaria Ardy. Piazza Sauli 4/2, tel. 0102468508. Old and rare books bought and sold.

Libreria Bardini. Salita del Fondaco 32 r., tel. 0102468956. Old, new and rare books.

Libreria di Piazza delle Erbe. Piazza delle Erbe 25 r., tel. 0102475347. Old and rare books; appraisals, valuations.

Migone. Piazza San Matteo 4 r., tel. 0102473282. Sale of wines, sparkling wines and spirits.

Vivioli Arte Antica. Palazzo Ducale, Piazza Matteotti 42 r., tel. 010587548. Antiques.

Eastern Genoa

🏛 Museums and cultural institutions

Galleria d'Arte Moderna. Villa Serra, Via Capolungo 3, tel. 0103726025. In preparation.

Museo Giannettino Luxoro. Via Aurelia 29, tel. 010322673. In preparation.

Raccolte Frugone. Villa Grimaldi Fassio, Via Capolungo 9, tel. 010322396. Closed Monday. Open: 9am-7pm; Sunday 9am-1pm.

🏛 Churches and monuments

Augustine monastery. Via al Capo di Santa Chiara 16, tel. 0103993315. Visits by prior arrangement.

Church of San Siro. Via dei Vassalli 1, tel. 010321502. Visits by prior arrangement.

Convent of San Francesco d'Albaro. Via Albaro 33, tel. 0103628624. Visits by prior arrangement.

🏃 Shows and other festivities

International Ballet Festival. Classical dance performed on the stage in the Nervi parks (some shows staged at the Teatro Carlo Felice); July.

⚖️ Arts and crafts

Vivai Olcese. Via Borghero 6, tel. 010380290. Tree and plant nursery.

Vivai Paesaggi. Corso Europa 1119, tel. 0103770553. Nursery (including bonsaï).

🏛 Markets and fairs

Euroflora. International flower and ornamental plant show. Last week in April. Every five years.

International Boat Show. Pleasure craft and nautical equipment. Third week in October, every year.

🦅 Nature sites, parks and reserves

Parchi di Nervi. Via Capolungo. Open: 8am-7.30pm; January, October 8am-5.30pm; February 8am-6pm; March, September 8am-6.30pm; April 8am-7pm; November-December 8am-5pm.

Western Genoa

🚢 Services and car hire

Hertz. Cristoforo Colombo Airport, Via Pionieri e Aviatori d'Italia, tel. 0106512422.

🧖 Spa establishments

Opera Pia Nostra Signora dell'Acquasanta. Via Acquasanta 273, tel. 010638178. Sulfur baths.

🏛 Museums and cultural institutions

Museo Civico di Archeologia Ligure. Via Pallavicini 11, tel. 0106981048. Closed Monday. Open: 9am-7pm (October-March 9am-5pm); Friday, Saturday and Sunday 9am-1pm.

Museo di Storia e Cultura Contadina (farming history). Salita al Garbo 47, tel. 0107401243. Closed Monday. Open: 9am-noon, 2-5pm; Sunday 9am-12.30pm, 2-5pm.

Museo Navale. Piazza Bonavino 7, tel. 0106969885. Closed Sunday and Monday. Open: 9am-1pm; Friday and Saturday 9am-7pm.

🏛 Churches and monuments

Lanterna (lighthouse). Piazzale S. Benigno, tel. 0102465346. Visits by prior arrangement.

Sanctuary of Nostra Signora della Guardia. Via Santuario di Nostra Signora della Guardia. Open: 8am-noon, 2-7pm; Sunday 8am-7pm.

Villa Brignole Sale. Via al Santuario delle Grazie. Open: 8am-7.30pm; January, October 8am-5.30pm; February 8am-6pm; March, September 8am-6.30pm; April 8am-7pm; November-December 8am-5pm.

🦅 Nature sites, parks and reserves

Parco Durazzo Pallavicini. Via Pallavicini 13, tel. 0106982776. Closed Monday. Open: 9am-7pm; October-March 10am-5pm.

Impèria

Page 139 ✉ 18100
ℹ *IAT*, Viale Matteotti 37, tel. 0183660140.

🏨 Hotels, restaurants, campsites and holiday camps

🛏 **Mira Maurizio.** Via Poggi 117, tel. 0183650509, fax 018362227. Seasonal.

at Onèglia

⭐⭐⭐ **Kristina.** Spianata Borgo Peri 8, tel. 0183293564, fax 0183293565. 34 rooms. Air conditioning, elevator; garden, private beach. A modern hotel near the sea, ideal for short-stay guests (B6).

🍴 **Salvo-Cacciatori.** Via Vieusseux 12, tel. 0183293763. Closed Sunday evening (in winter only), Monday, and for a period between July and August. Air conditioning. Ligurian cuisine. Well-established traditional family-run restaurant with two large dining-rooms and open kitchen (A6).

🍴 **Da Clorinda.** Via Garessio 98, tel. 0183291982. Closed Monday, and for a period in August. This trattoria, which serves delicious home-made dishes, has been run by the same family for a hundred years (A6, off map).

at Porto Maurizio

*** **Corallo.** Corso Garibaldi 29, tel. 0183666264, fax 0183666265. 42 rooms. Air conditioning, elevator; parking facilities, garden, private beach. This comfortable, functional hotel near the sea is well situated within easy reach of the main communication routes; independently-run restaurant (B2).

*** **Croce di Malta.** Via Scarincio 148, tel. 0183667020, fax 018363687. 39 rooms. Facilities for disabled. Air conditioning, elevator; parking facilities, private beach. A fully refurbished hotel near the sea with view over the port (B2).

¶¶ **Lanterna Blu-Da Tonino.** Via Scarincio 32, tel. 018363859, fax 018363859. Closed Wednesday, variable holiday closure. Air conditioning, parking facilities. Fresh fish, seafood and vegetables straight from the garden creatively prepared by the Sicilian-Neapolitan Fiorillo family, who established their famous restaurant here years ago (A-B2).

¶ **Tamerici.** Lungomare C. Colombo 142, tel. 0183667105. Closed Tuesday, and for periods in October and in February. A restaurant right by the sea, in a refurbished turn-of-the-century building; vaulted dining-room with old-style decorations and nautical trophies on the walls; typical Ligurian cuisine and traditional fish and seafood specialties revisited (B1, off map).

⌘ Cafés and pastry shops

Caffè Pasticceria Franchiolo. Via Cascione 14, tel. 0183650977.
Winston Churchill Pub. Via Airenti 380, tel. 0183666902.

⌂♀ Wineries

Enoteca Fratelli Lupi. Via Monti 13, tel. 0183291610 (Ligurian wines).

🏛 Museums and cultural institutions

Museo dell'Olivo. Via Garessio 11, tel. 0183720000. Closed Tuesday. Open: 9am-noon, 3-6.30pm.
Museo Navale Internazionale del Ponente Ligure. Piazza del Duomo 11, tel. 0183651541. Open: Tuesday 9am-noon; Wednesday and Saturday 3-7pm (June-September 9-11pm).
Pinacoteca Civica. Piazza Duomo, tel. 018361136. Closed Monday. Open: 4-7pm.

🏃 Shows and other festivities

Corpus Christi Flower Display. Procession in the flower-decked Via Carducci.
International Vintage Yacht Gathering. In September, every two years.

⚖ Arts and crafts

Azienda Floricola Gaggino. Via S. Agata 65, tel. 0183710790. Ornamental plants.
Lupi. Via Argine Sinistro 162, tel. 0183276090. Ligurian wines.
Soprano. Salita Monti 7, tel. 0183290176. Sale of porcelain.
Vivai Siccardi. Via Airenti 177, tel. 018363777. Plants.

Laiguèglia

Page 137   ✉ 17020
ℹ *IAT Laigueglia*, Via Roma 2, tel. 0182690059, fax 0182699191.

🏨🍴 Hotels, restaurants, campsites and holiday camps

⚜ **Splendid.** Piazza Badarò 3, tel. 0182690325, fax 0182690894. Seasonal. 48 rooms. Elevator; park-ing facilities, garden, open-air pool, private beach. This hotel, in a restored 19th-century monastery, is noted for its elegant interior and period furnishings. Good sea view.

*** **Mediterraneo.** Via A. Doria 18, tel. 0182690240, fax 0182499739. 32 rooms. Elevator; parking facilities, garden. A hotel set amid peaceful olive groves not far from the beach, for a comfortable relaxing stay.

¶¶¶ **Baiadelsole.** Piazza Cavour 8, tel. 0182690019, fax 0182690237. Closed Monday, 6 January-February, and mid-October to mid-December. This restaurant, in an 18th-century house with terrace over the sea and a beautiful brick-vaulted dining-room, serves light meals with all the typical Ligurian seafood specialties: grilled squid, gnocchi al pesto, tagliolini with vegetables and prawns, and a range of grilled or baked fish dishes served with seasonal vegetables (A-B2).

♨ **Capo Mele - P.V.** Via Aurelia at km 628, tel.
** 0182499997, fax 0182499997. All year.

La Spezia

Page 193   ✉ 19100
ℹ *APT Cinque Terre - Golfo dei Poeti*, Viale Mazzini 47, tel. 0187254311, fax 0187770908, and Piazza Stazione 1, tel. 0187718997. IAT, Viale Mazzini 45, tel. 0187770900. Website: www.aptcinqueterre.sp.it, e-mail info@aptcinqueterre.sp.it.

🏨🍴 Hotels, restaurants, campsites and holiday camps

⚜ **Ghironi.** Via Tino 62, tel. 0187504141, fax 0187524724. 47 rooms. Meublé. Air conditioning, elevator; parking facilities, garden. Modern and well equipped, with small meeting room, near the highway exit and the port (B5).

⚜ **Jolly.** Via XX Settembre 2, tel. 0187739555, fax 018722129. 110 rooms. Air conditioning, elevator; parking facilities. A modern, efficient hotel overlooking the port, with the chain's usual high level of comfort; busy Del Golfo restaurant (C3).

*** **Firenze & Continentale.** Via Paleocapa 7, tel. 0187713210, fax 0187714930. 66 rooms. Meublé. Air conditioning, elevator; parking facilities. Early 20th-century building enlarged and refurbished to provide all the modern, efficient services of a comfortable hotel (C2).

¶¶¶ **Parodi.** Via Amendola 210, tel. 0187715777. Closed Sunday, 15 August. Air conditioning, garden. An elegant dining-room with highly-trained staff: exquisite fresh fish specialties and admirable wine cellar (C1).

¶¶ **Il Forchettone.** Via Genova 288, tel. 0187718835. Closed Sunday, and mid-June to early July. Air conditioning. A small, intimate restaurant, at La Chiappa. Dishes include, surprisingly, some Sicilian specialties: buckwheat fish ravioli, fillet of bass stewed in caper and olive sauce, cod fricassee with vegetables (B1).

¶ **Antica Osteria Negrao.** Via Genova 428, tel. 0187701564. Closed Monday, Christmas-New Year and for a period in September. Parking facilities, garden. Characteristic restaurant serving traditional food; family run since 1950, excellent value for money (B1, off map).

🚗 Services and car hire

Hertz. Viale S. Bartolomeo 393, tel. 0187512140.
Navigazione Golfo dei Poeti. Via Mazzini 21, tel. 0187732987, fax 0187730336 (boat crossings and day trips: tour of the islands, Genoa Aquarium, Portofino, Cinque Terre, Moneglia, Deiva Marina, Bonassola, Levanto, Portovenere, Lerici).

🏛 Museums and cultural institutions

Museo Civico Archeologico Ubaldo Formentini. Castello di San Giorgio, Via XXVII Marzo, tel. 0187751142. Closed Tuesday, 1 January, 24 and 25 December. Open: Summer, 9.30am-12.30pm, 5-8pm; Winter, 9.30am-12.30pm, 2-5pm.

Museo Civico d'Arte Antica, Medievale e Moderna Amedeo Lia. Via Prione 234, tel. 0187731100. Closed Monday, 25 December, 1 January, 15 August. Open: 10am-6pm.

Museo Civico Giovanni Podenzana, ethnography and history section. Via Curtatone 9, tel. 0187739537. Closed Monday. Open: 8.30am-1pm.

Museo Tecnico Navale della Marina Militare. Viale Amendola 1, tel. 0187783016. Open: 9am-noon, 2-6pm; Monday, Friday 2-6pm; Sunday 8.30am-1.15pm.

⛪ Churches and monuments

Castello di S. Giorgio. Via XXVII Marzo.

🕺 Shows and other festivities

Sea Festival. Bay Boat Race. 1st Sunday in August.

⚖ Arts and crafts

Floricoltura La Pieve. Salita Castelvecchio 1, tel. 0187509771. Plants and flowers.

Fratelli Barite. Via Brizio Rebocco 20, tel. 0187711199. Wine production.

Vaccarone. Via Chiodo 13, tel. 018724062. Painter's studio.

🏛 Markets and fairs

Fiera di San Giuseppe. St. Joseph's Day Fair, 19 March.

👫 Local guides and excursions

at Campiglia, 7 km

Centro Turismo Equestre "Cinque Terre". Via della Castellana 2, tel. 0187758114. Excursions on horseback.

Lavagna

Page 183   ✉ 16033
i IAT, Piazza della Libertà 48/a, tel. 0185395070.

at Cavi, 4 km   ✉ 16090
IAT (seas.), Via Lombardia 53, tel. 0185395680.

🏨 Hotels, restaurants, campsites and holiday camps

*** **Admiral.** Via dei Devoto 89, tel. 0185306072, fax 0185306072. Seasonal. 22 rooms. Elevator; garden, open-air pool. A modern hotel, quietly situated by the marina, not far from the beach.

*** **Fieschi.** Via Rezza 12, tel. 0185304400, fax 0185313809. 13 rooms. Parking facilities, garden. A quiet, comfortable hotel in a 19th-century villa; food prepared and served by the owners themselves.

🍴🍴🍴 **Il Gabbiano.** Via S. Benedetto 26, tel. 0185390228. Closed Monday, for a period between February and March, and in November. Air conditioning, parking facilities, garden. This elegant, comfortable restaurant in a villa set in its own leafy grounds offers sophisticated Ligurian cuisine prepared by chef patron Dante Perrone; food served on the panoramic terrace in summer.

at Cavi, 4 km   ✉ 16030
*** **Doria.** Via Brigate Partigiane 9, tel. 0185392191, fax 0185 390095. Seasonal. 60 rooms. Elevator;

garage, garden. A quiet, comfortable hotel near the sea.

🍴🍴 **A Cantinna.** Via Torrente Barassi 8, tel. 0185390394. Closed Tuesday, February and for a period between November and December. Parking facilities, garden. Ligurian cuisine. An old trattoria brought up to date, with a bright verandah and attractive garden; family run since 1971.

🍴 **Rajeu.** Via Milite Ignoto 23, tel. 0185390145. Closed Monday, November and late February to early March. Parking facilities. Ligurian cuisine. A restaurant with a pleasant nautical atmosphere noted for its professional service; simple but tasty local dishes, based in many cases on ancient recipes; good selection of Italian and some French wines.

🕺 Shows and other festivities

Torta dei Fieschi. Re-enactment in historical costumes of the marriage of Count Opizzo Fieschi and Bianca de' Bianchi, after which all present receive a slice of wedding cake; 14 August.

Lerici

Page 197   ✉ 19032
i IAT, Via Biaggini 6, tel. and fax 0187967346.

🏨 Hotels, restaurants, campsites and holiday camps

*** **Byron.** Via Biaggini 19, tel. 0187967104, fax 0187967409. 26 rooms. Elevator. This comfortable, no-nonsense hotel is situated right by the sea and has an enviable view.

*** **Doria Park.** Via Privata Doria 2, tel. 0187967124, fax 0187966459. 42 rooms. Air conditioning, elevator; parking facilities, garden. Meticulously-organized, family-run hotel with good restaurant.

*** **Europa.** Via Carpanini 1, tel. 0187967800, fax 0187965957. 35 rooms. Air conditioning, parking facilities, garden. A comfortable hotel with attractive steps that lead among the olive groves down to the sea; typical Mediterranean restaurant; the picture windows offer views of the Bay of Poets.

*** **Florida.** Lungomare Biaggini 35, tel. 0187967332, fax 0187967344. 37 rooms. Meublé. Air conditioning, elevator; garage, private beach. A modern, comfortable hotel conveniently and panoramically situated by the sea,; sports facilities nearby.

*** **Shelley & delle Palme.** Lungomare Biaggini 5, tel. 0187968204, fax 0187964271. 49 rooms. Elevator; garage. Centrally situated, facing the sea and with large terrace; guests are warmly received as in a private residence; comfortable rooms. Independently-run restaurant.

🍴🍴🍴 **Miranda.** Via Fiascherino 92, tel. 0187964012. Closed Monday, December-mid-January. Air conditioning. Small, friendly hotel; quality cuisine, light but flavorful fish dishes. Other specialties include: risotto with celery and fennel, scampi in sweet garlic sauce and fish scallops.

🍴🍴 **Conchiglia.** Via Mazzini 2, tel. 0187967334. Closed Wednesday, and mid-January to mid-February. Ligurian cuisine. A restaurant in the port with a nautical atmosphere serving seafood and fish out on the pleasant terrace. Wide choice of wines.

🍴🍴 **La Barcaccia.** Piazza Garibaldi 8, tel. 0187967721. Closed Thursday, and for periods in February and November. A restaurant with a long tradition of fish specialties and courteous, professional service; extensive selection of wines.

⚲ *Gianna - P.V.* Locality Tellaro, Via Fiascherino, tel. 0187966411, fax 0187966411. Seasonal.
***

🚗 Services and car hire

Navigazione Golfo dei Poeti. Landing-stage south, tel. 0187967676.

🏛 Museums and cultural institutions

Museo Geopaleontologico. C/o Castello, Piazza del Poggio 1, tel. 0187969042. Closed Monday. Open: November-March 9am-1pm, 2.30-5.30pm, Sunday and holidays 9am-6pm. September, October, and April-June 9am-1pm, 3-7pm, Sunday and holidays 9am-7pm. July, August 10am-1pm, 5pm-midnight.

⚖ Arts and crafts

Baroni Franco. Via Cavour 18, tel. 0187966301. Winery and gourmet specialties.
Caselli Carlo. Piazza Battisti 10, tel. 0187964307. Painter's studio.
Il Sestante. Via Cavour 73, tel. 0187965274. Antiques and nautical instruments, in a characteristic interior.

✅ Sport

Golf Club Marigola. Via Biaggini 5, tel. 0187970193.

Levanto

Page 202 ✉ 19015
ℹ *IAT*, Piazza Cavour 12, tel. and fax 0187808125.

🏨 Hotels, restaurants, campsites and holiday camps

*** *Nazionale.* Via Jacopo da Levanto 20, tel. 0187808102, fax 0187800901. 39 rooms. Elevator; parking facilities, garden. A family-run hotel centrally situated near the sea.
** *Stella Maris.* Via Marconi 4, tel. 0187808258, fax 0187807351. 15 rooms. Garden. In a refurbished 19th-century building with large flower garden not far from the sea; frescoed ceilings in the dining-room and elsewhere; period furniture.
⚲ *Acqua Dolce.* Locality Acqua Dolce, Via Guido Semenza 5, tel. 0187808465, fax 0187807365.
* Seasonal.

🏛 Museums and cultural institutions

Mostra permanente della Cultura Materiale. Piazzetta Massola 4, tel. 0187817776. Closed Monday. Open: June-September 9-11pm; other times of the year by prior arrangement.

⚖ Arts and crafts

Cooperativa Agricoltori della Vallata di Levanto. Ghiare 20, tel. 0187800867. Local food specialties.
La Cantina Levantese. Via Zoppi 11, tel. 0187807137; at San Gottardo (2 km), tel. 0187801534. Sale of wines.

🏞 Nature sites, parks and reserves

Eastern Liguria Promontories and Islands Regional Nature Park Authority. Palazzo Comunale, Piazza Cavour 1, tel. 0187920893, e-mail webmaster@parco5terre.lig.it

Loano

Page 125 ✉ 17025
ℹ *IAT Loano*, Corso Europa 19, tel. 019676007, fax 019676818.

🏨 Hotels, restaurants, campsites and holiday camps

⚐ *G.H. Garden Lido.* Lungomare N. Sauro 9, tel. 019669666, fax 019668552. 77 rooms. Air conditioning, elevator; parking facilities, garden, open-air pool, private beach. A short walk from the beach, opposite the harbor, with an impressive array of leisure, sport and keep-fit facilities; dance evenings and other activities all year round.
*** *Perelli.* Lungomare G. Garbarino 13, tel. 019675708, fax 019675722. Seasonal. 41 rooms. Elevator; private beach. Centrally situated right by the beach; dining-room with large windows.
🍴 *Vecchia Trattoria.* Via Raimondi 3, tel. 019667162. Closed Monday (out of season), and for periods in May and November. Air conditioning. Small restaurant in the historic center with vaulted ceilings and brick floor; local cuisine (mostly fish and seafood specialties). Meticulously run by Davide Vay.
🏠 *Oasi.* Via Ugo Foscolo 40, tel. 019670619, fax
** 019670619. All year.

👫 Local guides and excursions

Pian delle Bosse Alpine Refuge. Locality Pian delle Bosse, tel. 0196 71790.

Lucinasco

Page 144 ✉ 18023

🏛 Museums and cultural institutions

Museo d'Arte Sacra Lazzaro Acquarone (Sacred Art). Piazza S. Antonino. Visits by prior arrangement, tel. 018352534.

Luni

Page 206 ✉ 19034

🏛 Museums and cultural institutions

Museo Archeologico Nazionale. Via S. Pero, archaeological site of Luni (Ortonovo), tel. 018766811. Closed Monday, 1 January, 1 May and 25 December. Open: 9am-7pm.

Manarola

Page 200 ✉ 19010

🏨 Hotels, restaurants, campsites and holiday camps

*** *Ca' d'Andrean.* Via Discovolo 101, tel. 0187920040, fax 0187920452. 10 rooms. Meublé. Garden. An old oil press and wine cellar now offers comfortable accommodation in a friendly, family environment.
🍴 *Marina Piccola.* Via Lo Scalo 16, tel. 0187920103. Closed Tuesday, early November-early December. Ligurian cuisine.
This recently renovated restaurant serves fish only on a bright verandah and terrace overlooking the sea.

Mele

Page 103 ✉ 16010

🏛 Museums and cultural institutions

Centro di Testimonianza ed Esposizione dell'Arte Cartaria della Valle del Leira (paper manufacture). Via Acquasanta 251, tel. 010638103. Visits by prior arrangement.

Millesimo

Page 119   ✉ 17017
ℹ️ *IAT Millesimo*, Piazza Italia 27, tel. 0195600078, fax 0195600970.

🏕 Nature sites, parks and reserves
Bric Tana Regional Nature Park. C/o Town Hall, Piazza Italia 14, tel. 019564007.

Molini di Triora

Page 158   ✉ 18010

🏨 Hotels, restaurants, campsites and holiday camps
🍴 **Santo Spirito.** Piazza Roma 23, tel. 018494092. Closed Wednesday. Ligurian cuisine - snails, mushrooms. This simple, traditional establishment has been run by the Zucchetto family for over a century. Specialties from the upper Argentina Valley prepared using fresh farm produce.

Monéglia

Page 185   ✉ 17025
ℹ️ *Pro Loco*, Corso Longhi 32, tel. 0185490576.

🏨 Hotels, restaurants, campsites and holiday camps
*** **Piccolo Hotel.** Corso L. Longhi 18/19, tel. 0185490432, fax 0185401292. 24 rooms. Air conditioning, elevator. A small, simply-furnished friendly hotel situated at the beginning of the celebrated Viale delle Palme.
*** **Villa Edera.** Via Venino 12, tel. 018549291, fax 018549470. Seasonal. 27 rooms. Facilities for disabled. Air conditioning, elevator; parking facilities, garden, open-air pool. A modernized hotel, offering a relaxing, quiet stay five minutes from the beach.
🍴 **Ruota.** At Lemeglio, tel. 0185495G5. Closed Wednesday, and late October-November. Parking facilities. Ligurian cuisine - fish and shellfish. A friendly restaurant in a leafy hillside setting, with à la carte menu; food served on the fine panoramic verandah in summer.
🏠 **Smeraldo - P.V.** Locality Preata, tel. 018549375, fax 0185490484. All year.

Monterosso al Mare

Page 201   ✉ 19016
ℹ️ *Pro Loco* (seas.), Via Fegina, tel. 0187817506, fax 0187817825.

🏨 Hotels, restaurants, campsites and holiday camps
*** **Porto Roca.** Via Corone 1, tel. 0187817502, fax 0187817692. Seasonal. 44 rooms. Air conditioning, elevator; garden, private beach. An elegant, comfortable hotel on the hillside overlooking the sea.
*** **La Colonnina.** Via Zuecca 6, tel. 0187817439, fax 0187817788. 20 rooms. Meublé. Elevator; garden. Centrally situated panoramic hotel run by a professional, friendly family.
🍴 **Miky.** Via Fegina 104, tel. 0187817608. Seasonal, closed Tuesday (except in summer). Garden. Ligurian cuisine - fresh pasta, fish. Characteristic restaurant, with verandah over the sea and inner garden. Also pizzeria with wood-fired oven.

🚐 Services and car hire
Navigazione Golfo dei Poeti (boat services). C/o "Fratelli Rossignoli", Via Molinelli 6, tel. 0187817582.

🍷 Wineries
Bar Enoteca 5 Terre. Via Fegina 92, tel. 0187818063. Wines and food specialties.
Enoteca Internazionale. Via Roma 62, tel. 0187817278.

⚖ Arts and crafts
Fabbrica d'Arte Monterosso. Via Vittorio Emanuele 27, tel. 0187817488. Artistic ceramics.

Nervi

Page 95   ✉ 16167

🏨 Hotels, restaurants, campsites and holiday camps
*** **Astor.** Viale delle Palme 16, tel. 010329011, fax 0103728486. 55 rooms. Facilities for disabled. Air conditioning, elevator; parking facilities, garden. Modern hotel complex, with meeting and reception rooms. Elegant restaurant, with summer garden near the seafront promenade (A1).
*** **Romantik Hotel Villa Pagoda.** Via Capolungo 15, tel. 0103726161, fax 010321218. 18 rooms. Air conditioning, elevator; parking facilities, garden, tennis. An elegant, well-equipped hotel in a completely refurbished 19th-century villa by the sea, suitable both for vacationing and congresses; Il Roseto restaurant (A3).
*** **Esperia.** Via Val Cismon 1, tel. 0103726071, fax 010321777. 25 rooms. Elevator; parking facilities, garden, private beach. A functional hotel in a leafy setting near the train station and seafront promenade (A2).

Noli

Page 120   ✉ 17026
ℹ️ *IAT Noli*, Corso Italia 8, tel. 0197499003, fax 0197493300.

🏨 Hotels, restaurants, campsites and holiday camps
*** **El Sito.** Via La Malfa 2, tel. 019748107, fax 0197485871. 14 rooms. Facilities for disabled. Air conditioning, parking facilities, garden, private beach. This hotel, pleasantly situated amidst the greenery above the town, has been completely refurbished to provide modern, comfortable accommodation.
🍴 **Lilliput.** At Voze, Via Zuglieno 49, tel. 019748009. Closed Monday, 6 January to mid-February and for a period in November. Parking facilities, garden. This rustically elegant restaurant serves food on the terrace in summer; garden, crazy golf and sea view; carefully prepared Ligurian and traditional cuisine, excellent choice of wines.
🍴 **La Scaletta.** Via Verdi 16, tel. 019748754. Closed Tuesday, October or November. Garden. Ligurian cuisine. Two dining rooms, one large, well-furnished with panoramic window, the other smaller and more intimate, and a cool covered outdoor area.

🏛 Churches and monuments
Church of San Paragorio. Via Cesari. Open: summer, Tuesday, Thursday, Saturday, Sunday 10am-noon, 3-5.30pm; winter, Thursday 10am-noon.

Shows and other festivities
Historical Regatta. First Sunday in September.

Ospedaletti

Page 152   ☒ 18014
📋 *IAT*, Corso Regina Margherita 13, tel. 0184689085.

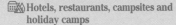Hotels, restaurants, campsites and holiday camps

*** **Le Rocce del Capo.** Lungomare C. Colombo 102, tel. 0184689733, fax 0184689024. 23 rooms. Air conditioning, elevator; parking facilities, indoor and outdoor pool, private beach. A modern, well-equipped hotel in a quiet area right by the sea; La Tolda restaurant and beauty center.

Perinaldo

Page 166   ☒ 18030
📋 *Pro Loco*, c/o Town Hall, Piazza S. Antonio 1, tel. 018467200.

🏛 Museums and cultural institutions
Museo Gian Domenico Cassini. Palazzo Comunale, Piazza S. Antonio 1, tel. 0184672001. Closed Sunday. Open: 8am-1.30pm.

Piana Crixia

Page 118   ☒ 17010

🔾 Nature sites, parks and reserves
Regional Nature Park Authority di Piana Crixia. C/o Town Hall, Via Chiarlone 17, tel. 019570021.

Pietra Ligure

Page 125   ☒ 17027
📋 *IAT Pietra Ligure*, Piazza Martiri della Libertà 31, tel. 019629003, fax 019629790.

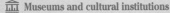Hotels, restaurants, campsites and holiday camps

*** **Royal.** Via Don G. Bado 129, tel. 019616192, fax 019616195. 105 rooms. Elevator; garage, garden, private beach. A hotel by the sea, 200 meters from the historic center, with modern, rational furnishings and comfortable rooms.
*** **Azucena.** Via della Repubblica 76, tel. 019615844, fax 019615810. 28 rooms. Elevator; parking facilities, garden, private beach. A well-organized family-run hotel (since 1972) in a quiet residential area near the sea.
⫶ **Buca di Bacco.** Corso Italia 113, tel. 019615307. Closed Monday (except holidays and in summer), and 6 January to mid-February. Air conditioning, parking facilities. Ligurian and traditional cuisine (mostly fish). Large dining-room with traditional decor; family run.
 Fiori. Viale Riviera 11, tel. 019625636, fax 019625636. All year.

Pigna

Page 166   ☒ 18037
📋 *Comune.* Via Isnardi 50, tel. 0184241016.
⚕ Spa establishment
Terme di Pigna. Regione Lago Pigo, tel. 0184240010.

⚖ Arts and crafts
Vini Annovazzi. Regione Canelli 26, tel. 0184240010. Sale of wines.

Pignone

Page 201   ☒ 19020
🌲 Farm holidays
Cinque Terre. At locality Giaggiolo, tel. 0187888087. Board and lodging in new buildings, camping area. Horse-riding, mountain bike hire; sale of wine, oil, honey, jam.

Portofino

Page 178   ☒ 16034
📋 *IAT*, Via Roma 35, t. 0185269024.

🏨 Hotels, restaurants, campsites and holiday camps

⚹ **Piccolo Hotel.** Via Duca degli Abruzzi 31, tel. 0185269015, fax 0185269621. 23 rooms. Facilities for disabled. Elevator; parking facilities, garden, private beach. All the rooms in this comfortable hotel set in its own grounds have balconies overlooking the sea (B2).
⚹ **Splendido.** Viale Baratta 16, tel. 0185267801, fax 0185267806. Seasonal. 69 rooms. Air conditioning, elevator; parking facilities, garden, open-air pool, tennis. A charming 19th-century villa in a splendid leafy setting with panoramic views, well equipped to satisfy all its guests' needs with elegance and efficiency (A2).
*** **Eden.** Vico Dritto 20, tel. 0185269091, fax 0185269047. 12 rooms. Meublé. Air conditioning, garden. Small hotel with its own attractive garden in the town a stone's throw from the famous "piazzetta" (B2).
⫶⫶⫶ **Puny.** Piazza Martiri dell'Olivetta 5, tel. 0185 269037. Closed Thursday, mid-December to mid-February. Two comfortable dining-rooms and a covered outdoor area from which to enjoy the sights and scents of the sea. Traditional cuisine, mostly fish (B2).
⫶⫶ **Da ü Batti.** Vico Nuovo 17, tel. 0185269379. Closed Monday, mid-November to mid-January. Garden. Ligurian cuisine. A small, intimate dining-room, with verandah; predominantly fish dishes (B2).

🏛 Museums and cultural institutions
Castello di S. Giorgio. Via La Penisola, tel. 0185269046. Closed Tuesday. Open: 10am-6pm; November-March 10am-5pm.

Portovenere

Page 196   ☒ 19025
📋 *IAT*, Piazza Bastreri 1, tel. 0187790691, fax 0187790215.

🏨 Hotels, restaurants, campsites and holiday camps

⚹ **G.H. Portovenere.** Via Garibaldi 5, tel. 0187792610, fax 0187790661. 54 rooms. Facilities for disabled. Air conditioning, elevator; garage. An old restored monastery, with comfortable rooms and also congress facilities; Il Convento restaurant has a terrace over the sea.
*** **Belvedere.** Via Garibaldi 26, tel. 0187790608, fax 0187791469. 18 rooms, of which 16 with bath or shower. Modernized to provide comfortable accommodation, quietly situated with a view of the sea.

¶¶¶ Taverna del Corsaro. Calata Doria 102, tel. 0187790622. Closed Monday, November-January. Ligurian cuisine - fish. Historic establishment in a medieval lookout tower on the promenade; panoramic verandah.

¶ Antica Osteria del Carrugio. Via Cappellini 66, tel. 0187790617. Closed Thursday, and November-early December. Local cuisine. A restaurant in a building dating back more than a century, with nautical furnishings and a room with Faenza majolica. Simple, traditional fare.

at Le Grazie, 3 km   ☒ 19022
*** Della Baia. Via Lungomare 111, tel. 0187790797, fax 0187790034. 34 rooms. Facilities for disabled. Air conditioning, elevator; open-air pool. Well situated with modern, functional services; busy restaurant.

🛏 Services and car hire
Navigazione Golfo dei Poeti. Passeggiata Aldo Moro 1, tel. 0187777727.

Rapallo

Page 179   ☒ 16035
𝑖 *IAT*, Lungomare V. Veneto 7, tel. 0185230346.

🏨 Hotels, restaurants, campsites and holiday camps
⚑⚑⚑ Excelsior Palace Hotel. Via S. Michele di Pagana 8, tel. 0185230666, fax 0185230214. 131 rooms. Facilities for disabled. Air conditioning, elevator; parking facilities, garden, indoor and outdoor pool, private beach. Elegant, completely refurbished hotel, with an extremely well equipped congress center and services for all working requirements, sporting activity or physical recuperation; busy Lord Byron and Eden Roc restaurants (C2).

⚑ Astoria. Via Gramsci 4, tel. 0185273533, fax 018562793. 18 rooms. Meublé. Air conditioning, elevator; parking facilities. Art Nouveau villa overlooking the sea, completely refurbished as a modern, elegant and comfortable hotel (B2).

⚑ Eurotel. Via Aurelia Occidentale 22, tel. 018560981, fax 018550635. 63 rooms. Air conditioning, elevator; parking facilities, garden, open-air pool. A modern, friendly, functional hotel in a peaceful, leafy setting overlooking the sea, and with a splendid view of the Tigullio Bay; adjoining Antica Aurelia restaurant (C1).

*** Riviera. Piazza IV Novembre 2, tel. 018550248, fax 018565668. 20 rooms. Air conditioning, elevator; parking facilities, garden. Centrally situated, late Art Nouveau building refurbished and modernized. Attractive rooms; four suites available (B2).

*** Stella. Via Aurelia Ponente 6, tel. 018550367, fax 0185272837. 27 rooms, of which 25 with bath or shower. Meublé. Elevator; garage. A well-established family hotel in an attractive early 20th-century building not far from the sea (B2).

¶¶ Roccabruna. Via Sotto la Croce 6, locality Savagna, tel. 0185261400. Closed Monday, and for a period in November. Parking facilities, garden. Refined cuisine. This restaurant, in an elegant villa, offers a range of dishes that cleverly combine the flavors of the land with those of the sea (A1, off map).

¶¶ Ü Giancu. At San Massimo, tel. 0185260505. Closed lunchtimes (except Saturday and Sunday) and Wednesday, variable holiday closure. Parking facilities, garden. Tigullio cuisine - fresh pasta, mushrooms. Ideal for families with children: good food in a happy atmosphere (A1, off map).

¶ Elite. Via Milite Ignoto 19, tel. 018550551. Closed Wednesday, November. Ligurian and traditional cuisine. This classy, meticulous restaurant has been run by the same family for thirty years (B3).(B2). Seasonal.

🏛 Museums and cultural institutions
Biblioteca Internazionale Città di Rapallo (library). Villa Tigullio, Parco Casale, tel. 018563304. Closed Sunday and Monday. Open: 2.30-6.30pm; Thursday 10am-noon. September closed.
Museo del Merletto. Villa Tigullio, Parco Casale, tel. 018563305. Closed Monday. Open: 15-18; Thursday 10am-noon; Sunday by prior arrangement. September closed.

✓ Sport
Golf Rapallo. Via Mameli 377, tel. 0185261777.

⚖ Arts and crafts
Gandolfi Emilio. Piazza Cavour 1, tel. 018550234. Lacework.

Recco

Page 98   ☒ 16036
𝑖 *IAT*, Piazza Nicoloso da Recco 13, tel. 0185722440.

🏨 Hotels, restaurants, campsites and holiday camps
⚑ La Villa. Via Roma 274, tel. 0185720779, fax 0185721095. 23 rooms. Facilities for disabled. Air conditioning, elevator; parking facilities, garden, open-air pool. An attractive modern, Genoese-style building, with a pleasant atmosphere and good services.

¶¶¶ Manuelina. Via Roma 278, tel. 018574128, fax 0185721677. Closed Wednesday, and for a period in January. Air conditioning, parking facilities, garden. Since 1882 four generations of the family of Emanuela Capurro ("Manuelina") have continued the tradition of offering the best in Ligurian cuisine with care and courtesy; interesting, carefully-chosen selection of wines.

¶¶¶ Vitturin. Via dei Giustiniani 48, tel. 0185720225, fax 0185723686. Closed Monday, variable holiday closure. Air conditioning, parking facilities, garden. Ligurian cuisine - fish, mushrooms. An establishment which has always been run by the same family, and with a long history of culinary excellence.

¶¶ Da ö Vittorio. Via Roma 160, tel. 018574029. Closed Thursday, and for a period between November and December. Air conditioning, parking facilities, garden. Rustic-style restaurant run by the same family for a century. Beautifully-prepared regional cuisine, noted in particular for its fresh fish and mushroom specialties; excellent Italian and foreign wines.

☕ Cafés and pastry shops
Cavassa. Via Saporito 8, tel. 018574280. Handmade ice cream.

Rezzo

Page 133   ☒ 18020
🏨 Hotels, restaurants, campsites and holiday camps
** Negro. At Cenova, Via Canada 11, tel. 018334089, fax 0183324802. Seasonal. 12 rooms. Parking facilities, garden, open-air pool. Hotel in a medieval farm, period interiors with modern furnishings and busy I Cavallini restaurant.

Rezzoaglio

Page 187   ✉ 16048
ℹ️ *Pro Loco* (seas.) Via Roma, tel. 0185870432.

⚒️ Arts and crafts
Caseificio Val d'Àveto. Via Rezzoaglio Inferiore 35, tel. 0185870390. Production and sale of cheeses and other dairy produce.

Riomaggiore

Page 200   ✉ 19017
🏨 Hotels, restaurants, campsites and holiday camps
at Campi, 9 km
*** Due Gemelli. Via Litoranea 1, tel. and fax 0187920678. 14 rooms. Parking facilities. Recently refurbished hotel in an enviable position among the vineyards, pine trees and chestnut woods high up over the sea.

🌲 Farm holidays
Riomaggiore. Via De Battè 61, tel. 0187718550. Apartments in a restored building, among the vineyards and vegetable gardens. Treks and walks organized; wine and jams sold.

⚒️ Arts and crafts
at Manarola, 6 km
Cooperativa Agricoltura delle Cinque Terre. At Groppo, tel. 0187920435. Wines (own production), local food specialties.

🐾 Nature sites, parks and reserves
National Cinque Terre Park Authority. For information contact municipal tourist office, tel. 0187920633.

San Bartolomeo al Mare

Page 143   ✉ 18016
ℹ️ *IAT*, piazza XXV Aprile 1, tel 0183400200.

🏨 Hotels, restaurants, campsites and holiday camps
*** Bergamo. Via Aurelia 15, tel. 0183400060, fax 01834010 21. Seasonal. 52 rooms. Elevator; garage, open-air pool. A friendly, functional ,family-run establishment centrally situated near the sea.
** Rosa - P.V. Via al Santuario 4, tel. 0183400473, fax 0183400475. All year.

Sanremo

Page 147   ✉ 18038
ℹ️ *APT Riviera dei Fiori*, largo Nuvoloni 1, tel. 0184571571.
Website www.apt.rivieradeifiori.it, e-mail apt-fiori@sistel.it.

🏨 Hotels, restaurants, campsites and holiday camps
*** Royal Hotel. Corso Imperatrice 80, tel. 01845391, fax 0184661445. 143 rooms. Facilities for disabled. Air conditioning, elevator; parking facilities, garden, open-air pool, tennis, private beach. A classic, top-ranking Sanremo hotel for over a century, offering elegance, comfort and a huge flower-filled park. Large, panoramic suites available. Fiori di Murano verandah-restaurant and Corallina poolside snack bar (C3).
*** Eveline Portosole. Corso Cavallotti 111, tel. 0184503430, fax 0184503431. 22 rooms. Meublé. Facilities for disabled. Air conditioning, elevator; parking facilities, garden. A stone's throw from the sea, this hotel, which has been under the same management for 50 years, shows originality and attention to detail; the silver decorations add extra sparkle to the romantic atmosphere (A6).

*** Miramare Palace. Corso Matuzia 9, tel. 0184667601, fax 0184667655. 59 rooms. Elevator; parking facilities, garden, indoor pool. A comfortable, refurbished late 19th-century Art Nouveau hotel set in a large park with tropical plants close to the elegant boulevard Corso Imperatrice; direct access to the beach (D2).

*** Nazionale. Corso Matteotti 3, tel. 0184577577, fax 0184541535. 78 rooms. Facilities for disabled. Air conditioning, elevator; parking facilities. An elegant hotel near the casino with eight high-class suites and a much-frequented restaurant (C3).

*** Nyala. Strada Solaro 134, tel. 0184667668, fax 0184666059. 80 rooms. Facilities for disabled. Air conditioning, elevator; parking facilities, garden, open-air pool. A modern hotel in a garden of age-old palm trees, with all the services of a modern, international establishment; in a quiet, panoramic position near the center and within easy reach of the highway. L'Asmara restaurant serves seafood and traditional cuisine (D1).

*** Lolli Palace. Corso Imperatrice 70, tel. 0184531496, fax 0184541574. 48 rooms. Facilities for disabled. Air conditioning, elevator; parking facilities, use of beach. Fine, completely refurbished early 20th-century Art Nouveau building, with a long-standing family-run tradition (C3).

*** Paradiso. Via Roccasterone 12, tel. 0184571211, fax 0184578176. 41 rooms. Elevator; parking facilities, garden, private beach. Beautifully situated in a quiet, leafy setting, not far from the sea and the town. Bright, tastefully-decorated interior, with fine verandah overlooking the garden (C2).

** Corso. Corso Cavallotti 194, tel. 0184509911, fax 0184509231. 16 rooms. Air conditioning, parking facilities. A well-equipped family-run hotel; rustic-style restaurant (A6).

🍴 **Giannino.** Corso Trento and Trieste 23, tel. 0184504014. Closed Sunday evening and Monday, variable holiday closure. Air conditioning. Highly sophisticated restaurant. Traditional cuisine, but with due attention to changes in eating habits; reasonably-priced business lunches (B5).

🍴 **Paolo e Barbara.** Via Roma 47, tel. 0184531653. Closed Wednesday, Thursday lunchtimes, and for periods in December, January and July. Air conditioning. Small but fascinating restaurant: Paolo, a committed chef who shuns fashions and appearances, uses almost exclusively local ingredients in the traditional recipes he revisits to create new culinary delights. Raviolini with spinach beet in curd sauce, trenette with mullet sauce, buckwheat pansotti with taleggio cheese filling, salt cod tripe with Pigna beans. Excellent desserts, including cassata in cornucopia sottile (C4).

🍴 **Il Bagatto.** Corso Matteotti 145, tel. 0184531925. Closed Sunday, July and for a period in January. Air conditioning. Two pleasant, carefully-furnished dining-rooms with vaulted ceilings in the 16th-century Palazzo Borea d'Olmo. Chef Ezio Ceniccola creates his imaginative versions of traditional dishes; good selection of wines (B4).

*** Dei Fiori. Locality Pian di Poma, Via Tiro a Volo 3, tel. 0184660635, fax 0184662377. All year.

📓 Cafés and pastry shops

Caffè Royal. C.so Imperatrice 80, tel. 01845391.

🍾🍷 Wineries

Enoteca Marone. Via S. Francesco 61, tel. 0184506916.
Mazzini Pub. Via S. Stefano 9, tel. 0184572007.

🏛 Museums and cultural institutions

Museo civico. Corso Matteotti, 143, tel. 0184531942. Closed Monday. Open: 9am-noon, 3-6pm.

at Coldirodi, 7 km

Pinacoteca e Biblioteca Rambaldi. Piazza S. Sebastiano 18. Closed Monday and Wednesday. Open: 10am-noon; Friday and Saturday also 3.30-6pm.

🏃 Shows and other festivities

Festival della Canzone Italiana (Song Festival). Last week in February.
Luigi Tenco Award. Singer-songwriter festival; last week in October.
Milano-Sanremo Cycle Race. Qualifier for the World Cycling Championships; third Saturday in March.
Sanremo Rally. World Racing Championship; in October.

✔️ Sport

Circolo Golf degli Ulivi. Via Campo Golf 59, tel. 0184557093. Golf Club.

⚖️ Arts and crafts

Fratelli Boeri. Via Palazzo 74, tel. 0184507663. Artistic porcelain and ceramics.
I Tasca. Frazione Bussana, Via Aurelia 95, tel. 0184510515. Artistic ceramics.
Stern & Dellerba. Via Privata delle Rose 7, tel. 0184661290. Cacti.
Studio Artistico Rapo. Via Massa 186, tel. 0184532394. Painting.
Wang Kristina. Frazione Bussana Vecchia, Via Vallao, tel. 0184510284. Artistic ceramics.
Weiser Wolfgang. Via Bussana Vecchia, tel. 0184 510388. Painting.
Zablach Vallejos Hector. Corso Marconi 9, tel. 0184662081. Latin American art.

Santa Margherita Ligure

Page 177   ✉ 16038
📍 *APT Tigullio*, Via XXV Aprile 4, tel. 01852929. Website www.apttigullio.liguria.it e-mail infoapt@apttigullio.liguria.it.

🏨🍴 Hotels, restaurants, campsites and holiday camps

⋆⋆ **Imperiale Palace Hotel.** Via Pagana 19, tel. 0185288991, fax 0185284223. Seasonal. 93 rooms. Air conditioning, elevator; parking facilities, garden, open-air pool, private beach. Late 19th-century building, in a superb position in a large, ancient park. De luxe interior with antique furnishings, extremely high level of comfort. Panoramic Novecento restaurant (A3).

⋆⋆⋆ **Continental.** Via Pagana 8, tel. 0185 286512, fax 0185284463. 76 rooms. Facilities for disabled. Air conditioning, elevator; parking facilities, garden, private beach. A grand, elegant hotel set amidst the palms and pine trees that run down to the sea (A-B3).

⋆⋆⋆ **G.H. Miramare.** Lungomare Milite Ignoto 30, tel. 0185287013, fax 0185284651. 81 rooms. Facilities for disabled. Air conditioning, elevator; parking facilities, garden, open-air pool, private beach. Imposing Art Nouveau-style building, situated opposite the sea, in a park with tropical plants and seawater swimming-pool; classy interior with period furniture; efficiently run (C3).

⋆⋆⋆ **Metropole.** Via Pagana 2, tel. 0185286134, fax 0185283495. 56 rooms. Air conditioning, elevator; parking facilities, garden, private beach. Beautifully situated in a huge park that leads down to the private beach. Comfortable, friendly and excellently managed by the owner. Snack-restaurant on beach, on a panoramic terrace; piano bar in summer (A3).

⋆⋆⋆ **Regina Elena.** Lungomare Milite Ignoto 44, tel. 0185287003, fax 0185284473. 105 rooms. Air conditioning, elevator; extensive parking facilities, garden, open-air pool, private beach. Another extremely friendly hotel run by the Ciana family; the garden leads directly to the private beach. Heated swimming-pool and whirlpool bath on the roof-solarium; splendid view over Tigullio Bay (C3).

⋆⋆⋆ **Minerva.** Via Maragliano 34/D, tel. 0185286073, fax 0185281697. 35 rooms. Elevator; parking facilities, garden. A hotel in a leafy setting near the port, with a relaxed atmosphere and well-equipped rooms (C2).

⋆⋆⋆ **Tigullio et de Milan.** Corso Rainusso 3, tel. 0185287455, fax 0185281860. 42 rooms. Air conditioning, elevator; parking facilities, garden. A modern, well-equipped hotel centrally situated close to the sea (A2).

⋆⋆ **Fasce.** Via Bozzo 3, tel. 0185286435, fax 0185283580. 12 rooms, of which 9 with bath or shower. Meublé. Parking facilities, garden. Run by the Fasce family which, for over forty years, has offered a highly professional service. Bicycles for hire (A1-2).

🍴 **Cambusa.** Via Bottaro 1, tel. 0185287410. Closed Thursday (in August Thursday lunchtime), and for a period between January and February. A characteristic restaurant by the sea, with a pleasant summer terrace with views of the port; simple, but carefully-prepared flavorful fish dishes (B2).

🍴 **L'Approdo da Felice.** Via Cairoli 26, tel. 0185281789. Closed Monday, for a period between February and March, and in December. Air conditioning, garden. Interesting traditional and seafood menu in the heart of the old town (B2).

🍴 **Trattoria Cesarina.** Via Mameli 2/C, tel. 0185286059. Closed Tuesday, mid-December to January. Ligurian cuisine - mushrooms, fish. Simple but tastefully furnished restaurant; traditional cuisine (C2).

📓 Cafés and pastry shops

Sabot American Bar. Piazza Martiri della Libertà 32, tel. 0185280747. Young person's bar.

🏛 Museums and cultural institutions

Villa Durazzo. Piazza S. Giacomo 1, tel. 0185205449. Closed Monday. Open: 9am-6pm, October-March 9.30am-12.30pm, 2.30-4.30pm.

⛪ Churches and monuments

Abbey of San Gerolamo della Cervara. Visits by prior arrangement, tel. 800652110.

🦌 Nature sites, parks and reserves

Regional Nature Park Authority of Portofino. Viale Rainusso 1, tel. 0185289479, website digilander.iol.it/parcoportofino, e-mail enteparco.portofino@labnet.comm2000.it.

Sant'Olcese

Page 104   ✉ 16010

🏛️ Churches and monuments
Villa Pinelli Gentile Serra. Open: 9am-5pm;
April and May 9am-7.30pm.

Santo Stefano d'Àveto

Page 187   ✉ 16049
📄 *IAT*, Piazza del Popolo 1, tel. 013588046.

🏨 Hotels, restaurants, campsites and
holiday camps
** **Leon d'Oro.** Via Razzetti 52, tel. 018588073, fax
018588041. 34 rooms. Elevator. Warm, friendly
family atmosphere; restaurant with Ligurian
and Emilian cuisine.
† **Doria.** Via Piaggio 4, tel. 018588052. Closed
Wednesday (except in summer), October-
November. Parking facilities, garden. Ligurian
cuisine - first courses. Simply designed family
run restaurant known for its professionalism. In
summer traditional local specialties revisited
are served in the garden.

🍰 Cafés and pastry shops
Bar Pasticceria Marrè. Via Mazzetti 30, tel.
018588169.
Pasticceria Chiesa. Via al Castello 27, tel.
018588056.

Sarzana

Page 204   ✉ 19038

🏨 Hotels, restaurants, campsites and
holiday camps
† **Girarrosto-da Paolo.** Via dei Molini 388, tel.
0187621088. Closed Wednesday, and for a period in July. Parking facilities. Lunigiana cuisine.
A well-established, authentic, family-run country trattoria in the green hills (A2, off map).
⚜ **Iron Gate - Marina 3 B - P.V.** Locality Falaschi,
** Viale XXV Aprile 54, tel. 0187676370, fax
0187675014. All year.

at Marinella di Sarzana, 10 km   ✉ 19030
*** **Rondine.** Viale Litoraneo 58, tel. 018764025, fax
018764256. 54 rooms. Facilities for disabled.
Elevator; garage, garden, private beach. Right
by the sea, simple, functional interior, panoramic restaurant on top floor.

🍰 Cafés and pastry shops
Gemmi. Via Mazzini 21, tel. 0187620165.

🏛️ Churches and monuments
at Sarzanello, 2 km
Fortezza di Sarzanello. tel. 0187409077. Open:
Saturday and Sunday 14.30-17.30.

🏛️ Markets and fairs
**La soffitta nella strada (The attic in the
street).** Open-air antiques fair in the historic
center. From first Saturday in August for three
weeks and during the Easter weekend.

🦌 Nature sites, parks and reserves
**Regional Nature Park Authority di Monte-
marcello-Magra.** Via Paci 2, tel. 0187691071, fax
0187606738, e-mail mcaleo@iclab.it.

Sassello

Page 118   ✉ 16038
📄 *IAT Sassello* (seas.), Via G. B. Badano, tel.
019724020, fax 019723832.

🏛️ Museums and cultural institutions
Museo Perrando. Via dei Perrando 33, tel.
019724100. Open: Friday, 3-5pm; Saturday 10am-
noon and 3-5pm; on other days by prior
arrangement.

🔶 Arts and crafts
Ceramiche 2G. Sorerolo Campi 31, tel.
019724671. Artistic ceramics.

🦌 Nature sites, parks and reserves
**Beigua Regional Nature Park Visitors'
Center.** Via Badano 45, tel. 019724020.

Savignone

Page 105   ✉ 16010

🏨 Hotels, restaurants, campsites and
holiday camps
*** **Palazzo Fieschi.** Piazza della Chiesa 14, tel.
0109360063, fax 010936821. 20 rooms. Facilities
for disabled. Elevator; parking facilities, garden.
A comfortable, beautifully-kept hotel in the
16th-century Palazzo Fieschi, which retains the
austere charm of the old patrician residence.

🏛️ Museums and cultural institutions
at San Bartolomeo, 2 km
Museo Storico dell'Alta Valle Scrivia. San
Bartolomeo di Vallecalda, tel. 0109360103.
Visits by prior arrangement.

Savona

Page 110   ✉ 17100
📄 *IAT Savona*, Via Guidobono 125r, tel.
0198402321, fax 0198403672.

🏨 Hotels, restaurants, campsites and
holiday camps
☆ **Mare.** Via Nizza 89, tel. 019264065, fax 019263277.
65 rooms. Meublé. Facilities for disabled. Air
conditioning, elevator; parking facilities, garden, private beach. Hotel with a complete
range of services including some rooms with
whirlpool bath; a number of elegant suites are
available (D1, off map).
*** **Motel Mirò.** Via Nizza 62, tel. 019861616, fax
019861632. 60 rooms. Facilities for disabled. Air
conditioning, elevator; parking facilities, garden, private beach. A comfortable, refurbished
hotel overlooking the sea and just 500 meters
from the highway exit; busy Club restaurant
(D1, off map).
*** **Riviera Suisse.** Via Paleocapa 24, tel.
019850853, fax 019853435. 80 rooms, of which
76 with bath or shower. Facilities for disabled.
Elevator; parking facilities. In a period building,
with functional, well-furnished rooms.
Professional, friendly staff (C2).
††† **A Spurcacciun-a.** Via Nizza 89/r, tel.
019264065, fax 019263277. Closed Wednesday,
and Christmas to mid-January. Air conditioning,
parking facilities, garden. Carefully prepared
traditional seafood dishes adapted to suit the
modern palate. Summer garden (D1, off map).
†† **Il Rigolo.** Corso Mazzini 62/r, tel. 019856406.
Closed Monday, January. Garden. A centrally-
located, friendly, intimate restaurant, with cool
garden in summer; cuisine based on local food.
Family run (C-D2).
†† **Molo Vecchio.** Via Baglietto 8/R, tel. 019854219.
Closed Tuesday, and for a period in September.

Air conditioning. New establishment in an old area which redevelopment has given a new lease of life. Traditional Ligurian cuisine revisited (B-C3).

⚲ ✱✱ Buggi International. At Zinola, Via N.S. del Monte 15, tel. 019860120. All year.

⌂ Youth hostels

Priamàr. Piazzale Priamàr 1, tel. 019812653. Open all year.

Villa de Franceschini. Via alla Strà 29, tel. 019263222. Open all year.

☕ Cafés and pastry shops

Ostaia du Cuu du Beuf. Calata Sbarbaro 34 r., tel. 019821091.

Osteria Bacco. Via Quarda Superiore 17, tel. 0198335350.

🏛 Museums and cultural institutions

Civico Museo Storico Archeologico. Corso Mazzini 1, tel. 019822708. Closed Monday. Open: from June to September, Tuesday-Saturday 10am-noon and 4-6pm, Sunday and holidays 4-6pm; from October to May, Tuesday-Saturday 10am-noon and 3-5pm, Sunday and holidays 3-5pm.

Museo d'Arte Sandro Pertini. Corso Mazzini 1, tel. 019811520. Closed Sunday and holidays. Open: 8.30am-1pm.

Museo del Tesoro della Cattedrale. Piazza Duomo, tel. 019825960. Visits by prior arrangement.

Museo del Tesoro del Santuario di Nostra Signora della Misericordia. Piazza Santuario 6, tel. 019879025. Open: Sunday and religious holidays 9am-noon, 3-6pm; on other days by prior arrangement.

Museo Renata Cuneo. Corso Mazzini 1. Closed for restoration.

Pinacoteca Civica. Corso Mazzini 1, tel. 019811520. Closed Sunday. Open: 8.30am-12.30pm, Thursday 8.30am-6pm.

Quadreria del Seminario Vescovile. Via Ponzone 5. Visits by prior arrangement, tel. 019821998.

⛪ Churches and monuments

Oratorio del Cristo Risorto. Via Aonzo, tel. 098335529. Open: 4-7pm and Sunday morning.

Oratorio di Nostra Signora di Castello. Via Manzoni, tel. 019813412. Open: Sunday and holidays, 8-10am.

🏃 Shows and other festivities

Teatro Comunale Gabriello Chiabrera. Piazza Diaz 2, tel. 019820409 (box office).

⚖ Arts and crafts

Canarini Luigi. Via Famagosta 18/20 r., tel. 019823793. Artistic windows.

Elde Ansgar. Piazza Santuario 7, tel. 019879277. Painter's studio.

Lorenzini Sandro. Via Milano 9 r., tel. 019811391. Sculptor's studio.

Stella d'Argento. Via Aonzo 24 r., tel. 019822482. Artistic ceramics.

🐿 Nature sites, parks and reserves

Beigua Regional Nature Park Authority. Corso Italia 3, tel. 01984187300, e-mail beigua@tin.it.

Sestri Levante

🏨 Hotels, restaurants, campsites and holiday camps

✱✱✱ G.H. dei Castelli. Via Penisola 26, tel. 0185487220, fax 018544767. Seasonal. 30 rooms. Elevator; parking facilities, garden, private beach. Medieval-style building, surrounded by a large park, well equipped to ensure a comfortable stay; independently-run restaurant (B2).

✱✱✱ G.H. Villa Balbi. Viale Rimembranza 1, tel. 018542941, fax 0185482459. 95 rooms. Air conditioning, elevator; parking facilities, garden, open-air pool, private beach. A complex of three buildings in a park with heated swimming-pool. The main building is a 17th-century villa whose spacious rooms and suites have period furnishings; Il Parco restaurant (B2).

✱✱✱ Vis à Vis. Via della Chiusa 28, tel. 018542661, fax 0185480853. 49 rooms. Air conditioning, elevator; parking facilities, garden, open-air pool. A panoramic, quietly situated hotel set in the hills amidst olive groves, with elevator to the town; friendly, professional service; modern congress facilities (B3).

✱✱✱ Due Mari. Vico Coro 18, tel. 018542695, fax 018542698. 26 rooms. Elevator; parking facilities, garden, private beach. Situated on the isthmus of the peninsula between the "two seas". 17th-century Genoese patrician residence completely refurbished and modernized; the dining-rooms face onto the fine inner garden (B-C2).

✱✱✱ Helvetia. Via Cappuccini 43, tel. 018541175, fax 0185457216. Seasonal. 24 rooms. Meublé. Air conditioning, elevator; parking facilities, garden, private beach. Comfortable, completely refurbished, functional hotel situated right by the sea in the Bay of Silence. (B2-3).

🍴🍴🍴 Fiammenghilla Fieschi. At Riva Trigoso, Via Pestella 6, tel. 0185481041. Closed Monday, and for periods between January and February and between October and November. Air conditioning, parking facilities, garden. Situated on the ground floor of a 17th-century villa, whose ancient structure and atmosphere it retains; extremely carefully-prepared food (mainly fish), excellent service (B3, off map).

🍴🍴 El Pescador. Via Pilade Queirolo 1, tel. 018542888. Closed Tuesday, and mid-December to early February. Air conditioning, parking facilities. Nautical atmosphere, high quality seafood and fish specialties, good selection of wines. Pleasant verandah overlooking the sea (B1).

🍴🍴 San Marco. Via Pilade Queirolo, tel. 018541459. Closed Wednesday, and for a period in November. A bright, cheerful restaurant overlooking the port with the sea on three sides, innovative mostly fish dishes (B1).

🍴 Mandrella. Viale Dante 37, tel. 018542716, fax 018542716. Closed Wednesday (except in July and August), and for periods in November and January. An elegantly decorated, friendly restaurant in an early 20th-century building; traditional cuisine including some interesting reworkings of ancient recipes (B3).

⚲ ✱✱✱ Tigullio - P.V. Via Sara 111/A, tel. 0185455455, fax 0185457257. All year.

⚲ ✱✱ Trigoso - P.V. A Riva Trigoso, Via Aurelia 251/A, tel. 018541047, fax 018541047. All year.

☕ Cafés and pastry shops

Rossignotti. Via Dante 2, tel. 018541034. Pastry shop noted for its nougat production.

🏛 Museums and cultural institutions

Galleria Rizzi. Via dei Cappuccini 8, tel. 018541300. Open: April and October Sunday 10am-1pm; 1 May-19 June and 11-30 September Wednesday 4-7pm; 20 June-10 September Friday and Saturday 9-11pm.

241

Arts and crafts

Asteria. Piazzetta Rizzi 16, tel. 0185457596. Artistic ceramics workshop.

Spotorno

Page 120 ✉ 17028
ℹ️ *IAT Spotorno*, Via Aurelia 119, tel. 0197415008, fax 0197415811.

Hotels, restaurants, campsites and holiday camps

⁑ **Tirreno.** Via Aurelia 2, tel. 019745106, fax 019745061. 38 rooms. Air conditioning, elevator; parking facilities, garden, private beach. A modern, functional and comfortable hotel by the seashore, with direct access to the beach; dining-room with bright, panoramic verandah, self-service lunches on the beach.

*** **Delle Palme.** Via Aurelia 39, tel. 019745161, fax 019745161. 32 rooms. Private beach. This modern establishment on the seafront promenade has been family run for 35 years; comfortable, panoramic rooms.

*** **La Torre.** Via alla Torre 25, tel. 019745390, fax 019746487. 24 rooms, of which 20 with bath or shower. Air conditioning, parking facilities, garden. Quietly situated, surrounded by pinewoods and gardens. Most rooms are doubles, with panoramic terrace; some are combined with single rooms sharing the same bathroom: ideal for families.

⑈ **A Sigögna.** Via Garibaldi 13, tel. 019745016. Closed Tuesday (except in summer), late October-early December. Garden. Friendly, family-run restaurant, serving expertly-prepared seafood.

⚓** **Rustia - P.V.** Locality Prelo, Via alla Torre 2, tel. 019745042. Seasonal.

Stellanello

Page 138 ✉ 17020
ℹ️ *Pro Loco Stellanello*, fraz. Rossi 1, tel. 0182668404.

Arts and crafts

Bestoso Domenico Dino. Via Borgonuovo 16, tel. 0182668031. Extra-virgin oil production.

Taggia

Page 156 ✉ 18018
at *Arma di Taggia, 3 km*
ℹ️ *IAT*, Villa Boselli, tel. 018443733.

Churches and monuments

Convent of San Domenico. Piazza Beato Cristoforo 6, tel. 0184476254. Open: 9am-noon, 3-5pm (until 6pm in summer).

Arts and crafts

Cantina Fratelli Ferraresi. Via Lungo Argentina 49, tel. 0184475290. Production and sale of wines.
Cooperativa Agricola Valverde. Via Revelli 96, tel. 0184476100. Flower bouquets prepared.
Corradi Umberto. At Arma di Taggia, Via Mimosa 10, tel. 018444294. Painting.

Toirano

Page 126 ✉ 17020
ℹ️ *Comune di Toirano*, tel. 018298722.

Museums and cultural institutions

Grotte di Toirano. Piazzale delle Grotte, tel. 018298062. Open: 9am-noon, 2-5pm.

Museo di Storia, Cultura e Tradizioni della Val Varatella. Via Polla 12, tel. 0182989968. Open: 10am-1pm, 3-6pm.

Torriglia

Page 106 ✉ 16029
ℹ️ *IAT*, Via N. S. della Provvidenza 3, tel. 010944931.

Hotels, restaurants, campsites and holiday camps

⑈ **Taverna dei Fieschi.** Via Magioncalda 30, tel. 010944815. Closed Monday, October and for a period in June. A characteristic restaurant with vaulted ceilings and period furniture in the heart of the old town. Simple, carefully-prepared Ligurian cuisine; family run since 1976.

Nature sites, parks and reserves

Centro Visite Parco Naturale Regionale dell'Antola. Via N. S. della Provvidenza 3, tel. 010944931, e-mail parco@telecentroantola. ge.it.

Tovo San Giacomo

Page 126 ✉ 17020
ℹ️ *Comune di Tovo San Giacomo*, tel. 019637140.

Museums and cultural institutions

at *Bardino Nuovo, 3 km*
Museo dell'Orologio da Torre Giovanni Battista Bergallo (tower clock museum). Piazza S. Sebastiano, tel. 019637140. Open: Wednesday-Sunday 9am-noon, 3-6pm; July and August 3-6pm, 8-11pm.

Triora

Page 158 ✉ 18010
ℹ️ *IAT*, Corso Italia 3, tel. 018494477.

Hotels, restaurants, campsites and holiday camps

** **Colomba d'Oro.** Corso Italia 66, tel. 018494051, fax 018494089. Seasonal. 37 rooms. Facilities for disabled. Garden. In an old convent, simple, sober interior.

Museums and cultural institutions

Museo Etnografico e della Stregoneria (witch-craft museum). C.so Italia 1, tel. 018494477. Open: 2.30-6pm (in summer 3-6.30pm); Saturday, Sunday and holidays also 10.30am-noon, 2.30-6pm.

Val Brevenna

Page 105 ✉ 16010

Museums and cultural institutions

at *Senarega, 7 km*
Museo Storico dell'Alta Valle Scrivia - Ethnology section. Visits by prior arrangement, tel. 0109672889.

Vallecrosia

Page 153 ✉ 18019

Hotels, restaurants, campsites and holiday camps

⑈⑈ **Giappun.** Via Maonaira 7, tel. 0184250560. Closed Wednesday, Thursday lunchtime, and for periods in July and November. Air conditioning, parking facilities. Intimate, friendly establishment run by the Lamberti family for over 80 years; Ligurian cuisine, a wide selection of fish dishes and a number of Provençale specialties.

Museums and cultural institutions

Museo della Canzone e della Riproduzione

Sonora (sound-recording museum). Via Roma 108, tel. 0184291000. Visits by prior arrangement.

⚖ Arts and crafts

Amato Vincenzo. Via Matteotti 2, tel. 0184290448. Painting.
Fratelli Tonet. Via Roma 107, tel. 0184253511. Ceramic art workshop.

Varazze

ℹ *IAT Varazze,* Viale Nazioni Unite 1, tel. 019935043, 019935916.

🏨 Hotels, restaurants, campsites and holiday camps

⁑   *Cristallo.* Via Cilea 4, tel. 01997264, fax 01996392. 45 rooms. Air conditioning, elevator; parking facilities, garden. Attractive outside, rational and comfortable inside; the centerpiece is the newly-opened gym; use of beach (A1).

⁑   *Eden.* Via Villagrande 1, tel. 019932888, fax 01996315. 45 rooms. Air conditioning, elevator; parking facilities, garden. functional, well-equipped hotel, catering mainly for business clientele; restaurant open in July and August (A1).

⁑   *Royal.* Via Cavour 25, tel. 019931166, fax 01996664. 33 rooms. Air conditioning, elevator; parking facilities. Functional, family-run hotel: fully soundproofed rooms all with sea view; busy restaurant (A3).

***   *Piccolo Hotel.* Via Padre Piazza 1, tel. 019932610, fax 0199355155. 36 rooms. Elevator; parking facilities, garden. Modern and functional, a stone's throw from the sea (A1).

⫟⫟   *Antico Genovese.* Corso Colombo 70, tel. 01996482. Closed Sunday, and for a period in September and in December. Air conditioning, parking facilities. Ligurian and traditional cuisine - fish. Friendly restaurant offering professional service (A1).

⫟⫟   *Cavetto.* Piazza S. Caterina 7, tel. 01997311. Closed Thursday, and for periods in January and in November. Meticulous service. Ligurian cuisine with good, often unusual fish specialties (A4).

🍵 Cafés and pastry shops

Confetteria Daniela & Daniela. Via Gavarone 16, tel. 01996239.
Magia Pub. Via Colombo 32, tel. 019930761.
Pasticceria Giordano. Via Mameli 18, tel. 019934642.

🏛 Museums and cultural institutions

at Alpicella, 8 km
Archaeological Exhibition. Piazza IV Novembre, tel. 01993901. Visits by prior arrangement.

⚖ Arts and crafts

Piccola Fornace. Via S. Ambrogio 41, tel. 01996607. Artistic ceramics.

👫 Local guides and excursions

at Alpicella, 8 km
Trekking Club Monte Beigua Vetta. C/o Albergo Monte Beigua, Via Monte Beigua 19, tel. 019931300. Horse-riding excursions (in season).

Varese Ligure

ℹ *IAT* (seas.), Via Portici 73, tel. and fax 0187842094.

🏨 Hotels, restaurants, campsites and holiday camps

⫟   *Amici.* Via Garibaldi 80, tel. 0187842139. Closed Wednesday in winter, Christmas-New Year. Parking facilities, garden. A friendly, family-run restaurant with a well-established tradition; Ligurian cuisine with specialties served in earthenware dishes.

🏛 Museums and cultural institutions

at Cassego, 10 km
Museo della Tradizione Contadina di Cassego (farming museum). Via Provinciale 150. Closed Sunday. Visits by prior arrangement, tel. 0187843005.

⚖ Arts and crafts

Cooperativa Agricola Casearia Val di Vara. Locality Perassa, tel. 0187842108. Cheeses and other dairy produce.

Varigotti

ℹ *IAT Varigotti* (seas.), Via Aurelia, tel. 019698013, fax 019698488.

🏨 Hotels, restaurants, campsites and holiday camps

**   *Holiday.* Via Ulivi 45, tel. 019698124, fax 019698124. Seasonal. 12 rooms. Garden. A comfortable hotel in a quiet, leafy setting, with typical Ligurian cuisine provided by the owners themselves.

⫟⫟⫟   *Muraglia-Conchiglia d'Oro.* Via Aurelia 133, tel. 019698015. Closed Wednesday (in winter also Tuesday), mid-January to mid-February. Parking facilities. Modern, elegant restaurant, with a cool outdoor area in summer. Fish, displayed in large wicker baskets and cooked on the large grille at the back of the dining-room, reigns supreme. The menu, which changes every day, offers the flavors of the sea enhanced with herbs.

⛪ Churches and monuments

San Lorenzo Vecchio. Strada per S. Lorenzo, tel. 019698252. Open: Sunday, 9am-2pm; on other days by prior arrangement.

Ventimiglia

ℹ *IAT*, Via Cavour 61, tel. 0184351183.

🏨 Hotels, restaurants, campsites and holiday camps

***   *Sole e Mare.* Via Marconi 12, tel. 0184351854, fax 0184230988. 28 rooms. Meublé. Facilities for disabled. Elevator; parking facilities, garden. Comfortable and functional, on the seafront promenade and not far from the center; adjoins the independently-run restaurant Pasta e Basta (B1).

⫟   *Marco Polo.* Passeggiata Cavallotti 2, tel. 0184352678. Closed Sunday evening and Monday (out of season), November and mid-January to mid-February. Garden. A restaurant overlooking the sea, serving regional cuisine (mostly fish) revisited (B3).

🏠   *Casa Giovannina.* At Castel d'Appio, Via Sant'Anna 205, tel. 0184356305, fax 018433575. All year.

at Castel d'Appio, 5 km
***   *La Riserva di Castel d'Appio.* tel. 0184229533,

fax 0184229712. Seasonal. 21 rooms. Parking facilities, garden, open-air pool. An ancient residence high up over the sea transformed into a comfortable, well-equipped hotel with superb views over the Blue Riviera and the Riviera of the Flowers; busy restaurant.

at Grimaldi Inferiore, 7 km   ✉ 18036
🍴 **Baia Beniamin.** Corso Europa 63, tel. 018438002, fax 018438027. Closed Sunday evening (out of season), Monday, and for periods in spring and November. Air conditioning, parking facilities, garden. This elegant restaurant, set in a large park by the seashore, serves light, mouth-watering fish dishes: moscardini with Pigna beans, scampi kebab with spelt, lasagnetta di astice and zucchini, seafood salad and, to finish with, sherbet with chocolates. Accommodation available.

at Ponte San Ludovico, km 8
🍴 **Balzi Rossi.** Via Balzi Rossi 2, tel. 018438132, fax 018438532. Closed Monday, Tuesday lunchtime (in high season also Sunday lunch), and for periods in March and December. Air conditioning. Refined atmosphere, excellent Ligurian cuisine, especially, prepared by Mamma Beglia; the terrace high up over the sea has an unforgettable view.

🍷 Wineries
La Cave. Via Cavour 54/A, tel. 0184351326.

🏛 Museums and cultural institutions
Museo Archeologico Gerolamo Rossi. Via Verdi 41, tel. 0184351181. Closed Monday. Open: 9am-12.30pm, 3-5pm; Sunday 10am-12.30pm.

at Mortola Inferiore, 6 km
Giardini Botanici Villa Hanbury. Corso Montecarlo 43, tel. 0184229507. Closed Wednesday in winter. Open: 10am-4pm; March-May 10am-5pm; June-September 10am-6pm.

at Ponte San Ludovico, 8 km
Museo Preistorico dei Balzi Rossi. Via Balzi Rossi 9, tel. 018438113. Closed Monday. Open: 9am-7pm.

⚖ Arts and crafts
Ceramica Corbo. Frazione Bevera, Via Maneira 11, tel. 0184210025. Artistic ceramics.
Coppo Etablissement de la Roya. Via Martiri della Libertà 20, tel. 0184358058. Sale of wines, spirits, and foodstuffs.
Statari Santo. Lungomare Varaldo 16, tel. 0184250667. Interior decoration.

Vernazza

Page 201   ✉ 19018

🏨 Hotels, restaurants, campsites and holiday camps
🍴 **Gambero Rosso.** Piazza Marconi 7, tel. 0187812265. Closed Monday (except August), December-February. Air conditioning. A friendly, professional restaurant in an ancient building that still has its old archways; fish specialties and excellent choice of wines.

⚖ Arts and crafts
Cantina del Molo. Via Gavino 19, tel. 0187821141. Wines.
Dolce Stil Novo. Locality Campo 3, tel. 0187821013. Artistic ceramics.

🌲 Farm holidays
at Corniglia, 6 km
Barrani Fabio. Via Fieschi 14, tel. 0187812063. Rooms in the village, food. Walks along the pathways connecting the Cinque Terre; sale of honey, D.O.C. wines, and oil.
La Rocca. Via Fieschi 222, tel. 0187812178. Accommodation in apartment and rooms in a house in the village. Walks and excursions; sale of D.O.C. wine and oil.

Vezzano Ligure

Page 207   ✉ 19020
ℹ *Pro Loco*, c/o Town Hall, tel. 0187993111.

⚖ Arts and crafts
Musante Francesco. Via Gramsci 41, tel. 0187993006. Artist's studio.

🚶 Local guides and excursions
Circolo Ippico Forte Bastia. Via Cerretta 1, tel. 0187994600. Horse-riding.

🤸 Shows and other festivities
Festival di Villa Faraldi. Theater and dance festival; in July.

Villanova d'Albenga

Page 131   ✉ 17038
ℹ *IAT Villanova d'Albenga* (seas.), Via Albenga 46, tel. and fax 0182582241.

🏨 Hotels, restaurants, campsites and holiday camps
*** **Hermitage.** Via Roma 152, tel. 0182582976, fax 0182582975. 11 rooms. Air conditioning, parking facilities, garden. Traditional, comfortable, family-run hotel, recently refurbished.
*** **C'era una volta.** Regione Fasceti, Strada per Ligo, tel. 0182580461, fax 0182582871. Seasonal.

⚖ Arts and crafts
Oleificio Baglietto & Secco. Via Roma 137, tel. 0182582838. Oil.

Vobbia

Page 105   ✉ 16010

🏛 Churches and monuments
Castello della Pietra. Locality Torre, tel. 010939479. Open: Sunday 10-17; June, July and September Saturday and Sunday 10am-6pm; August Thursday, Saturday and Sunday 10am-6pm.

Zoagli

Page 180   ✉ 18039
ℹ *IAT* (seas.), Piazza S. Martino 8, tel. 0185259127.

⚖ Arts and crafts
Gaggioli Giuseppe. Via Aurelia 208/A, tel. 0185259057. Damask, velvet, silk.
Seterie di Zoagli. Via S. Pietro 21, tel. 0185259141. Silk and velvet manufacture.

Index of names

The following index lists artists and architects mentioned in the guide, in order of surname, or – in cases where the surname is unfamiliar or unknown – by the pseudonym, nickname or first name followed by patronym or place of origin. The entries also contain a brief biographical note and references to the pages where the artists or their works are mentioned.

Abbreviations used:
A., architect(s); *act.*, active; *b.*, born; *bef.*, before; *ca.*, circa; *Carv.*, wood carver; *cent.*, century; *Cer.*, ceramicist(s); *d.*, died; *doc.*, documented; *Engn.*, engineer; *Engr.*, engraver; *fam.*, family; *P.*, painter(s); *S.*, sculptor(s); *Stg Des.*, stage designer; *Stucc.*, stucco artist.

Abate Ciccio, see *Solimena Francesco*
Adrechi Stefano, Nice (France), P., doc. 1512-41, p. 163
Albini Franco, Robbiate (Como), A., 1905-77, pp. 25, 27, 31, 53, 56, 64
Alessi Galeazzo, Perugia, A., ca. 1512-72, pp. 22, 24, 28, 48, 52, 62, 63, 77, 80, 95, 100, 102, 125, 177
Amoretti Gaetano, Oneglia (now Imperia), A., 1709-62, p. 140
Ansaldo Giovanni Andrea, Genoa Voltri, P., 1584-1638, pp. 29, 65, 67, 94, 102
Antonello da Messina (Antonello di Giovanni), Messina, P., ca. 1430-1479, p. 60
Antonio de Carabo, Comacin master, A., 16th cent., p. 179
Assereto Gioacchino, Genoa, P., 1600-49, pp. 29, 65, 73

Baiardo Giovanni Battista, Genoa, P., 1620-57, p. 59
Baliani Giovanni, Savona, A., 1583-?, p. 86
Barabino Carlo, Genoa, A., 1768-1835, pp. 24, 30, 66, 72, 73, 76, 79, 107
Barabino Nicolò, Genoa Sampierdarena, P., 1832-91, pp. 175, 178, 180
Barbagelata Giovanni, Genoa, P., 1484-1508, pp. 116, 125, 189
Bardi Donato de', Pavia, P., doc. from 1426, d. bef. 1451, pp. 27, 111
Barnaba da Modena, Modena, P., doc. 1361-83, pp. 27, 57, 115, 150, 183
Barocci or *Baroccio (Federico Fiori),* Urbino, P., bef. 1535-1612, p. 52
Baroni Eugenio, Taranto, S., 1888-1935, p. 95
Baudo Luca, Piedmont (Novara?), P., doc. from 1491, d. 1510, p. 144
Bellini Giovanni, Venice, P., ca. 1432-1516, p. 194
Belmonte Domenico, Gazzelli di Chiusanico (Imperia), A., 1725-95, pp. 145, 146
Benedetto da Rovezzano (Benedetto Grazzini), Pistoia, S. and A., 1474-after 1552, p. 76
Benso Giulio, Pieve di Teco (Imperia), P., 1601-68, p. 67
Benti Donato di Battista, Florence, S. and A., 1470-ca. 1536, p. 76
Bergamasco, il, see *Castello Giovanni Battista*
Bernini Gian Lorenzo, Naples, A., S. and P., 1598-1680, pp. 30, 115
Betti Sigismondo, Florence, P., doc. 1720-65, p. 60
Bianco Bartolomeo, Como, A., 1590-1657, pp. 57, 68, 86, 182, 183
Bianco Cipriano, A. act. in Genoa, 16th-17th cent., p. 83
Biazaci, fam. of P. from Busca (Cuneo), act. second half 15th cent., p. 28

Biazaci Matteo, Busca (Cuneo), P. act. second half 15th cent., p. 145
Biazaci Tomaso, Busca (Cuneo), P., doc. 1465-90, p. 145
Bisi Luigi, Milan, P. and A., 1814-86, p. 104
Bissoni, fam. of S. from Lombardy, 16th-17th cent., pp. 30, 62
Bissoni Domenico, known as *Domenico Veneto,* Lombardy, S., doc. from 1597, d. 1645, p. 57
Bocciardo Domenico, Finale Ligure (Savona), P., ca. 1686-1746, p. 141
Bocciardo Pasquale, Genoa, S., ca. 1710-91, p. 124
Boni Giacomo Antonio, Bologna, P., 1688-1766, pp. 61, 150
Borgianni Orazio, Rome, P., ca. 1578-1616, p. 115
Braccesco Carlo, Milan, P., doc. 1478-1501, pp. 27, 60, 145
Brea Antonio, Nice (France), P., doc. from 1495, d. 1527, pp. 143, 156
Brea Francesco, Nice (France), P., doc. 1512-55, pp. 156, 157, 158, 168
Brea Lodovico, Nice (France), P., doc. from 1475, d. 1522-23, pp. 28, 57, 83, 114, 115, 121, 156, 158, 163, 168, 169
Brilla Antonio, Savona, S., 1813-91, pp. 112, 113
Brozzi Paolo, Bologna, P., doc. 1650, p. 77
Brueghel Pieter, the Younger, Brussels (Belgium), P., ca. 1564-ca. 1638, p. 206
Brusco Paolo Gerolamo, Savona, P., 1742-1820, pp. 111, 113, 114

Caldera Simone, Andora (Savona), goldsmith, doc. from 1438, d. 1468, p. 53
Calvi, fam. of P. from Genoa, 16th-17th cent., p. 29
Calvi Felice, Genoa, P., doc. 1584, p. 74
Cambiaso Giovanni, Genoa, P., 1495-1579, pp. 74, 156, 157
Cambiaso Luca, Moneglia (Genoa), P. and S., 1527-85, pp. 29, 52, 54, 58, 63, 66, 74, 76, 77, 79, 80, 83, 95, 100, 108, 133, 156, 157, 158, 159, 177, 180, 183, 185, 186, 190, 201, 203
Canavesio Giovanni, Pinerolo (Turin), P., 1420/25-after 1499, pp. 28, 133, 156, 166, 169
Canova Antonio, Possagno (Treviso), S. and P., 1757-1822, p. 56
Cantone or *Cantoni Bernardino,* Cabbio (Canton Ticino, Switzerland), A. act. in Genoa, doc. 1537-72, pp. 60, 62, 63, 66, 74, 100
Cantoni or *Cantone Gaetano,* Muggio (Canton Ticino, Switzerland), A., 1745-1838, pp. 30, 141
Cantoni or *Cantone Simone,* Muggio (Canton Ticino, Switzerland), A., 1736-1818, pp. 30, 55

245

Index of places

This index comprises place names and isolated monuments mentioned in the itineraries and excursions; page numbers in *italics* refer to the "Other places: hotels, restaurants, curiosities. Addresses, opening times" section in which the place is listed. Monuments, churches and other places of interest in the region's most important towns (shown in blue) are grouped together in sub-indexes under the town's own heading.

Seterie di Zoagli Cordani

Silk manufacturing became popular in Genoa in the XVth century developing in the Eastern Riviera and especially in Zoagli with the velvet weaving. In 1890, 1236 looms had been registred in the Eastern Riviera, of which 1200 were distributed in Zoagli. In 1924 thanks to Domenico Cordani's sons Gio Batta and Luigi Eugenio entrepreneurial initiative was established the still existing **"Seterie di Zoagli Cordani"**. Their heirs, faithful to Zoagli and its heritage, are still sending their products to foreign markets all over the world, giving their names to a place of ancient and renowned tradition.

We are the only one in the world able to weave the famous smooth silk velvet like in the XVI century and as ancient time we continue weaving, with hand looms the jacquard velvets; we also realise high quality fabrics for dresses and design.

We have a special care to create a wide range of cloths for wedding and ceremony dresses.

In our point of sale you can also buy ties, foulards, scarves, personalized shirts and our exclusive tailored female models.

Via san Pietro, 21 - Tel. 0185 259141
www.teleconsiglio.com/cordani
E-mail: cordani-zoagli@libero.it
(Open from monday to saturday 9.00 am to 18.00 pm)

Picture credits: *AFE (G.B. Poletto)*, p. 36; *Agenzia In Liguria*, p. 38; *(APT Genova)*, p. 28 top; *(Marré Brunenghi)*, p. 89; *(F. Merlo)*, p. 188; *(M. Saponaro)*, pp. 84, 100, 103, 182; *APT La Spezia*, p. 199; *APT Savona*, pp. 24, 111, 119, 126, 135, 136, 170 right, 214, 215; *Archivi Alinari, (Tatge)*, p. 31; *Archivi Alinari/Seat*, pp. 27, 55, 59, 75, 79, 83, 141, 146, 195; *Archivio di Palazzo Rosso*, p. 53; *Archivio Fotografico Electa*, pp. 29, 64, 65, 68/69 top, 77, 94, 115, 145, 152, 156, 183; *Archivio TCI*, pp. 44, 80/81, 95, 101, 134, 173 top, 186; *G. L. Boetti*, pp. 16 bottom, 17 top, 22, 33 top, 117, 118, 122 bottom, 123, 124, 140, 160 right, 163 bottom; *Carfagna e Associati (G. Carfagna)*, pp. 19 bottom, 25, 46 bottom, 56; *K. Cattaneo*, pp. 23, 193; *Città dei Bambini*, p. 48; *Comune di Triora*, p. 158; *Cooperativa Omnia Ventimiglia*, p. 19 top; *Farabolafoto/Overseas*, pp. 46 top, 108, 137, 147 top, 174; *S. Finauri*, p. 82; *P. Gassani*, pp. 17 bottom, 21, 30, 37 top, 39, 49, 57, 61, 66, 87, 93, 96, 98, 99, 102, 104, 106, 109, 120, 132, 133 bottom, p. 139 left, 142, 144, 155, 156 top, 159, 169, 179, 181, 184 bottom, 189, 191, 197, 200, 205 top, 207; *V. Giannella*, pp. 33 bottom, 105; *L. Leonotti*, pp. 43, 54, 58, 72, 72/73, 73, 85 bottom, 92, 107, 139 right; *Lidiarte*, pp. 62/63; *R. Merlo*, p. 190; *P. Negri*, pp. 74, 133 top; *Old Post Cards*, p. 127; work by sculptor David Marani, p. 161; *P. Orlandi*, pp. 26, 37 bottom, 128, 160 left, 180; *Padiglione del Mare e della Navigazione*, pp. 40/41, 86; *A. Pastorino*, pp. 52, 166; *Rally Sanremo*, p. 149 bottom; *Realy Easy Star (L.A. Scatola)*, p. 149; *(T. Spagone)*, pp. 15, 129, 130, 198; *(R. Valterza)*, pp. 170 left, 171; *Studio Gatelli*, p. 153; *White Star (M. Bertinetti)*, pp. 78, 173 bottom, 175; *(A. Conway)*, pp. 16 top, 18, 28 bottom, 32, 69, 85 top, 112, 114, 122 top, 131, 146/147 bottom, 176, 184 top, 194, 201, 202, 205 bottom, 218, 219.

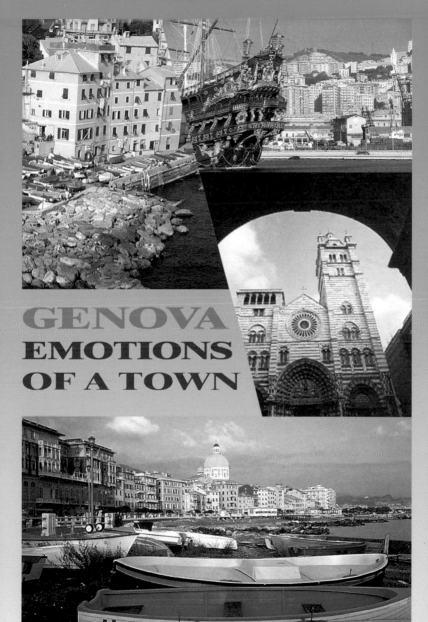

GENOVA
EMOTIONS
OF A TOWN

Azienda di Promozione Turistica
Tel. 010 248711 - Fax 010 2467658
E-mail: aptgenova@apt.genova.it
www.apt.genova.it

FRANTOIO DI SANT'AGATA D'ONEGLIA

Sant'Agata di Oneglia, a small village on the hill near the gulf of Imperia, is one of the oldest olive hill of Liguria.
In this place people make traditional dishes and old recipes. The Frantoio di Sant'Agata di Oneglia is a part of corporation "Maestri Oleari", an elite of original olive oil producers.

INCROCIO DI VIA SANT'AGATA, STRADA DEI FRANCESI, 48
TEL. 0183 293472 - FAX 0183 710963
18100 IMPERIA - LIGURIA - ITALIA
www.frantoiosantagata.com
e-mail: frantoio@frantoiosantagata.com